# FOREWORD

2018 started with a lot of questions waiting to be answered. Would Marc Márquez be able to break more records? Could Andrea Dovizioso begin where he left off in 2017? And what of Jorge Lorenzo, in his second year at Ducati, after having dominated the Sepang test in record-breaking style? Now, we have the answers – but it's been another incredible rollercoaster of a season to find them. I hope you've enjoyed it as much as I have.

The 2018 FIM MotoGP™ World Championship began with one rider immediately letting us know he was going to remain firmly in contention: Andrea Dovizioso. The Italian started the season by winning another duel against Marc Márquez at the final corner, becoming the first to top the standings and lighting the fuse on another incredible year. Later Lorenzo, after a more difficult start, would also emerge to battle the reigning Champion – and win his first races in red. Mugello saw the five-time World Champion back to his best, able to pull away and dominate for his first victory for Ducati. Honda vs Ducati became the key on-track battle in 2018, and each and every fight between the two gave us some of the most incredible racing we've ever seen.

The most incredible of all, however, must surely be the Dutch GP. The TT Circuit Assen always provides spectacular races but 2018 was the jewel in the crown of the season. There was a familiar victor by the name of Marc Márquez – maybe a clue as to who would also be able to come out on top over the course of the year – but it was, as ever, another amazing spectacle for us to enjoy.

Yamaha had a tough season in part but they brought their longest-ever losing streak to an end in Phillip Island. They had come close, but from Rossi's victory in Assen in 2017, they remained without a victory although the consistency of the number 46 shone through to ensure they remained in touch with those at the top. The man who ended the losing streak, however, was Maverick Viñales. The year had been looking up for Yamaha from Buriram on, but it took until the Australian GP to finally, fittingly, end that losing streak – after 25 races defeated, it was the number 25 who brought the drought to an end. And who can forget the incredible laptimes Rossi hammered out in Malaysia? The number 46 remains one of the hardest competitors to beat and it was a pleasure to once again see him end the year in the top three overall.

There were upturns elsewhere on the grid, too. After a difficult 2017 for Suzuki, it was fantastic to see both Álex Rins and Andrea Iannone taking multiple podium finishes and showing that the Hamamatsu factory were back in the mix, and Aprilia also had some good progress towards the latter part of the season. KTM, however, had some big mid-season struggles – with injuries affecting Pol Espargaró. That had a big impact on their second season, but then in the very last race of the year we got to witness some history made. Pol Espargaró gave the Austrian factory their first ever podium in MotoGP™, and it was his first podium too. It was an honour to see such hard work pay off on an important day for our newest manufacturer, and it will be exciting to see what they can achieve next year.

The Independent Team riders were also, once again, a cornerstone of this incredible season. Podium finishers and front row starters at many Grands Prix, it was Johann Zarco who beat Danilo Petrucci to the honour of top Independent Team rider in the season finale at Valencia. But the man who had been leading before injury curtailed his season before race day on Phillip Island, Cal Crutchlow, can't be overlooked as he became a three-time Grand Prix winner. That came in the dramatic and, at times, chaotic Grand Prix in Argentina, with Crutchlow a cut above.

In the end, despite that early drama for the Champion in Argentina, it was Márquez who began to make his mark on 2018 from then on, eventually making some more history on the way as the youngest to achieve the seven titles he has. But the story of the season is more than simply the story of the premier class. The talents and racing in MotoGP™ are born most often within the riders and races of the Moto2™ and Moto3™ World Championships, and both have been incredible in 2018. Italian Francesco 'Pecco' Bagnaia came out on top Moto2™ as he wrapped up the crown at Sepang, but Portuguese rider Miguel Oliveira pushed him during the season. Both now move up to the premier class, as well as 2018 Moto2™ Rookie of the Year Joan Mir and Fabio Quartararo, who won his first Grand Prix in Barcelona – four men who will undoubtedly now make their presence felt in MotoGP™. Bagnaia was also the final Champion of the Honda-powered era of the intermediate class, and we're delighted to now welcome Triumph for 2019 – beginning another new chapter with more new challenges on track and in the box.

As those stars of Moto2™ graduate to the premier class, Moto2™ receives its own fresh faces from the lightweight class, too. The Moto3™ season was one of the most dramatic as the pendulum of momentum swung between Jorge Martin and Marco Bezzecchi, with Fabio Di Giannantonio also gaining ground as the season went on. Incredible races and finishes – including some of the closest ever – made sure that every weekend was an exciting one, with Martin eventually able to pull the pin in Malaysia, winning the race and taking the crown. As happened so often this season, the Spaniard also made some history along the way.

Now another new era begins with more exciting changes. Champions graduate, riders change teams, some of those teams change machinery and we have a new team on the grid: Petronas Yamaha SRT. They welcome Rookie of the Year Franco Morbidelli and graduate Fabio Quartararo, as Andrea Iannone leaves Suzuki for Aprilia and Joan Mir takes his place. Tech 3 change to KTM machinery and Oliveira joins Hafizh Syahrin there, Bagnaia graduates at Pramac and Danilo Petrucci moves to the factory Ducati Team. But the man he replaces, Jorge Lorenzo, is undoubtedly one of the biggest headlines looking forward. Moving to Repsol Honda to partner reigning Champion Márquez, Lorenzo begins another new challenge – and the team now have the two men who have won every premier class title since 2010 bar one. Quite a line-up, and another incredible season to look forward to.

Before we quite say goodbye to 2018, however, we must say goodbye to some on the grid. Bradley Smith, who becomes a test rider, Scott Redding, who moves series, and Álvaro Bautista as he moves to WorldSBK. And, of course, one of the paddock's most successful riders: Dani Pedrosa. The three-time World Champion was named a MotoGP™ Legend before he retired at the end of the season, therefore becoming the first Legend to race full-time. We thank Pedrosa for his incredible contributions to the sport, on and off track, and we wish him all the best in his future as he becomes a test rider.

So as we wait for 2019 to begin in earnest, I hope you enjoy looking back through 2018 as much I as have and have the same great memories of more history made and titles conquered. Racing is a business so often decided by tenths or hundredths of a second, but off track we have the luxury of time to digest and reflect upon the year. And then, of course, we get ready for the lights to go out again in Qatar next year – and begin another chapter in the history of this incredible sport.

*CARMELO* | **EZPELETA**
**DORNA SPORTS CEO**
*NOVEMBER 2018*

© MAT OXLEY 2018

Published December 2018

A catalogue record for this book is available from the British Library

ISBN 978-1-5272-2827-6

**PUBLISHED BY** | Motocom Limited, Liscombe Park, Liscombe East, Soulbury, Bucks, LU7 0JL, UK
www.motocom.co.uk

**PRINTED & BOUND BY** | Gomer Press, Llandysul Enterprise Park, Llandysul, Ceredigion SA44 4JL

This product is officially licensed by Dorna SL, owners of the MotoGP trademark (© Dorna 2018)

**EDITOR & AUTHOR** | Mat Oxley

**DESIGN & ARTWORK** | Peter Neal

**SPECIAL SALES & ADVERTISING MANAGER** | David Dew
david@motocom.co.uk

**PHOTOGRAPHY** | Front cover and race action by Andrew Northcott/AJRN Sports Photography. Studio photos of bikes (pages 13 to 25), studio photos of riders (pages 28 to 34) and further race action by Dorna.

**AUTHOR'S ACKNOWLEDGEMENTS** | Thanks to photographer Andrew Northcott. Also to Lou Acedo, Romano Albesiano, Laura Beretta, Pol Bertran, Matt Birt, Peter Bom, Steve Booth, Majo Botella, Gino Borsoi, Alex Briggs, Davide Brivio, Federico Cappelli, Lucio Cecchinello, Peter Clifford, Andrea Coleman, Barry Coleman, Simon Crafar, Gigi Dall'Igna, Steve Day, Federica De Zottis, Matt Dunn, William Favero, Carlo Fiorani, Guido Giavazzi, Philippe Gruenberger, Francesco Guidotti, Ken Kawauchi, Tetsuhiro Kuwata, Isabelle Lariviere, Jose Maroto, Hector Martin, Neil Morrison, Josh Neville, Elisa Pavan, Paolo Pezzini, Herve Poncharal, Mathilde Poncharal, Ignacio Sagnier, Claire Sobas, Piero Taramasso, Julian Thomas, Federico Tondelli, Paul Trevathan, Irene Trimby, Mike Trimby, Kouichi Tsuji, Franco Uncini, Friné Velilla, Artur Vilalta, Tim Walpole, Mike Webb, Fran Wyld, Dr Michele Zasa, Andrea Zoccarato and all the riders, mechanics, Clinica Mobile staff, hospitality workers and everyone who keeps the MotoGP show on the road.

*MotoGP*™ *Season Review 2018*
Mat Oxley

# CONTENTS

# AS GOOD AS IT GETS?

***Closer than ever, thrillingly unpredictable and the finest array of talent seen on a grid since the days of Kevin Schwantz and Wayne Rainey***

MotoGP could hardly be in a better place. After a few challenging years – when the show was troubled by the global economic crisis, the unloved 800s and runaway electronics technology – the racing is reliably edge-of-the-seat entertainment.

The motorcycles are hyper-fast and super-challenging to ride, while the current breed of riders has drawn comparison with that other golden age of Grand Prix racing, when Kevin Schwantz did battle with Wayne Rainey, Mick Doohan, Eddie Lawson and Wayne Gardner.

Marc Márquez, Andrea Dovizioso, Valentino Rossi, Maverick Viñales, Jorge Lorenzo and Cal Crutchlow were often in the victory mix during 2018. These six men have different ways of riding their motorcycles and different ways of being human beings. MotoGP is very lucky to have such a rainbow of characters on the grid, from rock-star Rossi to crowd-pleasing Márquez and from the professorial Dovizioso to tell-it-like-he-sees-it Crutchlow. There's no such thing as a boring media conference when this lot is involved, which is another reason MotoGP stands out so brightly from other motorsport championships.

Once again Márquez was the main man. He was another year older and another year wiser. And so were his HRC engineers. He towered over the season, taking the title with a hat-trick of victories from COTA to Le Mans, back-to-back wins at Assen and Sachsenring

and another hat-trick from Aragón to Motegi. His consistency was remarkable for one who likes to live life on the edge.

His fifth premier-class title in six seasons wrote several new chapters in the sport's record books. To name but two: he is the youngest rider to reach such a milestone, taking the record from Rossi, and he is the youngest rider to win seven world championships across all classes, taking that record from Mike Hailwood. The 25-year-old already has his place in the pantheon.

This would be impressive in any era, but in an age when the racing is closer than ever, it is truly astonishing. The premier class has got progressively closer over the championship's 70 years, firstly thanks to more sponsorship that allowed independent teams to lease factory-spec bikes and more recently thanks to technical rules written specifically to tighten the grid.

The average winner-to-second-place gap has changed dramatically over the past seven decades. In 1949 it stood at two minutes and five seconds, by 1979 it had shrunk to 6.8 seconds, then to 3.6 seconds in 1991 and to a record 2.1 seconds in 2018. And this season broke more records: the closest-ever top-15 at Assen (16.043 seconds) and the closest top-ten at Brno (8.326 seconds).

So much for numbers. The story behind these statistics was some of the greatest racing ever seen. June's Dutch TT was the crown jewel of MotoGP's 70th season – a race that featured dozens of changes of leader and more than a hundred overtakes in total. This really was an edge-of-the-seat viewing experience – the racing was as thrilling as it gets, even a wee bit scary.

"Racing like this is the style of MotoGP now," said Suzuki's Andrea Iannone. "For sure the people watching on TV won't go to sleep on the sofa!"

The man who emerged as Assen victor was, of course, Márquez. The 125cc, Moto2 and MotoGP king has a unique ability to make sense of the chaos, to see through the maelstrom of man and machinery, rather like General Edward Cummings in Norman Mailer's seminal war novel The Naked and the Dead. "I like chaos, it's like the reagents foaming in the beaker before the precipitation of the crystals," said Cummings.

Márquez may turn out to be the best motorcycle racer of all time, because winning consistently when the machinery is so close requires a special kind of rider: thoughtful and clever in the garage, aggressive and clever on the racetrack.

The racing got even better in the second half of the season, once Ducati had fixed their issues to make Márquez's life more difficult. The Ducati versus Honda battles at Brno, Red Bull Ring, Aragón and Buriram were all decided on the last lap and by less than a second.

The Márquez/Dovizioso duels were so entertaining that older fans likened them to the Rainey versus Schwantz battles of the 1980s and 1990s. After the bitter taste of recent seasons, here were two racing heroes who fought like heavyweight boxers, then joked with each other on the podium. They both understand each other's character and technique, so they know what they're going to get. Usually it was Márquez divebombing Dovizioso, but occasionally it was the other way around.

"We always respect each other, but we have different riding styles and different bikes, so we have different strong points, which allows us to play in a good way," said Dovizioso.

Márquez had a more complicated relationship with Dovizioso's team-mate Lorenzo, especially after the turn-one incident at Aragón, where Márquez took the lead and Lorenzo crashed. Their arrival at Repsol Honda in 2019 is MotoGP's Senna-versus-Prost moment, in a good way. Never before have the winners of the last seven premier-class titles shared the same garage. The coming inhouse duel already has people making predictions, including one rash pundit who speculated that Lorenzo will never win a race on an RC213V. "Don't mess with the hammer or you risk to end up in the bigmouth club," was Lorenzo's reply.

Lorenzo's 2018 season turned upside down at Aragón. Literally. Two weeks later he hobbled into the Buriram paddock, where things only got worse. A stratospheric highside effectively ended his season, no doubt depriving us of further thrilling encounters with Márquez, Dovizioso and the rest.

In Lorenzo's absence, Suzuki stepped up. A midseason engine upgrade made Iannone and Álex Rins podium regulars. Their speed was so impressive that Márquez insists the GSX-RR could be a title contender in 2019.

Yamaha were mostly out of the game, enduring their longest losing streak since they entered the premier class in 1973. But as Lorenzo observed, "racing is like football, it works in cycles". Only recently had Ducati and Honda lived through their own victory droughts. Finally, Yamaha did make progress. Improvements in electronics and mechanical grip helped Maverick Viñales dominate in Australia and Valentino Rossi led most of the race in Malaysia.

Rossi is unique in motorsport, perhaps in any sport, with an unrivalled longevity and rate of success. In 2019 he will line up at the first race as a 40-year-old, hankering after the taste of victory just as he did when he dumped the clutch at the start of his first Grand Prix in March 1996.

The 2018 highlight for many was October's inaugural Thailand Grand Prix, where the South East Asian enthusiasm for motorcycles and for motorcycle racing transformed the weekend into something more like a rock festival. The lowlight was Silverstone, where tens of thousands of fans were denied a race at one of MotoGP's greatest circuits by poor track conditions.

The future of MotoGP certainly looks bright. And one part of that future arrives in 2019 with MotoGP's first electric-powered races. MotoE will be a one-make series, using Italian Energica motorcycles. It's a tentative step into a another world.

*CLOKWISE, FROM TOP LEFT* | *Rossi enjoys the taste of podium success; Márquez leads the race of the year at Assen; the Mugello top-three; the champ gets in the zone; Italian GP flyby; Márquez on another level*

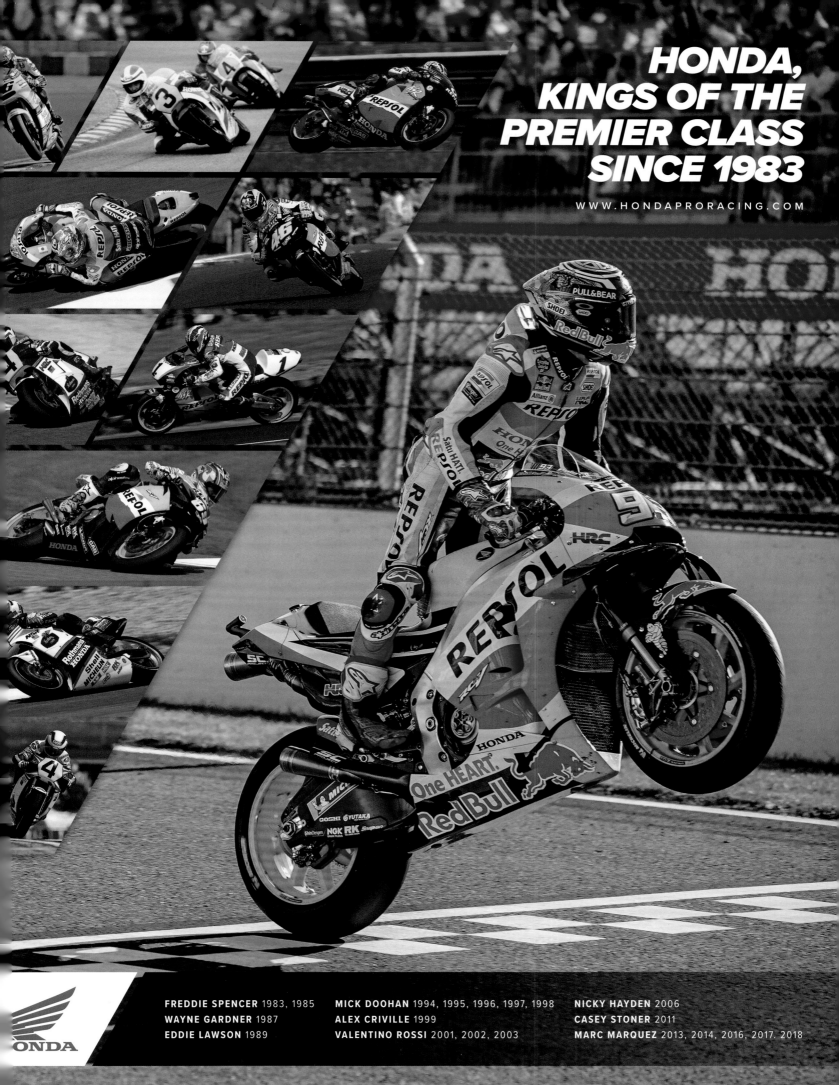

**HONDA, KINGS OF THE PREMIER CLASS SINCE 1983**

WWW.HONDAPRORACING.COM

FREDDIE SPENCER 1983, 1985
WAYNE GARDNER 1987
EDDIE LAWSON 1989

MICK DOOHAN 1994, 1995, 1996, 1997, 1998
ALEX CRIVILLE 1999
VALENTINO ROSSI 2001, 2002, 2003

NICKY HAYDEN 2006
CASEY STONER 2011
MARC MARQUEZ 2013, 2014, 2016, 2017. 2018

# J'5
## JOHANN ZARCO
### JOHANN ZARCO

## THE NEW RT-RACE PRO *AIR*

Adjustable calf
fastening system

D.F.C.
Double Flex
Control System

Replaceable
magnesium
heel slider

Michelin®
Burnout Sole

POWERED BY MICHELIN TECHNICAL SOLES

Replaceable magnesium
toe slider

F.F.C. Fasten Fit Control /
Internal lacing system

**SHARE YOUR PASSION #FOCUSONBOOTS** 📘 🐦 📷 📌 G+ ▶ YouTube

TCX
FOCUS ON BOOTS

# THE SEASON IN FOCUS

*From the factory stars to the wildcards and substitutes, the seasons of all 33 MotoGP riders analysed*

2018 FIM MotoGP™ WORLD CHAMPIONSHIP

## MotoGP™ WORLD CHAMPIONSHIP STANDINGS

| | RIDER | NAT | TEAM | POINTS |
|---|---|---|---|---|
| 1 | Marc Márquez | SPA | Repsol Honda Team | 321 |
| 2 | Andrea Dovizioso | ITA | Ducati Team | 245 |
| 3 | Valentino Rossi | ITA | Movistar Yamaha MotoGP | 198 |
| 4 | Maverick Viñales | SPA | Movistar Yamaha MotoGP | 193 |
| 5 | Álex Rins | SPA | Team SUZUKI ECSTAR | 169 |
| 6 | Johann Zarco | FRA | Monster Yamaha Tech 3 | 158 |
| 7 | Cal Crutchlow | GBR | LCR Honda CASTROL | 148 |
| 8 | Danilo Petrucci | ITA | Alma Pramac Racing | 144 |
| 9 | Jorge Lorenzo | SPA | Ducati Team | 134 |
| 10 | Andrea Iannone | ITA | Team SUZUKI ECSTAR | 133 |
| 11 | Dani Pedrosa | SPA | Repsol Honda Team | 117 |
| 12 | Álvaro Bautista | SPA | Ángel Nieto Team | 105 |
| 13 | Jack Miller | AUS | Alma Pramac Racing | 91 |
| 14 | Pol Espargaró | SPA | Red Bull KTM Factory Racing | 51 |
| 15 | Franco Morbidelli | ITA | EG 0,0 Marc VDS | 50 |
| 16 | Hafizh Syahrin | MAL | Monster Yamaha Tech 3 | 46 |
| 17 | Aleix Espargaró | SPA | Aprilia Racing Team Gresini | 44 |
| 18 | Bradley Smith | GBR | Red Bull KTM Factory Racing | 38 |
| 19 | Tito Rabat | SPA | Reale Avintia Racing | 35 |
| 20 | Takaaki Nakagami | JPN | LCR Honda IDEMITSU | 33 |
| 21 | Scott Redding | GBR | Aprilia Racing Team Gresini | 20 |
| 22 | Michele Pirro | ITA | Ducati Team | 14 |
| 23 | Karel Abraham | CZE | Ángel Nieto Team | 12 |
| 24 | Stefan Bradl | GER | Honda Racing Corporation | 10 |
| 25 | Mika Kallio | FIN | Red Bull KTM Factory Racing | 6 |
| 26 | Katsuyuki Nakasuga | JPN | Yamalube Yamaha Factory Racing | 2 |
| 27 | Xavier Siméon | GER | Reale Avintia Racing | 1 |
| 28 | Jordi Torres | SPA | Reale Avintia Racing | 1 |
| 29 | Thomas Lüthi | SWI | EG 0,0 Marc VDS | |
| 30 | Mike Jones | AUS | Ángel Nieto Team | |
| 31 | Sylvain Guintoli | FRA | Team SUZUKI ECSTAR | |
| 32 | Christophe Ponsson | FRA | Reale Avintia Racing | |
| 33 | Loris Baz | FRA | Red Bull KTM Factory Racing | |

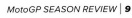

## 1ST MARC MÁRQUEZ
**REPSOL HONDA TEAM** | HONDA

Many fans are in awe of racers, but few racers are in awe of other racers. This is where Márquez is different: his greatest rivals know he isn't unbeatable but they are genuinely astounded by his talent to ride a motorcycle way beyond the limit and, mostly, get away with it. During his sixth premier-class season the Spaniard combined devastating speed with, mostly, unerring consistency. And the rest of the grid knows that he is still learning and getting better. He did have one bit of luck in 2018: that Ducati took until midseason to really get their act together.

**NATIONALITY** | SPANISH

**DATE OF BIRTH** | 17.02.93

**WEIGHT** | 65 KG   **HEIGHT** | 169 CM

**2018 SEASON** | 9 WINS, 14 PODIUMS, 7 POLE POSITIONS, 7 FASTEST LAPS

**TOTAL POINTS** | 321

## 2ND ANDREA DOVIZIOSO
**DUCATI TEAM** | DUCATI

MotoGP is very lucky to have Dovizioso taking on Márquez. He approaches racing from a very different angle: he doesn't ride through or around problems like magic Marc; he believes races can be won by thinking deeply about how to make the bike better, so he can ride faster without taking big risks. And he's right. His season was spoiled in the early stages by Michelin's softer 2018 rear and because he kept switching aero set-ups. Once he had found a consistent base he could challenge the more outlandish Márquez most weekends. If only he had got there earlier.

**NATIONALITY** | ITALIAN

**DATE OF BIRTH** | 23.03.86

**WEIGHT** | 67 KG   **HEIGHT** | 167 CM

**2018 SEASON** | 4 WINS, 9 PODIUMS, 2 POLE POSITIONS, 5 FASTEST LAPS

**TOTAL POINTS** | 245

## 5TH ÁLEX RINS
**TEAM SUZUKI ECSTAR** | SUZUKI

Step by step, Rins became a better and better rider during 2018. He is a quiet man and when he's racing he makes progress quietly; in such a way that you barely notice him. He is very smooth on the bike and smooth on the throttle, which is an important skill in the days of unified software. Rins doesn't make risky overtakes or get into arguments with rivals, he just gets faster and faster. At Sepang he set the fastest lap and at Valencia he made the front row and led the race, suggesting that both him and the Suzuki could be very close to the front in 2019.

**NATIONALITY** | SPANISH

**DATE OF BIRTH** | 08.12.95

**WEIGHT** | 68 KG   **HEIGHT** | 176 CM

**2018 SEASON** | 5 PODIUMS, 1 FASTEST LAP

**TOTAL POINTS** | 169

## 6TH JOHANN ZARCO
**MONSTER YAMAHA TECH 3** | YAMAHA

Started his second season in MotoGP the same way he started his first – leading the Qatar Grand Prix. The Frenchman was on stellar form during the early stages of the year – twice on the podium in the first four races, aboard an independent bike – but then seemed to lose his way after crashing out of his home GP in May. It wasn't until the flyaway section of the championship in October that he rediscovered his mojo. Seven days after that terrifying accident at the end of the start/finish straight at Phillip Island he was back on the podium at Sepang.

**NATIONALITY** | FRENCH

**DATE OF BIRTH** | 16.07.90

**WEIGHT** | 66 KG   **HEIGHT** | 171 CM

**2018 SEASON** | 3 PODIUMS, 2 POLE POSITIONS

**TOTAL POINTS** | 158

## 3RD | VALENTINO ROSSI
**MOVISTAR YAMAHA MotoGP** | YAMAHA

**46**

MotoGP's Peter Pan contested his 22nd season of GP racing in 2018. This alone was an amazing statistic – a rider who has no reason to prove anything and only continues racing towards his fifth decade because he adores going fast on motorcycles. However, this was his toughest season since his Ducati years. While Honda and Ducati pushed ahead, Yamaha were left struggling to keep up. Rossi kept his head high for much of the year but his frustration sometimes shone through. At least he finally got to "live the dream" for 16 laps at Sepang.

**NATIONALITY** | ITALIAN
**DATE OF BIRTH** | 16.02.79
**WEIGHT** | 69 KG   **HEIGHT** | 181 CM
**2018 SEASON** | 5 PODIUMS, 1 POLE POSITION
**TOTAL POINTS** | 198

## 4TH | MAVERICK VIÑALES
**MOVISTAR YAMAHA MotoGP** | YAMAHA

**25**

His second season with Yamaha didn't start as well as his first, but he got there in the end, thanks to a radical change of machine set-up during the final races, which helped him to his first victory in 18 months at Phillip Island. Viñales suffered more from his team's difficulties than his more experienced team-mate, so he plans to engage the services of a sports psychiatrist for 2019, to improve the consistency of his performances. If both the rider and his machine get better, there's no reason he shouldn't challenge for the championship very soon.

**NATIONALITY** | SPANISH
**DATE OF BIRTH** | 12.01.95
**WEIGHT** | 64 KG   **HEIGHT** | 171 CM
**2018 SEASON** | 1 WIN, 5 PODIUMS, 1 POLE POSITION, 2 FASTEST LAPS
**TOTAL POINTS** | 193

## 7TH | CAL CRUTCHLOW
**LCR HONDA CASTROL** | HONDA

 **35**

Rode the best season of his MotoGP career, until it was cruelly cut short by a nasty ankle fracture sustained in a high-speed accident at the Australian GP. Crutchlow's second season as a Honda Racing Corporation rider proved why the company signed him, because his aggressive riding style made him the only rider, apart from Marc Márquez, to get the maximum out of the RC213V. Came on strong late in the season with a run of strong performances, including podiums at Misano and Motegi. That form looked likely to continue until his injury.

**NATIONALITY** | BRITISH
**DATE OF BIRTH** | 29.10.85
**WEIGHT** | 68 KG   **HEIGHT** | 170 CM
**2018 SEASON** | 1 WIN, 3 PODIUMS, 1 POLE POSITION
**TOTAL POINTS** | 148

## 8TH | DANILO PETRUCCI
**ALMA PRAMAC RACING** | DUCATI

 **9**

Promoted to up-to-date machinery for the first time in his MotoGP career, the former Superstock rider had an up-and-down season. The highlight was undoubtedly Le Mans, where he chased winner Márquez all the way, helping cement his full-factory contract for 2019. However, much of his year was complicated by Michelin's slightly softer 2018 rear slick, which caused the heaviest rider on the grid difficulties in the later stages of some races, when the higher loads imposed by his extra weight made life much more complicated for his tyres.

**NATIONALITY** | ITALIAN
**DATE OF BIRTH** | 28/10/90
**WEIGHT** | 78 KG   **HEIGHT** | 181 CM
**2018 SEASON** | 1 PODIUM, 1 FASTEST LAP
**TOTAL POINTS** | 144

## 9TH — JORGE LORENZO
**DUCATI TEAM** | *DUCATI*

Lorenzo's 2018 season was a remarkable rollercoaster of up-and-down results, emotions and injury. He didn't finish in the top-ten until Le Mans, then he won the next two races at Mugello and Barcelona, at the very moment that he announced he would leave Ducati and join Honda in 2019. At Brno and the Red Bull Ring he proved he could defeat Márquez in hand-to-hand combat. And then everything went wrong again. Unlucky crashes and injuries ruined the last third of his season and deprived fans of what would've been some more great battles.

**NATIONALITY** | *SPANISH*
**DATE OF BIRTH** | *04.05.87*
**WEIGHT** | *65 KG*  **HEIGHT** | *171 CM*
**2018 SEASON** | *3 WINS, 4 PODIUMS, 4 POLE POSITIONS, 2 FASTEST LAPS*
**TOTAL POINTS** | *134*

## 10TH — ANDREA IANNONE
**TEAM SUZUKI ECSTAR** | *SUZUKI*

Suzuki's 2017 GSX-RR took a wrong turning on engine spec, which badly impacted Iannone's results. Sadly, the Italian's ever-improving form on the much-better 2018 GSX-RR came too late to save his ride with the smallest of the Japanese factory teams. Rode his greatest race at Phillip Island — a real rider's circuit — and might have won the event if he had chosen a different front tyre. Once Suzuki had got the GSX-RR sorted his talent was certainly not in doubt. If Aprilia can improve the RS-GP for 2019, Iannone will be a huge asset to the Italian factory.

**NATIONALITY** | *ITALIAN*
**DATE OF BIRTH** | *09.08.89*
**WEIGHT** | *74 KG*  **HEIGHT** | *178 CM*
**2018 SEASON** | *4 PODIUMS*
**TOTAL POINTS** | *133*

## 13TH — JACK MILLER
**ALMA PRAMAC RACING** | *DUCATI*

Miller immediately felt at home on a Desmosedici, after three seasons with Honda machinery. He found the bike less physical to ride and was up to speed right away, taking a top-ten first time out and a rodeo-style pole position at round two. Lost his way somewhat during the middle of the season, but front-row starts at Misano and Motegi proved he had rediscovered his speed, at least over one lap. He needs to work on his race-distance performance, but there's no doubt that Ducati see the young Australian as a long-term investment for the future.

**NATIONALITY** | *AUSTRALIAN*
**DATE OF BIRTH** | *18.01.95*
**WEIGHT** | *64 KG*  **HEIGHT** | *173 CM*
**2018 SEASON** | *1 POLE POSITION*
**TOTAL POINTS** | *91*

## 14TH — POL ESPARGARÓ
**RED BULL KTM FACTORY RACING** | *KTM*

Espargaró was KTM's biggest hope for 2018, but he suffered a nasty back injury during testing and had only just got back to full strength when he got hurt at Brno and again at Misano. This rash of injuries compromised his championship and had a serious effect on KTM's development programme. The younger Espargaró is fast, but life isn't easy when you are battling injuries and trying to develop a new motorcycle. His historic podium at the Valencia finale was hopefully the sign that his luck has changed and KTM will make bigger strides in 2019.

**NATIONALITY** | *SPANISH*
**DATE OF BIRTH** | *10.06.91*
**WEIGHT** | *64 KG*  **HEIGHT** | *171 CM*
**2018 SEASON** | *1 PODIUM*
**TOTAL POINTS** | *51*

## 11TH | DANI PEDROSA
**REPSOL HONDA TEAM** | *HONDA*

Pedrosa started his 13th season with Repsol Honda hoping against hope he might get another shot at the title. But once again, Lady Luck had other plans. He was knocked off in Argentina and got hurt. He was knocked off at Jerez and got hurt. So his title hopes were already over. He also struggled more than most with the Michelins and also with the unified software, which made the bikes more snappy and more difficult to control for the grid's smallest rider. No surprise that when he announced his retirement he admitted his heart was no longer in it.

**NATIONALITY** | *SPANISH*
**DATE OF BIRTH** | *29.09.85*
**WEIGHT** | *51 KG*   **HEIGHT** | *160 CM*
**TOTAL POINTS** | *117*

## 12TH | ÁLVARO BAUTISTA
**ÁNGEL NIETO TEAM** | *DUCATI*

Had a stellar ninth season in MotoGP, once he and his team had figured out how to get the best out of the GP17. From Jerez onward Bautista was a top-ten regular, often snapping at the heels of the lesser factory riders. His light weight certainly helped with tyre wear, sometimes giving him an important advantage in the later stages of races. Got his reward from Ducati when he took over Lorenzo's factory GP18 at Phillip Island, where he very nearly scored his first podium since 2014.

**NATIONALITY** | *SPANISH*
**DATE OF BIRTH** | *21.11.84*
**WEIGHT** | *58 KG*   **HEIGHT** | *169 CM*
**TOTAL POINTS** | *105*

## 15TH | FRANCO MORBIDELLI
**EG 0,0 MARC VDS** | *HONDA*

Brought the same calm, thoughtful approach to his apprentice MotoGP season that helped him dominate the 2017 Moto2 championship. And the youngster managed to maintain his focus despite a nasty midseason injury and the ructions within the upper echelons of his team. He rode his RC213V into the points more often than Honda's other two rookies, fully aware that his job was to keep climbing a steady learning curve. His eighth place at Phillip Island, battling with factory riders, was special. He changes to factory-spec Yamahas in 2019 and will be one to watch.

**NATIONALITY** | *ITALIAN*
**DATE OF BIRTH** | *04.12.94*
**WEIGHT** | *64 KG*   **HEIGHT** | *176 CM*
**TOTAL POINTS** | *50*

## 16TH | HAFIZH SYAHRIN
**MONSTER YAMAHA TECH 3** | *YAMAHA*

Called in at the last minute to replace Jonas Folger who had decided to step back from racing, Syahrin was thrown into the deep end at the penultimate pre-season test in February. But 'Pescao' didn't sink; he swam and he swam brilliantly. He scored points in his MotoGP debut and made the top-ten in his second race. In other words, he exceeded expectations and he did it with a smile – his Tech 3 crew loved his passion for racing and his appetite for fun. Syahrin will go down in history as the vanguard of South East Asian talent in bike racing's premier class.

**NATIONALITY** | *MALAYSIAN*
**DATE OF BIRTH** | *05.05.94*
**WEIGHT** | *65 KG*   **HEIGHT** | *180 CM*
**TOTAL POINTS** | *46*

## 17TH — ALEIX ESPARGARÓ
**APRILIA RACING TEAM GRESINI** | *APRILIA*

Aprilia had a pretty good 2017 season, the RS-GP putting Espargaró into the top-ten at almost half the races. However, the factory took a backward step in 2018, affecting Espargaró's results and then battering his motivation and his body. When Aprilia began to get the bike figured out he regained his determination. The Spaniard has a big heart and rides with a lot of emotion and aggression, like at Aragón where he finished sixth, just nine seconds behind the winner. During the final few races of the season he and his team made useful forward progress.

**NATIONALITY** | *SPANISH*
**DATE OF BIRTH** | *30.07.89*
**WEIGHT** | *66 KG*  **HEIGHT** | *180 CM*
**TOTAL POINTS** | *44*

## 18TH — BRADLEY SMITH
**RED BULL KTM FACTORY RACING** | *KTM*

Smith made a steady start to his second season with KTM, while still not totally at home with the Michelins. This is why he was one of the big losers in the earliest silly season in MotoGP history. By the time the paddock arrived at Jerez for the start of the European season he had been told that he would be replaced by Zarco for 2019. That left him to go 15 races with a factory that didn't want him; a far from easy situation for a rider. And yet Smith responded well, gradually picking up speed and consistency. It's not right that he won't be on the grid in 2019.

**NATIONALITY** | *BRITISH*
**DATE OF BIRTH** | *28.11.90*
**WEIGHT** | *68 KG*  **HEIGHT** | *180 CM*
**TOTAL POINTS** | *38*

## 21ST — SCOTT REDDING
**APRILIA RACING TEAM GRESINI** | *APRILIA*

The Briton was promised equal machinery by Aprilia but MotoGP's smallest factory struggled so much during most of 2018 that it wasn't easy for the team to properly look after its lead rider, let alone its newest rider. Redding showed some good speed when he managed to find some grip, but he spent much of the season searching for enough traction to last full-race distance. In the latter stages of the championship he did seem to lose some focus, but if his results suffered, his profile as an old-school motorcycle racer who likes to have fun certainly didn't.

**NATIONALITY** | *BRITISH*
**DATE OF BIRTH** | *04.01.93*
**WEIGHT** | *78 KG*  **HEIGHT** | *185 CM*
**TOTAL POINTS** | *20*

## 22ND — MICHELE PIRRO
**DUCATI TEAM** | *DUCATI*

Pirro has spent years helping Ducati move forward with the Desmosedici and the factory keeps him race-ready by having him contest (and win) the Italian superbike championship. His first 2018 MotoGP wild card at Mugello ended with a huge accident at the end of the main straight, which left him battered and bruised for a while. He returned to MotoGP action at Misano, where he made it into the points, and again at Valencia, where he qualified in Q2 and excelled in the rain-lashed race, finishing just one second off the podium. An invaluable asset.

**NATIONALITY** | *ITALIAN*
**DATE OF BIRTH** | *05.07.86*
**WEIGHT** | *69 KG*  **HEIGHT** | *177 CM*
**TOTAL POINTS** | *14*

## 19TH — TITO RABAT
**REALE AVINTIA RACING** | *DUCATI*

**53**

Like Miller, switched from Honda to Ducati machinery for 2018. His first few rides on the Desmosedici were sensational, but he struggled to maintain that level of results in the most gruelling category of them all. Rabat was just getting back to his best — he qualified 0.03 seconds off the second row at the Red Bull Ring — when he became the biggest victim of the atrocious track conditions during Saturday practice at Silverstone. A triple fracture of his right femur was a terrible injury. He showed astonishing bravery and resilience in his fightback to fitness.

**NATIONALITY** | *SPANISH*
**DATE OF BIRTH** | *25.05.89*
**WEIGHT** | *65 KG*  **HEIGHT** | *178 CM*
**TOTAL POINTS** | *35*

## 20TH — TAKAAKI NAKAGAMI
**LCR HONDA IDEMITSU** | *HONDA*

**30**

Honda have always wanted to conquer the premier class with a Japanese rider. Nakagami's promotion from Moto2 to HRC rider had him following in the wheel tracks of Takazumi Katayama, Tadayuki Okada, Makoto Tamada, Tohru Ukawa and the late, great Daijiro Kato. Nakagami had a promising pre-season and scored points in three of the first four races, but like many MotoGP newcomers he found it difficult to make consistent upward progress. His second MotoGP season — on a better-spec RC213V — will give him a better chance of showing his talent.

**NATIONALITY** | *JAPANESE*
**DATE OF BIRTH** | *09.02.92*
**WEIGHT** | *67 KG*  **HEIGHT** | *175 CM*
**TOTAL POINTS** | *33*

## 23RD — KAREL ABRAHAM
**ÁNGEL NIETO TEAM** | *DUCATI*

**17**

Did the best he could with his two-year-old Desmosedici GP16 machine, improving his speed in the latter stages of his sixth year in the premier-class championship. Abraham scored a few points on his best days and enjoyed by far his most impressive result of the season when he was loaned Bautista's GP17 for October's Australian Grand Prix. The equipment upgrade made a big difference to the Czech rider's performance, allowing him to battle with the GP18 of Petrucci and nearly make it into the top-ten at the end of the race.

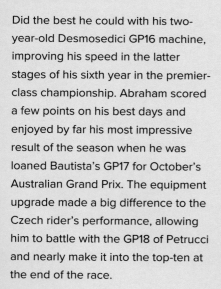

**NATIONALITY** | *CZECH*
**DATE OF BIRTH** | *02.01.90*
**WEIGHT** | *74 KG*  **HEIGHT** | *180 CM*
**TOTAL POINTS** | *12*

## 24TH — STEFAN BRADL
**HRC HONDA TEAM** | *HONDA*

**6**

MotoGP test teams grow with importance each year, as full-time riders and teams are allowed less and less time to go testing. HRC finally established its first Europe-based MotoGP test team in 2018, with former Moto2 champion Stefan Bradl as chief test rider. The German contested five GPs: two as an HRC tester, two with his old LCR team, substituting for the injured Crutchlow, and one with the EG 0,0 Marc VDS squad, subbing for Morbidelli. Although he didn't always make it to the finish, HRC were happy with his data and the quality of his feedback.

**NATIONALITY** | *GERMAN*
**DATE OF BIRTH** | *29.11.89*
**WEIGHT** | *63 KG*  **HEIGHT** | *170 CM*
**TOTAL POINTS** | *10*

## 25TH — MIKA KALLIO

**RED BULL KTM FACTORY RACING** | KTM

Beat his full-time team-mates at Jerez, riding a reverse-rotating crankshaft RC16, but his run of wild-card entries was ended by a high-speed crash at the Sachsenring.

**NAT** | FINNISH
**D.O.B** | 08.11.82
**WEIGHT** | 58 KG
**HEIGHT** | 166 CM
**TOTAL POINTS** | 6

## 26TH — KATSUYUKI NAKASUGA

**YAMALUBE YAMAHA FACTORY RACING** | YAMAHA

Sixteen years after his Grand Prix debut on a Yamaha TZ250, the Suzuka 8 Hours hero rode a development YZR-M1 at Motegi, where he managed to beat Nakagami.

**NAT** | JAPANESE
**D.O.B** | 09.08.81
**WEIGHT** | 64 KG
**HEIGHT** | 168 CM
**TOTAL POINTS** | 2

## 27TH — XAVIER SIMÉON

**REALE AVINTIA RACING** | DUCATI

The former Moto2 race winner didn't have an easy time in his apprentice MotoGP season. The Belgian scored his first premier-class point at the Australian GP.

**NAT** | BELGIAN
**D.O.B** | 31.08.89
**WEIGHT** | 68 KG
**HEIGHT** | 174 CM
**TOTAL POINTS** | 1

## 28TH — JORDI TORRES

**REALE AVINTIA RACING** | DUCATI

The MV Agusta World Superbike rider was called in to replace Ponsson, who had replaced Rabat. Adapted quickly to a MotoGP bike and impressed many with his pace.

**NAT** | SPANISH
**D.O.B** | 27.08.87
**WEIGHT** | 73 KG
**HEIGHT** | 180 CM
**TOTAL POINTS** | 1

## 29TH — THOMAS LÜTHI

**EG 0,0 MARC VDS** | HONDA

The 2005 125cc world champion finished runner-up in the 2016 and 2017 Moto2 world championships, but found MotoGP to be a much, much tougher challenge.

**NAT** | SWISS
**D.O.B** | 06.09.86
**WEIGHT** | 62 KG
**HEIGHT** | 172 CM
**TOTAL POINTS** | 0

## 30TH — MIKE JONES

**ÁNGEL NIETO TEAM** | DUCATI

Subbed for Hector Barbera in 2016, so this wasn't his first shot at MotoGP. Acquitted himself well at Phillip Island, but was unable to score a point as he had in 2016.

**NAT** | AUSTRALIAN
**D.O.B** | 25.02.94
**WEIGHT** | 60 KG
**HEIGHT** | 180 CM
**TOTAL POINTS** | 0

## 31ST — SYLVAIN GUINTOLI

**TEAM SUZUKI ECSTAR** | SUZUKI

The former 250 GP and MotoGP rider did sterling work as Suzuki's test rider, playing his part in the factory's impressive improvements throughout the 2018 season.

**NAT** | FRENCH
**D.O.B** | 24.06.82
**WEIGHT** | 62 KG
**HEIGHT** | 179 CM
**TOTAL POINTS** | 0

## 32ND — CHRISTOPHE PONSSON

**REALE AVINTIA RACING** | DUCATI

Agreed a deal to replace the injured Rabat for the last seven races of the season, but his pace was judged to be too slow, so he only contested one race, at Misano.

**NAT** | FRENCH
**D.O.B** | 23.12.95
**WEIGHT** | 73 KG
**HEIGHT** | 178 CM
**TOTAL POINTS** | 0

## 33RD — LORIS BAZ

**RED BULL KTM FACTORY RACING** | KTM

Got the Silverstone call-up to replace Espargaró. Qualified a very respectable 18th but dangerous track conditions denied him the chance of fighting for points.

**NAT** | FRENCH
**D.O.B** | 01.02.93
**WEIGHT** | 79 KG
**HEIGHT** | 191 CM
**TOTAL POINTS** | 0

# RACING

# AHEAD

# FLEXING THEIR MUSCLES

***Ducati and Honda pulled further ahead in the third season of MotoGP's latest technical regulations. But the biggest factor in chasing lap times remained the same: getting the bike turned in the middle of the corner***

MotoGP technology never stops changing and rarely stops moving forward. In 2016 the category's technological landscape was transformed by a change of tyre brand and a reduction in electronic rider aids. The next two seasons were dizzyingly unpredictable, as the factories tried to find a way through the labyrinth of Michelin tyres and unified software.

In 2016 independent teams inflicted more defeats on factory teams than in many decades. In 2017 there were nine different race winners, an all-time record. This new age of uncertainty was great for MotoGP – no one wants to turn on the telly on Sunday afternoon, already knowing who's going to win.

The 2018 season was a bit different. The latest technical regulations were into their third season, so this was a year of growing maturity for some factories, as the cleverest and best-funded engineers upped the pace and consistency of their motorcycles.

Ducati and Honda were the factories who drew furthest ahead, while Suzuki inched forward. Meanwhile Yamaha and Aprilia slid backwards, while injury-cursed newcomers KTM remained mostly static. The race for the constructors world championship was a close-run thing, with Ducati closer than at any time since the Casey Stoner era. But Honda finally took their seventh title in eight years.

What exactly were the technical challenges of 2018? The challenge is always the same, of course: to race around in circles

for 45 minutes or so and take the chequered flag before anyone else. But during the last three seasons it was incredibly difficult to meet this challenge. Was there ever a trickier age of premier-class Grand Prix racing for engineers? Perhaps, back in the 1970s and 1980s, when the two-stroke 500s were at their nastiest?

The challenge of the Michelins and unified software is great because the performance pyramid is so steep. Reaching the top of this pyramid and staying there is incredibly difficult, because the path is very narrow and the peak very pointy.

This affects everyone and everything: riders, engineers, engine design, chassis design, machine balance, suspension set-up, electronics settings and so on. When everyone has the same tyres and electronics, the riders and their motorcycles must adapt and be adapted to suit whatever is supplied by Michelin and Magneti Marelli, rather than the other way around.

Unified software has certainly made the riders work harder, relying more on their talent than the little black box hidden in the fairing nose. "With the factory software you were able to completely believe in the electronics and work in any way you wanted, using the electronics to be faster," explained Marc Márquez. "Now it's the opposite: you need to be quite free without using too much of the controls and also you need to be quite smooth, so that you don't work against the electronics."

However, it is the Michelins that have changed MotoGP the most since 2016, mostly for the better. By 2018 all the fastest riders had fully adjusted their technique to suit the French rubber.

"The limit with the front is very close," said Danilo Petrucci. "You have to stop the bike when it's upright, then, when you start

to lean into the corner, you have to release the brake as early as possible, because you can carry a lot of speed through the corner, but not with any brake. The most challenging thing is carrying a lot of speed through the corner and then opening the throttle as late as possible to save the rear tyre, so you have to mix the entry and the exit of the corner. It's very, very difficult and it's very challenging."

The Michelins certainly make the riders think more, not only about how they use the tyres through each corner but also how they use them throughout the race. The rider must be more gentle with the throttle to reduce wheelspin and he must listen to the rear tyre to understand how it's lasting, so he can decide at which parts of the track it's worth risking abusing the tyre to maintain his pace and at which parts of the track it's better to nurse the tyre, without slowing his pace. Then he needs to guesstimate – from his longer practice runs and from his own feeling of that specific tyre in that specific race – when he can afford to start using the grip he has saved up via his clever riding.

"With the Michelins the window is very, very narrow," affirmed Valentino Rossi's crew chief Silvano Galbusera. "It all depends on the track, the grip and the mu [the coefficient of friction]. And it's easier to be out of the window than inside the window. Before, we concentrated more on performance; now we work more on tyre life. We all must think much more. Now the rider who wins the race isn't always the fastest rider. The rider cannot ride the whole race at full gas because the tyres won't last, so he needs to play."

Michelin's tyre allocation policy is very different from that used by Bridgestone, MotoGP's previous tyre supplier. The scope of the company's standard allocation of three front slicks and three

rears is much narrower, because the French company wants all of those tyres to be potential race tyres, each helping different riders and bikes to perform at their best. Thus a greater variety of tyres usually gets chosen for the race, which makes the racing more exciting, because every rider has an advantage in different parts of the track and at different stages of the race.

By 2018 MotoGP's fastest factories had got the hang of the tyres, which completely changed machine balance. The Bridgestone front was better than the rear, while it's vice versa with the Michelins. Now engineers must ride a knife edge, just like the riders. Their main focus is getting the bike turned in the middle of the corner, so the front tyre isn't overloaded on the way in and the rear tyre isn't overloaded on the way out.

This requires a perfect combination of both engine and chassis. Factors like crankshaft inertia have always been important in racing but never more so than now: too much inertia and the motorcycle won't turn, too little and the rear tyre will spin too easily. Honda, Suzuki and most recently Yamaha have found this to their cost, by lightening the crankshaft too much in search of more outright engine performance and losing traction as a result.

Chassis flex was arguably the most important factor in chasing better lap times during 2018, with both Ducati and Suzuki introducing aluminium/carbon-fibre composite frames to change the amount of flex or move the area of flex. HRC suggested they may follow suit in 2019. Lateral flex isn't only vital to provide some suspension at full lean, when the forks and shock don't work effectively, but also to provide a self-turning effect. This is nicknamed the "banana effect" by some engineers, who design lateral flex into the chassis to allow its wheelbase to curve, by just a millimetre or two. This makes the bike go around corners better, while also stressing the front and rear tyres less, because the bike turns more naturally and the rider needs less spin to finish the corner. Thus flex is as big a factor in the turning conundrum as geometry and centre of mass.

"It's black magic!" said Paul Trevathan, crew chief to Pol Espargaró. "You have to take the load off the front tyre and start the process of getting the bike around the corner and rotating the load to the rear, because motorcycles don't turn from the front, they turn from the rear. This process of finding the right rear grip is the key, because the sooner you can do that, the sooner you can finish the corner and get onto the good [fatter] part of the tyre and then you can go. The more flexible you are in this area is the key to tyre life. We see on the data that from 50 degrees of lean to 35 degrees the difference in tyre performance is unbelievable, so you need to get into that better area, and the quicker you can get there the sooner you can use more throttle. The tyres are a massive part of what we're doing, trying to understand that part of the motorcycle.

"The engine and electronics also come into this. You are always looking for rideability from the engine, because the less the engine and electronics fight each other the smoother the whole corner-exit process. My belief with the Michelin rear is that you can't shock it into catching grip. You have to constantly load it. For example, if the traction control makes an ignition cut, then all of a sudden you've taken load off the rear tyre, so the bike goes into

a state of nothing, then the load comes back as a shock, and the tyre loses grip. If you have a good engine – a good, smooth heart to the motorcycle – then it makes it everything a lot easier."

Ducati and Honda both have former Magneti Marelli staff working within their MotoGP teams, which is certainly a factor in their recent successes. During the past two seasons their bikes exited corners faster than the rest because their electronics engineers found a way through the software that their rivals hadn't discovered. This is why their traction control didn't need to reduce torque so much or make so many ignition cuts to maintain grip.

MotoGP's unified electronics system will be completed next year by the introduction of a unified IMU, Magneti Marelli's six-axis IPS-160 unit. Most electronics engineers believe that all the factories were using their own IMUs to get more performance from the unified software, but no one admitted doing such things and no one accused anyone else of doing such things. Not surprisingly, the faster factories don't think the control IMU will make much difference, while the slower factories hope against hope that it will help them close the gap. Only time will tell...

**CLOCKWISE, FROM TOP LEFT** | *The Yamaha usually struggled to save its Michelins – note the slotted rear fender on Rossi's YZR-M1 designed to reduce rear-tyre temperature; HRC engineers hang on Márquez's every word at Motegi. Once again, the RC213V and the Spaniard were a match made in heaven; The GSX-RR was the biggest improver of the year: Suzuki added more horsepower to a fine-handling chassis and the bike ran near the front; Ducati won races with two riders using two different frames. Their big step forwards was turning performance, possibly a chassis-flex thing*

# REPLICA ✕ EDITION

# SHARK REPLICA HELMETS'

JORGE LORENZO

JOHANN ZARCO

SCOTT REDDING

MIGUEL OLIVEIRA

SAM LOWES

TOM SYKES

SYLVAIN GUINTOLI

JORDI TIXIER

**RACING**
DIVISION

MORE THAN **30** RIDERS IN THE WORLD SPEED CHAMPIONSHIP

**68** WORLD CHAMPION TITLES

REPLICA **37** ★ EDITION

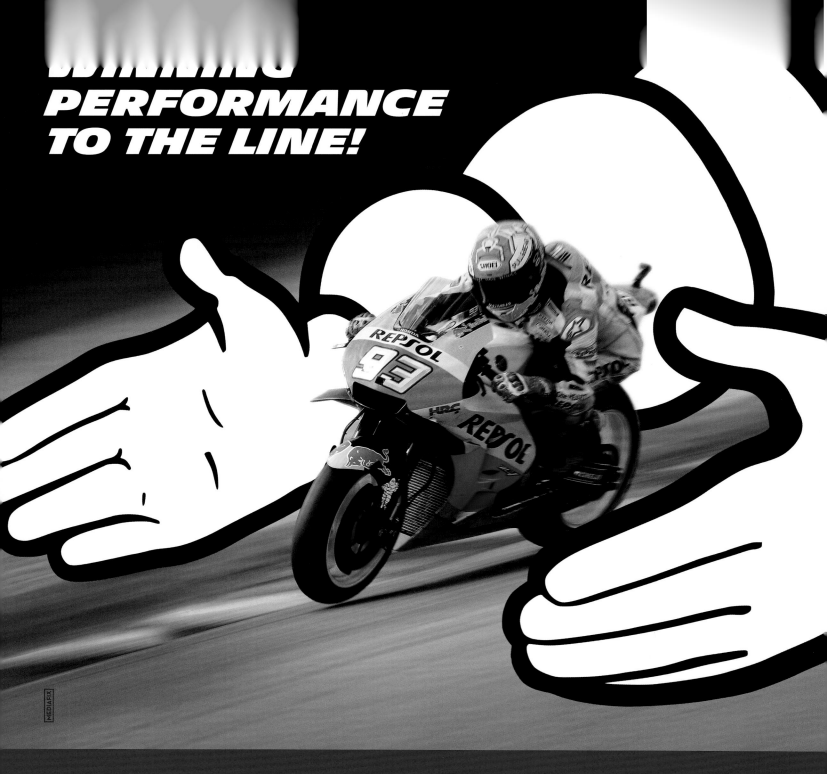

# WINNING
# PERFORMANCE
# TO THE LINE!

## WINNING PERFORMANCE
## TO THE LINE!

Congratulations from Michelin to **Marc Márquez** on winning the
**2018 MotoGP™ World Championship.**

You too can enjoy the performance and response delivered by MICHELIN tyres, from the first to
the very last kilometre!

www.michelinmotorsport.com

**MICHELIN**

# THE 2018 BIKES

HONDA | **RC213V**

**24**

YAMAHA | **YZR-M1**

**26**

DUCATI | **DESMOSEDICI GP**

**28**

SUZUKI | **GSX-RR**

**30**

KTM | **RC16**

**32**

APRILIA | **RS-GP**

**34**

# HONDA | *RC213V*

*The RC213V became more of a neutral bike in 2018, continuing down the same road Honda had taken in 2016, when MotoGP switched to Michelin tyres and unified software, which allowed less extreme corner entry and exit performance. "This year we tried to improve our bike to be competitive on all track layouts," said Marc Márquez. "Now we are stronger in what were our weak points, but also we suffer a bit more in what were our strong points."*

In 2016 HRC reversed the direction of crankshaft rotation, to improve machine balance and reduce wheelies, then in 2017 they switched from a screamer firing configuration to a big-bang configuration, to improve traction. Both these changes improved overall performance but reduced outright horsepower, thus HRC's main focus for 2018 was to improve horsepower to reduce the Ducati's advantage in acceleration and top-speed. This was vital, because if Márquez was faster on the straights, he could afford to take fewer risks in the corners.

"The power was much bigger than before," said HRC director Tetsuhiro Kuwata, without revealing exact figures. At Aragón, Márquez's top-speed deficit against the Ducati shrank from 4kmh/2.5mph in 2017 to 1.2kmh/0.7mph.

This helped Márquez and fellow HRC rider Cal Crutchlow, but they had to cope with a Ducati challenge that got stronger throughout the season. Both riders continued to make most of their time on corner entry. Following the switch to Michelins, Honda increased front load to stop and turn better, but this asked a lot of the front tyre, increasing tyre temperature, which is why Márquez and Crutchlow nearly always chose the hardest front option. Sometimes the hard front made the first few laps very risky. Thus improving the front end is a priority for 2019. "If we can better adjust the bike to the tyres that Michelin bring, it will be easier to manage the race," added Kuwata.

Chassis developments were subtle. Most noticeable was the carbon-fibre swingarm, which Márquez used with increasing frequency. "It's all related to how you want to load the tyres," he explained. "Sometimes the carbon-fibre swingarm gives you more initial grip but less at the end of the race; so you need to understand which swingarm is best, according to the tyres and the track." Next year HRC may try a carbon-fibre/aluminium composite frame, as they did with the troublesome RC212V.

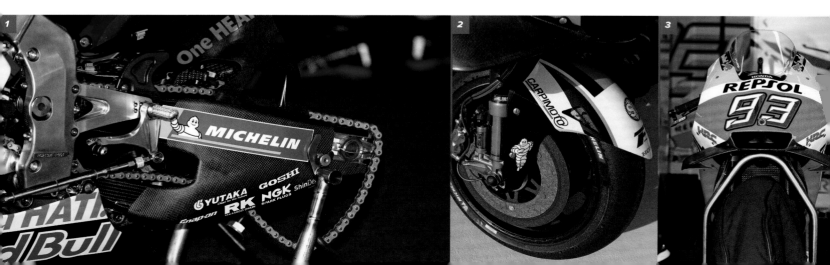

**1** | HRC's carbon-fibre swingarm was a gem. It changed grip characteristics and Márquez used it to win all of his victories

**2** | The RC213V is front-end heavy, which is why it can overheat even Michelin's hardest front slick; hence the cooling slots

**3** | Márquez used this new aero, which reduced wheelies and improved stability but could overheat the front tyre, from Le Mans

**4** | Márquez's RC213V gets different front springs and its brakes bled at Motegi, where HRC searched for better braking stability

**5** | Honda's radical V4 MotoGP concept scored its seventh constructors world championship in eight seasons

# YAMAHA | **YZR-M1**

*The 70th season of Grand Prix racing wasn't easy for Yamaha, who endured their worst losing streak in the 36 years since they unleashed their first factory 500 in April 1973.*

Yamaha's problem was very straightforward. They hadn't adapted as well as their rivals to the combination of Michelin tyres and unified software. In 2015, the final year of Bridgestone tyres and tailormade factory software, Yamaha won 11 races, a success rate of 71 percent. In the three seasons since their win rate has slumped to just over 20 percent.

The Michelins and lower-spec rider controls made life more challenging for engineers, especially for those at Iwata. The YZR-M1 is a corner-speed bike, which needs a lot of edge grip. The Michelins allow riders to use a lot of speed through the middle of the corner, but the M1's long, sweeping lines now carry a cost. "Our negative point is that our bike needs more lean angle to make the corner," said Yamaha motorsport manager Kouichi Tsuji. "So we use the edge of the tyre more, so edge grip drops down and the bike doesn't do what we want it to do."

Yamaha also had corner-exit traction problems, which reduced acceleration and top speed. "Electronics are only part of this problem, because you cannot create extra grip from electronics – what we need is more mechanical grip," added Tsuji.

Engine character was the third issue. It seemed Yamaha had made the same mistake Honda and Suzuki had made in recent years: reducing crankshaft inertia too much. Thus when the rider closes the throttle the engine shuts down too quickly, making the rear end snappy, and when he opens the throttle the engine picks up revs too quickly, causing wheelspin.

Yamaha have a lot of work to do. "We don't know exactly what's the problem: maybe engine character, maybe electronics, maybe chassis stiffness," explained Tsuji. "Something here, there and here."

Yamaha's 2018 season was further complicated by Michelin's softer-compound rear tyres, which also caused other factories problems.

The factory may have been in the grip of a downward circle during 2018, but they will surely find their way out, just as Honda and Ducati escaped from their doldrum periods in 2010 and 2016. Perhaps the biggest news for Yamaha going into 2019 is the arrival of MotoGP test rider Jonas Folger. Full-time MotoGP riders are allowed to do less and less testing, so quality feedback from someone like Folger could change everything.

**1** | As usual, the YZR-M1 looked more like a normal motorcycle than most of its MotoGP rivals. Could the bike be too conventional?

**2** | Yamaha aero fins appeared in preseason testing and worked well enough that Honda produced their own variation on the theme

**3** | The factory's permitted single aero update arrived at Buriram but was no better, so Rossi and Viñales returned to the original kit

**4** | Johann Zarco's Tech 3 M1 sometimes beat the Movistar M1s. No great surprise since both teams used very similar chassis

**5** | Test rider Katsuyuki Nakasuga's Motegi M1 didn't look much different but had different chassis stiffness to improve tyre life

# DUCATI | *DESMOSEDICI GP18*

*Five years ago Ducati's Desmosedici was the joke of the MotoGP grid. During the 2013 season the Italian V4 scored 155 points in the constructors world championship, compared to Honda's title-winning 389 points. In 2018, Ducati had surpassed that score before the championship had reached its halfway point. Andrea Dovizioso, who joined Ducati in 2013, still has vivid memories of the GP13. "It wasn't even a motorcycle!" he said.*

Ducati's renaissance began at the end of 2013 when Gigi Dall'Igna joined the factory. Every year since then Ducati have taken steps forward. In 2018, for the first time since 2007, the Desmosedici was almost certainly the best bike on the grid.

Their title challenge was blunted by a poor start. After winning the first race Dovizioso struggled until midseason. Firstly, he kept switching between different aero set-ups, which prevented him from finding a base setting. Secondly, Michelin's 2018 rear slick gave less grip in the later laps, so he had to revise his settings accordingly. "We didn't change a lot to win again," he explained after Misano. "Our good results came from analysing, then putting all the small details together, from bike settings to my lines."

Jorge Lorenzo's problem was ergonomics. The final piece to his Ducati jigsaw was the fat fuel tank, which arrived at Mugello, transforming him from loser to winner.

The Ducati's strong points remained the same as usual: braking stability and corner-exit traction. Its weak point also remained the same: mid-corner turning. Thus the bike required the same old stop-and-go riding technique. "You need to take profit of the braking stability, use no lean angle or corner speed, then take profit of the acceleration," said Lorenzo. This did have its advantages, because riders spent less time on the edge of the tyres, which improved tyre life.

The most obvious chassis upgrade was a frame with carbon-fibre inserts that revised stiffness to improve the bike's self-turning effect. This wasn't a complete success: Lorenzo liked it, Dovizioso not so much. Its plus point was faster changes of direction, the negative was corner-exit stability. Ducati's latest aero design, introduced at Brno in August, was that very rare thing in racing: a new part that had no negatives. It made turning lighter, while providing the same downforce to improve front-end load for better entry speed, especially in faster corners.

**1** | The GP18 was more competitive across more different tracks and conditions than any previous Ducati MotoGP bike

**2** | Ducati's first aero set of 2018 caused mid-corner problems for Lorenzo and the bike was still harder to steer

**3** | Second aero set arrived at Brno. Fork attachments arrived in Thailand to control flow separation and improve cooling

**4** | Dovizioso preferred the all-alloy frame. It gave him better corner-exit stability to take advantage of the GP18's drive grip

**5** | Lorenzo adopted the frame with carbon-fibre inserts, but wasn't really sure if its positives outweighed its negatives

# SUZUKI | *GSX-RR*

*Suzuki have ridden something of a rollercoaster since returning to MotoGP in 2015. The smallest of MotoGP's three Japanese factories scored a pole in 2015, won a race in 2016, then went backwards in 2017. Their 2018 campaign was therefore something of a comeback, with the GSX-RR fast enough to run close to the front when everything fell into place.*

Many rivals consider the Suzuki to be the best-handling MotoGP bike, with amazing corner-entry speed. The GSX-RR dives for the apex while many other machines struggle to turn when the rider releases the front brake. This helps explain the podiums achieved by Andrea Iannone and Álex Rins at serpentine tracks like Jerez, COTA, Assen and Aragón.

And yet Suzuki continued working very hard on chassis development. At Assen they raced their first carbon-fibre-reinforced frame. A second iteration arrived at the Red Bull Ring, for Rins only. This frame was a 2019 development item, but the Spaniard liked it so much at the post-Brno tests that he was allowed to race it immediately. "This frame gives me a bit more turning and a bit less spin," Rins explained. "With the old frame the tyre used to lose grip, recover grip, lose grip, recover grip, so the new frame gives us less movement on the exit." But the carbon-fibre sections weren't a long-term thing, merely an easy way to make changes while developing an all-alloy 2019 item.

Suzuki also managed to improve straight-line braking – a big bonus at Motegi – and this will continue to be a focus in 2019. "Braking stability is very, very important in MotoGP now," said Suzuki's technical manager Ken Kawauchi.

Late braking is obviously vital for overtaking and just as important for overcoming a top-speed disadvantage, even though Suzuki increased the inline four's horsepower significantly for 2018, halving their top-speed handicap from 10.4kmh/6.6mph to 5.4kmh/3.3mph.

The GSX-RR engine had been responsible for some of the bike's other woes. During 2016, when the factory had concessions (allowing in-season engine development), crankshaft inertia was too low, so the engine picked up revs too quickly, causing wheelspin. In 2017, when they no longer had concessions, crankshaft inertia was too high, making the bike unstable on the brakes and difficult to turn. In 2018 the balance was about right and the GSX-RR's multiple podiums take the factory into 2019 without concessions once again.

**1** | The GSX-RR at Buriram with no brakes and shallower aero side pods. Riders switched back and forth with aero sets

**2** | The deeper aero side pods first appeared at Misano and were somewhat inspired by Ducati's earlier creations

**3** | Carbon-fibre composite frames were a post-Brno feature to allow easier evaluation of different stiffness concepts

**4** | Iannone climbs aboard another composite bike at Motegi: main advantage was smoother drive grip out of turns

**5** | Test rider Sylvain Guintoli raced a prototype 2019 bike at Motegi, with all-aluminium frame and more powerful engine

# KTM | *RC16*

***Like rock bands have difficult second albums, so MotoGP factories have difficult second seasons. KTM impressed in its rookie 2017 campaign, narrowing the gap from 43 seconds in Argentina to 14 seconds at Aragón.***

But their 2018 season was marred by rider injuries. Pol Espargaró crashed at 250kmh/155mph during the Sepang preseason tests, his injuries requiring spinal surgery. He wasn't back to full strength until Mugello. Then test rider Mika Kallio smashed a knee at the Sachsenring, ending his season, and Espargaró broke a collarbone at Brno and again at Aragón.

All these injuries stalled KTM's development programme. Most important was a new engine with reverse-rotating crank, which Kallio raced at Jerez, beating both Espargaró and Bradley Smith. The new engine, which wasn't ready for the full-timers until later, improved turning and made the bike calmer, because it lifts the front less during acceleration. In doing so it changed the whole dynamics of the motorcycle – how the bike pitches and loads the tyres – so it required major changes to the chassis, electronics and suspension.

Even well into 2018, KTM riders often found themselves trying three different chassis during a race weekend. Sometimes an old, rejected chassis would be pulled out of the truck, in case it answered a new problem. "We are still at the tip of the iceberg," said Espargaró's crew chief Paul Travathan.

During 2018 the RC16's strongest point was corner entry, on the brakes, but even with the new engine its weakest point was running wide when the rider got on the throttle. "Turning with the throttle is killing us, especially when grip is low at the end of races," said Espargaró, who believes that adjusting swingarm stiffness could improve grip at this vital point. "Of course, the big thing for us is that gaining two tenths when you are a second behind is more difficult than gaining a second when you are three seconds behind. And also the other factories are always moving forward."

The 2019 season will be huge for KTM. They have Johann Zarco arriving in the factory team, with Tech 3 establishing the Austrian factory's first independent team. KTM have always been as good at organisation as they are at engineering. The factory has very little experience of premier-class racing, so they've signed a team that's been in the category for almost 20 years.

**1** | The RC16 may not have made much forward progress in 2018, but it was arguably the best-looking bike on the grid

**2** | Early 2018 aero used the 2017 upper fairing body with additional box-shaped lower sections for more downforce

**3** | KTM's aero update that arrived late in the season was similar to Honda's, which in turn looked like Yamaha's

**4** | Motegi is the toughest track on brakes, so 340mm discs are mandatory. Even so, air scoops are needed to avoid overheating

**5** | Did KTM use a carbon-fibre swingarm? No, the RC16 used a carbon skinned item, which probably tweaked stiffness

# APRILIA | RS-GP

**The 2018 season didn't go well for Aprilia. MotoGP's smallest factory team made major revisions to the RS-GP for its fourth campaign and the changes didn't work out as planned. Aleix Espargaró called 2018 "a disaster year".**

The Spaniard finished well inside the top ten at almost half of the 2017 rounds, but during 2018 he found it difficult just to get into the top ten. The problem was overall bike balance and dynamics. Aprilia had redesigned the chassis and rotated the engine backwards in the frame, to improve mass centralisation, but instead Espargaró found what had previously been the bike's strongest feature to be its weakest. After struggling so badly, the factory came close to reverting to the 2017 bike and used a 2017/2018/2019 hybrid machine at the final races.

"We improved braking stability with the 2018 bike, so I can brake later without crashing," said Espargaró, who reduced his crash rate by almost half. "But when I release the front brake the bike doesn't turn anymore and runs wide."

The change in machine balance had a dramatic effect on tyre temperature, with the front tyre running much cooler than before and the rear much hotter. The obvious conclusion is that Aprilia moved the RS-GP's centre of mass too far back. The riding position was also very different, which made it difficult for riders to get in the best position to help transfer load between the front and rear tyres.

"Front tyre temperature is lower because I can't apply enough force, which is why the bike won't turn," added Espargaró. "The biggest thing we lost was rear grip. In 2017 I was very strong in the last few laps, but no more. Tyre consumption is a lot higher and the pure grip, with new tyres, is also low." Perhaps increased tyre wear could also be attributed to Michelin's 2018 rubber and the aggressive throttle-opening technique Espargaró used to increase load transfer.

Aprilia made some improvements while testing at Misano during August, shifting mass forward to increase front tyre temperature and therefore improve turning. A revised frame was introduced at Silverstone, with shallower main beams for reduced lateral stiffness that made the bike more stable in corners, especially faster corners. But this was far from a final answer.

Straight-line performance was another issue. A new spec engine arrived late in the season but Espargaró was still battling an 8.9kmh/5.5mph top-speed handicap.

**1** | Some hard work on set-up at Misano allowed Espargaró to chase the leaders at Aragón for the first time all year

**2** | Carbon-fibre swingarm was designed to offer less lateral rigidity, but Aprilia struggled to get enough torsional rigidity

**3** | Aprilia undertook a major redesign for 2018, but the bike balance wasn't at all right, causing various tyre problems

**4** | Revised frame arrived at Silverstone, with shallower beams to reduce lateral stiffness for better cornering potential

<table>
<tr><td></td><td></td><td>**1 | QATAR** | 38</td></tr>
</table>

**GRAND PRIX OF QATAR**
*LOSAIL INTERNATIONAL CIRCUIT*

  **2 | ARGENTINA** | 46

**GRAN PREMIO MOTUL DE LA REPÚBLICA ARGENTINA**
*TERMAS DE RIO HONDO*

   **3 | USA** | 54

**RED BULL GRAND PRIX OF THE AMERICAS**
*CIRCUIT OF THE AMERICAS*

   **4 | SPAIN** | 62

**GRAN PREMIO RED BULL DE ESPAÑA**
*CIRCUITO DE JEREZ - ÁNGEL NIETO*

   **5 | FRANCE** | 70

**HJC HELMETS GRAND PRIX DE FRANCE**
*LE MANS*

  **6 | ITALY** | 78

**GRAN PREMIO D'ITALIA OAKLEY**
*AUTODROMO DEL MUGELLO*

  **7 | CATALUNYA** | 86

**GRAN PREMI MONSTER ENERGY DE CATALUNYA**
*CIRCUIT DE BARCELONA-CATALUNYA*

  **8 | NETHERLANDS** | 94

**MOTUL TT ASSEN**
*TT CIRCUIT ASSEN*

  **9 | GERMANY** | 102

**PRAMAC MOTORRAD GRAND PRIX DEUTSCHLAND**
*SACHSENRING*

  **10 | CZECH REPUBLIC** | 110

**MONSTER ENERGY GRAND PRIX ČESKÉ REPUBLIKY**
*AUTOMOTODROM BRNO*

# THE 2018 CALENDAR

**11 | AUSTRIA** 118
**EYETIME MOTORRAD GRAND PRIX VON ÖSTERREICH**
*RED BULL RING – SPIELBERG*

**12 | GREAT BRITAIN** 126
**GoPro BRITISH GRAND PRIX**
*SILVERSTONE CIRCUIT*

**13 | SAN MARINO** 134
**GP OCTO DI SAN MARINO E DELLA RIVIERA DI RIMINI**
*MISANO WORLD CIRCUIT MARCO SIMONCELLI*

**14 | ARAGÓN** 142
**GRAN PREMIO MOVISTAR DE ARAGÓN**
*MOTORLAND ARAGÓN*

**15 | THAILAND** 150
**PTT THAILAND GRAND PRIX**
*BURIRAM INTERNATIONAL CIRCUIT*

**16 | JAPAN** 158
**MOTUL GRAND PRIX OF JAPAN**
*TWIN RING MOTEGI*

**17 | AUSTRALIA** 166
**MICHELIN® AUSTRALIAN MOTORCYCLE GRAND PRIX**
*PHILLIP ISLAND*

**18 | MALAYSIA** 174
**SHELL MALAYSIA MOTORCYCLE GRAND PRIX**
*SEPANG INTERNATIONAL CIRCUIT*

**19 | VALENCIA** 182
**GRAN PREMIO MOTUL DE LA COMUNITAT VALENCIANA**
*CIRCUIT RICARDO TORMO*

The sprint to the finish: Dovizioso, Márquez and Rossi have just got the better of Zarco

# DOVIZIOSO OUTFOXES MÁRQUEZ

**The 2018 MotoGP season started the way the 2017 campaign had ended, with Dovizioso and Márquez battling all the way to the finish**

Once again, Andrea Dovizioso deployed his anti-Márquez tactic and once again it worked like a charm. The reigning world champion hurled his Honda RC213V inside the Italian's Ducati GP18 at the very last corner. Most riders would have tried a blocking move, but Dovizioso allowed the Honda through, Márquez couldn't quite hold his line, Dovizioso cut back inside and won the dash to the chequered flag: a perfect replica of his victories over Márquez at the 2017 Austrian and Japanese Grands Prix.

Dovizioso's first Qatar MotoGP victory had been a long time coming. He had finished a close second on his three previous visits, so with further off-season improvements to the Desmosedici it was no great surprise that he took the next step.

More surprising was Márquez, who crossed the line less than three hundredths of a second behind the Ducati. In his three previous visits to Losail he had been an average 5.3 seconds behind the winner. The theory went that the RC213V is better at in-and-out corners, not the long sweepers that characterise Losail. This result proved that Honda had made very significant advances during the off-season, transforming its bike into a potential winner at what had been one of its most unfavoured racetracks. For some people in the paddock, the writing on the wall was already there to see.

The start to Grand Prix racing's 70th season followed the usual rush of pre-season tests, which took riders to Sepang, Losail and Buriram in Thailand. Honda had been fast throughout, so perhaps Márquez's pace wasn't that much of a shock after all.

In practice the lead pack was separated by fractions – after FP1 the top ten was covered by seven tenths, by the end of FP3 that gap had shrunk to half a second. The pressure was on. And it told. In FP4 last year's rookie surprise Johann Zarco crashed and wasn't sure he would be able to regain his composure in time for qualifying. Luckily, he was wrong. The Frenchman took pole, while dragging Márquez and Danilo Petrucci onto the front row; the three of them just two tenths apart.

Zarco once again set the pace in the race, leading until the closing stages. All the riders knew this was a race of tyre management, so they were clicking off the laps, looking after their tyres and waiting to pull the pin. As Márquez said later, "Zarco led for so long because we wanted him to".

When the lead pack of Zarco, Dovizioso, Márquez, Valentino Rossi, Cal Crutchlow, Dani Pedrosa and Petrucci raced past the pits with five laps to go, Dovizioso used the Ducati's grunt to take the lead. Márquez knew he must go with him, so he too went past Zarco, but the pair collided as they braked for turn one. Márquez just about retained control and somehow kept a tight enough line to deny Zarco's counter-attack.

Zarco was suddenly going backwards, because he had burned his front tyre. Now Dovizioso tried to make the break. He set his fastest lap on lap 19 of 22, eking a lead of three tenths over Márquez, while Rossi was a further half second behind. By now the rest had lost touch. It would be a three-way fight.

But Dovizioso had nothing more to give. "When I got to the front I had finished my rear tyre," he said. "I couldn't take my [usual] lines, so I couldn't create the gap."

Márquez was like a dog with a bone. As usual he was faster through left-handers, which kept him right with the Ducati. As they started the last lap the gap was less than two tenths, with Rossi too far back to be in the game... unless the leaders got tangled up. They nearly did, but not quite, and Dovizioso took his seventh win from his last 14 races.

"I'm really happy because I was able to make a terrible start and gain a lot of positions, while at the same time saving my tyres and deciding my strategy," said the 31-year-old. "It's not so easy to do this in MotoGP."

Márquez knew his second place was at least as significant as Dovizioso's victory. "Twenty points at a very difficult track is like a victory," he grinned. "We did a great job, even though I struggled a lot with the hard front tyre, which gave me lots of risks in left-handers. My target was to control Andrea. When I went with him I was on the limit, sliding around, but I was able to stay there to try at the last corner."

Rossi was delighted to be on the podium for the fifth time in his last six outings at Losail. "I showed people I'm not too old!"

**CLOCKWISE, FROM TOP LEFT** *Márquez congratulates pole-position man Zarco after Q2; Zarco had winning pace, just like 2017; Syahrin scored points just weeks after his first ride on a MotoGP bike; Dovizioso worked his way into second at half-distance, chased by Márquez, Rossi, Crutchlow, Petrucci and Pedrosa*

'I'M REALLY HAPPY BECAUSE I WAS
ABLE TO MAKE A TERRIBLE START
AND GAIN A LOT OF POSITIONS'
ANDREA DOVIZIOSO

## GRAND PRIX
## RACING AT SUNSET

This was the start of Grand Prix racing's 70th season, so it was only fitting that the anniversary was celebrated by something new. This particular celebration wasn't actually intended, but it was nonetheless spectacular: Grand Prix racing at sunset.

The story goes back to the inaugural Qatar Grand Prix, in October 2004, when temperatures in pit lane nudged 50 degrees. Hence the first talk of moving the event to a night-time schedule, away from the cruel desert sun. The first floodlit Qatar GP went off smoothly in 2007, but the following year a surprise downpour just moments before the start of the MotoGP race caused the race to

grinned the veteran, who days before had inked a new two-year deal with Yamaha. "When Dovizioso got in front, the rhythm changed and that was the key moment for me. My idea was to stay close as possible to Andrea and Marc, because I knew Marc would try at the last corner..."

Honda's latest engine made all the difference for Márquez, who was hardly out of control all weekend and didn't fall once; a big change from 2017, when his average crash rate was 1.5 falls per weekend.

Crutchlow finished fourth, 2.9 seconds behind Rossi. Petrucci was a further second back, with Maverick Viñales right alongside after a stirring comeback from 14th. A last-minute set-up change had allowed him to use more corner speed which reduced his wheelspin problems. His last victim was Pedrosa. Zarco finished alone in eighth. Andrea Iannone was ninth, the lone Suzuki finisher after Álex Rins had slid off. Jack Miller completed the top ten in his first race with Ducati.

The top 15 riders across the finish line were only 23 seconds apart, an all-time record. This was a good time to make history, at the start of motorcycle Grand Prix racing's 70th season. The first premier-class world championship got underway in June 1949 at the Isle of Man TT. That year's 500cc Senior TT was won by factory Norton rider Harold Daniell and the top 15 finishers in the race were covered by no less than 14 minutes and 21 seconds. True, the 1949 Senior lasted three hours and two minutes, but nonetheless, the 2018 record proved beyond doubt that GP racing is closer than it's ever been.

*CLOCKWISE FROM TOP LEFT* | *Miller had a promising first outing with Ducati; two very happy Italians; class of 2018; Dovizioso went one better after finishing second in 2015, 2016 and 2017; Crutchlow and Petrucci dispute fourth place*

be rescheduled for Monday. MotoGP's safety officers had already decided that racing in the rain under powerful floodlights would cause vision problems for the riders.

The rain returned in 2017, once again playing havoc with the schedule, so during 2018 pre-season testing the Losail track was soaked by sprinkler trucks, allowing riders to try riding the glistening track under the lights. As first feared, this didn't work at all well. Thus the weekend schedule was amended, with the programme brought forward so that Moto2 (left) and Moto3 (right) would race in daylight and MotoGP at night-time, with the Moto2 race getting underway 20 minutes before sunset. It was a beautiful and somewhat surreal sight, watching Moto2 riders racing around as the flaming orange sun dipped below the horizon.

# 1 | QATAR

# RACE RESULTS

**2018 WINNER** ANDREA DOVIZIOSO

**CIRCUIT LENGTH** 5.4 KM | 3.34 MILES

**NO. OF LAPS** 22

**RACE DISTANCE** 118.4 KM | 73.5 MILES

**CIRCUIT RECORD LAP** 1'54.927 | 168.5 KM/H
JORGE LORENZO (2016)

**CIRCUIT BEST LAP** 1'53.680 | 170.3 KM/H
JOHANN ZARCO (2018)

**RACE CONDITION** DRY

**AIR** 21°C

**HUMIDITY** 46%

**GROUND** 23°C

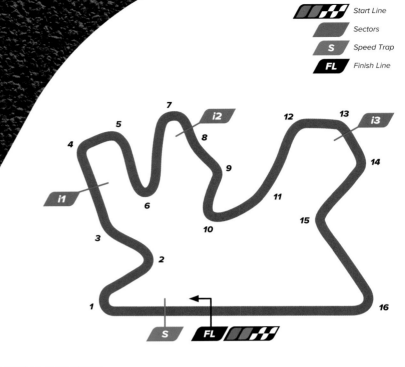

| | | Start Line |
| --- | --- | --- |
| | | Sectors |
| **S** | | Speed Trap |
| **FL** | | Finish Line |

TISSOT SWISS WATCHES SINCE 1853 / MotoGP

**OFFICIAL** TIMEKEEPER

MICHELIN / MotoGP

**OFFICIAL** MotoGP™ CLASS TYRE

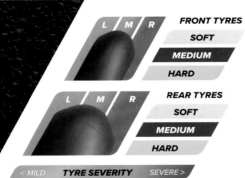

**FRONT TYRES**
SOFT
MEDIUM
HARD

**REAR TYRES**
SOFT
MEDIUM
HARD

< MILD  **TYRE SEVERITY**  SEVERE >

## QUALIFYING RESULTS

| | RIDER | NAT | TEAM | MACHINE | QP/TIME | GAP 1ST/PREV | |
| --- | --- | --- | --- | --- | --- | --- | --- |
| 1 | Johann Zarco | FRA | Monster Yamaha Tech 3 | YAMAHA | Q2 1'53.680 | | |
| 2 | Marc Márquez | SPA | Repsol Honda Team | HONDA | Q2 1'53.882 | 0.202 | 0.202 |
| 3 | Danilo Petrucci | ITA | Alma Pramac Racing | DUCATI | Q2 1'53.887 | 0.207 | 0.005 |
| 4 | Cal Crutchlow | GBR | LCR Honda CASTROL | HONDA | Q2 1'54.072 | 0.392 | 0.185 |
| 5 | Andrea Dovizioso | ITA | Ducati Team | DUCATI | Q2 1'54.074 | 0.394 | 0.002 |
| 6 | Álex Rins | SPA | Team SUZUKI ECSTAR | SUZUKI | Q2 1'54.339 | 0.659 | 0.265 |
| 7 | Dani Pedrosa | SPA | Repsol Honda Team | HONDA | Q2 1'54.368 | 0.688 | 0.029 |
| 8 | Valentino Rossi | ITA | Movistar Yamaha MotoGP | YAMAHA | Q2 1'54.389 | 0.709 | 0.021 |
| 9 | Jorge Lorenzo | SPA | Ducati Team | DUCATI | Q2 1'54.431 | 0.751 | 0.042 |
| 10 | Jack Miller** | AUS | Alma Pramac Racing | DUCATI | Q2 1'54.449 | 0.769 | 0.018 |
| 11 | Andrea Iannone | ITA | Team SUZUKI ECSTAR | SUZUKI | Q2 1'54.619 | 0.939 | 0.170 |
| 12 | Maverick Viñales** | SPA | Movistar Yamaha MotoGP | YAMAHA | Q2 1'54.707 | 1.027 | 0.088 |
| 13 | Aleix Espargaró | SPA | Aprilia Racing Team Gresini | APRILIA | Q1 1'55.140 | *0.506 | 0.503 |
| 14 | Franco Morbidelli | ITA | EG 0,0 Marc VDS | HONDA | Q1 1'55.169 | *0.535 | 0.029 |
| 15 | Hafizh Syahrin | MAL | Monster Yamaha Tech 3 | YAMAHA | Q1 1'55.258 | *0.624 | 0.089 |
| 16 | Tito Rabat | SPA | Reale Avintia Racing | DUCATI | Q1 1'55.273 | *0.639 | 0.015 |
| 17 | Scott Redding | GBR | Aprilia Racing Team Gresini | APRILIA | Q1 1'55.380 | *0.746 | 0.107 |
| 18 | Thomas Lüthi | SWI | EG 0,0 Marc VDS | HONDA | Q1 1'55.381 | *0.747 | 0.001 |
| 19 | Karel Abraham | CZE | Ángel Nieto Team | DUCATI | Q1 1'55.392 | *0.758 | 0.011 |
| 20 | Bradley Smith | GBR | Red Bull KTM Factory Racing | KTM | Q1 1'55.553 | *0.919 | 0.161 |
| 21 | Álvaro Bautista | SPA | Ángel Nieto Team | DUCATI | Q1 1'55.638 | *1.004 | 0.085 |
| 22 | Pol Espargaró | SPA | Red Bull KTM Factory Racing | KTM | Q1 1'55.706 | *1.072 | 0.068 |
| 23 | Takaaki Nakagami | JPN | LCR Honda IDEMITSU | HONDA | Q1 1'56.401 | *1.767 | 0.695 |
| 24 | Xavier Siméon | GER | Reale Avintia Racing | DUCATI | Q1 1'56.545 | *1.911 | 0.144 |

*Gap to the fastest rider in the Q1 session*
*** Went forward from Q1 to Q2*

**1 ANDREA DOVIZIOSO**
A typically intelligent victory from the thinking person's MotoGP rider. The Italian worked his way forward after a so-so start and timed his winning attack to perfection. And once again, he had Márquez under control.

**2 MARC MÁRQUEZ**
The reigning champion hadn't been close to winning at Losail since his sole Qatar MotoGP victory in 2014. Perhaps that removed some of the pressure for a man aiming for a fifth MotoGP championship in six years. His speed was ominous.

**3 VALENTINO ROSSI**
What can you say? Just weeks after the Italian had celebrated his 39th birthday he was once again in the mix. And once again with a bike that wasn't working so well. Perhaps the layout minimised the M1's problems.

**4 CAL CRUTCHLOW**
Like Márquez, Crutchlow was already loving the new RC213V engine, which gave more top speed, therefore reducing the need for risk-taking in the turns. This time the Briton didn't quite have the pace to go with the leaders.

**5 DANILO PETRUCCI**
Qualified on the front row and ran with the leaders, finishing less than four seconds behind the winner. This was an important result for the friendly Italian, who already knew that he was fighting for a 2019 ride.

**6 MAVERICK VIÑALES**
Apparently less calm than his team-mate in the face of adversity, Viñales had to go through Q1 qualifying, then spent most of his race fighting his way through the pack. At least he was fast: he ended up with the fifth-quickest lap of the race.

**7 DANI PEDROSA**
This was the start of Pedrosa's 13th season with Repsol Honda and once again it failed to deliver his first Losail victory. The Spaniard ran with the lead group but was later hampered by a lack of rear grip that slowed his pace.

**8 JOHANN ZARCO**
Zarco led the 2017 race, only to crash out. This year he led again, only to run short of front grip later on. The Frenchman is a corner-speed rider, so he can't do much once he loses confidence in the front.

**9 ANDREA IANNONE**
Iannone was overshadowed by his younger team-mate in qualifying and in the race, until Rins crashed out. The Italian showed good speed in the early stages of the race but used up his tyres too soon, which became a recurring theme.

**10 JACK MILLER**
After three challenging seasons on an independent Honda, the Aussie showed excellent promise in his first race with Ducati. The factory advised him to take it easy and build up to speed slowly but he was in a hurry!

**11 TITO RABAT**
The former Moto2 champion had taken the same journey as Miller, from Honda to Ducati machinery. The Spaniard fought his way through from 21st at the end of the first lap and finished closer to the race winner than ever before.

**12 FRANCO MORBIDELLI**
The reigning Moto2 champ and first VR46 rider in MotoGP had a superb debut MotoGP race, finishing 16 seconds behind Dovizioso – a difference of seven tenths a lap – and just 1.7 seconds outside the top ten.

## RACE LAP CHART

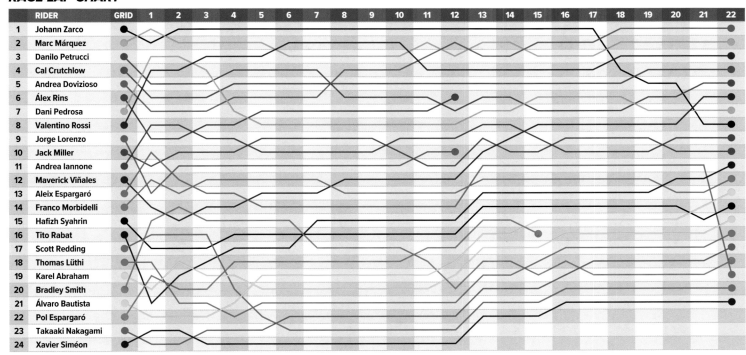

| | RIDER | GRID |
|---|---|---|
| 1 | Johann Zarco | |
| 2 | Marc Márquez | |
| 3 | Danilo Petrucci | |
| 4 | Cal Crutchlow | |
| 5 | Andrea Dovizioso | |
| 6 | Álex Rins | |
| 7 | Dani Pedrosa | |
| 8 | Valentino Rossi | |
| 9 | Jorge Lorenzo | |
| 10 | Jack Miller | |
| 11 | Andrea Iannone | |
| 12 | Maverick Viñales | |
| 13 | Aleix Espargaró | |
| 14 | Franco Morbidelli | |
| 15 | Hafizh Syahrin | |
| 16 | Tito Rabat | |
| 17 | Scott Redding | |
| 18 | Thomas Lüthi | |
| 19 | Karel Abraham | |
| 20 | Bradley Smith | |
| 21 | Álvaro Bautista | |
| 22 | Pol Espargaró | |
| 23 | Takaaki Nakagami | |
| 24 | Xavier Siméon | |

## RACE CLASSIFICATION AFTER 22 LAPS - 118.36 KM

| | RIDER | NAT | TEAM | MACHINE | TIME | + GAP | TYRES |
|---|---|---|---|---|---|---|---|
| 1 | Andrea Dovizioso | ITA | Ducati Team | DUCATI | 42'34.654 | | M/S |
| 2 | Marc Márquez | SPA | Repsol Honda Team | HONDA | 42'34.681 | 0.027 | H/S |
| 3 | Valentino Rossi | ITA | Movistar Yamaha MotoGP | YAMAHA | 42'35.451 | 0.797 | M/S |
| 4 | Cal Crutchlow | GBR | LCR Honda CASTROL | HONDA | 42'37.535 | 2.881 | M/S |
| 5 | Danilo Petrucci | ITA | Alma Pramac Racing | DUCATI | 42'38.475 | 3.821 | S/S |
| 6 | Maverick Viñales | SPA | Movistar Yamaha MotoGP | YAMAHA | 42'38.542 | 3.888 | M/S |
| 7 | Dani Pedrosa | SPA | Repsol Honda Team | HONDA | 42'39.275 | 4.621 | H/S |
| 8 | Johann Zarco | FRA | Monster Yamaha Tech 3 | YAMAHA | 42'41.766 | 7.112 | M/S |
| 9 | Andrea Iannone | ITA | Team SUZUKI ECSTAR | SUZUKI | 42'47.611 | 12.957 | M/S |
| 10 | Jack Miller | AUS | Alma Pramac Racing | DUCATI | 42'49.248 | 14.594 | M/S |
| 11 | Tito Rabat | SPA | Reale Avintia Racing | DUCATI | 42'49.835 | 15.181 | S/S |
| 12 | Franco Morbidelli | ITA | EG 0,0 Marc VDS | HONDA | 42'50.928 | 16.274 | M/S |
| 13 | Álvaro Bautista | SPA | Ángel Nieto Team | DUCATI | 42'54.442 | 19.788 | S/S |
| 14 | Hafizh Syahrin | MAL | Monster Yamaha Tech 3 | YAMAHA | 42'54.953 | 20.299 | M/S |
| 15 | Karel Abraham | CZE | Ángel Nieto Team | DUCATI | 42'57.941 | 23.287 | M/S |
| 16 | Thomas Lüthi | SWI | EG 0,0 Marc VDS | HONDA | 42'58.843 | 24.189 | M/S |
| 17 | Takaaki Nakagami | JPN | LCR Honda IDEMITSU | HONDA | 42'59.208 | 24.554 | M/S |
| 18 | Bradley Smith | GBR | Red Bull KTM Factory Racing | KTM | 43'06.358 | 31.704 | S/S |
| 19 | Aleix Espargaró | SPA | Aprilia Racing Team Gresini | APRILIA | 43'09.366 | 34.712 | S/S |
| 20 | Scott Redding | GBR | Aprilia Racing Team Gresini | APRILIA | 43'12.295 | 37.641 | S/S |
| 21 | Xavier Siméon | GER | Reale Avintia Racing | DUCATI | 43'21.360 | 46.706 | S/S |
| NC | Pol Espargaró | SPA | Red Bull KTM Factory Racing | KTM | 29'18.942 | 7 laps | S/S |
| NC | Álex Rins | SPA | Team SUZUKI ECSTAR | SUZUKI | 23'17.627 | 10 laps | M/S |
| NC | Jorge Lorenzo | SPA | Ducati Team | DUCATI | 23'20.011 | 10 laps | M/S |

## CHAMPIONSHIP STANDINGS

| | RIDER | NAT | TEAM | POINTS |
|---|---|---|---|---|
| 1 | Andrea Dovizioso | ITA | Ducati Team | 25 |
| 2 | Marc Márquez | SPA | Repsol Honda Team | 20 |
| 3 | Valentino Rossi | ITA | Movistar Yamaha MotoGP | 16 |
| 4 | Cal Crutchlow | GBR | LCR Honda CASTROL | 13 |
| 5 | Danilo Petrucci | ITA | Alma Pramac Racing | 11 |
| 6 | Maverick Viñales | SPA | Movistar Yamaha MotoGP | 10 |
| 7 | Dani Pedrosa | SPA | Repsol Honda Team | 9 |
| 8 | Johann Zarco | FRA | Monster Yamaha Tech 3 | 8 |
| 9 | Andrea Iannone | ITA | Team SUZUKI ECSTAR | 7 |
| 10 | Jack Miller | AUS | Alma Pramac Racing | 6 |
| 11 | Tito Rabat | SPA | Reale Avintia Racing | 5 |
| 12 | Franco Morbidelli | ITA | EG 0,0 Marc VDS | 4 |
| 13 | Álvaro Bautista | SPA | Ángel Nieto Team | 3 |
| 14 | Hafizh Syahrin | MAL | Monster Yamaha Tech 3 | 2 |
| 15 | Karel Abraham | CZE | Ángel Nieto Team | 1 |
| 16 | Thomas Lüthi | SWI | EG 0,0 Marc VDS | |
| 17 | Takaaki Nakagami | JPN | LCR Honda IDEMITSU | |
| 18 | Bradley Smith | GBR | Red Bull KTM Factory Racing | |
| 19 | Aleix Espargaró | SPA | Aprilia Racing Team Gresini | |
| 20 | Scott Redding | GBR | Aprilia Racing Team Gresini | |
| 21 | Xavier Siméon | GER | Reale Avintia Racing | |
| 22 | Pol Espargaró | SPA | Red Bull KTM Factory Racing | |
| 23 | Álex Rins | SPA | Team SUZUKI ECSTAR | |
| 24 | Jorge Lorenzo | SPA | Ducati Team | |

**13 | ÁLVARO BAUTISTA**
A gloomy first race under the team's new Ángel Nieto banner for the former 125 world champion, who found his GP17 a poorer fit than the GP16 he had ridden so well during the 2017 season His main issue was getting heat into the tyres.

**14 | HAFIZH SYAHRIN**
A remarkable debut. Only got the call-up to replace Jonas Folger during February. Syahrin made double history in this race: the first South East Asian to race in MotoGP and the first to score points.

**15 | KAREL ABRAHAM**
The Czech rider and Moto2 winner won the battle with two MotoGP rookies for the final world championship point after losing time and several positions with a near-collision and then a near-highside during the early laps of the race.

**16 | THOMAS LÜTHI**
Missed scoring points in his debut MotoGP race by less than a second; not bad considering that he had missed much of pre-season testing through injury. His only worries in the race were problems during braking.

**17 | TAKAAKI NAKAGAMI**
The last of Honda's three MotoGP rookies, but only just. The Japanese Moto2 race winner had been quick in pre-season testing, but a crash at the Losail test and another tumble during practice dented his form in his MotoGP race debut.

**18 | BRADLEY SMITH**
The Briton fought well to get into the points-scoring positions in the early stages, but lost front grip from the middle stages, causing serious understeer issues which made him an easy victim for his rivals.

**19 | ALEIX ESPARGARÓ**
Chased Miller for a top-ten, using a conservative engine-management map so he could save the full-power map for the end, but fuelling problems prevented him making the switch, then he ran short of gas on the final lap.

**20 | SCOTT REDDING**
Searched for grip throughout the weekend and battled against poor rear traction in the race, which left the Briton unable to run a good pace from start to finish. He ended up 15 seconds outside the points.

**21 | XAVIER SIMÉON**
The Belgian rookie wasn't able to complete a race simulation in pre-season testing, so this was his first full race run on a MotoGP bike; a huge physical test. He was at least happy that he rode his best lap on lap 19 of 22.

**DNF | POL ESPARGARÓ**
Already handicapped by a technical problem and then a crash during practice, the Spaniard fought his way through from 19th into the points, only to be KO'd by a reoccurrence of the same electronics glitch.

**DNF | ÁLEX RINS**
The youngster was enjoying a great start to his second MotoGP season, riding at the tail of the lead group. Losail's second corner is the most difficult corner of the year, according to Rins' crew chief.

**DNF | JORGE LORENZO**
A poor grid position left the Spaniard with a lot of work to do in the race, but by mid-race he was really flying. Indeed he was the fastest rider on track, until his front brake failed at speed and he had to abandon ship.

Crutchlow rode through the chaos, timing his winning move to perfection

# DRAMA, DRAMA, DRAMA!

*Termas has a habit of hosting controversial races, but the 2018 Argentine Grand Prix was just about as dramatic as it's possible to get*

Sometimes a little chaos creates something beautiful. The fifth Argentine Grand Prix at Termas de Rio Hondo was certainly that, for some at least, although not for others.

The race turned MotoGP upside down, with all the main protagonists out of the running, for one reason or another, leaving the race to the podium to Cal Crutchlow, Johann Zarco, Álex Rins and Jack Miller.

A hard-charging Marc Márquez was hit with three sanctions that left him out of the points, Valentino Rossi was hit by Márquez, Dani Pedrosa was hit by Zarco and Jorge Lorenzo was nowhere to be seen.

Who to blame for the chaos? The weather, mostly, and how most teams and riders reacted to it. A morning downpour had soaked the track, but by the time the MotoGP grid lined up the asphalt was drying fast. And yet the only man who went to the grid on slicks was Miller. The previous afternoon the 23-year-old had achieved his first premier class pole position – Australia's first since Casey Stoner's last at Phillip Island, 2012 – in jaw-dropping rodeo style, his Alma Pramac Ducati whipping this way and that on a mostly wet track, Miller refusing to shut the throttle, even when he was kicked out of the seat.

Miller was the only rider left on the grid when the other 23 bikes, wearing rain tyres, were wheeled back into pit lane, so their riders could swap to their second bikes, wearing slicks and dry settings. Finally, the race was delayed and the 23 formed up from the back row of the grid, in qualifying order, five rows behind Miller.

But the chaos was only just beginning. Márquez stalled his engine at the end of warm-up lap, then bumped it back into life as IRTA officials Tony Congram and Danny Aldridge chased him around the grid. When the lights went out, the world champion set off like a man possessed, possibly guessing a time penalty was coming his way. He was already looking for a way past Miller by turn 13 on the first lap, which is where Zarco did for Pedrosa.

Márquez had stretched a six second lead in five laps when the penalty came. After his ride-through he was 19th, 21 seconds down on Miller, who had Rins, Zarco and Crutchlow bearing down upon him. Now the race had two focus points: the four-way battle for victory and Márquez's rampant progress through the pack. By half-distance the leading quartet had bunched up, just eight tenths between them.

It was thrilling but scrappy stuff – Rins took the lead from Miller several times, only to run wide on damp patches of asphalt and allow the Aussie back in front. Rins wasn't the only one; all four were having moments in the sketchy conditions, getting sideways as they crossed the small river before the back straight and smoking rubber through turns six and 11. Miller's race went away from him on lap 18 of 24 when he nearly lost it on the soaking asphalt entering turn 13. That dropped him from first to fourth.

So now it was just the three of them. Crutchlow led, then Zarco, with Rins attacking Crutchlow for second. The Briton's winning move came on the last-but-one lap. Somehow he kept the power down across the turn-six river, which took him past Zarco. This was his fastest lap and it sealed his victory, although the Frenchman was still looking for a way past at the finish.

Crutchlow, the first British rider to lead the premier-class championship since Barry Sheene in the 1970s, had ridden a canny race in treacherous conditions. "The first ten laps I was sat in a comfortable position, not taking the same lines as them," he said after taking Honda's 750th Grand Prix win. "I was concerned that if one of them crashed on the water they would take me with them. We managed the situation very well: I won the race at the slowest possible speed."

Zarco had run out of steam by the final lap. "Cal had the better pace and I was a bit tired," he said. Rins was delighted, his first MotoGP podium and Suzuki's first top-three since Maverick Viñales finished third at Motegi in October 2016. "When Jack was leading I tried to overtake three or four times," said the 22-year-old. "But the track conditions were very bad – a lot of patches off the usual racing line."

The podium media conference was attended by fewer journalists than usual, because they thought they had a bigger story to tell.

**MAIN** Miller was the only man who stayed true to his original tyre choice; but all he got was a 100-metre start over his rivals

**TOP, FROM LEFT** Miller's pole-position lap on a damp track was something to behold: he was out of the seat more than once; Rins looks pensive before his best ride yet; Zarco tried everything he knew to get his first MotoGP victory

## WHEN STARTS GET TRICKY...

Regulations are adapted according to changing circumstances and unexpected incidents. MotoGP's start procedure was rewritten for 2005, introducing so-called flag-to-flag races, and again following the wet/dry 2014 German GP, which got underway with most of the grid starting from pit lane, elbow to elbow, after they had pitted at the end of the warm-up lap to change to their second bikes equipped with slicks. The rules were therefore rewritten to prevent another chaotic pit lane start: riders pitting after the warm-up lap must start in single file.

What happened this time was slightly different: the majority of riders left the grid to change bikes before the warm-up lap. A rule

Some way behind the lead group, life had become even more complicated for Márquez. On lap nine he thumped into Aleix Espargaró at turn 12, forcing his fellow Spaniard onto the asphalt runoff. At the time he was lapping almost four seconds faster than the Aprilia rider. Márquez was told to drop one position for his second sanction of the afternoon and he obeyed the signal. But worse was to come.

With five laps to go Márquez was catching sixth-placed Valentino Rossi at the rate of almost a second per lap. He closed on the Yamaha into turn 12 and went for the inside pass at turn 13. But there was no room and he nearly tucked the front on the wet asphalt. He thumped into Rossi, who wobbled off the track and toppled over on the wet grass. And this exactly three years after the pair's first clash, at turn six, which had left Márquez on the ground.

Rossi remounted to cross the line in 19th, while Márquez continued in full-attack mode, taking fifth from Viñales at the end of the final lap. However, it was obvious that there was another sanction coming Márquez's way. Race Direction gave him a 30-second penalty, which dropped him out of the points.

The atmosphere in pit lane was ugly. When Márquez visited Rossi's garage to apologise he was angrily shooed away by the nine-time world champion's friend and assistant Uccio Salucci. Rossi didn't hold back. "This is a very bad situation because he is destroying our sport. He doesn't have any respect for his rivals."

## 'WE MANAGED THE SITUATION VERY WELL: I WON THE RACE AT THE SLOWEST POSSIBLE SPEED'
CAL CRUTCHLOW

**CLOCKWISE, FROM TOP LEFT** | *Just like Sepang 2015, but the other way around; Márquez goes on his way as Rossi makes his feelings clear; Race Direction, IRTA and team managers try to make sense of the chaos on the grid; Miller leads before a mistake dropped him to fourth*

had been written to cope with this situation (all riders so doing must line up at the back of the grid in their qualifying positions), but 23 riders going through this procedure required a whole new grid to be arranged from the back row, hence the delayed start.

Once again, the rules were rewritten, this time to discourage riders from changing bikes at the last minute, which brings the risk of riders gambling with slicks on a damp track. Riders changing bikes before or after the warm-up lap must now serve a ride-through penalty during the race.

The rule concerning riders stalling engines after the warm-up lap was also tightened, making it 100 percent clear that riders aren't allowed to restart engines.

# 2 | ARGENTINA

# RACE RESULTS

**WINNER** | CAL CRUTCHLOW

**CIRCUIT LENGTH** | 4.8 KM | 2.99 MILES

**NO. OF LAPS** | 25

**RACE DISTANCE** | 120.2 KM | 74.8 MILES

**CIRCUIT RECORD LAP** | 1'39.019 | 174.7 KM/H
*VALENTINO ROSSI (2015)*

**CIRCUIT BEST LAP** | 1'37.683 | 177.1 KM/H
*MARC MÁRQUEZ (2014)*

**RACE CONDITION** | WET

**AIR** | 22°C

**HUMIDITY** | 94%

**GROUND** | 23°C

| | Start Line |
| | Sectors |
| S | Speed Trap |
| FL | Finish Line |

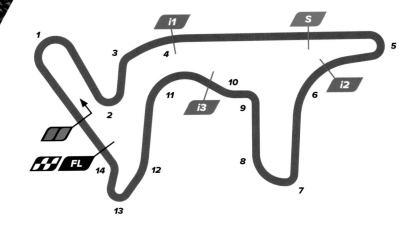

TISSOT
SWISS WATCHES SINCE 1853 | motoGP™

**OFFICIAL** TIMEKEEPER

MICHELIN | motoGP™

**OFFICIAL** MotoGP™ CLASS TYRE

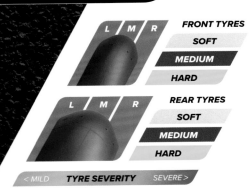

**FRONT TYRES**
L M R
SOFT
MEDIUM
HARD

**REAR TYRES**
L M R
SOFT
MEDIUM
HARD

< MILD | **TYRE SEVERITY** | SEVERE >

## QUALIFYING RESULTS

| | RIDER | NAT | TEAM | MACHINE | QP/TIME | GAP 1ST/PREV | |
|---|---|---|---|---|---|---|---|
| 1 | Jack Miller | AUS | Alma Pramac Racing | DUCATI | Q2 1'47.153 | | |
| 2 | Dani Pedrosa | SPA | Repsol Honda Team | HONDA | Q2 1'47.330 | 0.177 | 0.177 |
| 3 | Johann Zarco | FRA | Monster Yamaha Tech 3 | YAMAHA | Q2 1'47.365 | 0.212 | 0.035 |
| 4 | Tito Rabat | SPA | Reale Avintia Racing | DUCATI | Q2 1'47.681 | 0.528 | 0.316 |
| 5 | Álex Rins | SPA | Team SUZUKI ECSTAR | SUZUKI | Q2 1'47.743 | 0.590 | 0.062 |
| 6 | Marc Márquez | SPA | Repsol Honda Team | HONDA | Q2 1'47.754 | 0.601 | 0.011 |
| 7 | Aleix Espargaró** | SPA | Aprilia Racing Team Gresini | APRILIA | Q2 1'47.845 | 0.692 | 0.091 |
| 8 | Andrea Dovizioso** | ITA | Ducati Team | DUCATI | Q2 1'48.247 | 1.094 | 0.402 |
| 9 | Maverick Viñales | SPA | Movistar Yamaha MotoGP | YAMAHA | Q2 1'49.044 | 1.891 | 0.797 |
| 10 | Cal Crutchlow | GBR | LCR Honda CASTROL | HONDA | Q2 1'49.304 | 2.151 | 0.260 |
| 11 | Valentino Rossi | ITA | Movistar Yamaha MotoGP | YAMAHA | Q2 1'49.326 | 2.173 | 0.022 |
| 12 | Andrea Iannone | ITA | Team SUZUKI ECSTAR | SUZUKI | Q2 1'49.975 | 2.822 | 0.649 |
| 13 | Karel Abraham | CZE | Ángel Nieto Team | DUCATI | Q1 1'49.878 | *0.750 | 0.360 |
| 14 | Jorge Lorenzo | SPA | Ducati Team | DUCATI | Q1 1'50.063 | *0.935 | 0.185 |
| 15 | Scott Redding | GBR | Aprilia Racing Team Gresini | APRILIA | Q1 1'50.175 | *1.047 | 0.112 |
| 16 | Pol Espargaró | SPA | Red Bull KTM Factory Racing | KTM | Q1 1'50.324 | *1.196 | 0.149 |
| 17 | Xavier Siméon | GER | Reale Avintia Racing | DUCATI | Q1 1'50.364 | *1.236 | 0.040 |
| 18 | Danilo Petrucci | ITA | Alma Pramac Racing | DUCATI | Q1 1'50.449 | *1.321 | 0.085 |
| 19 | Alvaro Bautista | SPA | Ángel Nieto Team | DUCATI | Q1 1'50.606 | *1.478 | 0.157 |
| 20 | Thomas Lüthi | SWI | EG 0,0 Marc VDS | HONDA | Q1 1'50.833 | *1.705 | 0.227 |
| 21 | Bradley Smith | GBR | Red Bull KTM Factory Racing | KTM | Q1 1'51.007 | *1.879 | 0.174 |
| 22 | Franco Morbidelli | ITA | EG 0,0 Marc VDS | HONDA | Q1 1'51.012 | *1.884 | 0.005 |
| 23 | Hafizh Syahrin | MAL | Monster Yamaha Tech 3 | YAMAHA | Q1 1'51.142 | *2.014 | 0.130 |
| 24 | Takaaki Nakagami | JPN | LCR Honda IDEMITSU | HONDA | Q1 1'51.387 | *2.259 | 0.245 |

*\* Gap to the fastest rider in the Q1 session*
*\*\* Went forward from Q1 to Q2*

**1 | CAL CRUTCHLOW**
Crutchlow had finished on the podium at the previous three Argentine GPs, so it was no huge surprise to see him in contention for victory. He rode a canny race, letting the others lead in the tricky conditions, then pouncing at the end.

**2 | JOHANN ZARCO**
Like everyone else, didn't find the delayed start easy to deal with. He was tense at the start, which may explain his over-optimistic move on Pedrosa. On the last lap, he decided discretion is the better part of valour.

**3 | ÁLEX RINS**
Delighted with his first MotoGP podium result. Challenged for the win on many occasions, but always got into trouble with the damp parts of the track. As usual, he was fast and safe, treating his rivals with a lot of respect.

**4 | JACK MILLER**
The only man to make the correct tyre choice suffered for his decision more than anyone, but Miller was his usual philosophical self about that. Disappointed to miss the podium, but happy with his weekend overall.

**5 | MAVERICK VIÑALES**
Early signs of a problem that would haunt him as the season went on: he struggled in the early laps and only had front-running pace during the later stages of the race, when nonetheless he was overtaken by the flying Márquez.

**6 | ANDREA DOVIZIOSO**
A difficult weekend, with recurrent rain playing havoc with his hopes of getting his set-up right for the track. Didn't feel confident to push in the conditions but was lucky that Márquez and Rossi failed to score.

**7 | TITO RABAT**
Once again, showed how fast he can be on a Ducati. Third fastest on Friday, fourth quickest in Q2, then his best MotoGP result in the race. Also, his first ride in the lead group taught him many lessons he needed to learn for the future.

**8 | ANDREA IANNONE**
Spent the race trying to make up for a poor qualifying. Felt like he had the pace to run closer to the front, but was unable to use it because he had to dodge between the damp patches to pass other riders.

**9 | HAFIZH SYAHRIN**
Mightily impressive: a top-ten finish from his second MotoGP ride, despite only having his first ride on a MotoGP bike in February and despite starting from 25th on the grid. Spent much of the race chasing the factory Yamahas of Rossi and Viñales.

**10 | DANILO PETRUCCI**
Wet/dry qualifying left him 18th, with a lot of catching up to do. Worked his way into ninth and had his eyes set on Dovizioso, until he collided with Syahrin, which dropped him back to tenth at the flag.

**11 | POL ESPARGARÓ**
His first finish of the year and one place outside the top-ten, a position which would soon become very familiar to him. Believed he could have gone faster but for the RC16's inability to find grip when there's not much around.

**12 | SCOTT REDDING**
Made a good job of sussing out the conditions from the start, which put him in a fast group. Chased Pol Espargaró for much of the race and came within a few tenths of catching the KTM rider on the final lap.

## RACE LAP CHART

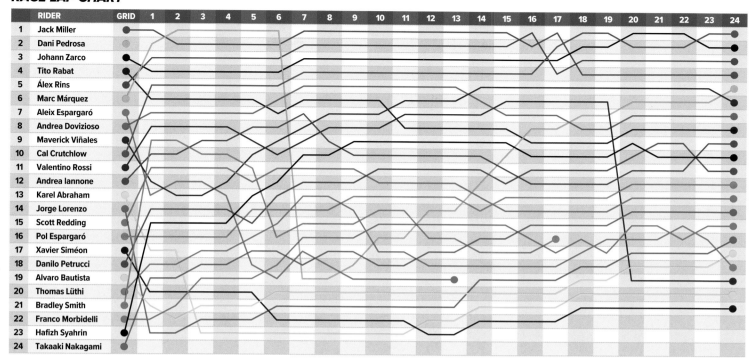

| RIDER | GRID | 1 | 2 | 3 | 4 | 5 | 6 | 7 | 8 | 9 | 10 | 11 | 12 | 13 | 14 | 15 | 16 | 17 | 18 | 19 | 20 | 21 | 22 | 23 | 24 |
|---|---|---|---|---|---|---|---|---|---|---|---|---|---|---|---|---|---|---|---|---|---|---|---|---|---|
| 1 Jack Miller | | | | | | | | | | | | | | | | | | | | | | | | | |
| 2 Dani Pedrosa | | | | | | | | | | | | | | | | | | | | | | | | | |
| 3 Johann Zarco | | | | | | | | | | | | | | | | | | | | | | | | | |
| 4 Tito Rabat | | | | | | | | | | | | | | | | | | | | | | | | | |
| 5 Álex Rins | | | | | | | | | | | | | | | | | | | | | | | | | |
| 6 Marc Márquez | | | | | | | | | | | | | | | | | | | | | | | | | |
| 7 Aleix Espargaró | | | | | | | | | | | | | | | | | | | | | | | | | |
| 8 Andrea Dovizioso | | | | | | | | | | | | | | | | | | | | | | | | | |
| 9 Maverick Viñales | | | | | | | | | | | | | | | | | | | | | | | | | |
| 10 Cal Crutchlow | | | | | | | | | | | | | | | | | | | | | | | | | |
| 11 Valentino Rossi | | | | | | | | | | | | | | | | | | | | | | | | | |
| 12 Andrea Iannone | | | | | | | | | | | | | | | | | | | | | | | | | |
| 13 Karel Abraham | | | | | | | | | | | | | | | | | | | | | | | | | |
| 14 Jorge Lorenzo | | | | | | | | | | | | | | | | | | | | | | | | | |
| 15 Scott Redding | | | | | | | | | | | | | | | | | | | | | | | | | |
| 16 Pol Espargaró | | | | | | | | | | | | | | | | | | | | | | | | | |
| 17 Xavier Siméon | | | | | | | | | | | | | | | | | | | | | | | | | |
| 18 Danilo Petrucci | | | | | | | | | | | | | | | | | | | | | | | | | |
| 19 Alvaro Bautista | | | | | | | | | | | | | | | | | | | | | | | | | |
| 20 Thomas Lüthi | | | | | | | | | | | | | | | | | | | | | | | | | |
| 21 Bradley Smith | | | | | | | | | | | | | | | | | | | | | | | | | |
| 22 Franco Morbidelli | | | | | | | | | | | | | | | | | | | | | | | | | |
| 23 Hafizh Syahrin | | | | | | | | | | | | | | | | | | | | | | | | | |
| 24 Takaaki Nakagami | | | | | | | | | | | | | | | | | | | | | | | | | |

## RACE CLASSIFICATION AFTER 24 LAPS⁺ = 115.344 KM

| | RIDER | NAT | TEAM | MACHINE | TIME | + GAP | TYRES |
|---|---|---|---|---|---|---|---|
| 1 | Cal Crutchlow | GBR | LCR Honda CASTROL | HONDA | 40'36.342 | | M/M |
| 2 | Johann Zarco | FRA | Monster Yamaha Tech 3 | YAMAHA | 40'36.593 | 0.251 | S/M |
| 3 | Álex Rins | SPA | Team SUZUKI ECSTAR | SUZUKI | 40'38.843 | 2.501 | M/M |
| 4 | Jack Miller | AUS | Alma Pramac Racing | DUCATI | 40'40.732 | 4.390 | M/M |
| 5 | Maverick Viñales | SPA | Movistar Yamaha MotoGP | YAMAHA | 40'51.283 | 14.941 | M/M |
| 6 | Andrea Dovizioso | ITA | Ducati Team | DUCATI | 40'58.875 | 22.533 | M/M |
| 7 | Tito Rabat | SPA | Reale Avintia Racing | DUCATI | 40'59.368 | 23.026 | M/M |
| 8 | Andrea Iannone | ITA | Team SUZUKI ECSTAR | SUZUKI | 41'00.263 | 23.921 | S/M |
| 9 | Hafizh Syahrin | MAL | Monster Yamaha Tech 3 | YAMAHA | 41'00.653 | 24.311 | S/M |
| 10 | Danilo Petrucci | ITA | Alma Pramac Racing | DUCATI | 41'02.345 | 26.003 | M/M |
| 11 | Pol Espargaró | SPA | Red Bull KTM Factory Racing | KTM | 41'07.364 | 31.022 | M/M |
| 12 | Scott Redding | GBR | Aprilia Racing Team Gresini | APRILIA | 41'08.233 | 31.891 | S/M |
| 13 | Takaaki Nakagami | JPN | LCR Honda IDEMITSU | HONDA | 41'08.794 | 32.452 | M/M |
| 14 | Franco Morbidelli | ITA | EG 0,0 Marc VDS | HONDA | 41'18.403 | 42.061 | M/M |
| 15 | Jorge Lorenzo | SPA | Ducati Team | DUCATI | 41'18.616 | 42.274 | M/M |
| 16 | Alvaro Bautista | SPA | Ángel Nieto Team | DUCATI | 41'18.967 | 42.625 | M/M |
| 17 | Thomas Lüthi | SWI | EG 0,0 Marc VDS | HONDA | 41'19.692 | 43.350 | M/M |
| 18 | Marc Márquez⁺⁺ | SPA | Repsol Honda Team | HONDA | 41'20.202 | 43.860 | M/M |
| 19 | Valentino Rossi | ITA | Movistar Yamaha MotoGP | YAMAHA | 41'28.424 | 52.082 | M/M |
| 20 | Karel Abraham | CZE | Ángel Nieto Team | DUCATI | 41'40.286 | 63.944 | M/M |
| 21 | Xavier Siméon | GER | Reale Avintia Racing | DUCATI | 41'46.486 | 70.144 | M/M |
| NC | Bradley Smith | GBR | Red Bull KTM Factory Racing | KTM | 29'19.028 | 7 laps | M/M |
| NC | Aleix Espargaró | SPA | Aprilia Racing Team Gresini | APRILIA | 22'32.967 | 11 laps | M/M |
| NC | Dani Pedrosa | SPA | Repsol Honda Team | HONDA | | | M/M |

## CHAMPIONSHIP STANDINGS

| | RIDER | NAT | TEAM | POINTS |
|---|---|---|---|---|
| 1 | Cal Crutchlow | GBR | LCR Honda CASTROL | 38 |
| 2 | Andrea Dovizioso | ITA | Ducati Team | 35 |
| 3 | Johann Zarco | FRA | Monster Yamaha Tech 3 | 28 |
| 4 | Maverick Viñales | SPA | Movistar Yamaha MotoGP | 21 |
| 5 | Marc Márquez | SPA | Repsol Honda Team | 20 |
| 6 | Jack Miller | AUS | Alma Pramac Racing | 19 |
| 7 | Danilo Petrucci | ITA | Alma Pramac Racing | 17 |
| 8 | Valentino Rossi | ITA | Movistar Yamaha MotoGP | 16 |
| 9 | Álex Rins | SPA | Team SUZUKI ECSTAR | 16 |
| 10 | Andrea Iannone | ITA | Team SUZUKI ECSTAR | 15 |
| 11 | Tito Rabat | SPA | Reale Avintia Racing | 14 |
| 12 | Dani Pedrosa | SPA | Repsol Honda Team | 9 |
| 13 | Hafizh Syahrin | MAL | Monster Yamaha Tech 3 | 9 |
| 14 | Franco Morbidelli | ITA | EG 0,0 Marc VDS | 6 |
| 15 | Pol Espargaró | SPA | Red Bull KTM Factory Racing | 5 |
| 16 | Scott Redding | GBR | Aprilia Racing Team Gresini | 4 |
| 17 | Alvaro Bautista | SPA | Ángel Nieto Team | 3 |
| 18 | Takaaki Nakagami | JPN | LCR Honda IDEMITSU | 3 |
| 19 | Karel Abraham | CZE | Ángel Nieto Team | 1 |
| 20 | Jorge Lorenzo | SPA | Ducati Team | 1 |
| 21 | Thomas Lüthi | SWI | EG 0,0 Marc VDS | |
| 22 | Bradley Smith | GBR | Red Bull KTM Factory Racing | |
| 23 | Aleix Espargaró | SPA | Aprilia Racing Team Gresini | |
| 24 | Xavier Siméon | GER | Reale Avintia Racing | |

+ Race shortened to 24 laps due to weather conditions and tyre changes after warm-up lap
++ FIM MotoGP Stewards Race penalties - Marc Márquez : ride-through penalty, drop one-position penalty and a ride-through 30 second penalty imposed

**13 | TAKAAKI NAKAGAMI**
Scored his first MotoGP points, despite starting from the very back of the grid following a disastrous qualifying. The former Moto2 race winner found that he got faster as the race went along, just as he had in his debut race in Qatar.

**14 | FRANCO MORBIDELLI**
His result wasn't as good as Qatar, but this was a more problematic weekend, with no testing beforehand, and the changeable weather causing more problems for rookies than for experienced riders.

**15 | JORGE LORENZO**
Lorenzo learned to be fast in the rain some years ago, but once again didn't find the going easy in mixed conditions. At the start was wary of crashing out, as he had done last year. Got faster as the race went on and the track dried.

**16 | ALVARO BAUTISTA**
Also lacked the confidence to push in the early laps. When Lorenzo passed him he tucked in behind, even though he wasn't getting much feel from the tyres. Riding faster warmed the tyres, helping him push harder.

**17 | THOMAS LÜTHI**
Like his fellow rookies, the rainy weekend didn't help him to make much forward progress. Spent some time fighting with Morbidelli but during the final stages of the race he found himself exhausted and fighting with the bike.

**18 | MARC MÁRQUEZ**
Three sanctions in one race may just be a record. Seemed intoxicated by his own speed as he found grip where the others found none. Some thought it was a remarkable ride, others thought the exact opposite.

**19 | VALENTINO ROSSI**
Rode a good race and was heading towards a fifth-place finish when Márquez came through like a bull in a china shop. After the race he announced that he was scared to share a racetrack with the reigning world champion.

**20 | KAREL ABRAHAM**
The race was chaotic for everyone, but more so for Abraham, who had a few collisions with other riders, then had his front brake fail. Ended up in the gravel, which concluded his hopes of making it into the points.

**21 | XAVIER SIMÉON**
Qualified well and was looking forward to the race. But things didn't go the way he had hoped. Made a mistake in the early stages, while getting used to carbon brakes, which had him off the track and at the back of the pack.

**DNF | BRADLEY SMITH**
Felt good on the bike and was fully committed in the treacherous early laps. That allowed him to make up positions, but he lost time through collisions. Finally got too greedy, ran wide at turn one and lost the front.

**DNF | ALEIX ESPARGARÓ**
Went well at the start but then ran into problems: the bike responded strangely to the throttle accelerating from low speed. After getting barged out of the way by Márquez and Petrucci, he finally fell victim to an electronics glitch.

**DNF | DANI PEDROSA**
Started well from the front row but his season went wrong on the first lap. The luckless Spaniard ran wide, opened the throttle and was thrown over the top, breaking his right wrist.

*Márquez – dangling a leg into the turn-11 hairpin – was out to make a point and he made it very well*

# THE QUIET AFTER THE STORM

**Two weeks after the Argentine Grand Prix, what the MotoGP paddock needed was a quieter weekend. It got it**

Tensions were still high and wounds still raw as riders and teams gathered at COTA, ten days after the chaos of Termas. Inevitably, Friday evening's safety meeting descended into a war of words between Valentino Rossi and Marc Márquez; the voice of reason turning out to be a young man who goes by the name of Jackass: Jack Miller.

"I want to refresh people's memories of Marco Simoncelli and Dani Pedrosa [who had a controversial coming together at Le Mans in 2011]," said Miller. "We are all here racing and risking our lives, and all these fans are picking sides and fighting each other, and also the riders are fighting each other. I think it's quite silly and immature. These riders need to remember that life is short and that we are risking our lives."

Against this background of bickering the 21-lap race turned into something of an uneventful procession, which, after the stress of Argentina, was exactly what much of the paddock wanted.

Márquez comfortably continued his unbeaten run of ten victories on US asphalt: six at COTA, three at Indianapolis and one at Laguna Seca; all of them anti-clockwise tracks, as is the American way. But for the first time he didn't start from pole at COTA. He was quickest on Saturday afternoon but was later handed his fourth penalty in two races, for slowing Maverick Viñales during Q2. The two Spaniards have a bit of history, just one of MotoGP's many festering sores.

Before Termas, Race Direction would most likely have limited disciplinary action for such a peccadillo to a personal warning, but Termas had changed everything, with Race Director Mike Webb promising tougher sanctions all round; hence Márquez's demotion to the second row.

It didn't make any difference. Márquez took the lead from Andrea Iannone after 12 corners and that was that. No one can get a bike turned as quickly through COTA's numerous zig-zags and no one looks quite as happy with the bike kicking sideways through left-handers.

Iannone tried going with the Repsol rider but it was a hopeless task and very soon his concern was holding off Viñales rather than holding onto Márquez. Viñales out-braked the GSX-RR as they approached the first corner for the seventh time and once again Iannone had no reply. Immediately it looked like the Italian would suffer the same fate with Rossi, who was also closing.

But Iannone dug deep to secure his first podium in blue, while Rossi's pace cooled after he nearly lost the front several times. The veteran's medium front slick was too soft, but he had to race the tyre because he couldn't get the hard option to work.

That switched attention to the battle for fifth place, featuring Johan Zarco, Cal Crutchlow, Andrea Dovizioso and the pinned-and-plated Pedrosa. Championship leader Crutchlow was the first to go, losing the front as he wrestled his RC213V into the final turn on lap eight. Pedrosa faded to a lonely eighth-place finish (no surprise there), which left just Dovizioso and Zarco. The Italian prevailed, but a distant fifth was hardly the kind of result the Qatar winner had been aiming for.

"The problem for us at COTA is that the bike doesn't turn when you're off the brakes and there are many changes of direction here without brakes," he revealed.

Team-mate Jorge Lorenzo had an even more humbling race. He came home 11th, half a minute behind Márquez, after having Tito Rabat, Miller and Aleix Espargaró get the better of him in the final stages. The three-times MotoGP king had gathered just six points from the first three races. There were already rumours of Suzuki looking to replace Iannone for 2019 – despite his top-three result – and now whispers started circulating about Lorenzo's future at Ducati.

As Márquez climbed the podium he was booed by some (so-called) fans; not that it worried him. "It's another motivation," grinned the world champion, who wanted to show everyone what he could do after the ignominy of Termas. "My strategy was clear. We worked all weekend to try and do this kind of a race: push from the beginning to try to open a gap. When I feel extra pressure I usually like it, it gives me an extra push. I feel sweet on this year's bike. Last year I felt good after Catalunya; this year I felt good from Qatar…"

**ABOVE, FROM LEFT** | Rossi was mobbed wherever he went, as usual; Iannone scored his first podium with Suzuki, at last; Dovizioso and Lorenzo weren't seeing eye to eye

**MAIN** | It's only the first corner but Márquez has already come through from the second row to grab second place, with Iannone just ahead and out of shot

'WHEN I FEEL EXTRA PRESSURE I USUALLY LIKE IT, IT GIVES ME AN EXTRA PUSH'
MARC MÁRQUEZ

## MotoGP'S OPEN-AIR DYNO

The final uphill straight at Brno is known to some paddock people as God's own dyno, but in fact the main straight at COTA is MotoGP's best dynamometer. Not only is the straight the longest in the championship – at 1.2km/0.74 miles – it is also mostly uphill and approached from a first-gear corner, so it's the best-possible test of engine horsepower, power delivery, electronics and aero.

No surprises that the fastest bike of the weekend was a Ducati – Danilo Petrucci's Pramac GP18, to be precise. The Italian reached 347.9kmh/216.1mph during the second free practice session, when the wind was most favourable. In fact Petrucci was only

Viñales led the Movistar team's best result since Phillip Island 2017. He thought that Yamaha had finally found something, with a revised frame and some new ideas with the unified software. "I can now ride a little more aggressively, like I did early last year, so I am pushing the bike more," he said.

Viñales's rider coach Wilco Zeelenberg explained the new electronics philosophy. "We were controlling the power too much, now it's more free," said the former 250 GP winner. "Maverick and Valentino can now spin more or less, as they want, so they can adjust the situation themselves. Also the 2018 chassis [essentially a 2016 item] has better balance, so they need less electronics, so they can play with the bike more."

It turned out to be a false dawn.

Iannone was delighted with his first top three on the GSX-RR, lamenting Suzuki's wasted 2017, which was largely the result of incorrect crankshaft mass. "Last year everything was difficult in every way," he said. "We struggled a lot, especially in braking, so it was difficult to overtake other riders. Now the balance of the bike is better."

Rabat's second top-eight finish in two races suggested a rider finally coming into his own on a MotoGP bike. He beat Miller by 0.134 seconds, with Espargaró a further two tenths down. "That was a lot of fun," beamed the 2015 Moto2 champion. "It was a real thrill to ride with Lorenzo and Miller, who I managed to pass on the final lap."

**ANTI-CLOCKWISE FROM TOP LEFT** | *Ezpeleta bestowed MotoGP Legend status on an emotional Randy Mamola; Viñales got his first podium of 2018; Espargaro was fast and aggressive on the RS-GP; Lorenzo had yet another grim weekend; former American world champions: Kenny Roberts Junior, Ben Spies and Colin Edwards; Márquez pays tribute to the late Nicky Hayden, 2006 MotoGP king*

equal fastest, because Honda's more powerful 2018 RC213V engine had bridged the gap with the Desmosedici, Cal Crutchlow recording the exact same top speed in the same session.

Suzuki's winter engine work – in fact much of it done in Japan before the end of the 2017 season – also seemed to have paid off because the factory was the third-fastest brand, sneaking ahead of Yamaha. Álex Rins had the quickest GSX-RR at 343.1 kmh/213.1mph, albeit behind Dani Pedrosa's RCV and the Ducatis of Tito Rabat, Andrea Dovizioso and Jack Miller.

Valentino Rossi had the fastest Yamaha, behind Rins and Jorge Lorenzo, at 342.4 kmh/212.7mph. Top KTM was Pol Espargaró, just a fraction slower at 342.3 kmh/212.5mph. Aleix Espargaró's Aprilia was the best RS-GP at 341.0 kmh/211.8mph

# RACE RESULTS

**WINNER** | *MARC MÁRQUEZ*

**CIRCUIT LENGTH** | 5.5 KM | 3.43 MILES

**NO. OF LAPS⁺** | 20

**RACE DISTANCE⁺** | 110.3 KM | 68.6 MILES

**CIRCUIT RECORD LAP** | 2'03.575 | 160.6 KM/H
MARC MÁRQUEZ (2014)

**CIRCUIT BEST LAP** | 2'02.135 | 162.4 KM/H
MARC MÁRQUEZ (2015)

**RACE CONDITION** | DRY

**AIR** | 22°C

**HUMIDITY** | 45%

**GROUND** | 35°C

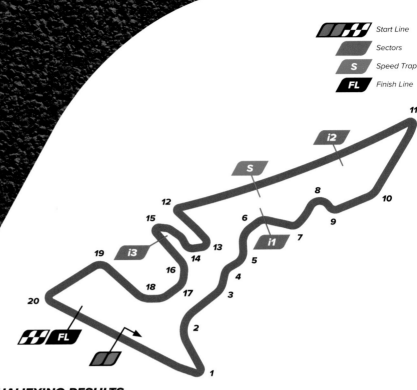

*Start Line*
*Sectors*
*S Speed Trap*
*FL Finish Line*

**TISSOT** SWISS WATCHES SINCE 1853 / *motoGP*

**OFFICIAL** TIMEKEEPER

**MICHELIN** / *motoGP*

**OFFICIAL** MotoGP™ CLASS TYRE

**FRONT TYRES**
L M R
SOFT
MEDIUM
HARD

**REAR TYRES**
L M R
SOFT
MEDIUM
HARD

< MILD **TYRE SEVERITY** SEVERE >

## QUALIFYING RESULTS

| | RIDER | NAT | TEAM | MACHINE | QP/TIME | | GAP 1ST/PREV | |
|---|---|---|---|---|---|---|---|---|
| 1 | **Marc Márquez** | SPA | Repsol Honda Team | HONDA | Q2 | 2'03.658 | | |
| 2 | **Maverick Viñales** | SPA | Movistar Yamaha MotoGP | YAMAHA | Q2 | 2'04.064 | 0.406 | 0.406 |
| 3 | **Andrea Iannone** | ITA | Team SUZUKI ECSTAR | SUZUKI | Q2 | 2'04.209 | 0.551 | 0.145 |
| 4 | **Johann Zarco** | FRA | Monster Yamaha Tech 3 | YAMAHA | Q2 | 2'04.210 | 0.552 | 0.001 |
| 5 | **Valentino Rossi** | ITA | Movistar Yamaha MotoGP | YAMAHA | Q2 | 2'04.229 | 0.571 | 0.019 |
| 6 | **Jorge Lorenzo** | SPA | Ducati Team | DUCATI | Q2 | 2'04.294 | 0.636 | 0.065 |
| 7 | **Cal Crutchlow** | GBR | LCR Honda CASTROL | HONDA | Q2 | 2'04.456 | 0.798 | 0.162 |
| 8 | **Andrea Dovizioso** | ITA | Ducati Team | DUCATI | Q2 | 2'04.865 | 1.207 | 0.409 |
| 9 | **Dani Pedrosa** | SPA | Repsol Honda Team | HONDA | Q2 | 2'04.963 | 1.305 | 0.098 |
| 10 | **Danilo Petrucci\*\*** | ITA | Alma Pramac Racing | DUCATI | Q2 | 2'05.058 | 1.400 | 0.095 |
| 11 | **Álex Rins** | SPA | Team SUZUKI ECSTAR | SUZUKI | Q2 | 2'05.260 | 1.602 | 0.202 |
| 12 | **Pol Espargaró\*\*** | SPA | Red Bull KTM Factory Racing | KTM | Q2 | 2'05.829 | 2.171 | 0.569 |
| 13 | **Takaaki Nakagami** | JPN | LCR Honda IDEMITSU | HONDA | Q1 | 2'05.457 | *0.288 | 0.212 |
| 14 | **Tito Rabat** | SPA | Reale Avintia Racing | DUCATI | Q1 | 2'05.686 | *0.517 | 0.229 |
| 15 | **Bradley Smith** | GBR | Red Bull KTM Factory Racing | KTM | Q1 | 2'05.761 | *0.592 | 0.075 |
| 16 | **Hafizh Syahrin** | MAL | Monster Yamaha Tech 3 | YAMAHA | Q1 | 2'05.873 | *0.704 | 0.112 |
| 17 | **Franco Morbidelli** | ITA | EG 0,0 Marc VDS | HONDA | Q1 | 2'05.943 | *0.774 | 0.070 |
| 18 | **Jack Miller** | AUS | Alma Pramac Racing | DUCATI | Q1 | 2'05.966 | *0.797 | 0.023 |
| 19 | **Aleix Espargaró** | SPA | Aprilia Racing Team Gresini | APRILIA | Q1 | 2'06.035 | *0.866 | 0.069 |
| 20 | **Thomas Lüthi** | SWI | EG 0,0 Marc VDS | HONDA | Q1 | 2'06.222 | *1.053 | 0.187 |
| 21 | **Álvaro Bautista** | SPA | Ángel Nieto Team | DUCATI | Q1 | 2'06.296 | *1.127 | 0.074 |
| 22 | **Scott Redding** | GBR | Aprilia Racing Team Gresini | APRILIA | Q1 | 2'06.370 | *1.201 | 0.074 |
| 23 | **Karel Abraham** | CZE | Ángel Nieto Team | DUCATI | Q1 | 2'06.537 | *1.368 | 0.167 |
| 24 | **Xavier Siméon** | GER | Reale Avintia Racing | DUCATI | Q1 | 2'06.726 | *1.557 | 0.189 |

*\* Gap to the fastest rider in the Q1 session*
*\*\* Went forward from Q1 to Q2*

**1 | MARC MÁRQUEZ**
Set out to make a point and made it. No one has got within a second of beating him at COTA, and that was in 2013, his second MotoGP race. A perfect weekend, apart from his misdemeanour in Q2, and an ominous performance for his rivals.

**2 | MAVERICK VIÑALES**
This seemed like a breakthrough race for Viñales, who bristled with confidence, even though he gave up chasing Márquez, after he had crashed out in 2017 doing just that. Believed his M1 had turned a corner.

**3 | ANDREA IANNONE**
Showed serious speed all weekend after making something of a breakthrough with front-end stability in the braking zone. Couldn't go with Márquez or Viñales in the race but his pace was good and he easily saw off Rossi's challenge.

**4 | VALENTINO ROSSI**
Was keener than ever for a podium to put the memories of Argentina behind him. Went into the race thinking he had the pace for third behind Márquez and Viñales but couldn't find a front tyre that worked.

**5 | ANDREA DOVIZIOSO**
Unusually, ran aero on his GP18 but struggled to find a set-up that would allow him to challenge for the podium, let alone the win. His second race off the pace was a worry, but he did head back to Europe leading the championship.

**6 | JOHANN ZARCO**
Chose the medium rear, like Rossi and Viñales, which gave him consistent enough grip, but the Frenchman didn't have the race set-up to capitalise on his front-row start (which was a present from Márquez).

**7 | DANI PEDROSA**
Once again, the Little Samurai gritted his teeth through the pain. He travelled from Spain unsure that he could ride, but exceeded expectations. Rode with a good group until his injury compromised his ability to control his bike.

**8 | TITO RABAT**
Found the track challenging in practice but kept building speed as his crew dialled in his GP17. Gambled on the hard rear for the race and was happy with his choice. Lost time in the early laps getting past Smith.

**9 | JACK MILLER**
From pole in Argentina to 18th on the grid, the Australian expected this to be a difficult race. It was, but he recovered superbly to lead Lorenzo and Rabat into the last lap, when he made a mistake that allowed the Avintia Duke past.

**10 | ALEIX ESPARGARÓ**
Tenth place – just metres off eighth – was a good result after starting from the seventh row of the grid. His secret was a very aggressive first few laps which got him into a fast group running a fast pace.

**11 | JORGE LORENZO**
This was the nadir of Lorenzo's time at Ducati, when it really did seem like he might be flummoxed by the Desmosedici. The Spaniard found the bike difficult to handle through the zig zags, especially with the hard rear tyre he chose.

**12 | DANILO PETRUCCI**
Struggled through practice, found in trouble in the race with the hard rear. Rabat's result suggested COTA was one of the tracks where the GP17 worked better than the GP18.

## RACE LAP CHART

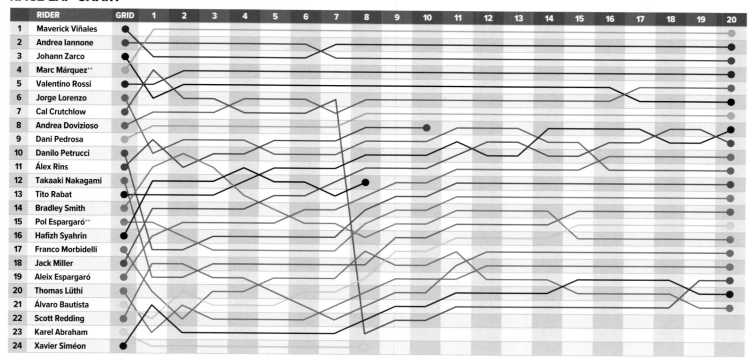

| | RIDER | GRID | 1 | 2 | 3 | 4 | 5 | 6 | 7 | 8 | 9 | 10 | 11 | 12 | 13 | 14 | 15 | 16 | 17 | 18 | 19 | 20 |
|---|---|---|---|---|---|---|---|---|---|---|---|---|---|---|---|---|---|---|---|---|---|---|---|
| 1 | Maverick Viñales | | | | | | | | | | | | | | | | | | | | | |
| 2 | Andrea Iannone | | | | | | | | | | | | | | | | | | | | | |
| 3 | Johann Zarco | | | | | | | | | | | | | | | | | | | | | |
| 4 | Marc Márquez++ | | | | | | | | | | | | | | | | | | | | | |
| 5 | Valentino Rossi | | | | | | | | | | | | | | | | | | | | | |
| 6 | Jorge Lorenzo | | | | | | | | | | | | | | | | | | | | | |
| 7 | Cal Crutchlow | | | | | | | | | | | | | | | | | | | | | |
| 8 | Andrea Dovizioso | | | | | | | | | | | | | | | | | | | | | |
| 9 | Dani Pedrosa | | | | | | | | | | | | | | | | | | | | | |
| 10 | Danilo Petrucci | | | | | | | | | | | | | | | | | | | | | |
| 11 | Álex Rins | | | | | | | | | | | | | | | | | | | | | |
| 12 | Takaaki Nakagami | | | | | | | | | | | | | | | | | | | | | |
| 13 | Tito Rabat | | | | | | | | | | | | | | | | | | | | | |
| 14 | Bradley Smith | | | | | | | | | | | | | | | | | | | | | |
| 15 | Pol Espargaró++ | | | | | | | | | | | | | | | | | | | | | |
| 16 | Hafizh Syahrin | | | | | | | | | | | | | | | | | | | | | |
| 17 | Franco Morbidelli | | | | | | | | | | | | | | | | | | | | | |
| 18 | Jack Miller | | | | | | | | | | | | | | | | | | | | | |
| 19 | Aleix Espargaró | | | | | | | | | | | | | | | | | | | | | |
| 20 | Thomas Lüthi | | | | | | | | | | | | | | | | | | | | | |
| 21 | Álvaro Bautista | | | | | | | | | | | | | | | | | | | | | |
| 22 | Scott Redding | | | | | | | | | | | | | | | | | | | | | |
| 23 | Karel Abraham | | | | | | | | | | | | | | | | | | | | | |
| 24 | Xavier Siméon | | | | | | | | | | | | | | | | | | | | | |

## RACE CLASSIFICATION AFTER 20 LAP = 110.26 KM

| | RIDER | NAT | TEAM | MACHINE | TIME | + GAP | TYRES |
|---|---|---|---|---|---|---|---|
| 1 | Marc Márquez | SPA | Repsol Honda Team | HONDA | 41'52.002 | | M/H |
| 2 | Maverick Viñales | SPA | Movistar Yamaha MotoGP | YAMAHA | 41'55.562 | 3.560 | M/M |
| 3 | Andrea Iannone | ITA | Team SUZUKI ECSTAR | SUZUKI | 41'58.706 | 6.704 | M/H |
| 4 | Valentino Rossi | ITA | Movistar Yamaha MotoGP | YAMAHA | 42'01.589 | 9.587 | M/M |
| 5 | Andrea Dovizioso | ITA | Ducati Team | DUCATI | 42'05.572 | 13.570 | M/H |
| 6 | Johann Zarco | FRA | Monster Yamaha Tech 3 | YAMAHA | 42'06.233 | 14.231 | M/M |
| 7 | Dani Pedrosa | SPA | Repsol Honda Team | HONDA | 42'10.203 | 18.201 | M/M |
| 8 | Tito Rabat | SPA | Reale Avintia Racing | DUCATI | 42'20.539 | 28.537 | M/H |
| 9 | Jack Miller | AUS | Alma Pramac Racing | DUCATI | 42'20.673 | 28.671 | M/H |
| 10 | Aleix Espargaró | SPA | Aprilia Racing Team Gresini | APRILIA | 42'20.877 | 28.875 | H/M |
| 11 | Jorge Lorenzo | SPA | Ducati Team | DUCATI | 42'23.357 | 31.355 | M/H |
| 12 | Danilo Petrucci | ITA | Alma Pramac Racing | DUCATI | 42'26.995 | 34.993 | M/H |
| 13 | Pol Espargaró | SPA | Red Bull KTM Factory Racing | KTM | 42'29.266 | 37.264 | S/M |
| 14 | Takaaki Nakagami | JPN | LCR Honda IDEMITSU | HONDA | 42'31.337 | 39.335 | S/M |
| 15 | Álvaro Bautista | SPA | Ángel Nieto Team | DUCATI | 42'32.889 | 40.887 | M/S |
| 16 | Bradley Smith | GBR | Red Bull KTM Factory Racing | KTM | 42'40.477 | 48.475 | M/M |
| 17 | Scott Redding | GBR | Aprilia Racing Team Gresini | APRILIA | 42'41.997 | 49.995 | H/H |
| 18 | Thomas Lüthi | SWI | EG 0,0 Marc VDS | HONDA | 42'43.117 | 51.115 | M/M |
| 19 | Cal Crutchlow++ | GBR | LCR Honda CASTROL | HONDA | 42'51.057 | 59.055 | M/H |
| 20 | Xavier Siméon | GER | Reale Avintia Racing | DUCATI | 42'51.749 | 59.747 | M/H |
| 21 | Franco Morbidelli | ITA | EG 0,0 Marc VDS | HONDA | 42'52.515 | 60.513 | M/M |
| NC | Álex Rins | SPA | Team SUZUKI ECSTAR | SUZUKI | 21'05.915 | 10 laps | M/H |
| NC | Hafizh Syahrin | MAL | Monster Yamaha Tech 3 | YAMAHA | 16'57.659 | 12 laps | M/M |
| NC | Karel Abraham | CZE | Ángel Nieto Team | DUCATI | 17'42.994 | 12 laps | M/S |

## CHAMPIONSHIP STANDINGS

| | RIDER | NAT | TEAM | POINTS |
|---|---|---|---|---|
| 1 | Andrea Dovizioso | ITA | Ducati Team | 46 |
| 2 | Marc Márquez | SPA | Repsol Honda Team | 45 |
| 3 | Maverick Viñales | SPA | Movistar Yamaha MotoGP | 41 |
| 4 | Cal Crutchlow | GBR | LCR Honda CASTROL | 38 |
| 5 | Johann Zarco | FRA | Monster Yamaha Tech 3 | 38 |
| 6 | Andrea Iannone | ITA | Team SUZUKI ECSTAR | 31 |
| 7 | Valentino Rossi | ITA | Movistar Yamaha MotoGP | 29 |
| 8 | Jack Miller | AUS | Alma Pramac Racing | 26 |
| 9 | Tito Rabat | SPA | Reale Avintia Racing | 22 |
| 10 | Danilo Petrucci | ITA | Alma Pramac Racing | 21 |
| 11 | Dani Pedrosa | SPA | Repsol Honda Team | 18 |
| 12 | Álex Rins | SPA | Team SUZUKI ECSTAR | 16 |
| 13 | Hafizh Syahrin | MAL | Monster Yamaha Tech 3 | 9 |
| 14 | Pol Espargaró | SPA | Red Bull KTM Factory Racing | 8 |
| 15 | Aleix Espargaró | SPA | Aprilia Racing Team Gresini | 6 |
| 16 | Jorge Lorenzo | SPA | Ducati Team | 6 |
| 17 | Franco Morbidelli | ITA | EG 0,0 Marc VDS | 6 |
| 18 | Takaaki Nakagami | JPN | LCR Honda IDEMITSU | 5 |
| 19 | Scott Redding | GBR | Aprilia Racing Team Gresini | 4 |
| 20 | Álvaro Bautista | SPA | Ángel Nieto Team | 4 |
| 21 | Karel Abraham | CZE | Ángel Nieto Team | 1 |
| 22 | Thomas Lüthi | SWI | EG 0,0 Marc VDS | |
| 23 | Bradley Smith | GBR | Red Bull KTM Factory Racing | |
| 24 | Xavier Siméon | GER | Reale Avintia Racing | |

+ New race distance for 2018
++ FIM MotoGP Stewards grid penalty - Pol Espargaró: three-position grid penalty for slowing a rival in Q1. Márquez: three-position grid penalty for slowing a rival in Q2.
++ FIM MotoGP Stewards race penalty - Crutchlow: 2.7 seconds penalty imposed

---

**13 | POL ESPARGARÓ**
COTA proved a big challenge for several factories, but especially KTM, with Espargaró 37 seconds down at the finish. The Spaniard found the RC16 particularly hard work through the multiple changes of direction.

**14 | TAKAAKI NAKAGAMI**
Made it through to Q2 for the first time, but a bad start left him 19th after the first lap. From there he doggedly pushed forward. Like Espargaró ahead of him, made the unusual choice of the soft front tyre and medium rear.

**15 | ÁLVARO BAUTISTA**
Once again, didn't feel at ease on the GP17, despite Rabat's speed on the same bike. Worked hard to improve front/rear balance, but although he could turn the bike better in the race he lacked good corner-exit traction.

**16 | BRADLEY SMITH**
No points for the third race in a row. While Espargaró ran the soft front, Smith went with the medium front. He briefly battled with Lorenzo but then the tyre lost grip, after which he had to deal with a major understeer problem.

**17 | SCOTT REDDING**
Struggled to find a good balance between set-up and tyres, so went into the race on a hard front and hard rear. The front worked well but the rear didn't, losing him places in the early laps, at one point dropping him to 22nd.

**18 | THOMAS LÜTHI**
There are few more complex tracks for a MotoGP rookie and the 2017 Moto2 runner-up found this to his cost. Lost out in the turn-one melee and from half distance his front tyre didn't give him the grip needed to get the bike turned.

**19 | CAL CRUTCHLOW**
Arrived at COTA leading the championship, left in fourth place. His early pace was strong, until he started having some issues with the front-brake lever and lost places. Lost the front at the last corner trying to make a run on Zarco.

**20 | XAVIER SIMÉON**
Decided to run the same hard rear used by most Ducati riders, even though he hadn't tried the tyre in practice. The tyre didn't give him confidence in the early stages but he raised his pace later in the race.

**21 | FRANCO MORBIDELLI**
A grim weekend for the Moto2 world champ, who had scored points in his first two MotoGP races. Got frustrated because he couldn't find a set-up that would give him a constant pace. He promised lessons would be learned.

**DNF | KAREL ABRAHAM**
Suffered a nasty 200kmh/125mph crash on Saturday, which left him battered and bruised. Opted to start the race but he was in no real shape to ride, so after a while his team sent him a dash message to return to the pits.

**DNF | HAFIZH SYAHRIN**
A big warm-up crash prevented the Malaysian from trying a final set-up change, so he went into the race with the bike too soft. Started superbly, battling with Rabat and then Miller. Lost the front trying to make up for a lack of top speed.

**DNF | ÁLEX RINS**
Down to earth with a bump after his first MotoGP podium, and for the second year running, because he broke a wrist at COTA 2017. Was ninth until he ran wide, then lost the front and crashed.

# KING MARC
# REIGNS IN SPAIN

*Márquez ran away for another dominant victory while all
hell broke loose in the battle for the lower steps of podium*

A month after the furore of Argentina, the Jerez race finished in another frenzy of controversy. Marc Márquez had already made good his escape, leaving Jorge Lorenzo, Andrea Dovizioso and Dani Pedrosa disputing second place.

Dovizioso had the best pace of the group. While Lorenzo had led the first few laps, his team-mate had to fight his way through from eighth place at the end of lap one. He made rapid progress, taking third place from Pedrosa at one-third distance. But Lorenzo proved a tougher nut to crack.

"Jorge was fast, but he was too slow in the middle of the corners because he was struggling with the front," said Dovizioso. "He also didn't want to let me pass; that's why we lost time with Marc. He kept slowing down to close the door, that's why I took ten laps to try to overtake him, because I didn't want to make a mistake. I was on the limit — the front tyre locked many times and I twice lost the front in the middle of corners. I just wanted to overtake Jorge, because I knew if I could make one lap in front of him then I would make a gap."

As the trio approached the Dry Sack hairpin during the 18th lap of 25, Dovizioso squeezed inside Lorenzo, only to run wide, because he had exceeded the front grip available. Lorenzo immediately swung to the apex, aiming to profit from Dovizioso's

*Márquez has just taken the lead from Lorenzo, who will prove
a more difficult obstacle for Dovizioso and Pedrosa*

mistake, while at the same time making sure he didn't make contact with his team-mate. But Pedrosa also went for the apex. The two collided, the ever-luckless Pedrosa ejected violently from his RC213V, while Lorenzo collected Dovizioso. Race Direction judged this a racing incident and that was probably the size of it.

"It was the three cleanest riders in the championship, so it was unlucky that we all finished on the ground," said Lorenzo. "Everything happened so fast. I was obviously cutting back, going for the best acceleration and then Dani was there. It was like dominoes and very unlucky, especially for Andrea who is fighting for the championship. But I don't have eyes in the back of my head."

While the two Ducati men and the battered Pedrosa got to their feet, Johann Zarco swept through, promoted from fifth to second place in an instant. The crowd's focus then switched to the four-way battle behind the Frenchman, which until that point had been a reasonably gentle skirmish for sixth place. Suddenly it was a much more urgent contest for the final spot on the podium, with Andrea Iannone, Danilo Petrucci, Valentino Rossi and Jack Miller all in with a chance.

Rossi and Miller were the first to slip behind as the battle intensified. "We cannot exit the corners fast enough," Rossi complained. "It could be a mechanical grip thing. Within the team there are different ideas, but for me it's more from the electronics side. At this moment we don't have the answer. Yamaha must work. In Saturday practice I followed Zarco; it looks like he stresses the tyres less, but also he is smaller and lighter on the bike."

Petrucci seemed to have got the better of Iannone in the final stages, but the Suzuki rider redeemed himself with a superb move on the final lap, diving inside the Ducati man at Ángel Nieto corner. A second consecutive podium was a big deal for a man written off by many at the end of 2017.

Márquez was imperious, leading Zarco by seven seconds on the penultimate lap, before easing the throttle on the final circuit to wave to his fans. And all this at the end of what hadn't been a straightforward weekend: he had crashed twice in practice and then again in morning warm-up. Three tumbles would have sewn seeds of doubts in the minds of most riders, but not Márquez, who has developed losing the front into an art form through which he finds the exact grip limit. Indeed at Jerez all his crashes came with the hard front tyre, which he knew he would have to use in the race, so he was merely working out how far he could push the tyre.

The reigning world champion had to work hard to pass Lorenzo, who was getting faster and faster on the Ducati but seemed unable to maintain his pace over race distance. We would soon find out why.

"It was nearly impossible to overtake Lorenzo because he was braking so late and exiting the corners so well," said Márquez,

**MAIN** | Lorenzo leads from Pedrosa, Zarco and Crutchlow

**BELOW, LEFT TO RIGHT** | Pedrosa dwarfed by his grid girl; Lorenzo was fast in and fast out; an ecstatic Márquez greets his ecstatic fans

'IT WAS NEARLY IMPOSSIBLE TO OVERTAKE LORENZO BECAUSE HE WAS BRAKING SO LATE AND EXITING THE CORNERS SO WELL'
MARC MÁRQUEZ

## WHY DUCATI LOVE AN AUSSIE

Jack Miller may have entertained people with his wild, pole-grabbing lap at Termas, but by Sunday night at Jerez it was obvious there's much more than that kind of thing to the young Aussie. Miller raced with Iannone, Petrucci and Rossi to score his fourth-consecutive top-ten finish. No wonder that Ducati already had long-term plans for him.

The Italian company certainly have a fondness for Australian riders. Casey Stoner and Troy Bayliss have helped build Ducati's legend over the past decade or so, but why do Aussies go so well on big red Dukes? It's no coincidence that some of the marque's greatest riders grew up flying around dirt racetracks in

who calmly awaited his moment, which came at one-third distance. "When I saw his tyres starting to drop, I said okay, now it's time to lead the race and try to open a gap."

Márquez slipped past at the Lorenzo hairpin and quickly built an unassailable lead. He only had one moment, but it was a big one. Rookie Tom Lüthi crashed at the last, fast right on lap 12, his cartwheeling bike spewing gravel onto the track. Marshals still hadn't cleared the mess when Márquez arrived on lap 13, going at full tilt. He saw the gravel too late to take avoiding action, so he ran through it at full speed, his rear wheel kicking out dirt-track style. Many others would have fallen, but not Márquez.

"I saw many stones on the track," he said. "But it was too late. Both wheels slid, but I stayed on.... Márquez style!"

Cal Crutchlow continued his strong form – a close fourth in Qatar, victory in Argentina and pole position at Jerez – at least until the race. He chose the hard front, like Márquez and most of the Honda riders, and was running with the leaders until he fell at one-third distance, because he was overheating the front tyre. He got going, only to crash again and put himself out of the race.

Jerez was the place where 12 months earlier Maverick Viñales' championship went awry. And it wasn't much different this time, Rossi's team-mate still confused by his lack of pace. "It's difficult, because when the bike goes well I can be very fast," he said after finishing seventh, almost four seconds down on Miller. "But when the bike doesn't work we have a lot of problems."

**CLOCKWISE FROM TOP LEFT** | *Viñales was still searching for solutions; Rossi and Ezpeleta mark the renaming of the circuit in honour of Spanish racing legend Ángel Nieto; the KTM freight train; sherry trophies on the podium; Márquez's first Jerez win since 2014; the first of Crutchlow's two crashes*

Australia, because dirt trackers use the rear brake all the time to help turn and control the bike.

"Jack's riding suits our bike perfectly: if the bike isn't turning then he makes it turn," explained Ducati MotoGP team manager Davide Tardozzi. "First, we asked him to be consistent, then he can work at being fast. We trust he has the talent to become a very fast Ducati rider."

Miller uses the rear brake so much that he has warped discs and pads. "I'd hate to see my rear brake temperature," he grinned at Jerez. "I'm burying the rear brake, I don't think it gets much of a rest. I used the brake with the Honda more to stop the bike and stop wheelies. With this bike it's more to help the bike turn, because you can get it to squat."

# 4 | SPAIN

# RACE RESULTS

**WINNER** MARC MÁRQUEZ

**CIRCUIT LENGTH** 4.4 KM | 2.75 MILES

**NO. OF LAPS**⁺ 25

**RACE DISTANCE**⁺ 110.6 KM | 68.8 MILES

**CIRCUIT RECORD LAP** 1'38.735 | 161.2 KM/H
JORGE LORENZO (2015)

**CIRCUIT BEST LAP** 1'37.653 | 163.0 KM/H
CAL CRUTCHLOW (2018)

**RACE CONDITION** DRY

**AIR** 25°C

**HUMIDITY** 41%

**GROUND** 40°C

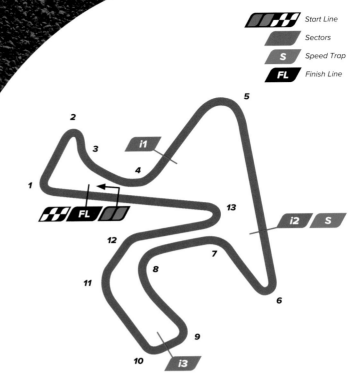

Start Line
Sectors
S Speed Trap
FL Finish Line

TISSOT
SWISS WATCHES SINCE 1853 / MotoGP™
**OFFICIAL** TIMEKEEPER

MICHELIN / MotoGP™
**OFFICIAL** MotoGP™ CLASS TYRE

**FRONT TYRES**
SOFT
MEDIUM
HARD

**REAR TYRES**
SOFT
MEDIUM
HARD

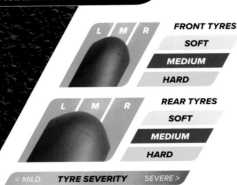

< MILD  **TYRE SEVERITY**  SEVERE >

## QUALIFYING RESULTS

| | RIDER | NAT | TEAM | MACHINE | QP/TIME | | GAP 1ST/PREV | |
|---|---|---|---|---|---|---|---|---|
| 1 | Cal Crutchlow | GBR | LCR Honda CASTROL | HONDA | Q2 | 1'37.653 | | |
| 2 | Dani Pedrosa | SPA | Repsol Honda Team | HONDA | Q2 | 1'37.912 | 0.259 | 0.259 |
| 3 | Johann Zarco | FRA | Monster Yamaha Tech 3 | YAMAHA | Q2 | 1'37.956 | 0.303 | 0.044 |
| 4 | Jorge Lorenzo | SPA | Ducati Team | DUCATI | Q2 | 1'37.969 | 0.316 | 0.013 |
| 5 | Marc Márquez | SPA | Repsol Honda Team | HONDA | Q2 | 1'37.977 | 0.324 | 0.008 |
| 6 | Álex Rins | SPA | Team SUZUKI ECSTAR | SUZUKI | Q2 | 1'37.984 | 0.331 | 0.007 |
| 7 | Andrea Iannone | ITA | Team SUZUKI ECSTAR | SUZUKI | Q2 | 1'37.987 | 0.334 | 0.003 |
| 8 | Andrea Dovizioso** | ITA | Ducati Team | DUCATI | Q2 | 1'38.029 | 0.376 | 0.042 |
| 9 | Danilo Petrucci | ITA | Alma Pramac Racing | DUCATI | Q2 | 1'38.086 | 0.433 | 0.057 |
| 10 | Valentino Rossi | ITA | Movistar Yamaha MotoGP | YAMAHA | Q2 | 1'38.267 | 0.614 | 0.181 |
| 11 | Maverick Viñales** | SPA | Movistar Yamaha MotoGP | YAMAHA | Q2 | 1'38.281 | 0.628 | 0.014 |
| 12 | Jack Miller | AUS | Alma Pramac Racing | DUCATI | Q2 | 1'38.522 | 0.869 | 0.241 |
| 13 | Aleix Espargaró | SPA | Aprilia Racing Team Gresini | APRILIA | Q1 | 1'38.389 | *0.315 | 0.040 |
| 14 | Takaaki Nakagami | JPN | LCR Honda IDEMITSU | HONDA | Q1 | 1'38.481 | *0.407 | 0.092 |
| 15 | Franco Morbidelli | ITA | EG 0,0 Marc VDS | HONDA | Q1 | 1'38.544 | *0.470 | 0.063 |
| 16 | Pol Espargaró | SPA | Red Bull KTM Factory Racing | KTM | Q1 | 1'38.598 | *0.524 | 0.054 |
| 17 | Tito Rabat | SPA | Reale Avintia Racing | DUCATI | Q1 | 1'38.610 | *0.536 | 0.012 |
| 18 | Thomas Lüthi | SWI | EG 0,0 Marc VDS | HONDA | Q1 | 1'38.752 | *0.678 | 0.142 |
| 19 | Mika Kallio | FIN | Red Bull KTM Factory Racing | KTM | Q1 | 1'38.759 | *0.685 | 0.007 |
| 20 | Álvaro Bautista | SPA | Ángel Nieto Team | DUCATI | Q1 | 1'38.838 | *0.764 | 0.079 |
| 21 | Bradley Smith | GBR | Red Bull KTM Factory Racing | KTM | Q1 | 1'38.961 | *0.887 | 0.123 |
| 22 | Hafizh Syahrin | MAL | Monster Yamaha Tech 3 | YAMAHA | Q1 | 1'39.135 | *1.061 | 0.174 |
| 23 | Karel Abraham | CZE | Ángel Nieto Team | DUCATI | Q1 | 1'39.146 | *1.072 | 0.011 |
| 24 | Xavier Siméon | GER | Reale Avintia Racing | DUCATI | Q1 | 1'39.708 | *1.634 | 0.562 |
| 25 | Scott Redding | GBR | Aprilia Racing Team Gresini | APRILIA | Q1 | 1'39.918 | *1.844 | 0.210 |

*Gap to the fastest rider in the Q1 session  ** Went forward from Q1 to Q2*

**1 | MARC MÁRQUEZ**
This was situation normal: a few low-side crashes before the race, almost a few more in the race, but first across the line and maximum points. Already it seemed like no else had the speed to stop him winning a fifth MotoGP title.

**2 | JOHANN ZARCO**
Made the factory Yamahas look slow once again, qualifying on the front row, while Rossi and Viñales were on row four, then taking his second runner-up finish in three races to move into second place in the championship.

**3 | ANDREA IANNONE**
The Italian went racing under a cloud at Jerez, with Suzuki apparently keen to replace him with Moto2 rookie Joan Mir. He rode well to score his second consecutive podium but this wouldn't be enough to save his GSX-RR ride.

**4 | DANILO PETRUCCI**
Like most of his rivals, profited from the pile-up, but he fought back well, joining the group that found itself fighting for the final place on the podium. Briefly got ahead of Rossi, joking later that the Italian has "a little more" experience.

**5 | VALENTINO ROSSI**
Qualified tenth, so was happy with fifth, after an entertaining tussle with fellow Italians Iannone and Petrucci. Raced with the medium/medium tyre combo used by most, remarkably recording his best lap on lap two.

**6 | JACK MILLER**
A poor start left him 13th after one lap, but he fought back well, joining the group that found itself fighting for the final place on the podium. Briefly got ahead of Rossi, joking later that the Italian has "a little more" experience.

**7 | MAVERICK VIÑALES**
After pole position and second place at COTA, this was back to earth with a bump. And the same old problem that had haunted him in Qatar: he lacked grip in the early stages of the race and gained grip as the laps ticked by.

**8 | ÁLVARO BAUTISTA**
Found a much better feeling with his Ducati GP17 than at the first three races, which helped him charge through from 18th on lap one to seventh, only to be knocked back one place by the slow-burning Viñales.

**9 | FRANCO MORBIDELLI**
This was another impressive performance from the Moto2 world champion, who achieved his first MotoGP top-ten finish, only 16 seconds down on the winner; the same gap he'd had in Qatar.

**10 | MIKA KALLIO**
When your test rider aboard your development bike beats your full-time riders it means he's faster, the bike is faster, or both. Maintained a fast, consistent pace, running an R&D RC16, allegedly with reverse-rotating crank.

**11 | POL ESPARGARÓ**
Spent much of the race swapping position with his KTM team-mates, only to lose out to Kallio in the final laps. Didn't have the grip he had expected from his tyre choice but took Kallio's pace on the R&D bike as a positive.

**12 | TAKAAKI NAKAGAMI**
Like fellow RC213V rookie Morbidelli, this was a strong ride from Nakagami, who spent most of the race chasing the trio of KTMs. The Japanese rider closed in on the group in the final laps, getting the better of Smith at the final corner.

# RACE LAP CHART

----- Dashed line: Lapped rider

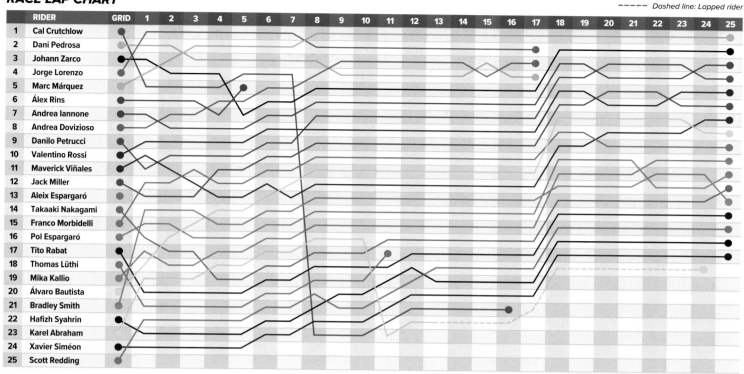

| | RIDER | GRID |
|---|---|---|
| 1 | Cal Crutchlow | |
| 2 | Dani Pedrosa | |
| 3 | Johann Zarco | |
| 4 | Jorge Lorenzo | |
| 5 | Marc Márquez | |
| 6 | Álex Rins | |
| 7 | Andrea Iannone | |
| 8 | Andrea Dovizioso | |
| 9 | Danilo Petrucci | |
| 10 | Valentino Rossi | |
| 11 | Maverick Viñales | |
| 12 | Jack Miller | |
| 13 | Aleix Espargaró | |
| 14 | Takaaki Nakagami | |
| 15 | Franco Morbidelli | |
| 16 | Pol Espargaró | |
| 17 | Tito Rabat | |
| 18 | Thomas Lüthi | |
| 19 | Mika Kallio | |
| 20 | Álvaro Bautista | |
| 21 | Bradley Smith | |
| 22 | Hafizh Syahrin | |
| 23 | Karel Abraham | |
| 24 | Xavier Siméon | |
| 25 | Scott Redding | |

## RACE CLASSIFICATION AFTER 25 LAPS = 110.575 KM

| | RIDER | NAT | TEAM | MACHINE | TIME | + GAP | TYRES |
|---|---|---|---|---|---|---|---|
| 1 | Marc Márquez | SPA | Repsol Honda Team | HONDA | 41'39.678 | | H/M |
| 2 | Johann Zarco | FRA | Monster Yamaha Tech 3 | YAMAHA | 41'44.919 | 5.241 | M/M |
| 3 | Andrea Iannone | ITA | Team SUZUKI ECSTAR | SUZUKI | 41'47.892 | 8.214 | M/H |
| 4 | Danilo Petrucci | ITA | Alma Pramac Racing | DUCATI | 41'48.295 | 8.617 | M/M |
| 5 | Valentino Rossi | ITA | Movistar Yamaha MotoGP | YAMAHA | 41'48.421 | 8.743 | M/M |
| 6 | Jack Miller | AUS | Alma Pramac Racing | DUCATI | 41'49.446 | 9.768 | H/H |
| 7 | Maverick Viñales | SPA | Movistar Yamaha MotoGP | YAMAHA | 41'53.221 | 13.543 | M/M |
| 8 | Álvaro Bautista | SPA | Ángel Nieto Team | DUCATI | 41'53.754 | 14.076 | M/M |
| 9 | Franco Morbidelli | ITA | EG 0,0 Marc VDS | HONDA | 41'56.500 | 16.822 | H/M |
| 10 | Mika Kallio | FIN | Red Bull KTM Factory Racing | KTM | 41'59.083 | 19.405 | M/M |
| 11 | Pol Espargaró | SPA | Red Bull KTM Factory Racing | KTM | 42'00.827 | 21.149 | M/M |
| 12 | Takaaki Nakagami | JPN | LCR Honda IDEMITSU | HONDA | 42'00.852 | 21.174 | M/M |
| 13 | Bradley Smith | GBR | Red Bull KTM Factory Racing | KTM | 42'01.443 | 21.765 | M/M |
| 14 | Tito Rabat | SPA | Reale Avintia Racing | DUCATI | 42'01.781 | 22.103 | M/M |
| 15 | Scott Redding | GBR | Aprilia Racing Team Gresini | APRILIA | 42'16.433 | 36.755 | H/H |
| 16 | Hafizh Syahrin | MAL | Monster Yamaha Tech 3 | YAMAHA | 42'21.539 | 41.861 | M/M |
| 17 | Xavier Siméon | GER | Reale Avintia Racing | DUCATI | 42'28.919 | 49.241 | M/M |
| 18 | Karel Abraham | CZE | Ángel Nieto Team | DUCATI | 42'22.308 | 1 lap | M/M |
| NC | Jorge Lorenzo | SPA | Ducati Team | DUCATI | 28'18.684 | 8 laps | S/M |
| NC | Andrea Dovizioso | ITA | Ducati Team | DUCATI | 28'18.820 | 8 laps | H/M |
| NC | Dani Pedrosa | SPA | Repsol Honda Team | HONDA | 28'19.015 | 8 laps | H/M |
| NC | Cal Crutchlow | GBR | LCR Honda CASTROL | HONDA | 27'18.708 | 9 laps | H/M |
| NC | Thomas Lüthi | SWI | EG 0,0 Marc VDS | HONDA | 18'35.074 | 14 laps | M/M |
| NC | Álex Rins | SPA | Team SUZUKI ECSTAR | SUZUKI | 8'23.946 | 20 laps | H/H |
| NC | Aleix Espargaró | SPA | Aprilia Racing Team Gresini | APRILIA | | | H/M |

+ New race distance for 2018

## CHAMPIONSHIP STANDINGS

| | RIDER | NAT | TEAM | POINTS |
|---|---|---|---|---|
| 1 | Marc Márquez | SPA | Repsol Honda Team | 70 |
| 2 | Johann Zarco | FRA | Monster Yamaha Tech 3 | 58 |
| 3 | Maverick Viñales | SPA | Movistar Yamaha MotoGP | 50 |
| 4 | Andrea Iannone | ITA | Team SUZUKI ECSTAR | 47 |
| 5 | Andrea Dovizioso | ITA | Ducati Team | 46 |
| 6 | Valentino Rossi | ITA | Movistar Yamaha MotoGP | 40 |
| 7 | Cal Crutchlow | GBR | LCR Honda CASTROL | 38 |
| 8 | Jack Miller | AUS | Alma Pramac Racing | 36 |
| 9 | Danilo Petrucci | ITA | Alma Pramac Racing | 34 |
| 10 | Tito Rabat | SPA | Reale Avintia Racing | 24 |
| 11 | Dani Pedrosa | SPA | Repsol Honda Team | 18 |
| 12 | Álex Rins | SPA | Team SUZUKI ECSTAR | 16 |
| 13 | Franco Morbidelli | ITA | EG 0,0 Marc VDS | 13 |
| 14 | Pol Espargaró | SPA | Red Bull KTM Factory Racing | 13 |
| 15 | Álvaro Bautista | SPA | Ángel Nieto Team | 12 |
| 16 | Hafizh Syahrin | MAL | Monster Yamaha Tech 3 | 9 |
| 17 | Takaaki Nakagami | JPN | LCR Honda IDEMITSU | 9 |
| 18 | Aleix Espargaró | SPA | Aprilia Racing Team Gresini | 6 |
| 19 | Mika Kallio | FIN | Red Bull KTM Factory Racing | 6 |
| 20 | Jorge Lorenzo | SPA | Ducati Team | 6 |
| 21 | Scott Redding | GBR | Aprilia Racing Team Gresini | 5 |
| 22 | Bradley Smith | GBR | Red Bull KTM Factory Racing | 3 |
| 23 | Karel Abraham | CZE | Ángel Nieto Team | 1 |
| 24 | Thomas Lüthi | SWI | EG 0,0 Marc VDS | |
| 25 | Xavier Siméon | GER | Reale Avintia Racing | |

---

**13 | BRADLEY SMITH**
Once Kallio had got the better of his full-time team-mates in the final laps, Smith and Espargaró duked it out until the last corner, where the Briton's last-gasp attack didn't quite go to plan and allowed Nakagami to come past on the rush to the finish line.

**14 | TITO RABAT**
Full of confidence after a strong November test at Jerez, but the hotter conditions changed everything and he never felt fully at ease. His only resolve to make it to the finish, which he did, three tenths behind Smith.

**15 | SCOTT REDDING**
Once again his crew focused its attention on searching for his RS-GP's missing rear grip, but made little progress. His only consolation was making it to the flag – 14 seconds down on Smith – and scoring the final championship point.

**16 | HAFIZH SYAHRIN**
Spoiled his weekend before it had even started after a nasty, high-speed cycling crash during training. Rode in agony throughout the three days but doggedly continued, completing the race just one place outside the points.

**17 | XAVIER SIMÉON**
Spent much of the weekend trying to find more rear grip. His crew made some final changes for the race, but they didn't work as expected, so the Belgian struggled more with each passing lap. His only positive was finishing the race.

**18 | KAREL ABRAHAM**
Made a great start from the eighth row of the grid to join the contest for the final points-scoring positions. However, he was struggling with front-end grip throughout and fell at turn one on lap 11. Remounted to finish last.

**DNF | JORGE LORENZO**
Led the race for seven laps and held onto second place for a further ten, working on the late-braking technique that would serve him so well a few races hence. There was little doubt that he was really starting to get the hang of the Ducati.

**DNF | ANDREA DOVIZIOSO**
Arguably MotoGP's latest braker, Dovizioso couldn't find a way around Lorenzo without losing the front into the corner. When he finally went for it, that's what happened, so he ran wide and then all hell broke loose.

**DNF | DANI PEDROSA**
Has there ever been a more serially unlucky rider in MotoGP? Exactly one month after he broke his right wrist after getting taken out by Zarco in Argentina, this time the Spaniard suffered a nasty right-hip injury, again through no fault of his own.

**DNF | CAL CRUTCHLOW**
Had a seriously good chance of making the podium, until he overheated the front tyre and fell at the first corner on lap eight. Remounted and got going again, but fell again, this time at the final corner, with nine laps remaining.

**DNF | THOMAS LÜTHI**
Found the going tough with a full fuel load, then lost the front. His crash debris nearly took out Márquez when the leader came around the next lap.

**DNF | ÁLEX RINS**
Swapped places with Dovizioso during the early laps, but then had his third crash and DNF from the first four races.

**DNF | ALEIX ESPARGARÓ**
Had hopes of a second top-ten but suffered a third technical in four races; this time a sensor cable failure.

*Three wins in a row; the last time Márquez did that was during his 2014 winning streak*

# MAGIC MARC'S VICTORY HAT-TRICK

**Once again Márquez crashed in practice and nearly in the race, but once again the Spanish magician rode the knife edge better and faster than anyone else**

Márquez was his usual miraculous self, tucking the front more than once on his way to his third consecutive victory. He failed at only one thing: he missed breaking the lap record, established 12 months earlier by 2017 French GP winner Maverick Viñales. Márquez came up 0.009 seconds short, not that it worried him as he climbed to the top of the podium.

More worried were those on the left side of the Movistar Yamaha garage, where Viñales sat, somewhat shell-shocked by his ride to seventh place. His fastest lap was 0.562 seconds slower than his 2017 best and he didn't seem to know why. "I was trying to crash at every corner, because I don't want to finish in seventh," he said. "I want to win, so I didn't care if I crashed or not."

Yamaha's continuing problems were soothed somewhat by Valentino Rossi's return to the podium with a strong ride to third, during which he chased Márquez and Danilo Petrucci, who was riding better than ever. However, Rossi had no great news for his embattled team. "I would like to say that our bike is now good for other racetracks," he said. "But unfortunately it's this racetrack that helps us."

Petrucci's first dry-weather runner-up finish (following three second-place results in rain-affected races) came at a critical

moment for the 27-year-old former Superstock champion, who spent his first three seasons in MotoGP aboard less competitive CRT bikes. The Le Mans paddock was aflame with contract rumours, concerning the second seats in the Honda, Suzuki and Ducati factory teams, after Ducati had announced during the weekend that Andrea Dovizioso would stay with them until the end of 2020.

Petrucci knew that this result was vital for his career prospects, but he was typically humorous about the situation. Asked if his performance might allow him to take Jorge Lorenzo's factory Ducati, he said, "If Ducati choose me instead of Jorge, it's because my salary will be less!". Most of the paddock – in fact probably all the paddock at this point – was blissfully unaware of the bomb that would be dropped a few weeks later.

Le Mans isn't the most picturesque of racetracks, its vast concrete grandstand towering over the paddock like the Maginot line, but this was a buzzing event, blessed by three days of blue skies and a frenzied crowd – 105,000 on race day – awaiting Johann Zarco's first MotoGP victory.

On Saturday afternoon Zarco became the first Frenchman to take a premier-class pole position since Christian Sarron at the 1988 French GP at Circuit Paul Ricard. He bettered Márquez by a tenth, with Petrucci a further nine hundredths behind, after coming through from the Q1 session.

Despite the sunshine, the Le Mans marshals were kept busy all weekend, with more than one hundred crashes across all classes. During practice several MotoGP riders fell while trying the medium front tyre. This convinced half the grid to choose the soft front, although the three riders most likely to win – Zarco, Márquez and fifth-fastest Andrea Dovizioso – all chose the medium.

Once again, Lorenzo won the drag race to the sweeping first turn and stayed out front for four laps, until Dovizioso swept ahead, only to lose the front when braking into the downhill turn six. "I wasn't pushing at that moment," he said. "I was pushing at 80 percent; that's why I'm disappointed." This seemed like a rare mistake by the 32-year-old Italian, whose strengths have always included calmness in the heat of battle and consistency in results. But perhaps the pressure was starting to tell.

That left Lorenzo ahead, with Zarco and Márquez snapping at his heels, until Zarco also lost the front, into another downhill corner, turn eight. Two laps later Márquez made an aggressive pass on Lorenzo and that was that; although he never got to relax. Petrucci was in storming form, closing to within half a second at half-distance, while Rossi came through to third as Lorenzo faded. "My main problem was that I couldn't keep my stamina during all the race," said Lorenzo. "The fuel tank on this year's bike is shorter and further forward, so it doesn't support me and it's more demanding for my arms."

The next man to pounce on Lorenzo was Petrucci's team-mate Jack Miller, having the ride of his life. True, the Aussie didn't win the race as he had at Assen in 2016, but this was a dry race and

*'I'M CURRENTLY EXPERIENCING A VERY SWEET PERIOD WITH MY BIKE'*
MARC MARQUEZ

## 109 CRASHES IN THE DRY! HOW COME?

MotoGP has gathered detailed crash statistics since the 1990s, to build a scientific database that helps reduce not so much the number of accidents but their severity. The all-time records for the greatest number of crashes during a weekend inevitably belong to events run in rain-swept conditions. There were 130 crashes at soaking Estoril in 2010 and 140 at sodden Misano in 2017.

Le Mans 2018 had the dubious honour of being the first MotoGP weekend untroubled by rain to exceed one hundred crashes. In total there were 109 falls, including several MotoGP highsides, which are usually prevented by traction-control systems. There

dry-race results mean much more to racers. During the final laps Miller actually closed on Rossi, missing the podium party by less than a second.

"To fight with those guys and to be able to see Márquez the whole race does so much for your confidence and self-belief," said the 23-year-old. "I felt I had better pace than Valentino at the end, but I wasn't able to stay in contention when he made mistakes, that's why I'm nicked off. It's the first time in my career I've wished for a race to be longer. When I looked up and it was the last lap, I was like, you're kidding!"

Dani Pedrosa crossed the line 1.1 seconds behind Miller, still struggling with the right-hip injury he sustained at Jerez. The hero of the day was Cal Crutchlow who came home eighth, behind Lorenzo and Viñales, following a purling highside during qualifying. The gritty Brit had blood on his lungs, so he was kept in hospital overnight, with doctors checking his bloods every two hours.

"I wasn't willing to push at the beginning of the race, because if I'd crashed I would've been in trouble," said Crutchlow, who nonetheless took Álex Rins and Aleix Espargaró in the final laps. "Once I started feeling comfortable, I started to push and was able to pick off some riders."

Following the exits of Dovizioso and Zarco, Márquez left Le Mans 36 points ahead in the championship, only six points less of an advantage than he had enjoyed after winning the first five races of 2014. "I'm currently experiencing a very sweet period with my bike, and when you've got that kind of feeling, you also work better; then you ride better, and the bike works better," he said ominously.

*CLOCKWISE, FROM TOP LEFT* | *Pedrosa had his best 2018 result so far; this seemed like a breakthrough race for Miller; Syahrin won a rookie battle with Morbidelli; Crutchlow raced with blood on his lungs after a purling crash; the podium men smile for the cameras; Márquez: no time to check the time*

were various reasons for this rash of crashes: a super-grippy asphalt that gave riders less feel when they pushed to the limit, a chilly breeze that cooled tyres on the track's two long straights and the tight stop-and-go layout, which had innumerable lap times cancelled for exceeding track limits during practice and numerous time penalties on race day for the same offence. The failure of MotoGP's lower-tech spec traction-control system to save several highsides, most notably Crutchlow's, was attributed to a combination of the tight corner exits that had riders turning down the TC, so they could use wheelspin to turn the bike.

The crash total was a shock, but more important was the lack of any injuries that prevented riders from racing. This, of course, is thanks to improvements in circuit safety and in riding gear.

# 5 | FRANCE

# RACE RESULTS

**WINNER** *MARC MÁRQUEZ*

**CIRCUIT LENGTH** *4.2 KM 2.6 MILES*

**NO. OF LAPS** *27*

**RACE DISTANCE** *113.0 KM 70.2 MILES*

**CIRCUIT RECORD LAP** *1'32.309 163.2 KM/H MAVERICK VIÑALES (2017)*

**CIRCUIT BEST LAP** *1'31.185 165.2 KM/H JOHANN ZARCO (2018)*

**RACE CONDITION** *DRY*

**AIR** *24°C*

**HUMIDITY** *41%*

**GROUND** *45°C*

Start Line
Sectors
**S** Speed Trap
**FL** Finish Line

**TISSOT** SWISS WATCHES SINCE 1853 / MotoGP™
**OFFICIAL** TIMEKEEPER

MICHELIN / MotoGP™
**OFFICIAL** MotoGP™ CLASS TYRE

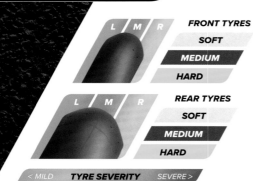

**FRONT TYRES**
SOFT
MEDIUM
HARD

**REAR TYRES**
SOFT
MEDIUM
HARD

< MILD **TYRE SEVERITY** SEVERE >

## QUALIFYING RESULTS

| | RIDER | NAT | TEAM | MACHINE | QP/TIME | | GAP 1ST/PREV | |
|---|---|---|---|---|---|---|---|---|
| 1 | Johann Zarco | FRA | Monster Yamaha Tech 3 | YAMAHA | Q2 | 1'31.185 | | |
| 2 | Marc Márquez | SPA | Repsol Honda Team | HONDA | Q2 | 1'31.293 | 0.108 | 0.108 |
| 3 | Danilo Petrucci** | ITA | Alma Pramac Racing | DUCATI | Q2 | 1'31.381 | 0.196 | 0.088 |
| 4 | Andrea Iannone | ITA | Team SUZUKI ECSTAR | SUZUKI | Q2 | 1'31.454 | 0.269 | 0.073 |
| 5 | Andrea Dovizioso | ITA | Ducati Team | DUCATI | Q2 | 1'31.553 | 0.368 | 0.099 |
| 6 | Jorge Lorenzo | SPA | Ducati Team | DUCATI | Q2 | 1'31.590 | 0.405 | 0.037 |
| 7 | Jack Miller | AUS | Alma Pramac Racing | DUCATI | Q2 | 1'31.683 | 0.498 | 0.093 |
| 8 | Maverick Viñales | SPA | Movistar Yamaha MotoGP | YAMAHA | Q2 | 1'31.784 | 0.599 | 0.101 |
| 9 | Valentino Rossi | ITA | Movistar Yamaha MotoGP | YAMAHA | Q2 | 1'31.900 | 0.715 | 0.116 |
| 10 | Dani Pedrosa** | SPA | Repsol Honda Team | HONDA | Q2 | 1'32.024 | 0.839 | 0.124 |
| 11 | Tito Rabat | SPA | Reale Avintia Racing | DUCATI | Q2 | 1'32.049 | 0.864 | 0.025 |
| 12 | Aleix Espargaró | SPA | Aprilia Racing Team Gresini | APRILIA | Q2 | 1'32.455 | 1.270 | 0.406 |
| 13 | Cal Crutchlow | GBR | LCR Honda CASTROL | HONDA | Q1 | 1'32.315 | *0.497 | 0.254 |
| 14 | Hafizh Syahrin | MAL | Monster Yamaha Tech 3 | YAMAHA | Q1 | 1'32.397 | *0.579 | 0.082 |
| 15 | Álex Rins | SPA | Team SUZUKI ECSTAR | SUZUKI | Q1 | 1'32.401 | *0.583 | 0.004 |
| 16 | Franco Morbidelli | ITA | EG 0,0 Marc VDS | HONDA | Q1 | 1'32.770 | *0.952 | 0.369 |
| 17 | Bradley Smith | GBR | Red Bull KTM Factory Racing | KTM | Q1 | 1'32.795 | *0.977 | 0.025 |
| 18 | Pol Espargaró | SPA | Red Bull KTM Factory Racing | KTM | Q1 | 1'32.988 | *1.170 | 0.193 |
| 19 | Takaaki Nakagami | JPN | LCR Honda IDEMITSU | HONDA | Q1 | 1'33.062 | *1.244 | 0.074 |
| 20 | Álvaro Bautista | SPA | Ángel Nieto Team | DUCATI | Q1 | 1'33.324 | *1.506 | 0.262 |
| 21 | Thomas Lüthi | SWI | EG 0,0 Marc VDS | HONDA | Q1 | 1'33.439 | *1.621 | 0.115 |
| 22 | Scott Redding | GBR | Aprilia Racing Team Gresini | APRILIA | Q1 | 1'33.676 | *1.858 | 0.237 |
| 23 | Xavier Siméon | GER | Reale Avintia Racing | DUCATI | Q1 | 1'33.802 | *1.984 | 0.126 |
| 24 | Karel Abraham | CZE | Ángel Nieto Team | DUCATI | Q1 | 1'33.839 | *2.021 | 0.037 |

*\* Gap to the fastest rider in the Q1 session*
*\*\* Went forward from Q1 to Q2*

**1 MARC MÁRQUEZ**
Pretty much a perfect weekend. Slid off at turn three in FP3 – in his usual exploration mode – after a typically gallant attempt to save the crash. What he learned from that allowed him to save an identical slide at the same corner in the race.

**2 DANILO PETRUCCI**
Spent much of practice fiddling with bike balance, finally getting it right in FP4 with a 5mm geometry adjustment. He crashed in practice with the medium front, so raced with the soft, the right choice for him.

**3 VALENTINO ROSSI**
Was at a loss to explain why his YZR-M1 regained its magic at Le Mans, but the short corner exits at the circuit's most important corners – turns eight and 14 – may have reduced Yamaha's troubling traction-control problems.

**4 JACK MILLER**
Learned plenty from following Rossi. He set the third fastest lap of the race, just 0.007 seconds slower than Rossi's best, using the soft front, like Petrucci, after a few moments with the medium during practice.

**5 DANI PEDROSA**
Needed his right hip draining after the Jerez pile-up but was unable to undergo the treatment due to testing at Jerez and Mugello and racing at Le Mans. The oft-beaten-up Spaniard therefore raced through the pain barrier once again.

**6 JORGE LORENZO**
Raced a different chassis. This was the chassis adopted by Dovizioso during preseason, with revised stiffness to improve turning and bump absorption. Bike ergonomics were again the main problem.

**7 MAVERICK VIÑALES**
The mystery continued for Viñales and his befuddled crew. He was slower than in 2017 and didn't know why. The only big difference between his Le Mans 2017 and 2018 bikes was a different front tyre, introduced at Mugello 2017.

**8 CAL CRUTCHLOW**
Most riders with blood on their lungs might've taken the day off. Crutchlow knew his body couldn't afford another battering, although that didn't stop him attacking in the final stages of the race.

**9 ALEIX ESPARGARÓ**
Got boxed in at the first chicane, which lost him several places on the first lap. As the race progressed his pace was affected by front-end chatter, which prevented him from resisting late-race attacks by Viñales and Crutchlow.

**10 ÁLEX RINS**
Missed the 2017 French GP through injury, so spent much of the weekend getting accustomed to the track on a MotoGP bike. Was also somewhat gun-shy after crashing out of the previous two races.

**11 POL ESPARGARÓ**
Fought back from 18th on the grid, helped by the RC16's impressive top speed: the bike was fourth fastest through the speed traps. And his pace was almost a second a lap better than it had been in 2017.

**12 HAFIZH SYAHRIN**
Another excellent ride by MotoGP's newest recruit: a sluggish start left the Malaysian 20th at the end of the first lap and he had to work hard to pick off rivals. His last victim was fellow beginner Morbidelli, his main rival for the Rookie of the Year prize.

## RACE LAP CHART

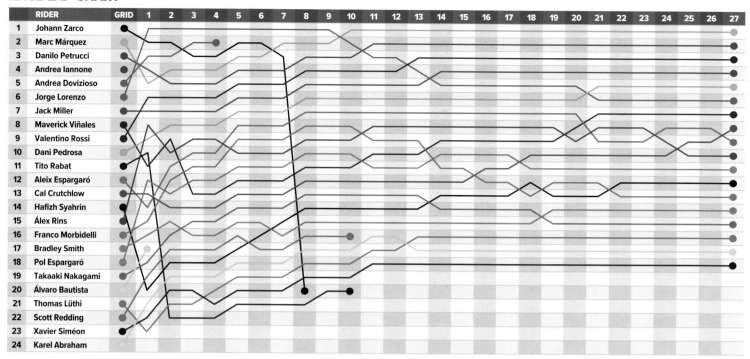

| | RIDER | GRID | 1 | 2 | 3 | 4 | 5 | 6 | 7 | 8 | 9 | 10 | 11 | 12 | 13 | 14 | 15 | 16 | 17 | 18 | 19 | 20 | 21 | 22 | 23 | 24 | 25 | 26 | 27 |
|---|---|---|---|---|---|---|---|---|---|---|---|---|---|---|---|---|---|---|---|---|---|---|---|---|---|---|---|---|---|
| 1 | Johann Zarco | | | | | | | | | | | | | | | | | | | | | | | | | | | | |
| 2 | Marc Márquez | | | | | | | | | | | | | | | | | | | | | | | | | | | | |
| 3 | Danilo Petrucci | | | | | | | | | | | | | | | | | | | | | | | | | | | | |
| 4 | Andrea Iannone | | | | | | | | | | | | | | | | | | | | | | | | | | | | |
| 5 | Andrea Dovizioso | | | | | | | | | | | | | | | | | | | | | | | | | | | | |
| 6 | Jorge Lorenzo | | | | | | | | | | | | | | | | | | | | | | | | | | | | |
| 7 | Jack Miller | | | | | | | | | | | | | | | | | | | | | | | | | | | | |
| 8 | Maverick Viñales | | | | | | | | | | | | | | | | | | | | | | | | | | | | |
| 9 | Valentino Rossi | | | | | | | | | | | | | | | | | | | | | | | | | | | | |
| 10 | Dani Pedrosa | | | | | | | | | | | | | | | | | | | | | | | | | | | | |
| 11 | Tito Rabat | | | | | | | | | | | | | | | | | | | | | | | | | | | | |
| 12 | Aleix Espargaró | | | | | | | | | | | | | | | | | | | | | | | | | | | | |
| 13 | Cal Crutchlow | | | | | | | | | | | | | | | | | | | | | | | | | | | | |
| 14 | Hafizh Syahrin | | | | | | | | | | | | | | | | | | | | | | | | | | | | |
| 15 | Álex Rins | | | | | | | | | | | | | | | | | | | | | | | | | | | | |
| 16 | Franco Morbidelli | | | | | | | | | | | | | | | | | | | | | | | | | | | | |
| 17 | Bradley Smith | | | | | | | | | | | | | | | | | | | | | | | | | | | | |
| 18 | Pol Espargaró | | | | | | | | | | | | | | | | | | | | | | | | | | | | |
| 19 | Takaaki Nakagami | | | | | | | | | | | | | | | | | | | | | | | | | | | | |
| 20 | Álvaro Bautista | | | | | | | | | | | | | | | | | | | | | | | | | | | | |
| 21 | Thomas Lüthi | | | | | | | | | | | | | | | | | | | | | | | | | | | | |
| 22 | Scott Redding | | | | | | | | | | | | | | | | | | | | | | | | | | | | |
| 23 | Xavier Siméon | | | | | | | | | | | | | | | | | | | | | | | | | | | | |
| 24 | Karel Abraham | | | | | | | | | | | | | | | | | | | | | | | | | | | | |

## RACE CLASSIFICATION AFTER 27 LAPS = 112.995 KM

| | RIDER | NAT | TEAM | MACHINE | TIME | + GAP | TYRES |
|---|---|---|---|---|---|---|---|
| 1 | Marc Márquez | SPA | Repsol Honda Team | HONDA | 41'49.773 | | M/H |
| 2 | Danilo Petrucci | ITA | Alma Pramac Racing | DUCATI | 41'52.083 | 2.310 | S/S |
| 3 | Valentino Rossi | ITA | Movistar Yamaha MotoGP | YAMAHA | 41'55.123 | 5.350 | M/S |
| 4 | Jack Miller | AUS | Alma Pramac Racing | DUCATI | 41'56.087 | 6.314 | S/S |
| 5 | Dani Pedrosa | SPA | Repsol Honda Team | HONDA | 41'57.192 | 7.419 | M/S |
| 6 | Jorge Lorenzo | SPA | Ducati Team | DUCATI | 42'00.128 | 10.355 | S/S |
| 7 | Maverick Viñales | SPA | Movistar Yamaha MotoGP | YAMAHA | 42'13.531 | 23.758 | S/S |
| 8 | Cal Crutchlow | GBR | LCR Honda CASTROL | HONDA | 42'15.568 | 25.795 | M/S |
| 9 | Aleix Espargaró | SPA | Aprilia Racing Team Gresini | APRILIA | 42'15.979 | 26.206 | M/S |
| 10 | Álex Rins | SPA | Team SUZUKI ECSTAR | SUZUKI | 42'17.710 | 27.937 | M/S |
| 11 | Pol Espargaró | SPA | Red Bull KTM Factory Racing | KTM | 42'22.077 | 32.304 | S/S |
| 12 | Hafizh Syahrin | MAL | Monster Yamaha Tech 3 | YAMAHA | 42'24.735 | 34.962 | S/S |
| 13 | Franco Morbidelli | ITA | EG 0,0 Marc VDS | HONDA | 42'27.654 | 37.881 | M/S |
| 14 | Bradley Smith | GBR | Red Bull KTM Factory Racing | KTM | 42'28.072 | 38.299 | S/S |
| 15 | Takaaki Nakagami | JPN | LCR Honda IDEMITSU | HONDA | 42'31.759 | 41.986 | M/S |
| 16 | Thomas Lüthi | SWI | EG 0,0 Marc VDS | HONDA | 42'35.033 | 45.260 | M/S |
| 17 | Karel Abraham | CZE | Ángel Nieto Team | DUCATI | 42'46.645 | 56.872 | S/S |
| 18 | Xavier Siméon | GER | Reale Avintia Racing | DUCATI | 43'01.890 | 72.117 | S/S |
| NC | Scott Redding⁺⁺ | GBR | Aprilia Racing Team Gresini | APRILIA | 15'50.276 | 17 laps | S/S |
| NC | Tito Rabat | SPA | Reale Avintia Racing | DUCATI | 17'02.377 | 17 laps | S/S |
| NC | Johann Zarco | FRA | Monster Yamaha Tech 3 | YAMAHA | 13'33.013 | 19 laps | M/S |
| NC | Andrea Dovizioso | ITA | Ducati Team | DUCATI | 6'15.860 | 23 laps | M/S |
| NC | Álvaro Bautista | SPA | Ángel Nieto Team | DUCATI | 1'41.096 | 26 laps | S/S |
| NC | Andrea Iannone | ITA | Team SUZUKI ECSTAR | SUZUKI | | | M/S |

+ New race distance for 2018
++ FIM MotoGP Stewards race penalty - Redding: 1.9 seconds penalty imposed

## CHAMPIONSHIP STANDINGS

| | RIDER | NAT | TEAM | POINTS |
|---|---|---|---|---|
| 1 | Marc Márquez | SPA | Repsol Honda Team | 95 |
| 2 | Maverick Viñales | SPA | Movistar Yamaha MotoGP | 59 |
| 3 | Johann Zarco | FRA | Monster Yamaha Tech 3 | 58 |
| 4 | Valentino Rossi | ITA | Movistar Yamaha MotoGP | 56 |
| 5 | Danilo Petrucci | ITA | Alma Pramac Racing | 54 |
| 6 | Jack Miller | AUS | Alma Pramac Racing | 49 |
| 7 | Andrea Iannone | ITA | Team SUZUKI ECSTAR | 47 |
| 8 | Cal Crutchlow | GBR | LCR Honda CASTROL | 46 |
| 9 | Andrea Dovizioso | ITA | Ducati Team | 46 |
| 10 | Dani Pedrosa | SPA | Repsol Honda Team | 29 |
| 11 | Tito Rabat | SPA | Reale Avintia Racing | 24 |
| 12 | Álex Rins | SPA | Team SUZUKI ECSTAR | 22 |
| 13 | Pol Espargaró | SPA | Red Bull KTM Factory Racing | 18 |
| 14 | Jorge Lorenzo | SPA | Ducati Team | 16 |
| 15 | Franco Morbidelli | ITA | EG 0,0 Marc VDS | 16 |
| 16 | Aleix Espargaró | SPA | Aprilia Racing Team Gresini | 13 |
| 17 | Hafizh Syahrin | MAL | Monster Yamaha Tech 3 | 13 |
| 18 | Álvaro Bautista | SPA | Ángel Nieto Team | 12 |
| 19 | Takaaki Nakagami | JPN | LCR Honda IDEMITSU | 10 |
| 20 | Mika Kallio | FIN | Red Bull KTM Factory Racing | 6 |
| 21 | Scott Redding | GBR | Aprilia Racing Team Gresini | 5 |
| 22 | Bradley Smith | GBR | Red Bull KTM Factory Racing | 5 |
| 23 | Karel Abraham | CZE | Ángel Nieto Team | 1 |
| 24 | Thomas Lüthi | SWI | EG 0,0 Marc VDS | |
| 25 | Xavier Siméon | GER | Reale Avintia Racing | |

**13 | FRANCO MORBIDELLI**
A tumble in practice put the Moto2 world champ on the back foot and he didn't find it easy to bounce back. Spent much of the race enjoying a battle with Syahrin and Smith, whom he beat by four tenths.

**14 | BRADLEY SMITH**
Like KTM team-mate Espargaró, the Briton was happy that his Le Mans pace had improved dramatically since the 2017 race. Was still hurting from a big highside in practice, again just like Espargaró.

**15 | TAKAAKI NAKAGAMI**
Another rider hurting from a practice fall, this time at turn 11. Felt better on his RC213V than he had during the Jerez weekend and tried chasing Crutchlow at one point, eventually overusing his front tyre.

**16 | THOMAS LÜTHI**
The many low-gear corners at Le Mans make life difficult for MotoGP rookies. Lüthi's race day started badly when he was taken out in warm-up by Zarco and he didn't want another fall in the race.

**17 | KAREL ABRAHAM**
Two crashes in practice left the Czech rider lacking confidence for the race and by half-distance he had lost touch with the group of riders fighting for the final world championship positions.

**18 | XAVIER SIMÉON**
The former Moto2 race winner once again struggled to be competitive on his Desmosedici, hampered by a right arm injury and a workload that was increased by the complexities of the tricky circuit.

**DNF | SCOTT REDDING**
Ended a mostly miserable weekend in the gravel at the turn-seven left-hander. He crashed twice on Friday, unable to find the grip he needed. He fell again in the race, losing the front with ten laps to go.

**DNF | TITO RABAT**
Fast in practice and confident for the race, he crashed when he lost the front on lap two while attacking Pedrosa and Rins. He bravely remounted but had to call it a day in the pits.

**DNF | JOHANN ZARCO**
The home hero's lap-eight crash triggered the loudest groan of the day. Zarco is usually good under pressure but this time it was too much. Dovizioso reckoned he was "too excited" in the race.

**DNF | ANDREA DOVIZIOSO**
Dovizioso knew he had the pace to win the race, even to beat Márquez, so he could hardly believe it when he fell, for his second consecutive no-score which left him 49 points behind the series leader.

**DNF | ÁLVARO BAUTISTA**
A crash in qualifying left him way back on the last-but-one row. He started with the aim of a top ten but lost the front and then the rear exiting turn six on only the second lap.

**DNF | ANDREA IANNONE**
Had high hopes of giving Suzuki a fourth consecutive podium for the first time since 1994, especially because Suzuki CEO Toshihiro Suzuki was present. But lost the rear on the first lap.

There's a lot of delight in that jump. Rossi shows respect, Dovizioso shows exhaustion

# AT LAST: JORGE WINS IN RED

**Lorenzo finally made his breakthrough at Ducati at the very moment he signed for Honda. This was a weird weekend...**

Mugello 2018 was one of MotoGP's strangest weekends in living memory. And that only applied to what we thought was happening. While Jorge Lorenzo made history for Ducati, 99 percent of the paddock believed he was signing a deal to ride an independent-team Yamaha in 2019. Three days after the race the bomb dropped: the 31-year-old Spaniard had signed with Repsol Honda for the next two seasons.

The Italian Grand Prix was Lorenzo's 24th race for Ducati and signalled the moment when the Borgo Panigale engineers finally got the bike just right for him, so he could lead from start to finish, chased home by Andrea Dovizioso, which gave the factory its first Mugello one-two. Meanwhile Valentino Rossi made it a perfect, sun-baked weekend for the fervent Italian crowd, which got to worship its greatest hero not once but twice: the veteran took pole on Saturday and the following day won a vicious battle for the final place in the podium party.

And yet it wasn't an easy home Grand Prix for Ducati. They may already have known they were losing Lorenzo when test-rider Michel Pirro suffered a terrifying FP2 crash following the flat-out kink that had claimed Marc Márquez five years previously. Pirro's bike flew into a vicious tank-slapper, which resulted in a 170mph tumble. The 31-year-old former Moto2 winner, a vital member

'THE TRICK TODAY WAS THAT I COMPLETELY CHANGED MY RIDING STYLE'

JORGE LORENZO

**MAIN** | *Márquez has just crashed out, leaving Rossi, Dovizioso and the rest to give vain chase to the flying number 99*

**BELOW, LEFT TO RIGHT** | *Dovizioso takes his place on the third row of the grid; Iannone started from the second row and missed the podium by 1.2 seconds; Pedrosa qualified lower than ever before and crashed trying to make up for it*

of the factory's R&D team, briefly lay unconscious, while the paddock anxiously awaited news. In fact Pirro got away with a nasty battering, including a dislocated right shoulder and two black eyes. Once again, modern track safety and riding gear had done their job.

The biggest technical challenge of the weekend was searching for front-end grip on the slippery asphalt, which on race day surpassed 50 degrees Celsius. Most riders were caught between two front tyres: the medium, which offered the best grip, and the hard, which offered better endurance.

While Lorenzo was the talk of the paddock, Italian Andrea Iannone was mostly the fastest man on track. He topped three of the four practice sessions, not only proving the pace of the Suzuki but also his own speed, an important factor at this particular moment because he was job-hunting. Iannone was unbeatable through most of the lap, but his GSX-RR still lacked grunt on Mugello's long, uphill start/finish straight.

On Sunday afternoon Ducati power once again gave Lorenzo the lead into the first corner, which was barely visible through a haze of yellow smoke. And there he stayed for the whole race; just like the old days with Yamaha. No one even got close to making a move on him. By the end of the first lap he was almost three tenths clear, by half distance he was more than a second in front and he took the flag 6.3 seconds ahead.

He had two winning secrets: an important change in bike ergonomics and a chameleon-like change of riding technique. "The trick today was that I completely changed my riding style," he beamed after his 66th Grand Prix win.

Dovizioso fought through from fifth on the first lap and tried to give chase but couldn't manage it. He ended the race defending second place from a hard-charging Rossi and Iannone. "I tried to catch Jorge, but I was slower in the last part of braking, in the middle of the corners," Dovizioso explained. "Jorge rode a very good race. It was a very particular race because the grip was low. You have to adapt to the conditions and he managed the medium front in a really good way. To keep his pace to the end with his tyres was very difficult."

Both Dovizioso and Rossi chose the hard front. Only too late did they realise they had made a mistake. "I saw Valentino lose the front too many times and he had the same tyre as me," said Dovizioso.

The battle behind the two Ducatis was fierce: Rossi, Iannone, Danilo Petrucci, Álex Rins and Cal Crutchlow all fighting to be part of the biggest celebration of the season: the Mugello podium.

Petrucci rode a hero's race. At the second corner of the first lap Márquez punted him onto the asphalt runoff, which relegated him to tenth. By half-distance he was third, but his remarkable fightback had burned his front tyre, so he didn't have enough grip for the torrid final laps.

## DUCATI'S PLASTIC FANTASTIC

In the age of carbon-fibre and hi-tech electronics it came as something of a shock that the difference between losing and winning could be a big lump of plastic attached to the rear of a fuel tank.

But that was the crucial change made to Jorge Lorenzo's GP18. The modification (right) was designed to give him better support in straight-line braking and shifting him several inches backwards to better position his arms and allow him to maintain maximum pace all the way to the finish.

"I feel better than ever with this bike," said Lorenzo. "Physically I have more energy to keep a more constant pace through more laps. With this modification I had the energy to keep pushing to the end. The ergonomics of last year's bike were different: the fuel

Thus the fight for third became a straight duel between Rossi and Iannone. "In the last laps you forget your strategy and it's all heart," said Rossi, whose last two laps were scintillating. "You enter the corners thinking, 'Maybe I will crash, but I must try'. You trust in the tyre and in the bike and it was okay."

And it was all worth it. "Ten minutes on the podium at Mugello in front of the crowd repays all the effort you make with training, travel and riding," he said after his 14th appearance high above the start/finish. "We suffered because we had to race with the hard front and I never had a good feeling with the hard in practice. It was one of my toughest races recently because the bike was very difficult to ride with low grip at the front."

Iannone's biggest worry was rear grip. "We struggled with the rear tyre because the track was really hot, so we lost out on acceleration, especially on the straight," he said.

Márquez didn't quite last five laps. He was chasing Lorenzo when he lost the front entering the downhill Scarperia right-hander. This was very nearly another moment of Márquez magic. The front tucked but he refused to surrender, holding onto the bike until it finally clattered into the gravel. The smear of rubber on the track and asphalt runoff measured 38 metres!

"This race is one to forget because the tyre allocation was so special for us; and that is not an excuse, because the allocation was the same for everybody," said Márquez, who remounted and set a good pace, but finished pointless. "The issue is that we stress the front even more than the others, with the Honda and my riding style."

**CLOCKWISE, FROM TOP LEFT** | *Iannone lost his podium fight with Rossi, then worked to keep Petrucci (wearing Lamborghini colours) behind him; "thanks and goodbye", mixed emotions for Gigi Dall'Igna; Pol Espargaró finished 11th for the third, but not the last, time; Viñales qualified well but went backwards in the race, again; Petrucci chased Rossi for third, but had burned his tyres fighting back from an off-track excursion; quite a view from the podium*

tank was higher and a different shape. Ducati had to modify the ergonomics and the shape of the fuel tank to fit the GP18 chassis. From the Buriram tests in February I said I have less support and get more tired during braking. We had some new parts at Jerez, then tried a slightly different shape fuel tank at the Barcelona tests before we came here and finally something bigger arrived."

There were two other factors in Lorenzo's change of fortune. The tank mod allowed him to adjust his riding technique to reduce stress on the front tyre, which was a problem for his rivals. And for the first time both his bikes were equipped with a later-spec frame that gave better tuning and bump absorption.

"This was a new experience which should help me to take the maximum with this bike in the future," said Lorenzo, without a hint of irony in his voice.

# 6 | ITALY

# RACE RESULTS

**WINNER** | JORGE LORENZO

**CIRCUIT LENGTH** | 5.2 KM | 3.26 MILES

**NO. OF LAPS** | 23

**RACE DISTANCE** | 120.6 KM | 75.0 MILES

**CIRCUIT RECORD LAP** | 1'47.639 | 175.4 KM/H
MARC MÁRQUEZ (2013)

**CIRCUIT BEST LAP** | 1'46.208 | 177.7 KM/H
VALENTINO ROSSI (2018)

**RACE CONDITION** | DRY

**AIR** | 29°C

**HUMIDITY** | 39%

**GROUND** | 51°C

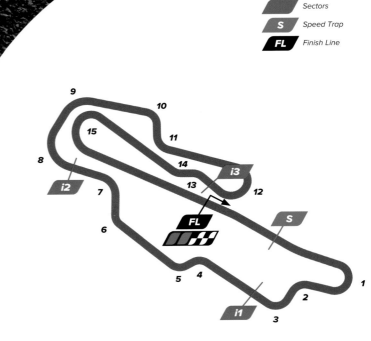

Start Line
Sectors
S — Speed Trap
FL — Finish Line

TISSOT / MotoGP
SWISS WATCHES SINCE 1853
**OFFICIAL** TIMEKEEPER

MICHELIN / MotoGP
**OFFICIAL** MotoGP™ CLASS TYRE

**FRONT TYRES**
L M R
SOFT
MEDIUM
HARD

**REAR TYRES**
L M R
SOFT
MEDIUM
HARD

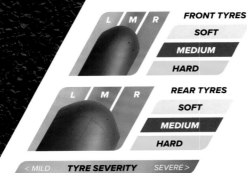

< MILD | **TYRE SEVERITY** | SEVERE >

## QUALIFYING RESULTS

| | RIDER | NAT | TEAM | MACHINE | QP/TIME | | GAP 1ST/PREV | |
|---|---|---|---|---|---|---|---|---|
| 1 | Valentino Rossi | ITA | Movistar Yamaha MotoGP | YAMAHA | Q2 | 1'46.208 | | |
| 2 | Jorge Lorenzo | SPA | Ducati Team | DUCATI | Q2 | 1'46.243 | 0.035 | 0.035 |
| 3 | Maverick Viñales** | SPA | Movistar Yamaha MotoGP | YAMAHA | Q2 | 1'46.304 | 0.096 | 0.061 |
| 4 | Andrea Iannone | ITA | Team SUZUKI ECSTAR | SUZUKI | Q2 | 1'46.347 | 0.139 | 0.043 |
| 5 | Danilo Petrucci | ITA | Alma Pramac Racing | DUCATI | Q2 | 1'46.445 | 0.237 | 0.098 |
| 6 | Marc Márquez | SPA | Repsol Honda Team | HONDA | Q2 | 1'46.454 | 0.246 | 0.009 |
| 7 | Andrea Dovizioso | ITA | Ducati Team | DUCATI | Q2 | 1'46.500 | 0.292 | 0.046 |
| 8 | Cal Crutchlow | GBR | LCR Honda CASTROL | HONDA | Q2 | 1'46.813 | 0.605 | 0.313 |
| 9 | Johann Zarco | FRA | Monster Yamaha Tech 3 | YAMAHA | Q2 | 1'46.830 | 0.622 | 0.017 |
| 10 | Álex Rins | SPA | Team SUZUKI ECSTAR | SUZUKI | Q2 | 1'46.909 | 0.701 | 0.079 |
| 11 | Jack Miller** | AUS | Alma Pramac Racing | DUCATI | Q2 | 1'46.998 | 0.790 | 0.089 |
| 12 | Franco Morbidelli | ITA | EG 0,0 Marc VDS | HONDA | Q2 | 1'47.002 | 0.794 | 0.004 |
| 13 | Tito Rabat | SPA | Reale Avintia Racing | DUCATI | Q1 | 1'46.908 | *0.137 | 0.102 |
| 14 | Hafizh Syahrin | MAL | Monster Yamaha Tech 3 | YAMAHA | Q1 | 1'47.188 | *0.417 | 0.280 |
| 15 | Pol Espargaró | SPA | Red Bull KTM Factory Racing | KTM | Q1 | 1'47.335 | *0.564 | 0.147 |
| 16 | Álvaro Bautista | SPA | Ángel Nieto Team | DUCATI | Q1 | 1'47.708 | *0.937 | 0.373 |
| 17 | Bradley Smith | GBR | Red Bull KTM Factory Racing | KTM | Q1 | 1'47.818 | *1.047 | 0.110 |
| 18 | Takaaki Nakagami | JPN | LCR Honda IDEMITSU | HONDA | Q1 | 1'47.868 | *1.097 | 0.050 |
| 19 | Thomas Lüthi | SWI | EG 0,0 Marc VDS | HONDA | Q1 | 1'47.989 | *1.218 | 0.121 |
| 20 | Dani Pedrosa | SPA | Repsol Honda Team | HONDA | Q1 | 1'48.065 | *1.294 | 0.076 |
| 21 | Aleix Espargaró | SPA | Aprilia Racing Team Gresini | APRILIA | Q1 | 1'48.286 | *1.515 | 0.221 |
| 22 | Karel Abraham | CZE | Ángel Nieto Team | DUCATI | Q1 | 1'48.532 | *1.761 | 0.246 |
| 23 | Scott Redding | GBR | Aprilia Racing Team Gresini | APRILIA | Q1 | 1'48.744 | *1.973 | 0.212 |
| 24 | Xavier Siméon | GER | Reale Avintia Racing | DUCATI | Q1 | 1'48.794 | *2.023 | 0.050 |
| 25 | Michele Pirro | ITA | Ducati Team | DUCATI | FP1 | 1'47.803 | 0.550 | |

*\* Gap to the fastest rider in the Q1 session*
*\*\* Went forward from Q1 to Q2*

**1 | JORGE LORENZO**
Pulled off a masterstroke of a race, discovering a new way of riding through the right-handers to reduce stress on the front tyre. And no, he didn't want to reveal the secret of this possibly decisive new riding technique!

**2 | ANDREA DOVIZIOSO**
Became the fastest man in the history of Grand Prix racing with a top speed of 356.5kmh/221.5mph during the race. Had to race the hard front, which didn't give him the grip he needed to fight for his second successive Mugello win.

**3 | VALENTINO ROSSI**
This was the home hero's best Mugello weekend since his last win in 2008: he started from pole for the second time in ten years and stood on the podium for the third time in ten years. Once again, he sent the crowd home happy.

**4 | ANDREA IANNONE**
The former Mugello Moto2 winner pushed from the beginning, asking a lot from his tyres, which forced him to reduce his pace at half-distance to cool the tyres. But he couldn't quite match Rossi's pace in the last laps.

**5 | ÁLEX RINS**
A big crash during Saturday practice left him battered, bruised and lacking strength and confidence. In these circumstances, his race to fifth place, just two hundredths of a second behind his team-mate, was remarkable.

**6 | CAL CRUTCHLOW**
Spent much of the race behind the dogfight for third place, the heat from the bikes ahead of him overheating his front tyre. This was another brave ride; after his Le Mans prang he was still coughing up blood.

**7 | DANILO PETRUCCI**
Aiming to repeat his 2017 podium and still job-hunting for 2019, Petrucci showed good pace and was optimistic for the race. He got a great start and was third on lap one when Márquez pushed him wide and dashed his hopes.

**8 | MAVERICK VIÑALES**
Once again dropped like a stone, from third to tenth, after losing the front and nearly crashing on lap one. Ended the race wondering if he needed to warm the tyres better on the sighting and warm-up laps.

**9 | ÁLVARO BAUTISTA**
Despite another so-so qualifying, had by far his best race of the year, finishing less than five seconds behind second-placed Dovizioso. Snuck in behind Viñales and tried to pass him at one point, nearly falling in the process.

**10 | JOHANN ZARCO**
Two weeks after crashing out of his home GP the Frenchman couldn't find the right feeling to push to the limit. Tried to stay with Viñales and Bautista when they came past, but couldn't manage it.

**11 | POL ESPARGARÓ**
Finished one place outside the top ten for the second time in three races. During the early laps made adjustments to his engine mapping to reduce wheelspin. Spent much of the race alone, just ahead of a big three-way battle.

**12 | HAFIZH SYAHRIN**
Like many riders, found that the rubber put down during the Moto2 race reduced grip. Didn't have the easiest of races but enjoyed the fight with Morbidelli and with Rabat, who he passed on the final lap.

# RACE LAP CHART

----- Dashed line: Lapped rider

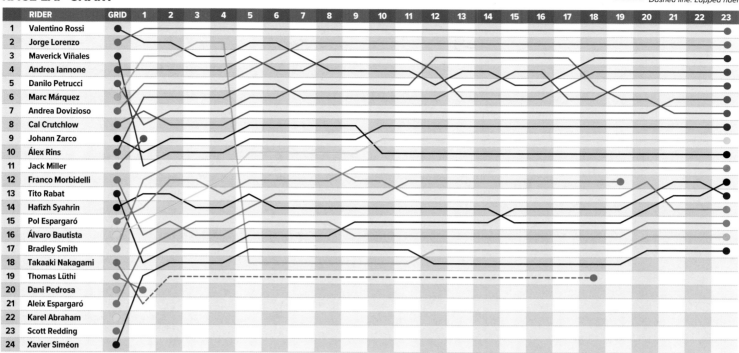

| | RIDER | GRID | 1 | 2 | 3 | 4 | 5 | 6 | 7 | 8 | 9 | 10 | 11 | 12 | 13 | 14 | 15 | 16 | 17 | 18 | 19 | 20 | 21 | 22 | 23 |
|---|---|---|---|---|---|---|---|---|---|---|---|---|---|---|---|---|---|---|---|---|---|---|---|---|---|
| 1 | Valentino Rossi | | | | | | | | | | | | | | | | | | | | | | | | |
| 2 | Jorge Lorenzo | | | | | | | | | | | | | | | | | | | | | | | | |
| 3 | Maverick Viñales | | | | | | | | | | | | | | | | | | | | | | | | |
| 4 | Andrea Iannone | | | | | | | | | | | | | | | | | | | | | | | | |
| 5 | Danilo Petrucci | | | | | | | | | | | | | | | | | | | | | | | | |
| 6 | Marc Márquez | | | | | | | | | | | | | | | | | | | | | | | | |
| 7 | Andrea Dovizioso | | | | | | | | | | | | | | | | | | | | | | | | |
| 8 | Cal Crutchlow | | | | | | | | | | | | | | | | | | | | | | | | |
| 9 | Johann Zarco | | | | | | | | | | | | | | | | | | | | | | | | |
| 10 | Álex Rins | | | | | | | | | | | | | | | | | | | | | | | | |
| 11 | Jack Miller | | | | | | | | | | | | | | | | | | | | | | | | |
| 12 | Franco Morbidelli | | | | | | | | | | | | | | | | | | | | | | | | |
| 13 | Tito Rabat | | | | | | | | | | | | | | | | | | | | | | | | |
| 14 | Hafizh Syahrin | | | | | | | | | | | | | | | | | | | | | | | | |
| 15 | Pol Espargaró | | | | | | | | | | | | | | | | | | | | | | | | |
| 16 | Álvaro Bautista | | | | | | | | | | | | | | | | | | | | | | | | |
| 17 | Bradley Smith | | | | | | | | | | | | | | | | | | | | | | | | |
| 18 | Takaaki Nakagami | | | | | | | | | | | | | | | | | | | | | | | | |
| 19 | Thomas Lüthi | | | | | | | | | | | | | | | | | | | | | | | | |
| 20 | Dani Pedrosa | | | | | | | | | | | | | | | | | | | | | | | | |
| 21 | Aleix Espargaró | | | | | | | | | | | | | | | | | | | | | | | | |
| 22 | Karel Abraham | | | | | | | | | | | | | | | | | | | | | | | | |
| 23 | Scott Redding | | | | | | | | | | | | | | | | | | | | | | | | |
| 24 | Xavier Siméon | | | | | | | | | | | | | | | | | | | | | | | | |

## RACE CLASSIFICATION AFTER 23 LAPS = 120.635 KM

| | RIDER | NAT | TEAM | MACHINE | TIME | + GAP | TYRES |
|---|---|---|---|---|---|---|---|
| 1 | Jorge Lorenzo | SPA | Ducati Team | DUCATI | 41'43.230 | | M/S |
| 2 | Andrea Dovizioso | ITA | Ducati Team | DUCATI | 41'49.600 | 6.370 | *HA/S |
| 3 | Valentino Rossi | ITA | Movistar Yamaha MotoGP | YAMAHA | 41'49.859 | 6.629 | *HA/M |
| 4 | Andrea Iannone | ITA | Team SUZUKI ECSTAR | SUZUKI | 41'51.115 | 7.885 | M/S |
| 5 | Álex Rins | SPA | Team SUZUKI ECSTAR | SUZUKI | 41'51.137 | 7.907 | M/S |
| 6 | Cal Crutchlow | GBR | LCR Honda CASTROL | HONDA | 41'52.350 | 9.120 | M/M |
| 7 | Danilo Petrucci | ITA | Alma Pramac Racing | DUCATI | 41'54.128 | 10.898 | M/S |
| 8 | Maverick Viñales | SPA | Movistar Yamaha MotoGP | YAMAHA | 41'54.290 | 11.060 | *HA/M |
| 9 | Álvaro Bautista | SPA | Ángel Nieto Team | DUCATI | 41'54.384 | 11.154 | M/S |
| 10 | Johann Zarco | FRA | Monster Yamaha Tech 3 | YAMAHA | 42'00.874 | 17.644 | M/M |
| 11 | Pol Espargaró | SPA | Red Bull KTM Factory Racing | KTM | 42'03.486 | 20.256 | H/S |
| 12 | Hafizh Syahrin | MAL | Monster Yamaha Tech 3 | YAMAHA | 42'05.665 | 22.435 | M/S |
| 13 | Tito Rabat | SPA | Reale Avintia Racing | DUCATI | 42'05.694 | 22.464 | M/S |
| 14 | Bradley Smith | GBR | Red Bull KTM Factory Racing | KTM | 42'05.725 | 22.495 | M/S |
| 15 | Franco Morbidelli | ITA | EG 0,0 Marc VDS | HONDA | 42'09.874 | 26.644 | M/S |
| 16 | Marc Márquez | SPA | Repsol Honda Team | HONDA | 42'22.541 | 39.311 | *HA/H |
| 17 | Xavier Siméon | GER | Reale Avintia Racing | DUCATI | 42'44.441 | 61.211 | M/S |
| 18 | Takaaki Nakagami | JPN | LCR Honda IDEMITSU | HONDA | 42'34.319 | 5 laps | M/S |
| NC | Aleix Espargaró | SPA | Aprilia Racing Team Gresini | APRILIA | 34'44.756 | 4 laps | M/S |
| NC | Jack Miller | AUS | Alma Pramac Racing | DUCATI | 1'56.650 | 22 laps | M/M |
| NC | Thomas Lüthi | SWI | EG 0,0 Marc VDS | HONDA | 1'59.032 | 22 laps | M/S |
| NC | Dani Pedrosa | SPA | Repsol Honda Team | HONDA | | | H/M |
| NC | Karel Abraham | CZE | Ángel Nieto Team | DUCATI | | | M/S |
| NC | Scott Redding | GBR | Aprilia Racing Team Gresini | APRILIA | | | M/S |

*HA - front hard asymmetric tyre

## CHAMPIONSHIP STANDINGS

| | RIDER | NAT | TEAM | POINTS |
|---|---|---|---|---|
| 1 | Marc Márquez | SPA | Repsol Honda Team | 95 |
| 2 | Valentino Rossi | ITA | Movistar Yamaha MotoGP | 72 |
| 3 | Maverick Viñales | SPA | Movistar Yamaha MotoGP | 67 |
| 4 | Andrea Dovizioso | ITA | Ducati Team | 66 |
| 5 | Johann Zarco | FRA | Monster Yamaha Tech 3 | 64 |
| 6 | Danilo Petrucci | ITA | Alma Pramac Racing | 63 |
| 7 | Andrea Iannone | ITA | Team SUZUKI ECSTAR | 60 |
| 8 | Cal Crutchlow | GBR | LCR Honda CASTROL | 56 |
| 9 | Jack Miller | AUS | Alma Pramac Racing | 49 |
| 10 | Jorge Lorenzo | SPA | Ducati Team | 41 |
| 11 | Álex Rins | SPA | Team SUZUKI ECSTAR | 33 |
| 12 | Dani Pedrosa | SPA | Repsol Honda Team | 29 |
| 13 | Tito Rabat | SPA | Reale Avintia Racing | 27 |
| 14 | Pol Espargaró | SPA | Red Bull KTM Factory Racing | 23 |
| 15 | Álvaro Bautista | SPA | Ángel Nieto Team | 19 |
| 16 | Hafizh Syahrin | MAL | Monster Yamaha Tech 3 | 17 |
| 17 | Franco Morbidelli | ITA | EG 0,0 Marc VDS | 17 |
| 18 | Aleix Espargaró | SPA | Aprilia Racing Team Gresini | 13 |
| 19 | Takaaki Nakagami | JPN | LCR Honda IDEMITSU | 10 |
| 20 | Bradley Smith | GBR | Red Bull KTM Factory Racing | 7 |
| 21 | Mika Kallio | FIN | Red Bull KTM Factory Racing | 6 |
| 22 | Scott Redding | GBR | Aprilia Racing Team Gresini | 5 |
| 23 | Karel Abraham | CZE | Ángel Nieto Team | 1 |
| 24 | Thomas Lüthi | SWI | EG 0,0 Marc VDS | |
| 25 | Xavier Siméon | GER | Reale Avintia Racing | |

**13 | TITO RABAT**
Rode at Mugello despite the effects of a big crash during testing at Barcelona-Catalunya. Went straight through to Q2 for the first time with Ducati and hoped for better in the race, in which he was unable to find much front grip.

**14 | BRADLEY SMITH**
Enjoyed the skirmish with Syahrin and Rabat, which he led until three laps from the end. The trio was covered by 0.06 seconds at the flag. Like most of his rivals, was affected by increasing front tyre pressure.

**15 | FRANCO MORBIDELLI**
Mugello isn't easy to master on a MotoGP bike, so any rookie that goes direct into Q2 is doing a very good job. Like Crutchlow, lost front grip when he was following other riders. Delighted to have made the finish and score a point.

**16 | MARC MÁRQUEZ**
Knew he would be in trouble as soon as he checked the front tyre allocation on arrival at Mugello, but was mystified by his crash, because he wasn't pushing so hard. Perhaps the Moto2 rubber was to blame.

**17 | XAVIER SIMÉON**
Got a great start from the back of the grid and quickly made up several positions, but then ran into rear-grip issues, which caused him problems on corner entry, rather than on corner exit. Rode most of the race alone.

**18 | TAKAAKI NAKAGAMI**
After getting taken out by a falling Pedrosa on the first lap, the rookie didn't give in. Returned to the pits for repairs and then continued to the finish, learning more and gathering more data along the way.

**DNF | ALEIX ESPARGARÓ**
Caught the Syahrin/Rabat/Smith freight train at one third-distance and was looking good until he ran out of rear grip, losing the rear into corners. The situation got so bad that he retired with four laps to go, rather than risk a fall.

**DNF | JACK MILLER**
Had high hopes of another strong ride to follow his superb Le Mans result. Started from the grid in ninth, aiming to move forward, but his forks bottomed while braking on the second lap and down he went.

**DNF | THOMAS LÜTHI**
Crashed in FP1 and again in FP2, which knocked his confidence for the remainder of the weekend. On the first lap he tried to get past Siméon on the way into Arrabbiata 1, where he lost the front and crashed once again.

**DNF | DANI PEDROSA**
Never had a good feeling until his crew made a final change for warm-up. However, starting from 20th brings risks. Tagged Bautista's rear tyre at turn two, which caused him to fall and take out Nakagami.

**DNF | KAREL ABRAHAM**
Laid low by sickness all weekend, was focused on getting through the race and moving on to the next round. However, it was not to be. Lost the rear entering the final corner for the first time and crashed out.

**DNF | SCOTT REDDING**
Not an easy first Italian Grand Prix with Aprilia. Qualified last but one, ahead of Siméon, and was just behind Abraham at the end of the first lap of the race when the Czech rider fell just ahead of him and brought him down heavily.

Lorenzo rode in glorious isolation once again — not even first-lap leader Márquez could stay with him

# LORENZO
# DOES IT AGAIN

**Just days after announcing his move to Repsol Honda, Lorenzo was totally dominant for the second race in a row and his rivals were looking worried**

The paddock was still somewhat in shock when it arrived at Barcelona-Catalunya, where soon-to-be team-mates Marc Márquez and Jorge Lorenzo met for the first time since the latter dropped his contract bombshell. Before practice got underway, Márquez joked that he liked having strong team-mates, but not that strong! And all through practice and the race he gave vain chase to Lorenzo, never quite able to match the Ducati rider's pace.

Márquez crashed twice in practice, then magicked his best-ever front-end save during FP4, tucking the front as he entered the final corner, smoke pouring off the front tyre as he jabbed his knee and elbow into the asphalt. As usual, he laughed off the incident — "It's all about the show!" — but his eyes told a different story. He knew he would struggle to beat Lorenzo in the race and he knew the championship landscape had changed more than anyone could have expected following his third win in a row at Le Mans.

Lorenzo usually rides in his self-styled hammer or mantequilla modes, but on the eve of this race he was so confident he talked of hammer-and-butter mode, which sounds messy, but was very effective. As Cal Crutchlow opined, "When Lorenzo is riding like this it's horrendous".

**MAIN** Márquez leads into the first corner but Lorenzo's body language says it all: he's already bursting with confidence

**BELOW, FROM LEFT** Zarco slightly distracted by the Monster girls; diligent workers Dovizioso and crew-chief Alberto Giribuola (left); Rossi took a third consecutive third-place finish

'NOW IT'S POSSIBLE – WE HAVE THE MOST COMPLETE DUCATI EVER AND WE HAVE NOTHING TO LOSE'

And it certainly was. Lorenzo was clear favourite after setting a blistering pace in FP4 and taking his first pole position for Ducati. The only thing that quite didn't go to plan was his getaway. This time MotoGP's fastest starter was only third into the first corner, where Andrea Iannone executed a no-nonsense overtaking manoeuvre. But it didn't matter, by the end of the first lap Lorenzo was already set to pounce on leader Márquez. The world champion did his best to stay with the Ducati and did close the gap at one point, only for Lorenzo to simply up his pace once more. By half-distance he was 1.6 seconds ahead, by the flag he was more than four seconds in front.

Lorenzo's winning secret was the same as at Mugello: his ability to decelerate faster than his rivals, so he could swoop into corners without overusing the front tyre. "I'm braking even better than at the last race," said the 31-year-old who used a soft/soft tyre combination that lasted every bit as well as Márquez's hard/hard combo.

After taking 30 points out of Márquez's championship lead in just two races, the 2010, 2011 and 2015 MotoGP king knew that the 2018 title was no longer out of reach. "Now it's possible," he said. "We have the most complete Ducati ever and we have nothing to lose."

Márquez admitted defeat just before half-distance, waving the white flag after several more front-end scares and a flurry of yellow warning flags. Wild cards Mika Kallio and Sylvain Guintoli were the first to crash out of the race, then Tom Lüthi, Aleix Espargaró, Xavier Siméon and Andrea Dovizioso. When Márquez's toughest 2017 rival hit the ground, he knew he was asking for trouble if he kept pushing too hard. Like most of the fallers, Dovizioso lost the front; his day ending at the downhill entry into turn five. By the end of the race ten riders had crashed out.

Third-placed Valentino Rossi put the blame for this rash of crashes on the front tyre. "The allocation here is not perfect because the soft is too soft and with the medium you are too slow," said the seven-times Catalan MotoGP winner, who chose the soft front like most of the grid. "You had to be very quiet to manage the front."

The track's new asphalt – smoother and grippier than the previous surface that had caused so many problems in 2017 – may also have claimed some of the victims. Most riders were satisfied with the improvement, but they were even happier about further changes to the circuit layout. Following Luis Salom's fatal accident in 2016 the track's fast and flowing final two right-handers had been interrupted by a chicane. For 2018, the old layout had been mostly restored, thanks to the removal of a grandstand to increase runoff at turn 12, now named Luis Salom corner and overlooked by a huge mural portrait of Salom.

Rossi managed his soft front better than most during the 24 laps, inheriting the final podium place from Dovizioso, who was distraught after his third DNF in four races.

## CELEBRATING 50 YEARS OF SPANISH VICTORIES

On 4th May 1968 Salvador Canellas rode his factory Bultaco TSS125 to victory in the Spanish 125cc Grand Prix at Montjuic Park, in Barcelona. He was the first Spaniard to win a world championship race, 19 years after the inaugural 1949 Grand Prix season.

Since then, Spanish riders have scored another 600 or so victories across all Grand Prix classes, making Spain the second most successful nation in bike racing, after Italy. It all started with Canellas, although Spain's obsession with motorcycle racing didn't really begin until the following year when Ángel Nieto won the 50cc title with Derbi.

However, Rossi was far from overjoyed with his third consecutive third-place finish. "We've only finished a maximum of third, so we are not strong enough to fight," he said. "We need to work in different areas to find two tenths. We need to work on acceleration, because when I follow the Ducati and Honda it looks like their engines and electronics work very well to give a lot of power, without spin. For me, this is the biggest difference."

During the closing laps, as Rossi tried to stay quiet with his front tyre, he had Cal Crutchlow closing on him. The Briton had come through from ninth on the first lap to catch Dani Pedrosa, who had been scrapping back and forth with Danilo Petrucci, who ruined his race when he ran wide at turn four on lap ten. Crutchlow took too long to get the better of Márquez's team-mate and although he was consistently faster than Rossi once he was past Pedrosa, he was still more than three seconds down on the Italian at the finish.

Maverick Viñales had yet another strange day. Swamped at the start, the former Moto3 world champion went backwards on the first lap, from fourth on the grid to tenth, then commenced a dogged climb through the pack, duelling with fellow M1 rider Johann Zarco along the way, but never getting fully into his groove until the last few laps. On laps 19, 22, 23 and 24 he was the fastest man on track. But that didn't do him much good.

Michelin suggested that Viñales and some other riders needed to increase their pace during the warm-up lap. Michelin motorsport manager Piero Taramasso advised riders to attack the warm-up lap at 95 percent of their race pace in order to bring the tyres to peak temperature and grip as quickly as possible.

**CLOCKWISE, FROM TOP LEFT** | *Márquez and Crutchlow bear flags commemorating teenager Andreas Perez, who lost his life during the previous weekend's Barcelona Moto3 junior world championship race; Marc's leathers bore the mark of another miracle save; Viñales was still looking for answers; Redding wasn't happy about crashing in warm-up; Lorenzo was in hammer mode and celebrated accordingly; Dovizioso chases hard, before crashing out*

A few days before the Catalan GP, Dorna organised a special event in Montjuic Park to celebrate the 50th anniversary of Spain's first Grand Prix victory. Canellas, dressed in his old leathers and pudding-basin helmet, sat on his TSS125 alongside Spain's seven factory MotoGP riders, who fill one quarter of this year's world championship grid: the Espargaró brothers, Lorenzo, Márquez, Pedrosa and Rins.

All but Majorcan Lorenzo are Catalans, and yet none of them knew the Montjuic racetrack, which is a public road now, just as it was way back then. "I was so surprised that none of them had taken a tour of the circuit, because to me Montjuic is like a temple," says Canellas, now 74. "The track seems very dangerous to them, but in fact it was safer than many of the street circuits on which we competed. Even so, in all these races we played with our lives."

# 7 | CATALUNYA

# RACE RESULTS

**WINNER** | JORGE LORENZO

**CIRCUIT LENGTH**⁺ | 4.6 KM | 2.88 MILES

**NO. OF LAPS**⁺ | 24

**RACE DISTANCE**⁺ | 111.0 KM | 69.1 MILES

**CIRCUIT RECORD LAP**⁺ | 1'40.021 | 166.5 KM/H
JORGE LORENZO (2018)

**CIRCUIT BEST LAP**⁺ | 1'38.680 | 168.8 KM/H
JORGE LORENZO (2018)

**RACE CONDITION** | DRY

**AIR** | 27˚C

**HUMIDITY** | 51%

**GROUND** | 45˚C

Start Line
Sectors
S | Speed Trap
FL | Finish Line

**TISSOT** SWISS WATCHES SINCE 1853 / motoGP™
**OFFICIAL** TIMEKEEPER

MICHELIN / motoGP™
**OFFICIAL** MotoGP™ CLASS TYRE

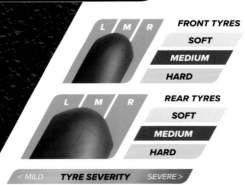

**FRONT TYRES**
SOFT
MEDIUM
HARD

**REAR TYRES**
SOFT
MEDIUM
HARD

< MILD   **TYRE SEVERITY**   SEVERE >

## QUALIFYING RESULTS

| | RIDER | NAT | TEAM | MACHINE | QP/TIME | GAP 1ST/PREV | |
|---|---|---|---|---|---|---|---|
| 1 | Jorge Lorenzo | SPA | Ducati Team | DUCATI | Q2 1'38.680 | | |
| 2 | Marc Márquez** | SPA | Repsol Honda Team | HONDA | Q2 1'38.746 | 0.066 | 0.066 |
| 3 | Andrea Dovizioso | ITA | Ducati Team | DUCATI | Q2 1'38.923 | 0.243 | 0.177 |
| 4 | Maverick Viñales | SPA | Movistar Yamaha MotoGP | YAMAHA | Q2 1'39.145 | 0.465 | 0.222 |
| 5 | Andrea Iannone | ITA | Team SUZUKI ECSTAR | SUZUKI | Q2 1'39.148 | 0.468 | 0.003 |
| 6 | Danilo Petrucci | ITA | Alma Pramac Racing | DUCATI | Q2 1'39.178 | 0.498 | 0.030 |
| 7 | Valentino Rossi | ITA | Movistar Yamaha MotoGP | YAMAHA | Q2 1'39.266 | 0.586 | 0.088 |
| 8 | Johann Zarco | FRA | Monster Yamaha Tech 3 | YAMAHA | Q2 1'39.331 | 0.651 | 0.065 |
| 9 | Tito Rabat | SPA | Reale Avintia Racing | DUCATI | Q2 1'39.504 | 0.824 | 0.173 |
| 10 | Cal Crutchlow | GBR | LCR Honda CASTROL | HONDA | Q2 1'39.556 | 0.876 | 0.052 |
| 11 | Dani Pedrosa | SPA | Repsol Honda Team | HONDA | Q2 1'39.695 | 1.015 | 0.139 |
| 12 | Takaaki Nakagami** | JPN | LCR Honda IDEMITSU | HONDA | Q2 1'39.888 | 1.208 | 0.193 |
| 13 | Jack Miller | AUS | Alma Pramac Racing | DUCATI | Q1 1'39.732 | *0.515 | 0.069 |
| 14 | Hafizh Syahrin | MAL | Monster Yamaha Tech 3 | YAMAHA | Q1 1'39.879 | *0.662 | 0.147 |
| 15 | Álex Rins | SPA | Team SUZUKI ECSTAR | SUZUKI | Q1 1'39.918 | *0.701 | 0.039 |
| 16 | Aleix Espargaró | SPA | Aprilia Racing Team Gresini | APRILIA | Q1 1'40.010 | *0.793 | 0.092 |
| 17 | Bradley Smith | GBR | Red Bull KTM Factory Racing | KTM | Q1 1'40.019 | *0.802 | 0.009 |
| 18 | Franco Morbidelli | ITA | EG 0,0 Marc VDS | HONDA | Q1 1'40.058 | *0.841 | 0.039 |
| 19 | Pol Espargaró | SPA | Red Bull KTM Factory Racing | KTM | Q1 1'40.178 | *0.961 | 0.120 |
| 20 | Scott Redding | GBR | Aprilia Racing Team Gresini | APRILIA | Q1 1'40.300 | *1.083 | 0.122 |
| 21 | Karel Abraham | CZE | Ángel Nieto Team | DUCATI | Q1 1'40.449 | *1.232 | 0.149 |
| 22 | Álvaro Bautista | SPA | Ángel Nieto Team | DUCATI | Q1 1'40.524 | *1.307 | 0.075 |
| 23 | Mika Kallio | FIN | Red Bull KTM Factory Racing | KTM | Q1 1'40.572 | *1.355 | 0.048 |
| 24 | Thomas Lüthi | SWI | EG 0,0 Marc VDS | HONDA | Q1 1'40.590 | *1.373 | 0.018 |
| 25 | Sylvain Guintoli | FRA | Team SUZUKI ECSTAR | SUZUKI | Q1 1'40.834 | *1.617 | 0.244 |
| 26 | Xavier Siméon | GER | Reale Avintia Racing | DUCATI | Q1 1'41.369 | *2.152 | 0.535 |

*Gap to the fastest rider in the Q1 session   ** Went forward from Q1 to Q2*

**1 | JORGE LORENZO**
Lorenzo gave Ducati back-to-back Mugello/Catalunya victories, just as Dovizioso had done in 2017. His dominance was ominous, breaking away out front and comfortably pulling away from Márquez.

**2 | MARC MÁRQUEZ**
It's not often that the world champ gives it everything and comes up short, but this was one of those occasions. His tyres didn't give him the grip that Lorenzo had, so this time Márquez put discretion before valour.

**3 | VALENTINO ROSSI**
Four podiums from the first seven races might be considered a strong start to the season, but not strong enough for Rossi, even though this time he quickly came through from the third row of the grid.

**4 | CAL CRUTCHLOW**
Now fully recovered from his horrible Le Mans shunt, had his best ride since his Argentine victory. He was one of eight riders who chose the medium front instead of the soft and he made it work for him.

**5 | DANI PEDROSA**
Many people expected something special in his first race since Repsol Honda announced it would not renew his contract. But he suffered from a lack of grip, especially in the middle and the exit of corners.

**6 | MAVERICK VIÑALES**
Qualified fourth quickest, but once again couldn't get going until the late stages of the race, when he was as fast or faster than anyone. Ended the weekend as mystified as he had ended the previous few weekends.

**7 | JOHANN ZARCO**
Another difficult race for the Frenchman, who lost positions in the first-lap charge. Battled with Viñales for many laps, had his eyes on catching Pedrosa and Crutchlow, but succumbed to Viñales in the final laps.

**8 | DANILO PETRUCCI**
Ran as high as fourth in the early stages while trying to save his rear tyre, then battled with Crutchlow and Pedrosa. In the end a lack of front grip caused him to lose that fight and slipped steadily backwards.

**9 | ÁLVARO BAUTISTA**
A crash in qualifying left him 22nd on the grid, with a lot of work to do. Started the race steadily to avoid overheating his tyres and came through thanks to fine riding and the exit of many of his rivals.

**10 | ANDREA IANNONE**
Couldn't sustain his impressive start, when he briefly lay second. Went steadily backwards as his tyres went away, especially under acceleration, but somehow managed to set his best lap on lap 18.

**11 | POL ESPARGARÓ**
Was happy that he was much closer to the winner than he had been at Catalunya 2017, even though he was in cruise mode due to excessive wheelspin, especially through the circuit's numerous long corners.

**12 | SCOTT REDDING**
Equalled his best performance so far with Aprilia, apparently more able than his rivals to deal with the lack of grip, because he was accustomed to the issue. Spent most of the race chasing the KTM ahead of him.

# RACE LAP CHART

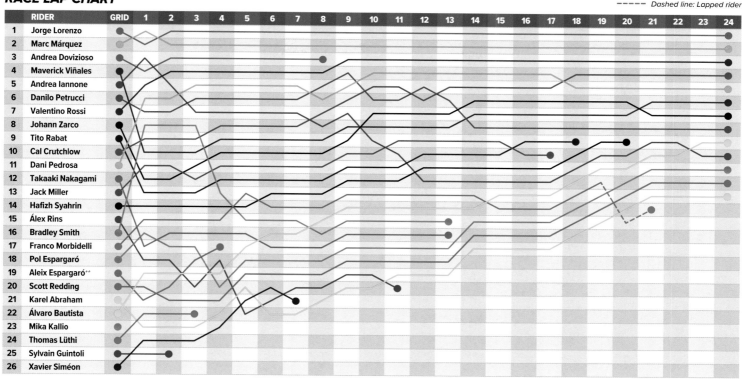

| | RIDER | GRID | 1 | 2 | 3 | 4 | 5 | 6 | 7 | 8 | 9 | 10 | 11 | 12 | 13 | 14 | 15 | 16 | 17 | 18 | 19 | 20 | 21 | 22 | 23 | 24 |
|---|---|---|---|---|---|---|---|---|---|---|---|---|---|---|---|---|---|---|---|---|---|---|---|---|---|---|
| 1 | Jorge Lorenzo | | | | | | | | | | | | | | | | | | | | | | | | | |
| 2 | Marc Márquez | | | | | | | | | | | | | | | | | | | | | | | | | |
| 3 | Andrea Dovizioso | | | | | | | | | | | | | | | | | | | | | | | | | |
| 4 | Maverick Viñales | | | | | | | | | | | | | | | | | | | | | | | | | |
| 5 | Andrea Iannone | | | | | | | | | | | | | | | | | | | | | | | | | |
| 6 | Danilo Petrucci | | | | | | | | | | | | | | | | | | | | | | | | | |
| 7 | Valentino Rossi | | | | | | | | | | | | | | | | | | | | | | | | | |
| 8 | Johann Zarco | | | | | | | | | | | | | | | | | | | | | | | | | |
| 9 | Tito Rabat | | | | | | | | | | | | | | | | | | | | | | | | | |
| 10 | Cal Crutchlow | | | | | | | | | | | | | | | | | | | | | | | | | |
| 11 | Dani Pedrosa | | | | | | | | | | | | | | | | | | | | | | | | | |
| 12 | Takaaki Nakagami | | | | | | | | | | | | | | | | | | | | | | | | | |
| 13 | Jack Miller | | | | | | | | | | | | | | | | | | | | | | | | | |
| 14 | Hafizh Syahrin | | | | | | | | | | | | | | | | | | | | | | | | | |
| 15 | Álex Rins | | | | | | | | | | | | | | | | | | | | | | | | | |
| 16 | Bradley Smith | | | | | | | | | | | | | | | | | | | | | | | | | |
| 17 | Franco Morbidelli | | | | | | | | | | | | | | | | | | | | | | | | | |
| 18 | Pol Espargaró | | | | | | | | | | | | | | | | | | | | | | | | | |
| 19 | Aleix Espargaró++ | | | | | | | | | | | | | | | | | | | | | | | | | |
| 20 | Scott Redding | | | | | | | | | | | | | | | | | | | | | | | | | |
| 21 | Karel Abraham | | | | | | | | | | | | | | | | | | | | | | | | | |
| 22 | Álvaro Bautista | | | | | | | | | | | | | | | | | | | | | | | | | |
| 23 | Mika Kallio | | | | | | | | | | | | | | | | | | | | | | | | | |
| 24 | Thomas Lüthi | | | | | | | | | | | | | | | | | | | | | | | | | |
| 25 | Sylvain Guintoli | | | | | | | | | | | | | | | | | | | | | | | | | |
| 26 | Xavier Siméon | | | | | | | | | | | | | | | | | | | | | | | | | |

## RACE CLASSIFICATION AFTER 24 LAPS = 111.048 KM

| | RIDER | NAT | TEAM | MACHINE | TIME | + GAP | TYRES |
|---|---|---|---|---|---|---|---|
| 1 | Jorge Lorenzo | SPA | Ducati Team | DUCATI | 40'13.566 | | S/S |
| 2 | Marc Márquez | SPA | Repsol Honda Team | HONDA | 40'18.045 | 4.479 | H/H |
| 3 | Valentino Rossi | ITA | Movistar Yamaha MotoGP | YAMAHA | 40'19.664 | 6.098 | S/S |
| 4 | Cal Crutchlow | GBR | LCR Honda CASTROL | HONDA | 40'23.371 | 9.805 | M/S |
| 5 | Dani Pedrosa | SPA | Repsol Honda Team | HONDA | 40'24.206 | 10.640 | M/M |
| 6 | Maverick Viñales | SPA | Movistar Yamaha MotoGP | YAMAHA | 40'24.364 | 10.798 | S/S |
| 7 | Johann Zarco | FRA | Monster Yamaha Tech 3 | YAMAHA | 40'26.998 | 13.432 | S/M |
| 8 | Danilo Petrucci | ITA | Alma Pramac Racing | DUCATI | 40'28.621 | 15.055 | S/S |
| 9 | Álvaro Bautista | SPA | Ángel Nieto Team | DUCATI | 40'35.623 | 22.057 | S/S |
| 10 | Andrea Iannone | ITA | Team SUZUKI ECSTAR | SUZUKI | 40'37.707 | 24.141 | S/S |
| 11 | Pol Espargaró | SPA | Red Bull KTM Factory Racing | KTM | 40'50.126 | 36.560 | S/S |
| 12 | Scott Redding | GBR | Aprilia Racing Team Gresini | APRILIA | 40'51.795 | 38.229 | H/S |
| 13 | Karel Abraham | CZE | Ángel Nieto Team | DUCATI | 41'35.092 | 81.526 | M/S |
| 14 | Franco Morbidelli | ITA | EG 0,0 Marc VDS | HONDA | 41'54.234 | 3 laps | H/H |
| NC | Hafizh Syahrin | MAL | Monster Yamaha Tech 3 | YAMAHA | 33'47.459 | 4 laps | S/S |
| NC | Tito Rabat | SPA | Reale Avintia Racing | DUCATI | 30'24.107 | 6 laps | S/S |
| NC | Jack Miller | AUS | Alma Pramac Racing | DUCATI | 28'43.087 | 7 laps | S/S |
| NC | Bradley Smith | GBR | Red Bull KTM Factory Racing | KTM | 22'09.417 | 11 laps | M/S |
| NC | Takaaki Nakagami | JPN | LCR Honda IDEMITSU | HONDA | 22'09.554 | 11 laps | M/S |
| NC | Álex Rins | SPA | Team SUZUKI ECSTAR | SUZUKI | 19'27.527 | 13 laps | S/S |
| NC | Andrea Dovizioso | ITA | Ducati Team | DUCATI | 13'28.202 | 16 laps | S/S |
| NC | Xavier Siméon | GER | Reale Avintia Racing | DUCATI | 12'06.906 | 17 laps | S/S |
| NC | Aleix Espargaró | SPA | Aprilia Racing Team Gresini | APRILIA | 6'53.385 | 20 laps | M/S |
| NC | Thomas Lüthi | SWI | EG 0,0 Marc VDS | HONDA | 5'13.932 | 21 laps | M/S |
| NC | Sylvain Guintoli | FRA | Team SUZUKI ECSTAR | SUZUKI | 3'34.230 | 22 laps | S/S |
| NC | Mika Kallio | FIN | Red Bull KTM Factory Racing | KTM | | | M/S |

## CHAMPIONSHIP STANDINGS

| | RIDER | NAT | TEAM | POINTS |
|---|---|---|---|---|
| 1 | Marc Márquez | SPA | Repsol Honda Team | 115 |
| 2 | Valentino Rossi | ITA | Movistar Yamaha MotoGP | 88 |
| 3 | Maverick Viñales | SPA | Movistar Yamaha MotoGP | 77 |
| 4 | Johann Zarco | FRA | Monster Yamaha Tech 3 | 73 |
| 5 | Danilo Petrucci | ITA | Alma Pramac Racing | 71 |
| 6 | Cal Crutchlow | GBR | LCR Honda CASTROL | 69 |
| 7 | Jorge Lorenzo | SPA | Ducati Team | 66 |
| 8 | Andrea Dovizioso | ITA | Ducati Team | 66 |
| 9 | Andrea Iannone | ITA | Team SUZUKI ECSTAR | 66 |
| 10 | Jack Miller | AUS | Alma Pramac Racing | 49 |
| 11 | Dani Pedrosa | SPA | Repsol Honda Team | 40 |
| 12 | Álex Rins | SPA | Team SUZUKI ECSTAR | 33 |
| 13 | Pol Espargaró | SPA | Red Bull KTM Factory Racing | 28 |
| 14 | Tito Rabat | SPA | Reale Avintia Racing | 27 |
| 15 | Álvaro Bautista | SPA | Ángel Nieto Team | 26 |
| 16 | Franco Morbidelli | ITA | EG 0,0 Marc VDS | 19 |
| 17 | Hafizh Syahrin | MAL | Monster Yamaha Tech 3 | 17 |
| 18 | Aleix Espargaró | SPA | Aprilia Racing Team Gresini | 13 |
| 19 | Takaaki Nakagami | JPN | LCR Honda IDEMITSU | 10 |
| 20 | Scott Redding | GBR | Aprilia Racing Team Gresini | 9 |
| 21 | Bradley Smith | GBR | Red Bull KTM Factory Racing | 7 |
| 22 | Mika Kallio | FIN | Red Bull KTM Factory Racing | 6 |
| 23 | Karel Abraham | CZE | Ángel Nieto Team | 4 |
| 24 | Thomas Lüthi | SWI | EG 0,0 Marc VDS | |
| 25 | Xavier Siméon | GER | Reale Avintia Racing | |
| 26 | Sylvain Guintoli | FRA | Team SUZUKI ECSTAR | |

+ New track layout and race distance for 2018   ++ FIM MotoGP Stewards grid penalty for Aleix Espargaró

---

**13 | KAREL ABRAHAM**
Lost time on the first lap when Kallio highsided in front of him, which left him alone for much of the race. He got a good enough view of several riders crashing to convince him to focus on making it to the finish.

**14 | FRANCO MORBIDELLI**
A torrid weekend for the rookie, who had three crashes in practice, one of which required a trip to hospital, and another in the race. He continued to finish the race three laps down: last man home and two points.

**DNF | HAFIZH SYAHRIN**
Was riding a great race, holding ninth place between Petrucci and Iannone, when he had a nasty highside at turn four. The bike flicked him off after he ran wide onto the dirty asphalt and was returning to the racing line.

**DNF | TITO RABAT**
Ended free practice tenth fastest, ahead of Márquez, which put him into Q2. Qualified alongside Rossi and Zarco. In the race his Desmosedici caught fire and he had to abandon ship in the turn-one gravel trap.

**DNF | JACK MILLER**
Worked hard to save his tyres for later in the race while running with Zarco and Viñales in the early stages, only to be slowed by a fuel-pump problem which put him out of the race with seven laps remaining.

**DNF | BRADLEY SMITH**
Got a remarkable start from the sixth row to complete the first lap in eighth position. Was battling for the final point with team-mate Espargaró, Nakagami and Redding when Nakagami fell and took him out.

**DNF | TAKAAKI NAKAGAMI**
Made it into Q2 for the second time to qualify 12th fastest. Like many of his rivals, struggled with front-end grip and kept losing the front. Finally pushed it too far while attacking Smith, falling and wiping out the Brit.

**DNF | ÁLEX RINS**
Had a difficult home race, starting from the fifth row of the grid. Found the going tough on Sunday afternoon, circulating outside the points until an electrical problem forced him to pull into the pits and retire.

**DNF | ANDREA DOVIZIOSO**
Seemed the only man capable of racing with Lorenzo and Márquez. Lost the front trying to keep up.

**DNF | XAVIER SIMÉON**
Felt better aboard his Desmosedici than in previous races, but lost the front at turn two at one-third distance.

**DNF | ALEIX ESPARGARÓ**
His first race as a dad didn't go well. Was penalised in warm-up, then crashed out on lap five.

**DNF | THOMAS LÜTHI**
Needed a confidence boost after crashing out of two of the previous three races, but didn't get one.

**DNF | SYLVAIN GUINTOLI**
Suzuki's test rider wanted to finish the race to gather maximum data but fell at turn seven on the third lap.

**DNF | MIKA KALLIO**
Fell on lap one. His development RC16 was once again passed to the full-timers for post-race testing.

Lap two and Márquez has grabbed the lead from Lorenzo. The top seven remained this close throughout the 26 laps. Epic!

# MotoGP's MAGNIFICENT SEVEN

***Assen's 70th world championship round served up a race that will be remembered for decades***

Qualifying suggested that this would be a special race, but no one could've guessed quite how special. The fastest ten riders in Q2 were covered by 0.376 seconds, the closest top ten since Jerez 2007.

In fact, perhaps the biggest surprise of the weekend wasn't the epic race but the epic weather, which had the Dutch TT baking in a midsummer heatwave for the first time in decades. Consistent conditions allowed riders and teams to focus on extracting maximum performance from themselves and their machinery, which had the gaps shrinking.

Qualifying was exciting enough in itself, with a flurry of fast laps in the dying seconds of the session. When the chequered flag was waved, Andrea Iannone held pole position, with Jorge Lorenzo second, but there was "a bunch of animals!" (according to Cal Crutchlow) chasing Marc Márquez and pole. By the time that bunch had finished their final laps, Iannone and Lorenzo were ninth and tenth. On top was Márquez, for the 75th time in his Grand Prix career. The front row was covered by less than six hundredths of a second.

Lorenzo was dismayed by his rapid relegation, but 24 hours later he made amends with probably the best start of his career: from the outside of the fourth row to second place at the second corner and then diving past Márquez to lead the first lap. Many people in pit lane had predicted that Márquez had shown enough pace throughout free practice to break away, which is why Lorenzo and the rest were determined to not let that happen.

During the first few laps Lorenzo and Márquez fought back and forth, the former champion doing everything in his power to upset the momentum of the reigning champion. The ploy worked. Soon the two Spaniards had another half dozen riders with them: Valentino Rossi, Andrea Dovizioso, Maverick Viñales, Álex Rins, Johann Zarco and Crutchlow. And that's pretty much how it stayed for most of the race.

For days afterwards, pundits and fans argued about how many overtakes had been made by the lead group. Some said over one hundred, others reckoned more like 120; but what was certain was that this was one of the all-time great races.

There were a number of factors involved in creating this always thrilling, sometimes scary spectacle: the similarity in machinery, the layout of the track and the windy conditions, which hurt anyone who tried to break away out front by causing them to run wide through several corners.

There were numerous heart-in-the-mouth moments, when riders made contact with each other around Assen's mega-fast curves. But the biggest scare happened on lap five of 26, when Rossi rammed Lorenzo on the exit of the fifth-gear Meeuwenmeer right-hander. Lorenzo had tucked the front on the inside kerb and only just managed to stay onboard. As he slowed in recovery mode, Rossi's M1 clattered the rear of his Desmosedici. After the race Rossi was seen crossing himself in the Yamaha garage — he knew he had had a lucky escape.

Just before half-distance Márquez had a similarly close call when Rins snuck inside him at De Strubben. On the exit the pair tangled, pulling Márquez halfway off his bike. It was a mystery how he stayed on, let alone how he kept the throttle open.

The tempo of the race never diminished as each member of the lead group had a go at pushing his way to the front. Rossi ran rampant into the chicane, running fast through the preceding right-hander to pounce on the brakes, time and time again. The 39-year-old was one of half a dozen riders to lead the race, searching for a ninth Assen MotoGP win.

Lorenzo led most of the first half but was never able to eke an advantage of more than a few tenths. And then his rear tyre started losing grip and he started losing places. As he went backwards, team-mate Dovizioso moved forwards, the two Ducatis trading paint as they disputed the lead for several laps. Lorenzo had chosen the soft rear to Dovizioso's hard, and the Spaniard's hopes of victory were over.

With eight laps to go Viñales hit the front for the first time, which was also the first time either Movistar Yamaha had led

**MAIN** Márquez looks for a way past Lorenzo at Strubben

**BELOW, LEFT-RIGHT** Viñales was back in the top three for the first time since COTA, while Crutchlow was top indie rider again; Zarco crashes in FP2; Rossi and Silvano Galbusera were still searching for answers

'THE RIDING STYLE OF ALL THE RIDERS WAS COMPLETELY DIFFERENT, SO THE RACE WAS CRAZY FOR THAT REASON'

ANDREA DOVIZIOSO

## THE TYRE MARKS OF HISTORY

MotoGP left behind its oldest venues long ago, with the exception of just one: Assen. The roads around the town hosted their first Dutch TT in July 1925 and their first world championship round in July 1949. The organisers got permission from the Isle of Man to use the Tourist Trophy name, which they've stuck with ever since.

The 2018 Dutch TT was doubly historic: it was the 70th running of the Assen world round and it was the closest premier-class race in history, with the top 15 riders separated by 16 seconds. Comparing the 1949 and 2018 Dutch TTs shows how much racing has changed: this year's top five finishers were separated

a race all season. Finally, he was looking fully confident and committed. However, the M1's difficulties were easy to see as he got the rear spinning and sliding, which made him easy prey for Márquez. But still he wouldn't give in. The two Spaniards collided as they disputed the lead, which had them both onto the asphalt runoff at De Bult, allowing Rossi to take over out front, chased by Dovizioso.

Márquez's moment with Viñales made up his mind. It was time to pull the pin. On lap 22 he grabbed the lead from Dovizioso and by the start of the final lap he was two seconds in front. Meanwhile Rins was his usual stealthy self. Under the radar for much of the race he timed his podium push to perfection, moving into third on the penultimate lap and snatching second from Viñales as they attacked Ramshoek for the final time.

Rossi's hopes of repeating his 2017 win evaporated at the start of the last-but-one lap when Dovizioso forced him wide at turn one. The veteran fought back to pass his compatriot at the final chicane but the onslaught went awry and Dovizioso finished fourth, 0.114 seconds off the podium.

"The riding style of all the riders was completely different, so the race was crazy for that reason," said Dovizioso, summing up the thoughts of everyone.

**CLOCKWISE FROM TOP LEFT** | *Viñales had his best ride of the year so far; so did Scott Redding; and also Álex Rins, who snatched second from Viñales; Zarco fought in the lead group again; Pol Espargaró scored points for the seventh consecutive race; the Lorenzo versus Dovizioso duel was red hot*

by 2.9 seconds, while in 1949 the first five past the chequered flag were covered by four minutes and 37.9 seconds. The winner was Gilera's Nello Pagani.

The first Assen circuit was a triangle of roads between the villages of Rolde, Borger and Schoonlo. The track – dusty at best, muddy at worst – included three bridges that were so narrow they only had room for one rider at a time. And the roads were only closed to normal traffic on race day, so riders had to practice alongside cars, bicycles and the horse-drawn carts of local farmers. In 1926 the racing was moved to a shorter ten-mile roads course, linking three different villages. In 1955 Assen shrank again with the creation of a purpose-built short circuit, which was shortened in 1983 and once more in 2006.

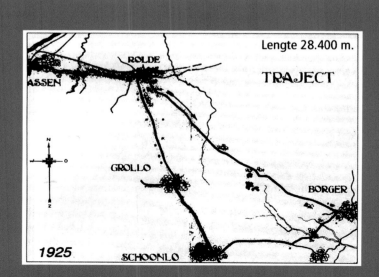

# RACE RESULTS

**WINNER** | *MARC MÁRQUEZ*

**CIRCUIT LENGTH** | 4.5 KM | 2.82 MILES

**NO. OF LAPS** | 26

**RACE DISTANCE** | 118.1 KM | 73.3 MILES

**CIRCUIT RECORD LAP** | 1'33.617 | 174.6 KM/H
*MARC MÁRQUEZ (2015)*

**CIRCUIT BEST LAP** | 1'32.627 | 176.5 KM/H
*VALENTINO ROSSI (2015)*

**RACE CONDITION** | DRY

**AIR** | 23°C

**HUMIDITY** | 32%

**GROUND** | 40°C

Start Line
Sectors
S Speed Trap
FL Finish Line

**OFFICIAL** TIMEKEEPER

**OFFICIAL** MotoGP™ CLASS TYRE

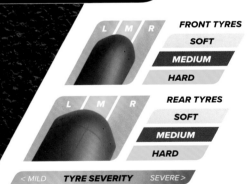

**FRONT TYRES**
SOFT
MEDIUM
HARD

**REAR TYRES**
SOFT
MEDIUM
HARD

< MILD **TYRE SEVERITY** SEVERE >

## QUALIFYING RESULTS

| | RIDER | NAT | TEAM | MACHINE | QP/TIME | | GAP 1ST/PREV | |
|---|---|---|---|---|---|---|---|---|
| 1 | Marc Márquez | SPA | Repsol Honda Team | HONDA | Q2 | 1'32.791 | | |
| 2 | Cal Crutchlow | GBR | LCR Honda CASTROL | HONDA | Q2 | 1'32.832 | 0.041 | 0.041 |
| 3 | Valentino Rossi | ITA | Movistar Yamaha MotoGP | YAMAHA | Q2 | 1'32.850 | 0.059 | 0.018 |
| 4 | Andrea Dovizioso | ITA | Ducati Team | DUCATI | Q2 | 1'32.870 | 0.079 | 0.020 |
| 5 | Álex Rins** | SPA | Team SUZUKI ECSTAR | SUZUKI | Q2 | 1'32.933 | 0.142 | 0.063 |
| 6 | Maverick Viñales | SPA | Movistar Yamaha MotoGP | YAMAHA | Q2 | 1'32.984 | 0.193 | 0.051 |
| 7 | Aleix Espargaró | SPA | Aprilia Racing Team Gresini | APRILIA | Q2 | 1'33.029 | 0.238 | 0.045 |
| 8 | Johann Zarco** | FRA | Monster Yamaha Tech 3 | YAMAHA | Q2 | 1'33.072 | 0.281 | 0.043 |
| 9 | Andrea Iannone | ITA | Team SUZUKI ECSTAR | SUZUKI | Q2 | 1'33.120 | 0.329 | 0.048 |
| 10 | Jorge Lorenzo | SPA | Ducati Team | DUCATI | Q2 | 1'33.167 | 0.376 | 0.047 |
| 11 | Danilo Petrucci | ITA | Alma Pramac Racing | DUCATI | Q2 | 1'33.292 | 0.501 | 0.125 |
| 12 | Álvaro Bautista | SPA | Ángel Nieto Team | DUCATI | Q2 | 1'34.015 | 1.224 | 0.723 |
| 13 | Takaaki Nakagami | JPN | LCR Honda IDEMITSU | HONDA | Q1 | 1'33.625 | *0.047 | 0.025 |
| 14 | Tito Rabat | SPA | Reale Avintia Racing | DUCATI | Q1 | 1'33.666 | *0.088 | 0.041 |
| 15 | Hafizh Syahrin | MAL | Monster Yamaha Tech 3 | YAMAHA | Q1 | 1'33.666 | *0.088 | 0.000 |
| 16 | Jack Miller | AUS | Alma Pramac Racing | DUCATI | Q1 | 1'33.672 | *0.094 | 0.006 |
| 17 | Scott Redding | GBR | Aprilia Racing Team Gresini | APRILIA | Q1 | 1'33.995 | *0.417 | 0.323 |
| 18 | Dani Pedrosa | SPA | Repsol Honda Team | HONDA | Q1 | 1'34.125 | *0.547 | 0.130 |
| 19 | Karel Abraham | CZE | Ángel Nieto Team | DUCATI | Q1 | 1'34.145 | *0.567 | 0.020 |
| 20 | Bradley Smith | GBR | Red Bull KTM Factory Racing | KTM | Q1 | 1'34.149 | *0.571 | 0.004 |
| 21 | Pol Espargaró | SPA | Red Bull KTM Factory Racing | KTM | Q1 | 1'34.268 | *0.690 | 0.119 |
| 22 | Thomas Lüthi | SWI | EG 0,0 Marc VDS | HONDA | Q1 | 1'35.192 | *1.614 | 0.924 |
| 23 | Xavier Siméon | GER | Reale Avintia Racing | DUCATI | Q1 | 1'35.646 | *2.068 | 0.454 |
| 24 | Franco Morbidelli | ITA | EG 0,0 Marc VDS | HONDA | FP1 | 1'34.820 | 0.593 | |

*\* Gap to the fastest rider in the Q1 session*
*\*\* Went forward from Q1 to Q2*

**1 | MARC MÁRQUEZ**
Another perfect race from masterful Marc: enjoyed the skirmish more than most and bided his time until he knew he had enough grip left to make the break. That ensured there would be no last-lap nightmares at the final chicane.

**2 | ÁLEX RINS**
Recovered from stomach problems to ride his best MotoGP race yet; the youngster learning plenty from his more experienced rivals. And his easy-handling GSX-RR was at its best through Assen's serpentine twists.

**3 | MAVERICK VIÑALES**
Finally raced the carbon-fibre forks preferred by most riders since summer 2017 and for once wasn't left behind at the start. Had race-winning speed at the end too, but his hopes were dashed when he ran off-track with Márquez.

**4 | ANDREA DOVIZIOSO**
Ducati's full aero helped him control the bike better, despite the wind. Believed he could've fought for the win if he hadn't run out of rear tyre – the crucial difference between his 2017 and 2018 performances.

**5 | VALENTINO ROSSI**
Did well to retain his composure after ramming Lorenzo at high speed, then worked to save his soft tyre. Was looking good for a podium until his end-of-race moment with Dovizioso. Was a bit too vocal in his criticism of his compatriot.

**6 | CAL CRUTCHLOW**
Focused on looking after his front tyre while keeping his place in the lead group and waiting for the final laps when he pushed hard for a podium finish, until he almost lost control on the penultimate lap.

**7 | JORGE LORENZO**
Ran out of rear tyre earlier than most of his rivals and from then on wasn't able to compensate for his lack of speed through the crucial final section, where the Ducati struggled to match its rivals through the fast changes of direction.

**8 | JOHANN ZARCO**
Regained the feeling he had lost following Le Mans and was back in the lead group. However, his M1 wasn't working how he'd like, so he spent too much energy fighting it, rather than fighting with his rivals.

**9 | ÁLVARO BAUTISTA**
Continued his adaptation to the GP17, finding the set-up he had failed to find during the early stages of the season. Spent quite some time passing Miller, after which he was running a similar pace to the eight-man lead group.

**10 | JACK MILLER**
The Ducati isn't the easiest of machines at Assen, with the track's high-speed direction changes. Miller couldn't find a set-up that allowed him to get around this problem and couldn't get the right feeling.

**11 | ANDREA IANNONE**
Once again, had impressive single-lap pace, but was unable to sustain it, even over just a few laps. Had issues with bike stability and tyre longevity, suggesting he needed to take a long, hard look at his young team-mate's data.

**12 | POL ESPARGARÓ**
Delighted not to finish 11th again, even though he was 12th! His race pace was good (15.8 seconds behind the winner) but what he needed to work on was qualifying, by improving the RC16's pace with a new rear tyre.

## RACE LAP CHART

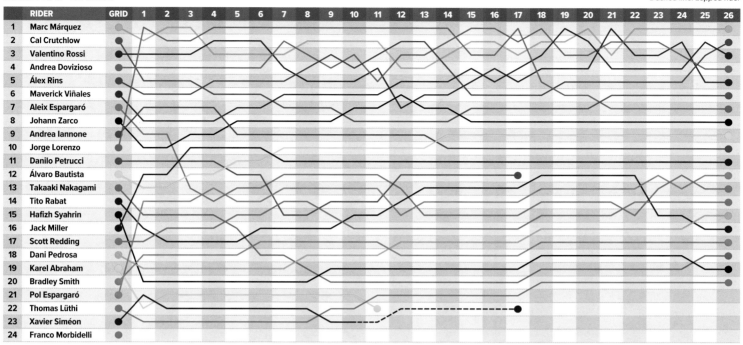

| | RIDER | GRID | 1 | 2 | 3 | 4 | 5 | 6 | 7 | 8 | 9 | 10 | 11 | 12 | 13 | 14 | 15 | 16 | 17 | 18 | 19 | 20 | 21 | 22 | 23 | 24 | 25 | 26 |
|---|---|---|---|---|---|---|---|---|---|---|---|---|---|---|---|---|---|---|---|---|---|---|---|---|---|---|---|---|
| 1 | Marc Márquez | | | | | | | | | | | | | | | | | | | | | | | | | | | |
| 2 | Cal Crutchlow | | | | | | | | | | | | | | | | | | | | | | | | | | | |
| 3 | Valentino Rossi | | | | | | | | | | | | | | | | | | | | | | | | | | | |
| 4 | Andrea Dovizioso | | | | | | | | | | | | | | | | | | | | | | | | | | | |
| 5 | Álex Rins | | | | | | | | | | | | | | | | | | | | | | | | | | | |
| 6 | Maverick Viñales | | | | | | | | | | | | | | | | | | | | | | | | | | | |
| 7 | Aleix Espargaró | | | | | | | | | | | | | | | | | | | | | | | | | | | |
| 8 | Johann Zarco | | | | | | | | | | | | | | | | | | | | | | | | | | | |
| 9 | Andrea Iannone | | | | | | | | | | | | | | | | | | | | | | | | | | | |
| 10 | Jorge Lorenzo | | | | | | | | | | | | | | | | | | | | | | | | | | | |
| 11 | Danilo Petrucci | | | | | | | | | | | | | | | | | | | | | | | | | | | |
| 12 | Álvaro Bautista | | | | | | | | | | | | | | | | | | | | | | | | | | | |
| 13 | Takaaki Nakagami | | | | | | | | | | | | | | | | | | | | | | | | | | | |
| 14 | Tito Rabat | | | | | | | | | | | | | | | | | | | | | | | | | | | |
| 15 | Hafizh Syahrin | | | | | | | | | | | | | | | | | | | | | | | | | | | |
| 16 | Jack Miller | | | | | | | | | | | | | | | | | | | | | | | | | | | |
| 17 | Scott Redding | | | | | | | | | | | | | | | | | | | | | | | | | | | |
| 18 | Dani Pedrosa | | | | | | | | | | | | | | | | | | | | | | | | | | | |
| 19 | Karel Abraham | | | | | | | | | | | | | | | | | | | | | | | | | | | |
| 20 | Bradley Smith | | | | | | | | | | | | | | | | | | | | | | | | | | | |
| 21 | Pol Espargaró | | | | | | | | | | | | | | | | | | | | | | | | | | | |
| 22 | Thomas Lüthi | | | | | | | | | | | | | | | | | | | | | | | | | | | |
| 23 | Xavier Siméon | | | | | | | | | | | | | | | | | | | | | | | | | | | |
| 24 | Franco Morbidelli | | | | | | | | | | | | | | | | | | | | | | | | | | | |

## RACE CLASSIFICATION AFTER 26 LAPS = 118.092 KM

| | RIDER | NAT | TEAM | MACHINE | TIME | + GAP | TYRES |
|---|---|---|---|---|---|---|---|
| 1 | Marc Márquez | SPA | Repsol Honda Team | HONDA | 41'13.863 | | M/S |
| 2 | Álex Rins | SPA | Team SUZUKI ECSTAR | SUZUKI | 41'16.132 | 2.269 | M/H |
| 3 | Maverick Viñales | SPA | Movistar Yamaha MotoGP | YAMAHA | 41'16.171 | 2.308 | M/S |
| 4 | Andrea Dovizioso | ITA | Ducati Team | DUCATI | 41'16.285 | 2.422 | M/H |
| 5 | Valentino Rossi | ITA | Movistar Yamaha MotoGP | YAMAHA | 41'16.826 | 2.963 | M/S |
| 6 | Cal Crutchlow | GBR | LCR Honda CASTROL | HONDA | 41'17.739 | 3.876 | M/S |
| 7 | Jorge Lorenzo | SPA | Ducati Team | DUCATI | 41'18.325 | 4.462 | S/S |
| 8 | Johann Zarco | FRA | Monster Yamaha Tech 3 | YAMAHA | 41'20.864 | 7.001 | M/H |
| 9 | Álvaro Bautista | SPA | Ángel Nieto Team | DUCATI | 41'21.404 | 7.541 | S/S |
| 10 | Jack Miller | AUS | Alma Pramac Racing | DUCATI | 41'26.919 | 13.056 | M/H |
| 11 | Andrea Iannone++ | ITA | Team SUZUKI ECSTAR | SUZUKI | 41'28.118 | 14.255 | M/H |
| 12 | Pol Espargaró | SPA | Red Bull KTM Factory Racing | KTM | 41'29.739 | 15.876 | M/H |
| 13 | Aleix Espargaró | SPA | Aprilia Racing Team Gresini | APRILIA | 41'29.849 | 15.986 | M/S |
| 14 | Scott Redding | GBR | Aprilia Racing Team Gresini | APRILIA | 41'29.882 | 16.019 | M/S |
| 15 | Dani Pedrosa | SPA | Repsol Honda Team | HONDA | 41'29.906 | 16.043 | M/S |
| 16 | Tito Rabat | SPA | Reale Avintia Racing | DUCATI | 41'30.279 | 16.416 | M/S |
| 17 | Bradley Smith | GBR | Red Bull KTM Factory Racing | KTM | 41'42.936 | 29.073 | M/S |
| 18 | Hafizh Syahrin | MAL | Monster Yamaha Tech 3 | YAMAHA | 41'47.687 | 33.824 | S/S |
| 19 | Takaaki Nakagami++ | JPN | LCR Honda IDEMITSU | HONDA | 41'47.900 | 34.037 | M/H |
| 20 | Thomas Lüthi | SWI | EG 0,0 Marc VDS | HONDA | 42'01.716 | 47.853 | M/H |
| NC | Danilo Petrucci | ITA | Alma Pramac Racing | DUCATI | 27'06.105 | 9 laps | M/H |
| NC | Xavier Siméon | GER | Reale Avintia Racing | DUCATI | 29'33.533 | 9 laps | S/S |
| NC | Karel Abraham | CZE | Ángel Nieto Team | DUCATI | 18'03.887 | 15 laps | M/H |

++ FIM MotoGP Stewards race penalties:
*Takaaki Nakagami 1.5 seconds penalty imposed. Andrea Iannone 2 seconds penalty imposed.*

## CHAMPIONSHIP STANDINGS

| | RIDER | NAT | TEAM | POINTS |
|---|---|---|---|---|
| 1 | Marc Márquez | SPA | Repsol Honda Team | 140 |
| 2 | Valentino Rossi | ITA | Movistar Yamaha MotoGP | 99 |
| 3 | Maverick Viñales | SPA | Movistar Yamaha MotoGP | 93 |
| 4 | Johann Zarco | FRA | Monster Yamaha Tech 3 | 81 |
| 5 | Andrea Dovizioso | ITA | Ducati Team | 79 |
| 6 | Cal Crutchlow | GBR | LCR Honda CASTROL | 79 |
| 7 | Jorge Lorenzo | SPA | Ducati Team | 75 |
| 8 | Danilo Petrucci | ITA | Alma Pramac Racing | 71 |
| 9 | Andrea Iannone | ITA | Team SUZUKI ECSTAR | 71 |
| 10 | Jack Miller | AUS | Alma Pramac Racing | 55 |
| 11 | Álex Rins | SPA | Team SUZUKI ECSTAR | 53 |
| 12 | Dani Pedrosa | SPA | Repsol Honda Team | 41 |
| 13 | Álvaro Bautista | SPA | Ángel Nieto Team | 33 |
| 14 | Pol Espargaró | SPA | Red Bull KTM Factory Racing | 32 |
| 15 | Tito Rabat | SPA | Reale Avintia Racing | 27 |
| 16 | Franco Morbidelli | ITA | EG 0,0 Marc VDS | 19 |
| 17 | Hafizh Syahrin | MAL | Monster Yamaha Tech 3 | 17 |
| 18 | Aleix Espargaró | SPA | Aprilia Racing Team Gresini | 16 |
| 19 | Scott Redding | GBR | Aprilia Racing Team Gresini | 11 |
| 20 | Takaaki Nakagami | JPN | LCR Honda IDEMITSU | 10 |
| 21 | Bradley Smith | GBR | Red Bull KTM Factory Racing | 7 |
| 22 | Mika Kallio | FIN | Red Bull KTM Factory Racing | 6 |
| 23 | Karel Abraham | CZE | Ángel Nieto Team | 4 |
| 24 | Thomas Lüthi | SWI | EG 0,0 Marc VDS | |
| 25 | Xavier Siméon | GER | Reale Avintia Racing | |
| 26 | Sylvain Guintoli | FRA | Team SUZUKI ECSTAR | |

---

**13 | ALEIX ESPARGARÓ**
Was happy with his weekend until the race. The Spaniard had spent Friday and Saturday working with the soft rear tyre, but concerns over tyre life forced him to race with the hard, which didn't provide good grip from the start.

**14 | SCOTT REDDING**
His best ride so far on the Aprilia, averaging six tenths slower than the winner. Chased the Espargaró brothers during most of the second half of the race and was able to fend off Pedrosa's attacks in the final laps.

**15 | DANI PEDROSA**
The grimmest result so far of a grim year. Once again the former 125/250cc champ struggled to be fast on new tyres, so he was slow in qualifying and again in the early stages. Got faster as the fuel load went down and grip came up.

**16 | TITO RABAT**
His first finish on the Ducati outside the points. Struggled all weekend to get enough feeling to allow him to push. Felt better in the race while chasing Petrucci, but was later bothered by the wind.

**17 | BRADLEY SMITH**
Chased his team-mate, Redding and Rabat during the early stages, but then suffered a serious loss of rear traction which caused him wheelspin problems, even in a straight line, killing his hopes of making it into the points.

**18 | HAFIZH SYAHRIN**
Made a hash of the first corner, which allowed several riders to come past and dropped him to 20th. After that he had a tough time, especially when he ran short of front grip from the tenth lap.

**19 | TAKAAKI NAKAGAMI**
Opted for the hard rear which didn't give him the grip and traction he had expected, even though he had tried the same tyre twice during practice. Stayed inside the points-scoring positions for the first few laps but from then it was all downhill.

**20 | THOMAS LÜTHI**
Another difficult weekend for the rookie, who found it impossible to push hard without losing control. He dedicated the race to working on his riding technique, experimenting with different riding positions and so on.

**DNF | DANILO PETRUCCI**
Went into the race as the only rider, apart from Viñales, to have scored points at every race. A mistake in Q2 left him on the fourth row of the grid. He was running the same pace as the leading group when he crashed out at turn five.

**DNF | XAVIER SIMÉON**
Had high hopes of his best MotoGP race yet at a track he loves and after completing a promising race simulation during the Barcelona tests. But was forced out of the race by a technical problem.

**DNF | KAREL ABRAHAM**
Made a good start but the Czech rider's hopes of a good race were thwarted when his Desmosedici began to cut out. After returning to the pits the problem was traced to a faulty rear-wheel sensor interfering with the electronics.

**DNF | FRANCO MORBIDELLI**
A nasty, high-speed crash during Saturday's FP3 session left the reigning Moto2 world champion nursing a fracture in his left hand. Had finished his first day on a MotoGP bike at Assen 19th fastest.

# NINE TIMES LORD OF THE 'RING

**Márquez continued his remarkable run of victories at the Sachsenring – unbeaten since 2010**

On race day a group of local politicians arrived at Sachsenring, hoping to thrash out a deal to keep the venue in MotoGP. It's tempting to wonder if Marc Márquez considered donating a few hundred thousand Euros to ensure the track remained a Grand Prix venue, because there's nowhere else in Europe where he's more likely to score 25 points. In the end there was no need, because the politicians and MotoGP did thrash out a deal.

Márquez likes going left because he has spent much of his life tearing around anti-clockwise dirt-track ovals, learning the art of controlling a motorcycle that's teetering on the brink through left-handers. Indeed his record at anti-clockwise tracks is very special. Although only a quarter of MotoGP circuits go left, his Sachsenring victory was his 22nd at an anti-clockwise venue from his total of 40 MotoGP wins.

This was Márquez's ninth consecutive pole position and victory at the twisty little German track. The last time he didn't climb the top step of the podium at the Sachsenring was in July 2009 when he slid off on the penultimate lap while fighting for what could've been the second podium finish of his career.

And yet 2018 didn't go quite as smoothly as his previous visits. He was sixth in free practice, then slid off in FP4, although this

*Márquez in his element: going left, going fast, at Sachsenring's final corner*

**ABOVE, LEFT-RIGHT** | Bautista made Ducati's factory riders look slow, on a second-hand GP17; Lorenzo led the way, until he ran out of rear grip; Bradl dropped the mic and picked up his helmet to replace the injured Morbidelli

**MAIN** | Lorenzo led into the first corner for the sixth race in a row

was more of a trademark Márquez grip test than a mistake. In qualifying he used a three-run strategy, stealing Danilo Petrucci's first pole by 0.025 seconds. He later apologised to the Italian!

Two weeks after that heart-stopper of a race at Assen, this wasn't another wild dogfight, even though it started the same way, with Jorge Lorenzo storming into the lead — for the sixth race in a row — while Petrucci edged out Márquez at the first turn. Ducati have always suffered at the Sachsenring because the Desmosedici's turning issues become a real problem when there are 13 corners packed into a circuit measuring just 3.7km/2.3 miles.

This didn't seem to worry Lorenzo, who 12 months earlier had struggled home 11th on the GP17, 25 seconds behind the winner. The GP18 certainly turns better, at least when it has grip, plus Lorenzo used Ducati's latest ergonomic add-on — yet more rubber pads that widened the fuel tank to give him better support through the corners — which were rushed overnight from Bologna.

The former world champion stayed out front for 12 laps, with Márquez right behind him, looking perfectly comfortable as he awaited the right moment to attack. The biggest performance factor at the Sachsenring is always the left side of the rear tyre, so every rider on the grid knew the race would be a waiting game: look after the rear tyre, get through the first 20 laps, then see how much grip remains for the final push.

In fact, Márquez made his move earlier than he had planned. Valentino Rossi was flying in third place, having dispensed with Petrucci at one-third distance. When the reigning world champion's pit board told him that the former world champion was coming after him, Márquez pounced on Lorenzo at turn 13 on lap 13.

Two laps later Lorenzo nearly ran off the track at turn ten, laying a big smear of rubber as he recovered, but he couldn't prevent Rossi from going past. It looked like Lorenzo's choice of the softest front tyre had worked against him, but in fact this wasn't the case.

"The front was perfect all the way to the end," he said. "My problem was the rear tyre. The medium was our only choice, but from mid-race it was impossible to have normal acceleration. Even if I was smooth with the throttle in the pick-up area the rear of the bike was shaking, with no traction."

At most tracks riders can reduce wear at the edge of the tyre by picking up the bike earlier than usual when exiting corners, but this isn't really an option at the Sachsenring where riders are turning nearly all the time, so they can't help but use the edge of the tyre.

With five laps to go Lorenzo had exhausted his rear grip and succumbed to Petrucci, Maverick Viñales and GP17 rider Álvaro Bautista.

Rossi was delighted with second, his best-yet 2018 result, but he once again took aim at Yamaha, still mired in their electronics

'FROM MID-RACE IT WAS IMPOSSIBLE TO HAVE NORMAL ACCELERATION, EVEN IF I WAS SMOOTH WITH THE THROTTLE'

JORGE LORENZO

## THE LITTLE SAMURAI SAYS GOODBYE

After weeks of speculation Dani Pedrosa finally announced his retirement during an emotional press conference on Thursday afternoon. The 32-year-old Spaniard, who made his Grand Prix debut at Suzuka in 2001, won the 125cc world championship in 2003 and took back-to-back 250cc crowns in 2004 and 2005 before graduating to MotoGP with Repsol Honda, where he stayed for 13 seasons. It seemed certain he would conquer the premier class, but it never quite happened. He never bettered second overall despite 31 race wins, which makes him the most successful rider never to wear the crown. He is also the only rider to have won at least one GP a year over 16 seasons.

nightmare. "We have had this problem from August 2017 and more or less we are where we were last year," he said. "To me the problem is very clear and I have said this many times to Yamaha."

During the final laps Rossi came under pressure from his team-mate, the Italian slowing as he lost rear grip. "I can stop the bike when the rear tyre is new, but once the tyre goes I can't," he explained.

As usual, it was the opposite story for Viñales who was faster with less rear grip. The Spaniard scored his second successive podium and made it two Yamaha riders on the podium for the first time since Phillip Island 2017. "I feel a bit better when the rear tyre drops because it takes the stress off the front tyre," he said.

Viñales had all but given up on Yamaha making an electronics breakthrough, so he had taken it upon himself to compensate for the lack of electronics assistance with improved wrist action. "I am being much smoother with the gas, to do what the electronics can't do," he added.

Petrucci was happy to be fourth and top Ducati, well clear of Bautista, Lorenzo and Andrea Dovizioso, who had his worst finish of the year. And yet Dovizioso was at least content that he had been seven seconds faster than in 2017, when the race time was four seconds slower. "We are much faster here than last year, which is a big positive," he said. "But our bike still has the same DNA, so that here we can't accelerate out of the fast corners like the Hondas and Yamahas."

Incredibly, Márquez chose the softest rear tyre for one of the toughest races of the year. "Because I felt the medium rear to be softer than the soft rear," he said.

**CLOCKWISE FROM TOP LEFT** | *Rabat was still missing his early season form; Syahrin regained the lead in the rookies contest; two Yamahas made the podium for the first time all year; which pleased the Rossi fans; Petrucci equalled his best qualifying performance; Rossi and Viñales celebrate*

One factor conspired against Pedrosa in MotoGP: he stands 160 centimetres tall and weighs 51 kilos. "Normal-sized riders can move around the bike, so they can change how the bike works, how it turns and how it grips into corners and out of corners," said Öhlins engineer Mats Larsson. "Dani can't do that, simple as that."

Controlling the bike and getting heat into the tyres was always a challenge for Pedrosa, who suffered numerous injuries that cruelly ended his title hopes on several occasions. "Whenever Dani has a crash the bike always flicks him into the air because the bike's so much bigger than him," said Jack Miller. "It's like when he got highsided in Argentina this year, or anywhere else."

# 9 | GERMANY

# RACE RESULTS

**WINNER** *MARC MÁRQUEZ*

**CIRCUIT LENGTH** *3.7 KM 2.28 MILES*

**NO. OF LAPS** *30*

**RACE DISTANCE** *110.1 KM 68.4 MILES*

**CIRCUIT RECORD LAP** *1'21.442 162.2 KM/H*
*JONAS FOLGER (2017)*

**CIRCUIT BEST LAP** *1'20.270 164.6 KM/H*
*MARC MÁRQUEZ (2018)*

**RACE CONDITION** *DRY*

**AIR** *27°C*

**HUMIDITY** *48%*

**GROUND** *48°C*

**TISSOT** | **motoGP™**
SWISS WATCHES SINCE 1853

**OFFICIAL** TIMEKEEPER

**MICHELIN** | **motoGP™**

**OFFICIAL** MotoGP™ CLASS TYRE

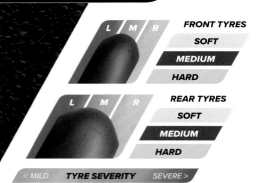

**FRONT TYRES**

L M R

SOFT

MEDIUM

HARD

**REAR TYRES**

L M R

SOFT

MEDIUM

HARD

< MILD **TYRE SEVERITY** SEVERE >

Start Line
Sectors
**S** Speed Trap
**FL** Finish Line

## QUALIFYING RESULTS

| | RIDER | NAT | TEAM | MACHINE | QP/TIME | GAP 1ST/PREV | |
|---|---|---|---|---|---|---|---|
| 1 | Marc Márquez | SPA | Repsol Honda Team | HONDA | Q2 1'20.270 | | |
| 2 | Danilo Petrucci | ITA | Alma Pramac Racing | DUCATI | Q2 1'20.295 | 0.025 | 0.025 |
| 3 | Jorge Lorenzo | SPA | Ducati Team | DUCATI | Q2 1'20.327 | 0.057 | 0.032 |
| 4 | Maverick Viñales | SPA | Movistar Yamaha MotoGP | YAMAHA | Q2 1'20.441 | 0.171 | 0.114 |
| 5 | Andrea Dovizioso** | ITA | Ducati Team | DUCATI | Q2 1'20.444 | 0.174 | 0.003 |
| 6 | Valentino Rossi | ITA | Movistar Yamaha MotoGP | YAMAHA | Q2 1'20.532 | 0.262 | 0.088 |
| 7 | Cal Crutchlow | GBR | LCR Honda CASTROL | HONDA | Q2 1'20.675 | 0.405 | 0.143 |
| 8 | Andrea Iannone | ITA | Team SUZUKI ECSTAR | SUZUKI | Q2 1'20.682 | 0.412 | 0.007 |
| 9 | Álvaro Bautista | SPA | Ángel Nieto Team | DUCATI | Q2 1'20.700 | 0.430 | 0.018 |
| 10 | Dani Pedrosa | SPA | Repsol Honda Team | HONDA | Q2 1'20.831 | 0.561 | 0.131 |
| 11 | Álex Rins | SPA | Team SUZUKI ECSTAR | SUZUKI | Q2 1'20.847 | 0.577 | 0.016 |
| 12 | Takaaki Nakagami** | JPN | LCR Honda IDEMITSU | HONDA | Q2 1'20.938 | 0.668 | 0.091 |
| 13 | Aleix Espargaró | SPA | Aprilia Racing Team Gresini | APRILIA | Q1 1'20.972 | *0.221 | 0.009 |
| 14 | Johann Zarco | FRA | Monster Yamaha Tech 3 | YAMAHA | Q1 1'21.059 | *0.308 | 0.087 |
| 15 | Jack Miller | AUS | Alma Pramac Racing | DUCATI | Q1 1'21.183 | *0.432 | 0.124 |
| 16 | Pol Espargaró | SPA | Red Bull KTM Factory Racing | KTM | Q1 1'21.242 | *0.491 | 0.059 |
| 17 | Bradley Smith | GBR | Red Bull KTM Factory Racing | KTM | Q1 1'21.287 | *0.536 | 0.045 |
| 18 | Hafizh Syahrin | MAL | Monster Yamaha Tech 3 | YAMAHA | Q1 1'21.460 | *0.709 | 0.173 |
| 19 | Tito Rabat | SPA | Reale Avintia Racing | DUCATI | Q1 1'21.546 | *0.795 | 0.086 |
| 20 | Scott Redding | GBR | Aprilia Racing Team Gresini | APRILIA | Q1 1'21.749 | *0.998 | 0.203 |
| 21 | Stefan Bradl | GER | EG 0,0 Marc VDS | HONDA | Q1 1'21.802 | *1.051 | 0.053 |
| 22 | Thomas Lüthi | SWI | EG 0,0 Marc VDS | HONDA | Q1 1'22.012 | *1.261 | 0.210 |
| 23 | Karel Abraham | CZE | Ángel Nieto Team | DUCATI | Q1 1'22.159 | *1.408 | 0.147 |
| 24 | Xavier Siméon | GER | Reale Avintia Racing | DUCATI | Q1 1'22.709 | *1.958 | 0.550 |

*\* Gap to the fastest rider in the Q1 session*
*\*\* Went forward from Q1 to Q2*

**1 | MARC MÁRQUEZ**
His race was harder than expected after he lost several places early on. Expected the rear tyre to drop after nine laps and again with five laps to go. Managed the situation perfectly despite pressure from Rossi.

**2 | VALENTINO ROSSI**
The Sachsenring isn't usually kind to the Yamaha, but Rossi was inspired by watching Jonas Folger's excellent ride to second place in 2017. If Folger could do it, so could he! Did not make a single mistake during the 30 laps.

**3 | MAVERICK VIÑALES**
As usual, was slow in the early laps, dropping to eighth, leaving him with a lot of work to do. And as usual, the bike got better and he made several brave passes into the fourth-gear turn eight at the bottom of the hill.

**4 | DANILO PETRUCCI**
Made a better job of set-up than Ducati's factory riders and rode a very strong race, overtaking Márquez on the first lap. By two-thirds distance he looked safe in third place but succumbed to Viñales with just two laps to go.

**5 | ÁLVARO BAUTISTA**
Humbled the factory Ducati riders aboard his GP17, scoring by far the best result of his season so far. This was the culmination of following the same set-up he found at Jerez, after a difficult start to the year.

**6 | JORGE LORENZO**
Ran out of rear grip sooner than he had expected, for which he accepted the blame – during practice he had focused too much on improving front grip, so he had neglected the rear. Once he lost grip he was an easy target for his rivals.

**7 | ANDREA DOVIZIOSO**
Accustomed to difficult races at the 'Ring, he was happy about this outing, at least the first half. Mid-race he was 1.8 seconds behind the leader, by the end he was 7.9 down. Rear grip was the issue.

**8 | DANI PEDROSA**
The former king of the Sachsenring (250 winner in 2004/2005 and MotoGP victor in 2010/2011/2012) had another tough race, three days after announcing his retirement. Never felt comfortable but finally got the better of Zarco.

**9 | JOHANN ZARCO**
Felt happy with his race, which said a lot for a rider who had finished on the podium at two of the first four races of the year. Once again felt he couldn't get the bike quite right to allow him to run a good race pace.

**10 | BRADLEY SMITH**
His first top-ten finish of the year equalled his best two results with KTM in 2017, at Misano and Phillip Island. Chased Pedrosa and Zarco until half distance, then made a small mistake that let Syahrin past. He soon retook the Malaysian.

**11 | HAFIZH SYAHRIN**
An excellent ride moved him back into the lead of the Rookie of the Year contest, with rival Morbidelli absent. Regained the confidence he had at the first races. Lost his pace when the rear tyre dropped.

**12 | ANDREA IANNONE**
His race was effectively over at turn three on the first lap, when Pol Espargaró nearly took him out. Quick reactions prevented Iannone from joining the Spaniard on the floor, but he ended the first lap way down in 18th.

## RACE LAP CHART

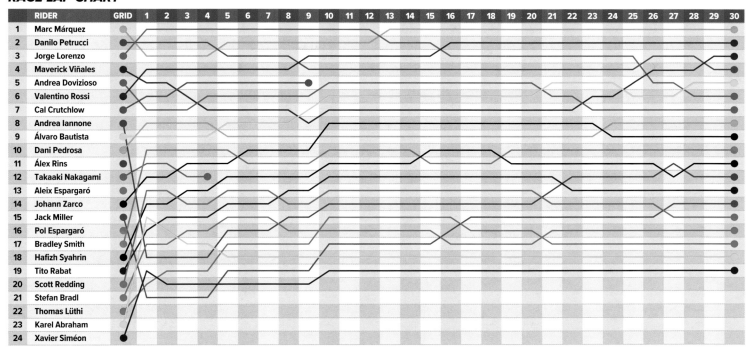

| | RIDER | GRID | 1 | 2 | 3 | 4 | 5 | 6 | 7 | 8 | 9 | 10 | 11 | 12 | 13 | 14 | 15 | 16 | 17 | 18 | 19 | 20 | 21 | 22 | 23 | 24 | 25 | 26 | 27 | 28 | 29 | 30 |
|---|---|---|---|---|---|---|---|---|---|---|---|---|---|---|---|---|---|---|---|---|---|---|---|---|---|---|---|---|---|---|---|---|
| 1 | Marc Márquez | | | | | | | | | | | | | | | | | | | | | | | | | | | | | | | |
| 2 | Danilo Petrucci | | | | | | | | | | | | | | | | | | | | | | | | | | | | | | | |
| 3 | Jorge Lorenzo | | | | | | | | | | | | | | | | | | | | | | | | | | | | | | | |
| 4 | Maverick Viñales | | | | | | | | | | | | | | | | | | | | | | | | | | | | | | | |
| 5 | Andrea Dovizioso | | | | | | | | | | | | | | | | | | | | | | | | | | | | | | | |
| 6 | Valentino Rossi | | | | | | | | | | | | | | | | | | | | | | | | | | | | | | | |
| 7 | Cal Crutchlow | | | | | | | | | | | | | | | | | | | | | | | | | | | | | | | |
| 8 | Andrea Iannone | | | | | | | | | | | | | | | | | | | | | | | | | | | | | | | |
| 9 | Álvaro Bautista | | | | | | | | | | | | | | | | | | | | | | | | | | | | | | | |
| 10 | Dani Pedrosa | | | | | | | | | | | | | | | | | | | | | | | | | | | | | | | |
| 11 | Álex Rins | | | | | | | | | | | | | | | | | | | | | | | | | | | | | | | |
| 12 | Takaaki Nakagami | | | | | | | | | | | | | | | | | | | | | | | | | | | | | | | |
| 13 | Aleix Espargaró | | | | | | | | | | | | | | | | | | | | | | | | | | | | | | | |
| 14 | Johann Zarco | | | | | | | | | | | | | | | | | | | | | | | | | | | | | | | |
| 15 | Jack Miller | | | | | | | | | | | | | | | | | | | | | | | | | | | | | | | |
| 16 | Pol Espargaró | | | | | | | | | | | | | | | | | | | | | | | | | | | | | | | |
| 17 | Bradley Smith | | | | | | | | | | | | | | | | | | | | | | | | | | | | | | | |
| 18 | Hafizh Syahrin | | | | | | | | | | | | | | | | | | | | | | | | | | | | | | | |
| 19 | Tito Rabat | | | | | | | | | | | | | | | | | | | | | | | | | | | | | | | |
| 20 | Scott Redding | | | | | | | | | | | | | | | | | | | | | | | | | | | | | | | |
| 21 | Stefan Bradl | | | | | | | | | | | | | | | | | | | | | | | | | | | | | | | |
| 22 | Thomas Lüthi | | | | | | | | | | | | | | | | | | | | | | | | | | | | | | | |
| 23 | Karel Abraham | | | | | | | | | | | | | | | | | | | | | | | | | | | | | | | |
| 24 | Xavier Siméon | | | | | | | | | | | | | | | | | | | | | | | | | | | | | | | |

## RACE CLASSIFICATION AFTER 30 LAPS = 110.13 KM

| | RIDER | NAT | TEAM | MACHINE | TIME | + GAP | TYRES |
|---|---|---|---|---|---|---|---|
| 1 | Marc Márquez | SPA | Repsol Honda Team | HONDA | 41'05.019 | | H/S |
| 2 | Valentino Rossi | ITA | Movistar Yamaha MotoGP | YAMAHA | 41'07.215 | 2.196 | M/M |
| 3 | Maverick Viñales | SPA | Movistar Yamaha MotoGP | YAMAHA | 41'07.795 | 2.776 | M/S |
| 4 | Danilo Petrucci | ITA | Alma Pramac Racing | DUCATI | 41'08.395 | 3.376 | M/M |
| 5 | Álvaro Bautista | SPA | Ángel Nieto Team | DUCATI | 41'10.202 | 5.183 | M/M |
| 6 | Jorge Lorenzo | SPA | Ducati Team | DUCATI | 41'10.799 | 5.780 | S/M |
| 7 | Andrea Dovizioso | ITA | Ducati Team | DUCATI | 41'12.960 | 7.941 | M/M |
| 8 | Dani Pedrosa | SPA | Repsol Honda Team | HONDA | 41'17.730 | 12.711 | H/M |
| 9 | Johann Zarco | FRA | Monster Yamaha Tech 3 | YAMAHA | 41'19.447 | 14.428 | M/S |
| 10 | Bradley Smith | GBR | Red Bull KTM Factory Racing | KTM | 41'26.493 | 21.474 | M/M |
| 11 | Hafizh Syahrin | MAL | Monster Yamaha Tech 3 | YAMAHA | 41'30.828 | 25.809 | M/S |
| 12 | Andrea Iannone | ITA | Team SUZUKI ECSTAR | SUZUKI | 41'30.982 | 25.963 | M/M |
| 13 | Tito Rabat | SPA | Reale Avintia Racing | DUCATI | 41'34.059 | 29.040 | M/M |
| 14 | Jack Miller | AUS | Alma Pramac Racing | DUCATI | 41'34.344 | 29.325 | M/M |
| 15 | Scott Redding | GBR | Aprilia Racing Team Gresini | APRILIA | 41'39.142 | 34.123 | H/M |
| 16 | Stefan Bradl | GER | EG 0,0 Marc VDS | HONDA | 41'43.226 | 38.207 | M/M |
| 17 | Thomas Lüthi | SWI | EG 0,0 Marc VDS | HONDA | 41'54.388 | 49.369 | M/M |
| 18 | Karel Abraham | CZE | Ángel Nieto Team | DUCATI | 42'06.041 | 61.022 | M/M |
| 19 | Xavier Siméon | GER | Reale Avintia Racing | DUCATI | 42'21.711 | 76.692 | M/M |
| NC | Cal Crutchlow | GBR | LCR Honda CASTROL | HONDA | 12'21.278 | 21 laps | H/S |
| NC | Takaaki Nakagami | JPN | LCR Honda IDEMITSU | HONDA | 5'33.378 | 26 laps | H/S |
| NC | Álex Rins | SPA | Team SUZUKI ECSTAR | SUZUKI | | | M/S |
| NC | Pol Espargaró | SPA | Red Bull KTM Factory Racing | KTM | | | M/M |

## CHAMPIONSHIP STANDINGS

| | RIDER | NAT | TEAM | POINTS |
|---|---|---|---|---|
| 1 | Marc Márquez | SPA | Repsol Honda Team | 165 |
| 2 | Valentino Rossi | ITA | Movistar Yamaha MotoGP | 119 |
| 3 | Maverick Viñales | SPA | Movistar Yamaha MotoGP | 109 |
| 4 | Andrea Dovizioso | ITA | Ducati Team | 88 |
| 5 | Johann Zarco | FRA | Monster Yamaha Tech 3 | 88 |
| 6 | Jorge Lorenzo | SPA | Ducati Team | 85 |
| 7 | Danilo Petrucci | ITA | Alma Pramac Racing | 84 |
| 8 | Cal Crutchlow | GBR | LCR Honda CASTROL | 79 |
| 9 | Andrea Iannone | ITA | Team SUZUKI ECSTAR | 75 |
| 10 | Jack Miller | AUS | Alma Pramac Racing | 57 |
| 11 | Álex Rins | SPA | Team SUZUKI ECSTAR | 53 |
| 12 | Dani Pedrosa | SPA | Repsol Honda Team | 49 |
| 13 | Álvaro Bautista | SPA | Ángel Nieto Team | 44 |
| 14 | Pol Espargaró | SPA | Red Bull KTM Factory Racing | 32 |
| 15 | Tito Rabat | SPA | Reale Avintia Racing | 30 |
| 16 | Hafizh Syahrin | MAL | Monster Yamaha Tech 3 | 22 |
| 17 | Franco Morbidelli | ITA | EG 0,0 Marc VDS | 19 |
| 18 | Aleix Espargaró | SPA | Aprilia Racing Team Gresini | 16 |
| 19 | Bradley Smith | GBR | Red Bull KTM Factory Racing | 13 |
| 20 | Scott Redding | GBR | Aprilia Racing Team Gresini | 12 |
| 21 | Takaaki Nakagami | JPN | LCR Honda IDEMITSU | 10 |
| 22 | Mika Kallio | FIN | Red Bull KTM Factory Racing | 6 |
| 23 | Karel Abraham | CZE | Ángel Nieto Team | 4 |
| 24 | Thomas Lüthi | SWI | EG 0,0 Marc VDS | |
| 25 | Stefan Bradl | GER | Honda Racing Corporation | |
| 26 | Xavier Siméon | GER | Reale Avintia Racing | |
| 27 | Sylvain Guintoli | FRA | Team SUZUKI ECSTAR | |

**13 TITO RABAT**
Still working to regain his early season form. Had a complicated weekend, trying in vain to find the grip he wanted. Finally his crew changed the set-up at the last minute which was enough for three points.

**14 JACK MILLER**
Another rider involved in the first-lap Pol Espargaró incident and another lucky to stay onboard. Suffered even worse than Iannone, running off-track and completing the first lap dead last. His fightback from there kept him in the overall top ten.

**15 SCOTT REDDING**
Felt better than he had in practice, which gave him the confidence to push hard in the early laps. Spent most of the race breathing Rabat's exhaust fumes and planning an attack, until he lost rear-end grip.

**16 STEFAN BRADL**
An unusual weekend: started out doing commentary duties for German television, then climbed into his leathers for FP2, taking over from the injured Morbidelli! Did very well to miss out on championship points by just one position.

**17 THOMAS LÜTHI**
Came into the race weekend from a useful test at Brno and had good pace, moving from 20th to 15th, looking good for his first MotoGP points. But like most riders, struggled when he lost rear grip.

**18 KAREL ABRAHAM**
The Czech rider got a great start to finish the first lap in 15th place and when Miller came past he tried his very best to stay with the Australian, but he couldn't find enough traction to get good drive out of the last turn and then his tyre dropped.

**19 XAVIER SIMÉON**
Another troubled weekend for the rookie who expected better than another last-place finish. Couldn't understand why he lost so much time on the riders ahead of him. Seemed to be going backwards, not forwards.

**DNF CAL CRUTCHLOW**
Was in the middle of the Rossi/Petrucci/Dovizioso group and feeling good when he went down hard at the penultimate corner on the ninth lap of the race. Perhaps his front tyre overheated while running behind two other bikes.

**DNF ÁLEX RINS**
When Espargaró hit Iannone and fell at turn three on the first lap, Rins had nowhere to go and joined the KTM on the ground. This was a big comedown for the Spaniard who had scored his best-ever result at the previous race.

**DNF HAFIZH SYAHRIN**
Made Q2 again, got a great start and managed to avoid the Espargaró incident to chase Zarco, only to lose the front at turn 13. This was a busy time for the rookie who immediately flew to Japan for the Suzuka 8 Hours.

**DNF ÁLEX RINS**
When Espargaró hit Iannone and fell at turn three on the first lap, Rins had nowhere to go and joined the KTM on the ground. This was a big comedown for the Spaniard who had scored his best-ever result at the previous race.

**DNF POL ESPARGARÓ**
The architect of the downfall of several of his rivals rammed Iannone at the third turn of the first lap.

**DNS ALEIX ESPARGARÓ**
A nasty crash in morning warm-up had him helicoptered to Chemnitz hospital, where he remained for five days, with chest and thoracic injuries.

**DNS MIKA KALLIO**
KTM's much-valued test rider had a horror crash in FP2, careering into an air-fence at speed. A nasty knee injury ended his season.

The summer break was over and Ducati were back, stronger than ever

# DUCATI'S PERFECT DAY

*Another one-two for the Bolognese, with two riders riding the Desmosedici in different ways*

MotoGP reconvened after its midseason break with Europe in the grip of an epic heatwave. On Saturday track temperature reached 50 degrees, so the riders knew that this race, more than any other, would be a race of tyre conservation.

Some riders find that Michelin's soft rear can work very well on super-hot asphalt, because grip levels tend to decrease as track temperature reaches a certain point, after which the soft compound can grip better than a hard compound. This, however, wasn't one of those occasions; for once, very nearly all the front-runners chose the hard rear.

Much of the race was fought out in a kind of slow-motion dance, with riders exchanging the gentlest of moves, trying not to overstress their tyres to ensure they had enough rubber left for the final push. Tyre-management mode also kept the lead group bunched up for most of the race, until the fastest men pulled the pin with five laps to go.

On Saturday Andrea Dovizioso was surprised to be on pole — he was so quick through the first split of his fastest lap that he thought his onboard timer was broken — and on Sunday he was surprised to win the race. "I expected to be fast but not this fast," said the Italian after scoring his first win since Qatar and his first podium since Mugello.

**'EVERYONE WAS MANAGING THEIR ENERGY AND ESPECIALLY THE REAR TYRE'**

*ANDREA DOVIZIOSO*

He led most of the race, disputing the lead with Valentino Rossi during the first half, then dealing with Marc Márquez and finally Jorge Lorenzo in the second half. There was much at stake here and not just championship points, because once again the two factory Ducati men had been exchanging insults in the media.

Lorenzo rode a very unusual race. He let his team-mate and his compatriot do most of the work while he looked after the right side of his front tyre, which had shown worrying signs of graining during practice.

When the leading trio upped their pace they finally left behind Cal Crutchlow and Rossi, who had been taking it to the limit trying to hang on.

As the leaders reached three-quarters distance Dovizioso could hear Márquez's RC213V engine barking behind him, so he assumed the reigning champion would be his main contender for the win. But it was Lorenzo who had saved his tyres better.

"Jorge came through with really good speed and we started battling," said Dovizioso. "It wasn't easy for me because I had been leading, so I didn't know the strong points and weak points of the other guys."

Of course, Márquez hadn't given up, yet. On the last lap he cut inside Lorenzo at turn three, only for Lorenzo to counter-attack two corners later. That little conflab probably gave Dovizioso the space he needed to maintain his advantage to the flag, even though Lorenzo set the fastest lap of the race. Indeed each of the podium men set their best laps on the final lap.

"It's been a perfect weekend," grinned Dovizioso, as relieved as he was happy, because he seemed to have solved the rear-tyre management issues that had been hampering him. "We started with good speed in FP1, which really helped because it gave us the possibility to work in a perfect way for the race: putting in lots of laps on tyres and having a good qualifying, which is important because starting from the front row helps you manage the tyres in the best way. No one could push from beginning to end because consumption of the rear tyre was a bit high. Everyone was managing their energy and especially the rear tyre."

Lorenzo was happy enough, having struggled through the first day, which he ended 15th fastest. "We were quite lost on Friday, but we improved the setting and my riding during the weekend," he said after his best result since his back-to-back wins in June. "I decided to stay in third for a long time to save the tyres. This was very new for me, but the strategy paid off because I had very good speed at the end. But maybe I waited too long, because with one more lap..."

Both Ducati men raced with the factory's latest aerodynamic update, which was a rare thing in racing: all positives, no negatives, with the same downforce as the previous iteration, but less drag for easier handling through changes of direction and better straight-line speed.

Márquez had known all along that he faced an uphill battle

*TOP, LEFT-RIGHT* | The paddock sweltered all weekend; Márquez and Lorenzo give their version of events to the TV cameras; Iannone and Suzuki had another tough one

*MAIN* | I can see clearly now - Dovizioso removes a tear-off

## AN UNHAPPY GARAGE

Five-times 500cc world champion Mick Doohan once said that motorcycle racing is 90 percent psychological, while the Australian's faithful crew chief Jeremy Burgess opined, "If your rider wants golden handlebars, you give him golden handlebars".

There's a lot of truth in those statements, because for all kinds of reasons the psyche of a racer is his most important weapon. And, as the old paddock cliché has it, a happy rider is a fast rider. Maverick Viñales is a fast motorcycle racer, but by Brno 2018 he hadn't won a race in 23 outings. His excellent start to his Yamaha career — three victories from four races in early 2017 — was but a distant memory, serving only to highlight his lack of form since then.

with the Ducatis, especially on the crucial uphill blast towards the final esses. He may have had better corner speed than the Desmosedicis but that was about it.

"I felt strong with my bike and was able to ride well and save the tyres," he said. "But the problem was fighting against the Ducati riders because they have really strong acceleration, even stronger top speed and also really strong braking performance. But OK, I decided to try, but I didn't want to be too crazy! The good thing was that Valentino was behind me and my main target was to try to increase my advantage in the championship."

Márquez took the flag just 0.368 seconds behind the winner, which made this the eighth closest premier-class podium in Grand Prix history. Not only that, the race featured the closest-ever top ten; with just 8.3 seconds separating Dovizioso from tenth-placed Andrea Iannone.

Rossi crossed the line fourth, 2.5 seconds behind Márquez after reclaiming the position from Crutchlow at the final esses. Both the Italian and the Briton had been unable to run the leading pace during the first 16 laps and save their rear tyres, so when the leading trio took off, they didn't have the grip to go with them.

At three-quarters distance Danilo Petrucci and Johann Zarco were right behind the leading quintet but just as the fourth- and fifth-placed finishers couldn't go with the leaders, the Pramac and Tech 3 riders couldn't go with those just ahead of them. Zarco was the only rider in the lead group to run the soft rear and the tyre worked well for him, his pace just three tenths a lap slower than the winner's.

The following morning the overture for MotoGP 2019 began, with most of the grid riding out for the traditional post-Brno test.

**CLOCKWISE FROM TOP LEFT** | *The podium party was messy; this race was all about saving rubber; monsters of rock; Rossi did Crutchlow on the last lap; the first lap pile-up wasn't Smith's fault; the final laps were mesmerising*

What happened to Viñales after Le Mans 2017? Was the bike wrong, was it the change of front tyre, was it his crew chief or was it the rider? Between Germany and Brno 2018 the 23-year-old Spaniard finally decided that he wanted to terminate his association with Ramon Forcada at the end of 2018, although he never told Forcada, who was informed by Yamaha management.

No wonder that the atmosphere in Vinales' garage remained ugly all weekend. On Saturday morning he failed to make it into Q2, which inevitably raised blood pressure still further. He ended up qualifying way down in 12th, which put him at the back of the third row, a fraction of a second ahead of rookie Franco Morbidelli. A horrible weekend was completed in the worst way when Vinales got taken out three corners after the start.

# 10 | CZECH REPUBLIC

# RACE RESULTS

**WINNER** ANDREA DOVIZIOSO

**CIRCUIT LENGTH** 5.4 KM | 3.36 MILES

**NO. OF LAPS**[+] 21

**RACE DISTANCE**[+] 113.5 KM | 70.6 MILES

**CIRCUIT RECORD LAP** 1'56.027 | 167.6 KM/H
DANI PEDROSA (2014)

**CIRCUIT BEST LAP** 1'54.596 | 169.7 KM/H
MARC MÁRQUEZ (2016)

**RACE CONDITION** DRY

**AIR** 28°C

**HUMIDITY** 44%

**GROUND** 41°C

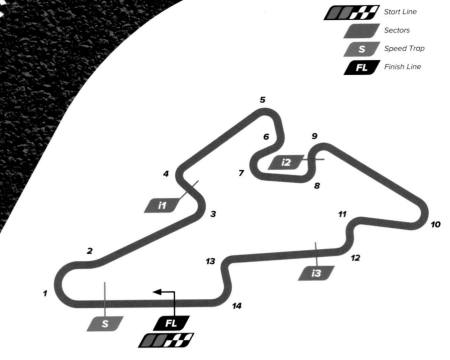

| | Start Line |
| | Sectors |
| S | Speed Trap |
| FL | Finish Line |

**TISSOT** SWISS WATCHES SINCE 1853 / MotoGP
**OFFICIAL** TIMEKEEPER

**MICHELIN** / MotoGP
**OFFICIAL** MotoGP™ CLASS TYRE

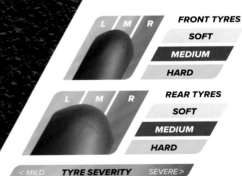

**FRONT TYRES**
SOFT
MEDIUM
HARD

**REAR TYRES**
SOFT
MEDIUM
HARD

< MILD | **TYRE SEVERITY** | SEVERE >

## QUALIFYING RESULTS

| | RIDER | NAT | TEAM | MACHINE | QP/TIME | GAP 1ST/PREV | |
|---|---|---|---|---|---|---|---|
| 1 | Andrea Dovizioso | ITA | Ducati Team | DUCATI | Q2 1'54.689 | | |
| 2 | Valentino Rossi | ITA | Movistar Yamaha MotoGP | YAMAHA | Q2 1'54.956 | 0.267 | 0.267 |
| 3 | Marc Márquez | SPA | Repsol Honda Team | HONDA | Q2 1'54.961 | 0.272 | 0.005 |
| 4 | Jorge Lorenzo | SPA | Ducati Team | DUCATI | Q2 1'55.038 | 0.349 | 0.077 |
| 5 | Cal Crutchlow | GBR | LCR Honda CASTROL | HONDA | Q2 1'55.055 | 0.366 | 0.017 |
| 6 | Danilo Petrucci | ITA | Alma Pramac Racing | DUCATI | Q2 1'55.203 | 0.514 | 0.148 |
| 7 | Johann Zarco | FRA | Monster Yamaha Tech 3 | YAMAHA | Q2 1'55.221 | 0.532 | 0.018 |
| 8 | Andrea Iannone | ITA | Team SUZUKI ECSTAR | SUZUKI | Q2 1'55.270 | 0.581 | 0.049 |
| 9 | Álex Rins** | SPA | Team SUZUKI ECSTAR | SUZUKI | Q2 1'55.431 | 0.742 | 0.161 |
| 10 | Dani Pedrosa | SPA | Repsol Honda Team | HONDA | Q2 1'55.474 | 0.785 | 0.043 |
| 11 | Tito Rabat | SPA | Reale Avintia Racing | DUCATI | Q2 1'55.686 | 0.997 | 0.212 |
| 12 | Maverick Viñales** | SPA | Movistar Yamaha MotoGP | YAMAHA | Q2 1'55.823 | 1.134 | 0.137 |
| 13 | Franco Morbidelli | ITA | EG 0,0 Marc VDS | HONDA | Q1 1'56.029 | *0.491 | 0.177 |
| 14 | Álvaro Bautista | SPA | Ángel Nieto Team | DUCATI | Q1 1'56.031 | *0.493 | 0.002 |
| 15 | Bradley Smith | GBR | Red Bull KTM Factory Racing | KTM | Q1 1'56.218 | *0.680 | 0.187 |
| 16 | Hafizh Syahrin | MAL | Monster Yamaha Tech 3 | YAMAHA | Q1 1'56.285 | *0.747 | 0.067 |
| 17 | Jack Miller | AUS | Alma Pramac Racing | DUCATI | Q1 1'56.316 | *0.778 | 0.031 |
| 18 | Stefan Bradl | GER | HRC Honda Team | HONDA | Q1 1'56.330 | *0.792 | 0.014 |
| 19 | Pol Espargaró | SPA | Red Bull KTM Factory Racing | KTM | Q1 1'56.353 | *0.815 | 0.023 |
| 20 | Takaaki Nakagami | JPN | LCR Honda IDEMITSU | HONDA | Q1 1'56.512 | *0.974 | 0.159 |
| 21 | Sylvain Guintoli | FRA | Team SUZUKI ECSTAR | SUZUKI | Q1 1'57.037 | *1.499 | 0.525 |
| 22 | Thomas Lüthi | SWI | EG 0,0 Marc VDS | HONDA | Q1 1'57.208 | *1.670 | 0.171 |
| 23 | Karel Abraham | CZE | Ángel Nieto Team | DUCATI | Q1 1'57.217 | *1.679 | 0.009 |
| 24 | Aleix Espargaró | SPA | Aprilia Racing Team Gresini | APRILIA | Q1 1'57.250 | *1.712 | 0.033 |
| 25 | Scott Redding | GBR | Aprilia Racing Team Gresini | APRILIA | Q1 1'57.438 | *1.900 | 0.188 |
| 26 | Xavier Siméon | GER | Reale Avintia Racing | DUCATI | Q1 1'58.048 | *2.510 | 0.610 |

---

**1 ANDREA DOVIZIOSO**
A perfect weekend from the thinking man's MotoGP rider, including his first pole-to-victory ride since Sepang 2016. Used his usual technique to save edge grip, so he had enough speed to resist Lorenzo's advances.

**2 JORGE LORENZO**
Nursed his front tyre very well, then unleashed his attack, but perhaps just a little too late. He had more corner speed than Dovizioso, which helped, but this was only a real advantage when he had a clear track ahead of him.

**3 MARC MÁRQUEZ**
While Dovizioso and Lorenzo were prepared to risk just about anything to beat each other, Márquez's target was a good points haul at a difficult track. In his 100th MotoGP ride he increased his lead to 49 points.

**4 VALENTINO ROSSI**
Chose the medium front tyre because he couldn't get the hard to work. Could run low 1m 57s laps, but when the top three dipped into the 56s he wasn't able to go with them. Finished top Yamaha for the sixth time in ten races.

**5 CAL CRUTCHLOW**
Another strong ride; his fourth finish in five races within nine seconds of the winner. Ran out of rear tyre in the final laps, so his bike was floating through the turns and he couldn't exit as fast as the leaders.

**6 DANILO PETRUCCI**
His feedback from testing Ducati's new aero on Friday encouraged Dovizioso and Lorenzo to try the bodywork on Saturday, so he played his part in the factory's latest one-two. Didn't quite have the pace to go with the men at the front.

**7 JOHANN ZARCO**
Determined to find his missing mojo after the summer break and wasn't far off. Felt better on the bike and ran well in the race but didn't have the pace to battle for the podium as he had done earlier in the season.

**8 DANI PEDROSA**
The hotter the track, the more comfortable he felt, so Sunday's cooler track conditions (nine degrees down on qualifying) didn't help him at all. Only when the rear tyres of his rivals dropped was he able to make forward progress.

**9 ÁLVARO BAUTISTA**
Had a race of two halves: found it difficult to attack the corners during the first half and had almost given up when his bike and tyres responded and he was able to surge forward, from 13th to less than a 0.1 seconds behind Pedrosa.

**10 ANDREA IANNONE**
Against all predictions, Iannone bettered his team-mate in a tyre-management race that should've suited Rins. At one point lapped close to the leading pace, but he was unable to maintain that pace for more than a lap or two.

**11 ÁLEX RINS**
Like Iannone, suffered especially on corner exits, with too much wheelspin. The GSX-RR also seemed to suffer more than usual on top speed, possibly due to the very high ambient temperatures.

**12 JACK MILLER**
A crash during the Q1 qualifying session left the Australian way back on the sixth row of the grid, which gave him far too much work to do at the start of the race. Survived the frantic first few laps and from there just kept plugging away.

## RACE LAP CHART

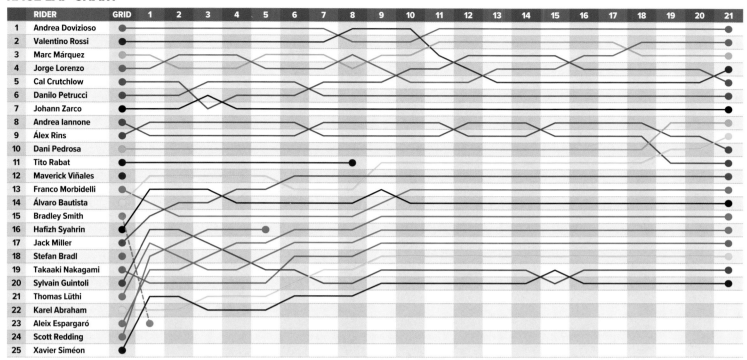

| | RIDER | GRID | 1 | 2 | 3 | 4 | 5 | 6 | 7 | 8 | 9 | 10 | 11 | 12 | 13 | 14 | 15 | 16 | 17 | 18 | 19 | 20 | 21 |
|---|---|---|---|---|---|---|---|---|---|---|---|---|---|---|---|---|---|---|---|---|---|---|---|
| 1 | Andrea Dovizioso | | | | | | | | | | | | | | | | | | | | | | |
| 2 | Valentino Rossi | | | | | | | | | | | | | | | | | | | | | | |
| 3 | Marc Márquez | | | | | | | | | | | | | | | | | | | | | | |
| 4 | Jorge Lorenzo | | | | | | | | | | | | | | | | | | | | | | |
| 5 | Cal Crutchlow | | | | | | | | | | | | | | | | | | | | | | |
| 6 | Danilo Petrucci | | | | | | | | | | | | | | | | | | | | | | |
| 7 | Johann Zarco | | | | | | | | | | | | | | | | | | | | | | |
| 8 | Andrea Iannone | | | | | | | | | | | | | | | | | | | | | | |
| 9 | Álex Rins | | | | | | | | | | | | | | | | | | | | | | |
| 10 | Dani Pedrosa | | | | | | | | | | | | | | | | | | | | | | |
| 11 | Tito Rabat | | | | | | | | | | | | | | | | | | | | | | |
| 12 | Maverick Viñales | | | | | | | | | | | | | | | | | | | | | | |
| 13 | Franco Morbidelli | | | | | | | | | | | | | | | | | | | | | | |
| 14 | Álvaro Bautista | | | | | | | | | | | | | | | | | | | | | | |
| 15 | Bradley Smith | | | | | | | | | | | | | | | | | | | | | | |
| 16 | Hafizh Syahrin | | | | | | | | | | | | | | | | | | | | | | |
| 17 | Jack Miller | | | | | | | | | | | | | | | | | | | | | | |
| 18 | Stefan Bradl | | | | | | | | | | | | | | | | | | | | | | |
| 19 | Takaaki Nakagami | | | | | | | | | | | | | | | | | | | | | | |
| 20 | Sylvain Guintoli | | | | | | | | | | | | | | | | | | | | | | |
| 21 | Thomas Lüthi | | | | | | | | | | | | | | | | | | | | | | |
| 22 | Karel Abraham | | | | | | | | | | | | | | | | | | | | | | |
| 23 | Aleix Espargaró | | | | | | | | | | | | | | | | | | | | | | |
| 24 | Scott Redding | | | | | | | | | | | | | | | | | | | | | | |
| 25 | Xavier Siméon | | | | | | | | | | | | | | | | | | | | | | |

## RACE CLASSIFICATION AFTER 21 LAPS = 113.463 KM

| | RIDER | NAT | TEAM | MACHINE | TIME | + GAP | TYRES |
|---|---|---|---|---|---|---|---|
| 1 | Andrea Dovizioso | ITA | Ducati Team | DUCATI | 41'07.728 | | H/H |
| 2 | Jorge Lorenzo | SPA | Ducati Team | DUCATI | 41'07.906 | 0.178 | H/H |
| 3 | Marc Márquez | SPA | Repsol Honda Team | HONDA | 41'08.096 | 0.368 | H/H |
| 4 | Valentino Rossi | ITA | Movistar Yamaha MotoGP | YAMAHA | 41'10.630 | 2.902 | M/H |
| 5 | Cal Crutchlow | GBR | LCR Honda CASTROL | HONDA | 41'10.686 | 2.958 | H/H |
| 6 | Danilo Petrucci | ITA | Alma Pramac Racing | DUCATI | 41'11.496 | 3.768 | H/H |
| 7 | Johann Zarco | FRA | Monster Yamaha Tech 3 | YAMAHA | 41'13.887 | 6.159 | M/S |
| 8 | Dani Pedrosa | SPA | Repsol Honda Team | HONDA | 41'15.207 | 7.479 | H/H |
| 9 | Álvaro Bautista | SPA | Ángel Nieto Team | DUCATI | 41'15.303 | 7.575 | M/S |
| 10 | Andrea Iannone | ITA | Team SUZUKI ECSTAR | SUZUKI | 41'16.054 | 8.326 | H/H |
| 11 | Álex Rins | SPA | Team SUZUKI ECSTAR | SUZUKI | 41'16.381 | 8.653 | M/H |
| 12 | Jack Miller | AUS | Alma Pramac Racing | DUCATI | 41'24.277 | 16.549 | H/H |
| 13 | Franco Morbidelli | ITA | EG 0,0 Marc VDS | HONDA | 41'27.331 | 19.603 | H/H |
| 14 | Hafizh Syahrin | MAL | Monster Yamaha Tech 3 | YAMAHA | 41'29.109 | 21.381 | H/H |
| 15 | Aleix Espargaró | SPA | Aprilia Racing Team Gresini | APRILIA | 41'30.887 | 23.159 | H/H |
| 16 | Thomas Lüthi | SWI | EG 0,0 Marc VDS | HONDA | 41'35.401 | 27.673 | H/H |
| 17 | Takaaki Nakagami | JPN | LCR Honda IDEMITSU | HONDA | 41'36.039 | 28.311 | H/H |
| 18 | Karel Abraham | CZE | Ángel Nieto Team | DUCATI | 41'48.900 | 41.172 | H/H |
| 19 | Sylvain Guintoli | FRA | Team SUZUKI ECSTAR | SUZUKI | 41'50.139 | 42.411 | M/H |
| 20 | Xavier Siméon | GER | Reale Avintia Racing | DUCATI | 41'58.669 | 50.941 | H/H |
| NC | Tito Rabat | SPA | Reale Avintia Racing | DUCATI | 15'47.185 | 13 laps | M/H |
| NC | Scott Redding | GBR | Aprilia Racing Team Gresini | APRILIA | 9'59.699 | 16 laps | H/H |
| NC | Bradley Smith | GBR | Red Bull KTM Factory Racing | KTM | 8'48.917 | 20 laps | M/S |
| NC | Maverick Viñales | SPA | Movistar Yamaha MotoGP | YAMAHA | | | M/S |
| NC | Stefan Bradl | GER | HRC Honda Team | HONDA | | | H/H |

*Gap to the fastest rider in the Q1 session   **Went forward from Q1 to Q2   +New race distance for 2018*

## CHAMPIONSHIP STANDINGS

| | RIDER | NAT | TEAM | POINTS |
|---|---|---|---|---|
| 1 | Marc Márquez | SPA | Repsol Honda Team | 181 |
| 2 | Valentino Rossi | ITA | Movistar Yamaha MotoGP | 132 |
| 3 | Andrea Dovizioso | ITA | Ducati Team | 113 |
| 4 | Maverick Viñales | SPA | Movistar Yamaha MotoGP | 109 |
| 5 | Jorge Lorenzo | SPA | Ducati Team | 105 |
| 6 | Johann Zarco | FRA | Monster Yamaha Tech 3 | 97 |
| 7 | Danilo Petrucci | ITA | Alma Pramac Racing | 94 |
| 8 | Cal Crutchlow | GBR | LCR Honda CASTROL | 90 |
| 9 | Andrea Iannone | ITA | Team SUZUKI ECSTAR | 81 |
| 10 | Jack Miller | AUS | Alma Pramac Racing | 61 |
| 11 | Álex Rins | SPA | Team SUZUKI ECSTAR | 58 |
| 12 | Dani Pedrosa | SPA | Repsol Honda Team | 57 |
| 13 | Álvaro Bautista | SPA | Ángel Nieto Team | 51 |
| 14 | Pol Espargaró | SPA | Red Bull KTM Factory Racing | 32 |
| 15 | Tito Rabat | SPA | Reale Avintia Racing | 30 |
| 16 | Hafizh Syahrin | MAL | Monster Yamaha Tech 3 | 24 |
| 17 | Franco Morbidelli | ITA | EG 0,0 Marc VDS | 22 |
| 18 | Aleix Espargaró | SPA | Aprilia Racing Team Gresini | 17 |
| 19 | Bradley Smith | GBR | Red Bull KTM Factory Racing | 13 |
| 20 | Scott Redding | GBR | Aprilia Racing Team Gresini | 12 |
| 21 | Takaaki Nakagami | JPN | LCR Honda IDEMITSU | 10 |
| 22 | Mika Kallio | FIN | Red Bull KTM Factory Racing | 6 |
| 23 | Karel Abraham | CZE | Ángel Nieto Team | 4 |
| 24 | Thomas Lüthi | SWI | EG 0,0 Marc VDS | |
| 25 | Stefan Bradl | GER | Honda Racing Corporation | |
| 26 | Xavier Siméon | GER | Reale Avintia Racing | |
| 27 | Sylvain Guintoli | FRA | Team SUZUKI ECSTAR | |

**13 | FRANCO MORBIDELLI**
A strong ride in his return from injuries sustained at Assen. Complained of over-aggressive riding by some of his rivals on the first lap, after which he rode hard, despite tucking the front too often.

**14 | HAFIZH SYAHRIN**
Spent most of the race with fellow rookie Morbidelli. After half distance the Malaysian's M1 lost stability during acceleration, so he tried controlling the bike by modifying his riding position, but he wasn't able to resist the Italian's attacks.

**15 | ALEIX ESPARGARÓ**
An unhappy weekend for the Spaniard, still in pain from his German GP crash. Struggled to get the bike turned as he released the brakes. Chose the hard front for this race, which was probably a mistake.

**16 | THOMAS LÜTHI**
The Moto2 runner-up's difficult MotoGP apprenticeship continued with his third 16th-place finish of the year, just one position away from scoring his first points. Was at least happy to finish closer than usual to the winner.

**17 | TAKAAKI NAKAGAMI**
The strain of months of travelling to Japan and back, switching between endurance and MotoGP bikes, finally told. Days after finishing second in the Suzuka 8 Hours found it too tricky to adapt to MotoGP once more.

**18 | KAREL ABRAHAM**
Lost ground during the Bradl/Viñales/Smith pile-up, then chased after Nakagami and had a bit of a duel with Guintoli, whom he got the better of after changing the engine mapping to help reduce a rear-grip problem.

**19 | SYLVAIN GUINTOLI**
His second wild card/testing race of the year followed a crash during the previous weekend's Suzuka 8 Hours. Was in so much pain that he visited the Clinica Mobile, who found two broken ribs. Had an agonising race.

**20 | XAVIER SIMÉON**
Spent most of the race chasing after Abraham and Guintoli. But like many riders he suffered from a serious loss of rear traction during the closing stages, so he lost touch completely during the final laps of the race.

**DNF | TITO RABAT**
His engine stopped again. Took the positives from the weekend – discovered some useful set-up improvements during practice.

**DNF | SCOTT REDDING**
Suffered from the same problem as his team-mate, during the crucial brake-release phase of corner entry.

**DNF | BRADLEY SMITH**
Completed KTM's miserable weekend when Bradl took him out at the third corner, before he took out Viñales.

**DNF | MAVERICK VIÑALES**
Undoubtedly the worst weekend of his MotoGP career. Announced his split with his crew chief and ended his race at turn three.

**DNF | STEFAN BRADL**
His data-gathering exercise lasted as far as the third corner. He claimed he was rammed from behind.

**DNS | POL ESPARGARÓ**
The Spaniard crashed during warm-up, breaking a collarbone and suffering nerve damage.

# STILL DUCATI'S LAND

**Márquez risked everything to inflict a first defeat on Ducati at Spielberg. It nearly worked**

"This is Ducati's land," announced Marc Márquez after taking pole position. The world champion may have bettered Andrea Dovizioso by two thousandths of a second but he knew the Red Bull Ring might as well have been designed specifically for the Desmosedici. The breathtakingly beautiful mountainside circuit has three slow-speed corners followed by high-speed straights that allow the Italian V4 to fully exploit its horsepower and aerodynamics advantages.

And yet, Márquez had a glint in his eye. The previous year he had taken pole, only to be outfoxed by Andrea Dovizioso at the final corner. This time it seemed like he only christened the track in Ducati's name so he could contradict himself the next day.

This wasn't foolish optimism. Honda's 2018 RC213V had better straight-line speed than its predecessor, thanks to improved horsepower, aerodynamics and wheelie control. Thus Márquez knew he could just about hold the Ducatis on the straights, then use his superior speed through the track's two left-handers to make the difference.

"We have better acceleration this year, but the key to better acceleration isn't always more torque, the key is controlling wheelies," he said. "When we manage wheelies in a good way our acceleration is much better, so I don't feel a big difference

*'IF WE ARE LUCKY AND WE CAN RECOVER A LOT OF POINTS ON MARC, MAYBE WE CAN FIGHT FOR THE CHAMPIONSHIP'*
*JORGE LORENZO*

against the Ducatis, until fourth, fifth and sixth gears. We know Ducati will be faster in some parts of the track, so we will work to be faster in other parts."

For once, no one else was in the race: it was a straight three-way shootout, just like the final laps at Brno. By lap five of 28 the lead trio was already 1.6 seconds ahead of the pack, with Márquez trying to make the break. He upped his pace repeatedly to build an advantage of nine tenths. But that's as good as it got.

Now the Ducatis came after him, Lorenzo a fraction ahead of Dovizioso, the Italian trying everything but failing to get past his team-mate, just like at Jerez.

By lap 18 Márquez's lead had disappeared and he nearly collided with Lorenzo as they rode through the flat-out kink before the dead-stop turn three. The next lap Lorenzo attacked at turn one, cutting inside the Honda. Dovizioso wanted to go with him but ran wide. One tiny mistake and he was out of the fight.

Márquez counter-attacked two corners later, then Lorenzo forced ahead at turn nine and tried to escape. But there was no way Márquez was going to let him go. He seemed prepared to risk everything to win, never mind the championship. After all, he had taken a 49-point lead over Valentino Rossi into the race, so perhaps he had decided that a DNF was worth the risk, especially to beat his soon-to-be team-mate.

The last three laps were explosive. On lap 26 the lead changed twice, Lorenzo once again finding room to retake the advantage at turn nine, squeezing ahead as Márquez fought to hold his slithering RCV to its line. On the penultimate lap Márquez put a block pass on the Ducati at turn three, Lorenzo returning the compliment as they swept into turn one for the final time.

Márquez already realised he no longer had an advantage through the turn six and seven left-handers, so he unleashed his final attack at the turn-three right. He did get ahead, for a moment, but Lorenzo had the better drive and was back in front. His last seven corners were perfection, so there was no way past for the world champion.

"I didn't expect Marc to be so fast for the whole race," said Lorenzo who may have found the winning difference while sat in his motorhome during the weekend. He knew his weak point was the two left-handers, so he watched videos of practice, examining the lines, technique and body position of his fastest rivals through those corners.

Unlike Brno, where the podium men all chose the same rear, the top three all chose different tyres, confirming Michelin's work to create an allocation of compounds that can all be used for the race. Lorenzo chose the soft (as he did when he won at Mugello and Barcelona), Márquez the hard and Dovizioso the medium.

"Today I tried," said Márquez. "At Brno I didn't try so much because I didn't feel good on the bike, so there was more

## A PSYCHOLOGY TEST: DRAW YOUR OWN RACETRACK

MotoGP fans have been able to ask questions at pre-event media conferences since the start of 2017. Sometimes the questions are funny, other times not so funny. Occasionally they are brilliant.

In Austria each rider in the conference was asked to draw his ideal racetrack. The results revealed a great deal about the riders, their riding techniques and their bikes.

Marc Márquez drew a heptagon, an anti-clockwise circuit of seven left-handers; in other words, an asphalted dirt track. "For me, it's easy," he laughed. "All left corners and very, very slippery!"

chance to lose points than to win. Today I tried to open a gap but my tyre dropped. I gave it everything and I enjoyed it a lot."

Not so Dovizioso. "I'm very disappointed," said the Brno winner who finished alone in third. "I used my rear tyre too much trying to get past Jorge, so I had to slow down." Perhaps this was one of those races where the soft caused less spin than the medium.

Lorenzo's third win changed the dynamics of the championship. Márquez may have extended his points lead over Rossi, but that was almost irrelevant. By now it was obvious that the only people who might threaten him were Lorenzo and Dovizioso.

"If we are lucky and we recover a lot of points on Marc then maybe we can fight to the end," said Lorenzo.

Cal Crutchlow finished fourth, 9.4 seconds down, after comfortably outpacing Danilo Petrucci. Rossi came home in sixth, completing another miserable weekend for Yamaha, who were getting worryingly close to their longest victory drought since the factory entered the premier class in 1973.

The situation was so bad that M1 project leader Kouji Tusya made a surprise appearance at the team's Saturday media debrief. "We have to apologise to our riders for the poor acceleration performance," he said. "We are investigating how to solve this problem..."

Although Rossi and Maverick Viñales had consistently blamed poor electronics for their corner-exit problems, their criticism changed direction in Austria.

"It's not just the electronics," said Rossi. "It's also the engine. Honda and Ducati have changed very, very much over the last year. It's a combination of engine and electronics – this is the way."

**CLOCKWISE FROM TOP LEFT** | *The Márquez/Lorenzo duel was a stunner; two Ducatis in victory lane again; Miller leads Bautista before he overheated his front tyre; Viñales looks far from happy; Morbidelli was still not back to full strength; Smith was KTM's lone representative at their home race*

Lorenzo drew two very different circuits: his 2018 layout was a square, while his 2019 design was all twists and turns. "For this year I prefer all right-handers: straight, hard braking, straight, hard braking..." he said. "For next year, the opposite: corner, corner, corner, like the Sachsenring."

Márquez and fellow Honda rider Cal Crutchlow weren't so sure. "I said to Jorge that the Honda won't work in some corners in your 2019 layout," said Márquez. "If you want to have good turning in long corners you need to choose a Yamaha!"

Crutchlow was even more outspoken. "Jorge is going to have the biggest shock of his life next year!" he said. "I told him he's going to have to work on his biceps. He has the best turning bike on the grid, so he needs to ask Marc how hard our bike is to turn. He is absolutely dreaming!"

# 11 | AUSTRIA

# RACE RESULTS

| | | |
|---|---|---|
| | | Start Line |
| | | Sectors |
| S | | Speed Trap |
| FL | | Finish Line |

**WINNER** | JORGE LORENZO

**CIRCUIT LENGTH** | 4.3 KM 2.68 MILES

**NO. OF LAPS** | 28

**RACE DISTANCE** | 120.9 KM 75.0 MILES

**CIRCUIT RECORD LAP** | 1'24.277 184.4 KM/H
ANDREA DOVIZIOSO (2018)

**CIRCUIT BEST LAP** | 1'23.142 186.9 KM/H
ANDREA IANNONE (2016)

**RACE CONDITION** | DRY

**AIR** | 27°C

**HUMIDITY** | 41%

**GROUND** | 43°C

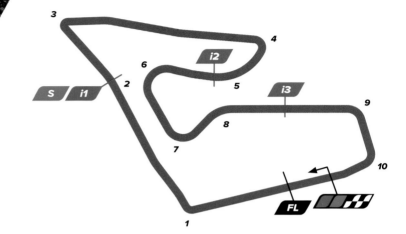

**TISSOT** | **motogp**
SWISS WATCHES SINCE 1853

**OFFICIAL** TIMEKEEPER

**MICHELIN** | **motogp**

**OFFICIAL** MotoGP™ CLASS TYRE

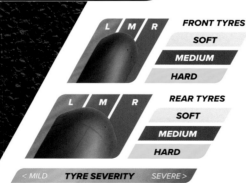

**FRONT TYRES**
SOFT
MEDIUM
HARD

**REAR TYRES**
SOFT
MEDIUM
HARD

< MILD    **TYRE SEVERITY**    SEVERE >

## QUALIFYING RESULTS

| | RIDER | NAT | TEAM | MACHINE | QP/TIME | | GAP 1ST/PREV | |
|---|---|---|---|---|---|---|---|---|
| 1 | Marc Márquez | SPA | Repsol Honda Team | HONDA | Q2 | 1'23.241 | | |
| 2 | Andrea Dovizioso | ITA | Ducati Team | DUCATI | Q2 | 1'23.243 | 0.002 | 0.002 |
| 3 | Jorge Lorenzo | SPA | Ducati Team | DUCATI | Q2 | 1'23.376 | 0.135 | 0.133 |
| 4 | Danilo Petrucci | ITA | Alma Pramac Racing | DUCATI | Q2 | 1'23.503 | 0.262 | 0.127 |
| 5 | Cal Crutchlow | GBR | LCR Honda CASTROL | HONDA | Q2 | 1'23.812 | 0.571 | 0.309 |
| 6 | Johann Zarco | FRA | Monster Yamaha Tech 3 | YAMAHA | Q2 | 1'23.887 | 0.646 | 0.075 |
| 7 | Tito Rabat | SPA | Reale Avintia Racing | DUCATI | Q2 | 1'23.922 | 0.681 | 0.035 |
| 8 | Andrea Iannone | ITA | Team SUZUKI ECSTAR | SUZUKI | Q2 | 1'24.091 | 0.850 | 0.169 |
| 9 | Dani Pedrosa | SPA | Repsol Honda Team | HONDA | Q2 | 1'24.124 | 0.883 | 0.033 |
| 10 | Álex Rins** | SPA | Team SUZUKI ECSTAR | SUZUKI | Q2 | 1'24.227 | 0.986 | 0.103 |
| 11 | Maverick Viñales | SPA | Movistar Yamaha MotoGP | YAMAHA | Q2 | 1'24.284 | 1.043 | 0.057 |
| 12 | Álvaro Bautista** | SPA | Ángel Nieto Team | DUCATI | Q2 | 1'24.342 | 1.101 | 0.058 |
| 13 | Bradley Smith | GBR | Red Bull KTM Factory Racing | KTM | Q1 | 1'24.245 | *0.050 | 0.015 |
| 14 | Valentino Rossi | ITA | Movistar Yamaha MotoGP | YAMAHA | Q1 | 1'24.309 | *0.114 | 0.064 |
| 15 | Aleix Espargaró | SPA | Aprilia Racing Team Gresini | APRILIA | Q1 | 1'24.762 | *0.567 | 0.453 |
| 16 | Franco Morbidelli | ITA | EG 0,0 Marc VDS | HONDA | Q1 | 1'24.767 | *0.572 | 0.005 |
| 17 | Jack Miller | AUS | Alma Pramac Racing | DUCATI | Q1 | 1'24.805 | *0.610 | 0.038 |
| 18 | Hafizh Syahrin | MAL | Monster Yamaha Tech 3 | YAMAHA | Q1 | 1'24.834 | *0.639 | 0.029 |
| 19 | Xavier Siméon | GER | Reale Avintia Racing | DUCATI | Q1 | 1'24.868 | *0.673 | 0.034 |
| 20 | Scott Redding | GBR | Aprilia Racing Team Gresini | APRILIA | Q1 | 1'25.067 | *0.872 | 0.199 |
| 21 | Takaaki Nakagami | JPN | LCR Honda IDEMITSU | HONDA | Q1 | 1'25.178 | *0.983 | 0.111 |
| 22 | Thomas Lüthi | SWI | EG 0,0 Marc VDS | HONDA | Q1 | 1'25.310 | *1.115 | 0.132 |
| 23 | Karel Abraham | CZE | Ángel Nieto Team | DUCATI | Q1 | 1'25.339 | *1.144 | 0.029 |

*\* Gap to the fastest rider in the Q1 session*
*\*\* Went forward from Q1 to Q2*

---

**1 | JORGE LORENZO**
Another amazing ride from the man once known as a one-trick pony. Erased his weak points, chose the soft rear and backed it in with the best of them. If only he hadn't lost all those points earlier on.

**2 | MARC MÁRQUEZ**
Threw everything at victory, but didn't quite have the bike or the grip. Seemed confident with his pace and probably didn't expect such race-long speed from Lorenzo. But what really mattered was that he increased his title lead.

**3 | ANDREA DOVIZIOSO**
Got stuck behind his team-mate and that finished his race. Believed he had better pace but Lorenzo was impossible to pass. In trying to out-drive Lorenzo he over-used his rear tyre. Looked very grim after the race.

**4 | CAL CRUTCHLOW**
The best of the rest, but this time a long way behind the lead group. Maybe he could've gone with them if he hadn't almost crashed on the left side of his hard front tyre on the first lap. Was very happy with his seventh top-six finish.

**5 | DANILO PETRUCCI**
Quickly got the better of Rins and then chased after Crutchlow. He had the pace to stay with the Briton until half distance, but his rear tyre didn't last as well, so his pace dropped and he had to be content with fifth.

**6 | VALENTINO ROSSI**
Didn't even make it into Q2, so this was always going to be a difficult race. In fact the nine-times champion enjoyed himself during the race, attacking and overtaking riders throughout. Another few laps and he would've had Petrucci.

**7 | DANI PEDROSA**
Rossi wasn't only in a hurry to catch Petrucci, he also got his head down because Pedrosa was closing. As usual, the little Spaniard lacked grip and feeling with new tyres, but found a good rhythm later in the race.

**8 | ÁLEX RINS**
Chose the medium rear like most of the grid. Made a great start, from tenth on the grid to fifth at the end of the first lap, then followed Petrucci for much of the race. When his rear tyre dropped couldn't quite hold off Rossi or Pedrosa.

**9 | JOHANN ZARCO**
Comfortably out-qualified both Movistar Yamahas for a second-row start, but his longed-for return to form didn't come. Struggled with the soft rear, but enjoyed an end-of-race skirmish with Bautista and Rabat.

**10 | ÁLVARO BAUTISTA**
Qualified well and expected a good result, until another rider barged into him at turn three, relegating him to 16th. The Spaniard spent the race catching up. Caught Zarco and Rabat, but Zarco did them both at the final turn.

**11 | TITO RABAT**
Started well in seventh and ran a strong pace, just three seconds behind Crutchlow at mid-distance. But when his rear tyre dropped, Rossi and Pedrosa came past, then Zarco and Bautista on the last lap.

**12 | MAVERICK VIÑALES**
Had a miserable qualifying, ending up on the fourth row, and a miserable race, scoring his worst result since Valencia 2017 and Germany 2016. Had more electronics issues when the bike seemed to lose power at the start.

## RACE LAP CHART

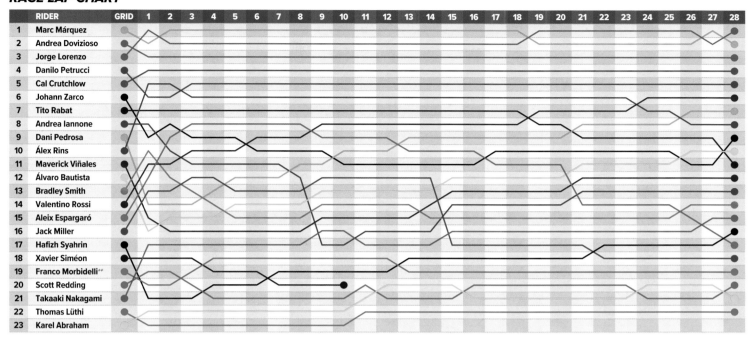

| | RIDER | GRID | 1 | 2 | 3 | 4 | 5 | 6 | 7 | 8 | 9 | 10 | 11 | 12 | 13 | 14 | 15 | 16 | 17 | 18 | 19 | 20 | 21 | 22 | 23 | 24 | 25 | 26 | 27 | 28 |
|---|---|---|---|---|---|---|---|---|---|---|---|---|---|---|---|---|---|---|---|---|---|---|---|---|---|---|---|---|---|---|
| 1 | Marc Márquez | | | | | | | | | | | | | | | | | | | | | | | | | | | | | |
| 2 | Andrea Dovizioso | | | | | | | | | | | | | | | | | | | | | | | | | | | | | |
| 3 | Jorge Lorenzo | | | | | | | | | | | | | | | | | | | | | | | | | | | | | |
| 4 | Danilo Petrucci | | | | | | | | | | | | | | | | | | | | | | | | | | | | | |
| 5 | Cal Crutchlow | | | | | | | | | | | | | | | | | | | | | | | | | | | | | |
| 6 | Johann Zarco | | | | | | | | | | | | | | | | | | | | | | | | | | | | | |
| 7 | Tito Rabat | | | | | | | | | | | | | | | | | | | | | | | | | | | | | |
| 8 | Andrea Iannone | | | | | | | | | | | | | | | | | | | | | | | | | | | | | |
| 9 | Dani Pedrosa | | | | | | | | | | | | | | | | | | | | | | | | | | | | | |
| 10 | Álex Rins | | | | | | | | | | | | | | | | | | | | | | | | | | | | | |
| 11 | Maverick Viñales | | | | | | | | | | | | | | | | | | | | | | | | | | | | | |
| 12 | Álvaro Bautista | | | | | | | | | | | | | | | | | | | | | | | | | | | | | |
| 13 | Bradley Smith | | | | | | | | | | | | | | | | | | | | | | | | | | | | | |
| 14 | Valentino Rossi | | | | | | | | | | | | | | | | | | | | | | | | | | | | | |
| 15 | Aleix Espargaró | | | | | | | | | | | | | | | | | | | | | | | | | | | | | |
| 16 | Jack Miller | | | | | | | | | | | | | | | | | | | | | | | | | | | | | |
| 17 | Hafizh Syahrin | | | | | | | | | | | | | | | | | | | | | | | | | | | | | |
| 18 | Xavier Siméon | | | | | | | | | | | | | | | | | | | | | | | | | | | | | |
| 19 | Franco Morbidelli++ | | | | | | | | | | | | | | | | | | | | | | | | | | | | | |
| 20 | Scott Redding | | | | | | | | | | | | | | | | | | | | | | | | | | | | | |
| 21 | Takaaki Nakagami | | | | | | | | | | | | | | | | | | | | | | | | | | | | | |
| 22 | Thomas Lüthi | | | | | | | | | | | | | | | | | | | | | | | | | | | | | |
| 23 | Karel Abraham | | | | | | | | | | | | | | | | | | | | | | | | | | | | | |

## RACE CLASSIFICATION AFTER 28 LAPS = 120.904 KM

| | RIDER | NAT | TEAM | MACHINE | TIME | + GAP | TYRES |
|---|---|---|---|---|---|---|---|
| 1 | Jorge Lorenzo | SPA | Ducati Team | DUCATI | 39'40.688 | | S/S |
| 2 | Marc Márquez | SPA | Repsol Honda Team | HONDA | 39'40.818 | 0.130 | M/H |
| 3 | Andrea Dovizioso | ITA | Ducati Team | DUCATI | 39'42.344 | 1.656 | M/M |
| 4 | Cal Crutchlow | GBR | LCR Honda CASTROL | HONDA | 39'50.12 | 9.434 | H/M |
| 5 | Danilo Petrucci | ITA | Alma Pramac Racing | DUCATI | 39'53.857 | 13.169 | M/M |
| 6 | Valentino Rossi | ITA | Movistar Yamaha MotoGP | YAMAHA | 39'54.714 | 14.026 | M/M |
| 7 | Dani Pedrosa | SPA | Repsol Honda Team | HONDA | 39'54.844 | 14.156 | M/M |
| 8 | Álex Rins | SPA | Team SUZUKI ECSTAR | SUZUKI | 39'57.332 | 16.644 | H/M |
| 9 | Johann Zarco | FRA | Monster Yamaha Tech 3 | YAMAHA | 40'01.448 | 20.760 | M/S |
| 10 | Álvaro Bautista | SPA | Ángel Nieto Team | DUCATI | 40'01.532 | 20.844 | S/S |
| 11 | Tito Rabat | SPA | Reale Avintia Racing | DUCATI | 40'01.802 | 21.114 | S/S |
| 12 | Maverick Viñales | SPA | Movistar Yamaha MotoGP | YAMAHA | 40'03.627 | 22.939 | M/S |
| 13 | Andrea Iannone | ITA | Team SUZUKI ECSTAR | SUZUKI | 40'07.211 | 26.523 | M/M |
| 14 | Bradley Smith | GBR | Red Bull KTM Factory Racing | KTM | 40'09.856 | 29.168 | M/S |
| 15 | Takaaki Nakagami | JPN | LCR Honda IDEMITSU | HONDA | 40'10.760 | 30.072 | M/M |
| 16 | Hafizh Syahrin | MAL | Monster Yamaha Tech 3 | YAMAHA | 40'11.031 | 30.343 | M/S |
| 17 | Aleix Espargaró | SPA | Aprilia Racing Team Gresini | APRILIA | 40'12.463 | 31.775 | M/M |
| 18 | Jack Miller | AUS | Alma Pramac Racing | DUCATI | 40'15.063 | 34.375 | M/S |
| 19 | Franco Morbidelli | ITA | EG 0,0 Marc VDS | HONDA | 40'20.859 | 40.171 | M/S |
| 20 | Scott Redding | GBR | Aprilia Racing Team Gresini | APRILIA | 40'33.708 | 53.020 | H/M |
| 21 | Karel Abraham | CZE | Ángel Nieto Team | DUCATI | 40'33.949 | 53.261 | S/S |
| 22 | Thomas Lüthi | SWI | EG 0,0 Marc VDS | HONDA | 40'35.043 | 54.355 | M/M |
| NC | Xavier Siméon | GER | Reale Avintia Racing | DUCATI | 14'29.160 | 18 laps | S/S |

++ FIM MotoGP Stewards grid penalty for Franco Morbidelli

## CHAMPIONSHIP STANDINGS

| | RIDER | NAT | TEAM | POINTS |
|---|---|---|---|---|
| 1 | Marc Márquez | SPA | Repsol Honda Team | 201 |
| 2 | Valentino Rossi | ITA | Movistar Yamaha MotoGP | 142 |
| 3 | Jorge Lorenzo | SPA | Ducati Team | 130 |
| 4 | Andrea Dovizioso | ITA | Ducati Team | 129 |
| 5 | Maverick Viñales | SPA | Movistar Yamaha MotoGP | 113 |
| 6 | Danilo Petrucci | ITA | Alma Pramac Racing | 105 |
| 7 | Johann Zarco | FRA | Monster Yamaha Tech 3 | 104 |
| 8 | Cal Crutchlow | GBR | LCR Honda CASTROL | 103 |
| 9 | Andrea Iannone | ITA | Team SUZUKI ECSTAR | 84 |
| 10 | Alex Rins | SPA | Team SUZUKI ECSTAR | 66 |
| 11 | Dani Pedrosa | SPA | Repsol Honda Team | 66 |
| 12 | Jack Miller | AUS | Alma Pramac Racing | 61 |
| 13 | Álvaro Bautista | SPA | Ángel Nieto Team | 57 |
| 14 | Tito Rabat | SPA | Reale Avintia Racing | 35 |
| 15 | Pol Espargaró | SPA | Red Bull KTM Factory Racing | 32 |
| 16 | Hafizh Syahrin | MAL | Monster Yamaha Tech 3 | 24 |
| 17 | Franco Morbidelli | ITA | EG 0,0 Marc VDS | 22 |
| 18 | Aleix Espargaró | SPA | Aprilia Racing Team Gresini | 17 |
| 19 | Bradley Smith | GBR | Red Bull KTM Factory Racing | 15 |
| 20 | Scott Redding | GBR | Aprilia Racing Team Gresini | 12 |
| 21 | Takaaki Nakagami | JPN | LCR Honda IDEMITSU | 11 |
| 22 | Mika Kallio | FIN | Red Bull KTM Factory Racing | 6 |
| 23 | Karel Abraham | CZE | Ángel Nieto Team | 4 |
| 24 | Thomas Lüthi | SWI | EG 0,0 Marc VDS | |
| 25 | Stefan Bradl | GER | Honda Racing Corporation | |
| 26 | Xavier Siméon | GER | Reale Avintia Racing | |
| 27 | Sylvain Guintoli | FRA | Team SUZUKI ECSTAR | |

**13 | ANDREA IANNONE**
Lacked rear traction from the early laps, so he went backwards. Shortly after Pedrosa overtook him he ran off the track, losing more places, then with free space ahead he dropped his times by half a second.

**14 | BRADLEY SMITH**
All alone at Red Bull's and KTM's home race, with Espargaró and Kallio both recovering from injury. Was more competitive on a cooler track when grip levels were high, but found things more difficult with the track coated with Moto2 rubber.

**15 | TAKAAKI NAKAGAMI**
This was the rookie's first point since Le Mans, which had been his fourth points-scoring ride from five starts. The Suzuka 8 Hours had certainly been a distraction. Finally he was back on track and took the last point.

**16 | HAFIZH SYAHRIN**
Like Rossi and the rest, found the track's low-gear acceleration zones difficult for the Yamaha. His race was compromised by a lowly grid slot, which put him down in 21st on lap one. Very nearly got the better of Nakagami on the final lap.

**16 | ALEIX ESPARGARÓ**
Had a great start, taking Rossi and Iannone on lap two to run in the top ten for the first half of the race. But the RS-GP once again ate its rear tyre too quickly, leaving Espargaró unable to resist attacks from rivals.

**18 | JACK MILLER**
Made an aggressive start from 16th on the grid, passing four rivals at the very first corner. Spent the first third of the race with Pedrosa, but had overheated his front tyre, which forced him to drop his pace significantly as the race went on.

**19 | FRANCO MORBIDELLI**
Chose the soft tyre, which clearly wasn't the right choice for a Honda. Never got into the points-scoring positions. This was his worst result since COTA but he was happy with the way he rode with the lack of grip.

**20 | SCOTT REDDING**
Found it impossible to be competitive, except on a wet track in practice. After the race he let his frustration get to him and said some rather rude things about the Aprilia RS-GP, which cost him a large chunk of his contract fee.

**21 | KAREL ABRAHAM**
The Czech rider's fourth successive race without scoring points came despite the Red Bull Ring suiting his riding style. Got baulked by a rival in Q1 which left him on the back row. Lost out to Redding on the last lap.

**22 | THOMAS LÜTHI**
The 2017 Moto2 runner-up had his first ride on a MotoGP bike at the Red Bull Ring in 2016, when he evaluated an early KTM prototype, but that bit of MotoGP knowledge didn't help him. In the race he couldn't get heat into his tyres

**DNF | XAVIER SIMÉON**
The only non-finisher of the race was chasing Syahrin when he crashed out just before half-distance. He had chosen the soft-option front, which kept tucking on him, until finally he lost the front and fell at turn nine.

**GoPro BRITISH GRAND PRIX**
SILVERSTONE CIRCUIT
*24/25/26 AUGUST*

# THE RACE THAT NEVER WAS

**A newly resurfaced Silverstone promised even better racing than usual, but it didn't quite turn out like that**

This was a weekend like no MotoGP rider had known before. The last time a Grand Prix was abandoned after the riders had arrived at the circuit was the Austrian round of the 1980 world championships. On that occasion the paddock assembled as usual at the stunningly beautiful Salzburgring, only to find the circuit covered in almost a metre of snow.

That year's Austrian Grand Prix was supposed to be the second round of the world championships, following the season-opening Venezuelan Grand Prix, which had been cancelled for financial reasons, so the racing didn't get underway until the Italian Grand Prix at Misano in May.

Valentino Rossi was the only current MotoGP star born at that time and Grand Prix racing has changed beyond recognition since then. The championship is infinitely better organised and infinitely safer, but no motorcycle-racing event will ever be entirely immune from the kind of curveball that hit Silverstone.

What should have been Britain's 70th world championship round in the 70th year of Grand Prix racing was cancelled due to poor track conditions.

Silverstone is a favourite among riders because it is very fast and immensely challenging. However, it was also very bumpy, which

**CLOCKWISE, FROM TOP LEFT** Crutchlow salutes the fans, before they got wet; MotoGP's big guns launch the new Petronas Yamaha SIC team; Lorenzo's second Ducati pole; Rabat before his horror smash; even the safety car slipped and slithered; Márquez helped Two Wheels for Life raise €325,000; Crutchlow returns a battered Smith to pit lane; standing water was everywhere; Rossi and others enjoy a live chat with astronaut and MotoGP fan Drew Feustel.

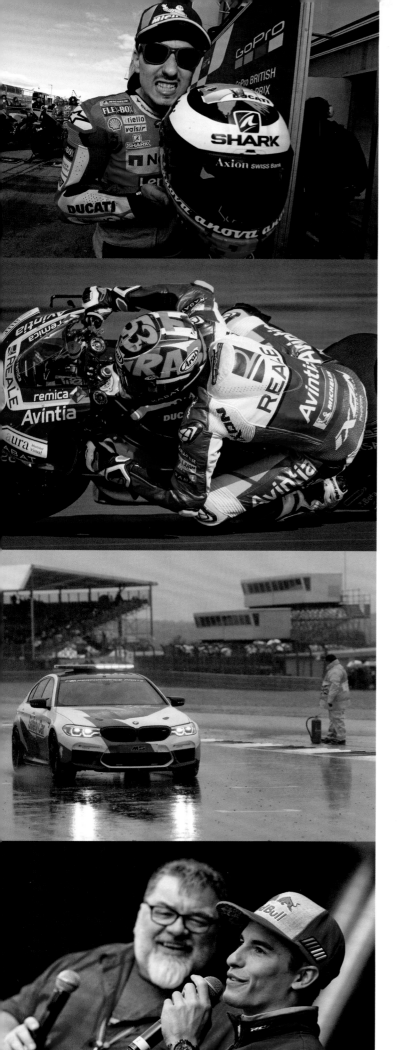

is why it was fully resurfaced for 2018; ironically with the specific aims of removing the bumps and improving drainage.

The new surface was laid in February and later checked by FIM Grand Prix Safety Officer Franco Uncini. But from the start of practice on Friday morning it was immediately apparent that the new asphalt was bumpier in places.

"It's a shame because Silverstone is a very nice track with some very fast corners," said Aleix Espargaró. "But now we are trying to avoid crashing on the bumps instead of focusing on being fast."

Despite the bumps, lap times had reached lap-record pace by the end of FP3. Andrea Dovizioso led the way, while Maverick Viñales topped the FP4 session, chased by Jorge Lorenzo, Marc Márquez, Jack Miller, Andrea Dovizioso and local hero Cal Crutchlow. Less than six tenths of a second covered the fastest seven riders, suggesting another epic battle lay ahead.

Sadly, lap times were soon not the main concern. Rain hit the circuit during the final minutes of FP4, triggering a horrific series of events at Stowe corner. Álex Rins was the first to fall. When he braked from 290kmh/180mph his GSX-RR hit a small lake of standing water and began to aquaplane. The Spaniard jumped off at 160kmh/100mph to avoid riding into the trackside barrier. Moments later Tito Rabat had the same problem and abandoned ship, at around 270kmh/170mph.

"I remember changing into sixth, the bike started aquaplaning uncontrollably, so I decided to throw myself on the ground," said Rabat. Remarkably the former Moto2 world champion wasn't badly hurt in the fall, but as he stood up he was hit by the bike of Franco Morbidelli, who had also lost control and crashed. Rins had been waving frantically, trying to warn Rabat, but to no good. Rabat broke his right femur in three places, as well as his right tibia and fibula.

Morbidelli had done everything he could to avoid crashing. "I had already changed into sixth gear, so 290 or 300kmh when I saw the yellow flags and everything, so I braked and had a major front aquaplaning. Immediately I went into panic mode, because of the people on the ground, so I braked with the rear and I had a highside crash."

Qualifying got underway an hour late, on a track that was dry in some places and wet in others. Pole position changed hands eight times, with Lorenzo snatching pole from Dovizioso on his final lap. Once again, here was proof that the three-times MotoGP champion was a changed a man: not only had he transformed his riding style to suit the Ducati, now he could ride in the kind of tricky mixed conditions that once confounded him.

However, heavier rain was forecast for Sunday afternoon, so in light of what had happened at Stowe, Race Direction announced on Saturday evening that the MotoGP race would start at 11.30am, in the hope of beating the weather. Meanwhile Dorna

## THE LONG ROAD TO RACING SAFETY

Not all the riders voted to abandon Silverstone, but the fact that the entire grid acted as one was a good thing.

Grand Prix riders haven't always worked together. Decades ago, when riders went on strike following deaths caused by poor track safety (an all-too-frequent occurrence) promoters toured the paddock, offering better prize money to the poverty-stricken privateers, hoping they would put on a show, while the stars remained in their caravans. Usually the privateers accepted the cash, because they needed to put food in their stomachs and fuel in their vans.

Promoters could be shockingly callous. When Jarno Saarinen

and Silverstone staff worked into the night, trying to improve drainage in the danger zone at the end of Hangar Straight.

But the rain arrived early, not long before riders set out on their sighting laps. It was soon obvious that the track was in a bad condition, with dangerous amounts of standing water all around the circuit. A plan to start at 2pm was also thwarted by further rain. Riders and teams discussed the possibility of racing in the evening, once the rain had passed, but at around 4pm the riders voted – albeit not unanimously – to abandon the event. Dorna had earlier asked the teams if they would race on Monday, but this option was voted down by Honda and Yamaha.

"When we left the box and rode to the grid on Sunday morning there was too much water everywhere," said Maverick Viñales. "When we raced in the rain at Silverstone in 2015 the amount of water on the track was normal, whereas this year with maybe less rain the water remained on the track."

The tens of thousands of fans that went home without seeing any racing weren't happy, although most understood that track conditions simply weren't safe.

Silverstone immediately began an investigation into the track surface, which had also been heavily criticised by drivers during the previous month's British Formula 1 GP.

**CLOCKWISE FROM TOP LEFT** | *Miller was one of the few who wanted to have a go at racing; Zarco looks concerned; Race Direction speaks following the cancellation; KTM sub Loris Baz and Smith; the Sunday morning grid was all chaos; riders emerge from their final meeting: there will be no race.*

and Renzo Pasolini died during the 1973 Italian Grand Prix at Monza the race wasn't even stopped. When Barry Sheene led a strike at the 1977 Austrian GP, following the death of Swiss rider Hans Stadelmann, the Briton was given an official warning.

The man who did most to get riders working together to improve safety was three-times 500cc world champion 'King' Kenny Roberts (pictured skirting the guardrail, or "death rails" as the riders called them). At the end of 1979 the American and others attempted to create a breakaway world championship, which scared the racing establishment into changing its ways.

"The old promoters treated us like s**t!" Roberts recalls. "It was just wrong, they had everybody by the balls, so I told Sheene and the guys we should organise our own series. We got close

enough to making it happen to scare them. After that it was like heaven; we turned it around from not being able to talk to the promoters about safety to being able to talk to them. Until then it was a nightmare."

In 1982 the top riders hired Mike Trimby to lead the fight for justice, but there was still a long road ahead. "I remember at Mugello in 1983, the circuit people took out the fencing, then told us: right, your haybales are on that tractor over there, so go and put them out, which we did – us and the riders," says Trimby, now CEO of IRTA (International Road Racing Teams Association). "Once IRTA was launched in 1986 we had a formal voice. The other turning point was 1992 when Dorna came in. The deal with them was that we didn't have to race anywhere we didn't want to race."

# 12 | **GREAT BRITAIN**

## **RACE RESULTS**

Start Line
Sectors
**S** Speed Trap
**FL** Finish Line

**WINNER** NA

**CIRCUIT LENGTH** 5.9 KM 3.67 MILES

**NO. OF LAPS** 20

**RACE DISTANCE** 118.0 KM 73.4 MILES

**CIRCUIT RECORD LAP** 2'01.560 174.7 KM/H
MARC MÁRQUEZ (2017)

**CIRCUIT BEST LAP** 1'59.941 177.0 KM/H
MARC MÁRQUEZ (2017)

**RACE CONDITION** NA

**AIR** NA

**HUMIDITY** NA

**GROUND** NA

**OFFICIAL** TIMEKEEPER

**OFFICIAL** MotoGP™ CLASS TYRE

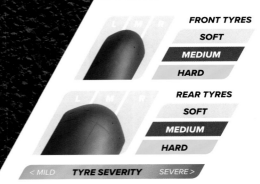

**FRONT TYRES**
SOFT
MEDIUM
HARD

**REAR TYRES**
SOFT
MEDIUM
HARD

< MILD  **TYRE SEVERITY**  SEVERE >

### QUALIFYING RESULTS

| | RIDER | NAT | TEAM | MACHINE | QP/TIME | | GAP 1ST/PREV | |
|---|---|---|---|---|---|---|---|---|
| 1 | Jorge Lorenzo | SPA | Ducati Team | DUCATI | Q2 | 2'10.155 | | |
| 2 | Andrea Dovizioso | ITA | Ducati Team | DUCATI | Q2 | 2'10.314 | 0.159 | 0.159 |
| 3 | Johann Zarco | FRA | Monster Yamaha Tech 3 | YAMAHA | Q2 | 2'10.439 | 0.284 | 0.125 |
| 4 | Cal Crutchlow | GBR | LCR Honda CASTROL | HONDA | Q2 | 2'10.615 | 0.460 | 0.176 |
| 5 | Marc Márquez | SPA | Repsol Honda Team | HONDA | Q2 | 2'11.083 | 0.928 | 0.468 |
| 6 | Danilo Petrucci | ITA | Alma Pramac Racing | DUCATI | Q2 | 2'11.317 | 1.162 | 0.234 |
| 7 | Andrea Iannone | ITA | Team SUZUKI ECSTAR | SUZUKI | Q2 | 2'11.495 | 1.340 | 0.178 |
| 8 | Bradley Smith** | GBR | Red Bull KTM Factory Racing | KTM | Q2 | 2'11.514 | 1.359 | 0.019 |
| 9 | Jack Miller | AUS | Alma Pramac Racing | DUCATI | Q2 | 2'12.173 | 2.018 | 0.659 |
| 10 | Álex Rins** | SPA | Team SUZUKI ECSTAR | SUZUKI | Q2 | 2'12.504 | 2.349 | 0.331 |
| 11 | Maverick Viñales | SPA | Movistar Yamaha MotoGP | YAMAHA | Q2 | 2'12.514 | 2.359 | 0.010 |
| 12 | Valentino Rossi | ITA | Movistar Yamaha MotoGP | YAMAHA | Q2 | 2'13.504 | 3.349 | 0.990 |
| 13 | Franco Morbidelli | ITA | EG 0,0 Marc VDS | HONDA | Q1 | 2'13.945 | *0.605 | 0.232 |
| 14 | Scott Redding | GBR | Aprilia Racing Team Gresini | APRILIA | Q1 | 2'14.171 | *0.831 | 0.226 |
| 15 | Thomas Lüthi | SWI | EG 0,0 Marc VDS | HONDA | Q1 | 2'14.198 | *0.858 | 0.027 |
| 16 | Dani Pedrosa | SPA | Repsol Honda Team | HONDA | Q1 | 2'14.866 | *1.526 | 0.668 |
| 17 | Aleix Espargaró | SPA | Aprilia Racing Team Gresini | APRILIA | Q1 | 2'15.141 | *1.801 | 0.275 |
| 18 | Loris Baz | FRA | Red Bull KTM Factory Racing | KTM | Q1 | 2'15.299 | *1.959 | 0.158 |
| 19 | Takaaki Nakagami | JPN | LCR Honda IDEMITSU | HONDA | Q1 | 2'15.377 | *2.037 | 0.078 |
| 20 | Karel Abraham | CZE | Angel Nieto Team | DUCATI | Q1 | 2'15.721 | *2.381 | 0.344 |
| 21 | Álvaro Bautista | SPA | Angel Nieto Team | DUCATI | Q1 | 2'16.106 | *2.766 | 0.385 |
| 22 | Xavier Siméon | GER | Reale Avintia Racing | DUCATI | Q1 | 2'16.451 | *3.111 | 0.345 |
| 23 | Hafizh Syahrin | MAL | Monster Yamaha Tech 3 | YAMAHA | Q1 | 2'16.483 | *3.143 | 0.032 |
| 24 | Tito Rabat | SPA | Reale Avintia Racing | DUCATI | FP3 | 2'02.640 | 1.255 | |

Michelin tyre severity not available due to new surface

*Gap to the fastest rider in the Q1 session
**Went forward from Q1 to Q2

## RACE LAP CHART

| | RIDER | GRID | 1 | 2 | 3 | 4 | 5 | 6 | 7 | 8 | 9 | 10 | 11 | 12 | 13 | 14 | 15 | 16 | 17 | 18 | 19 | 20 |
|---|---|---|---|---|---|---|---|---|---|---|---|---|---|---|---|---|---|---|---|---|---|---|
| 1 | Jorge Lorenzo | | | | | | | | | | | | | | | | | | | | | |
| 2 | Andrea Dovizioso | | | | | | | | | | | | | | | | | | | | | |
| 3 | Johann Zarco | | | | | | | | | | | | | | | | | | | | | |
| 4 | Cal Crutchlow | | | | | | | | | | | | | | | | | | | | | |
| 5 | Marc Márquez | | | | | | | | | | | | | | | | | | | | | |
| 6 | Danilo Petrucci | | | | | | | | | | | | | | | | | | | | | |
| 7 | Andrea Iannone | | | | | | | | | | | | | | | | | | | | | |
| 8 | Bradley Smith | | | | | | | | | | | | | | | | | | | | | |
| 9 | Jack Miller | | | | | | | | | | | | | | | | | | | | | |
| 10 | Álex Rins | | | | | | | | | | | | | | | | | | | | | |
| 11 | Maverick Viñales | | | | | | | | | | | | | | | | | | | | | |
| 12 | Valentino Rossi | | | | | | | | | | | | | | | | | | | | | |
| 13 | Franco Morbidelli | | | | | | | | | | | | | | | | | | | | | |
| 14 | Scott Redding | | | | | | | | | | | | | | | | | | | | | |
| 15 | Thomas Lüthi | | | | | | | | | | | | | | | | | | | | | |
| 16 | Dani Pedrosa | | | | | | | | | | | | | | | | | | | | | |
| 17 | Aleix Espargaró | | | | | | | | | | | | | | | | | | | | | |
| 18 | Loris Baz | | | | | | | | | | | | | | | | | | | | | |
| 19 | Takaaki Nakagami | | | | | | | | | | | | | | | | | | | | | |
| 20 | Karel Abraham | | | | | | | | | | | | | | | | | | | | | |
| 21 | Álvaro Bautista | | | | | | | | | | | | | | | | | | | | | |
| 22 | Xavier Siméon | | | | | | | | | | | | | | | | | | | | | |
| 23 | Hafizh Syahrin | | | | | | | | | | | | | | | | | | | | | |
| 24 | Tito Rabat | | | | | | | | | | | | | | | | | | | | | |

**CANCELLED**

## RACE CLASSIFICATION

| | RIDER | NAT | TEAM | MACHINE | TIME | + GAP | TYRES |
|---|---|---|---|---|---|---|---|
| 1 | | | | | | | |
| 2 | | | | | | | |
| 3 | | | | | | | |
| 4 | | | | | | | |
| 5 | | | | | | | |
| 6 | | | | | | | |
| 7 | | | | | | | |
| 8 | | | | | | | |
| 9 | | | | | | | |
| 10 | | | | | | | |
| 11 | | | | | | | |
| 12 | | | | | | | |
| 13 | | | | | | | |
| 14 | | | | | | | |
| 15 | | | | | | | |
| 16 | | | | | | | |
| 17 | | | | | | | |
| 18 | | | | | | | |
| 19 | | | | | | | |
| 20 | | | | | | | |
| 21 | | | | | | | |
| 22 | | | | | | | |
| 23 | | | | | | | |
| 24 | | | | | | | |

**CANCELLED**

*FIM MotoGP Officials - Race cancelled due to track conditions*

## CHAMPIONSHIP STANDINGS

| | RIDER | NAT | TEAM | POINTS |
|---|---|---|---|---|
| 1 | Marc Márquez | SPA | Repsol Honda Team | 201 |
| 2 | Valentino Rossi | ITA | Movistar Yamaha MotoGP | 142 |
| 3 | Jorge Lorenzo | SPA | Ducati Team | 130 |
| 4 | Andrea Dovizioso | ITA | Ducati Team | 129 |
| 5 | Maverick Viñales | SPA | Movistar Yamaha MotoGP | 113 |
| 6 | Danilo Petrucci | ITA | Alma Pramac Racing | 105 |
| 7 | Johann Zarco | FRA | Monster Yamaha Tech 3 | 104 |
| 8 | Cal Crutchlow | GBR | LCR Honda CASTROL | 103 |
| 9 | Andrea Iannone | ITA | Team SUZUKI ECSTAR | 84 |
| 10 | Álex Rins | SPA | Team SUZUKI ECSTAR | 66 |
| 11 | Dani Pedrosa | SPA | Repsol Honda Team | 66 |
| 12 | Jack Miller | AUS | Alma Pramac Racing | 61 |
| 13 | Álvaro Bautista | SPA | Angel Nieto Team | 57 |
| 14 | Tito Rabat | SPA | Reale Avintia Racing | 35 |
| 15 | Pol Espargaró | SPA | Red Bull KTM Factory Racing | 32 |
| 16 | Hafizh Syahrin | MAL | Monster Yamaha Tech 3 | 24 |
| 17 | Franco Morbidelli | ITA | EG 0,0 Marc VDS | 22 |
| 18 | Aleix Espargaró | SPA | Aprilia Racing Team Gresini | 17 |
| 19 | Bradley Smith | GBR | Red Bull KTM Factory Racing | 15 |
| 20 | Scott Redding | GBR | Aprilia Racing Team Gresini | 12 |
| 21 | Takaaki Nakagami | JPN | LCR Honda IDEMITSU | 11 |
| 22 | Mika Kallio | FIN | Red Bull KTM Factory Racing | 6 |
| 23 | Karel Abraham | CZE | Angel Nieto Team | 4 |
| 24 | Thomas Lüthi | SWI | EG 0,0 Marc VDS | |
| 25 | Stefan Bradl | GER | Honda Racing Corporation | |
| 26 | Xavier Siméon | GER | Reale Avintia Racing | |
| 27 | Sylvain Guintoli | FRA | Team SUZUKI ECSTAR | |

# DESMO DOVI DOMINATES

*Ducati made history at Misano, achieving their first MotoGP victory hat-trick with different riders*

MotoGP is always changing. At the first ten races of 2018 the same three riders didn't appear together on the podium once. But the next three races all featured the exact same men on the podium: world championship leader Marc Márquez and Ducati team-mates Andrea Dovizioso and Jorge Lorenzo; or at least they would have done if Lorenzo hadn't thrown it away on the penultimate lap at Misano.

For all kinds of reasons this trio had worked out how to get ahead of the rest. Most importantly, Brno and Misano winner Dovizioso had finally solved the conundrum that had him flummoxed for much of the first half of the season: how to eke the best race-long performance from Michelin's slightly softer 2018 rear slicks.

Lorenzo started from pole and was race favourite. But he made a rare mistake. In fact, two rare mistakes. The Misano surface had changed since Ducati and others had tested at the track in August, convincing him that Michelin's soft-option tyres, which he prefers (he used them at Mugello and Catalunya), wouldn't last the distance.

Once again, the leading trio bolted from the rest of the pack, just as they had done in Austria. Lorenzo led from Dovizioso who on the first lap had scythed past Márquez, who was riding the outer

*Since the summer break Dovizioso had become the strongest rider in MotoGP*

'DUCATI ARE VERY STRONG HERE – THEY HAVE GOOD TURNING, SO THEY DON'T LOSE THERE LIKE BEFORE'

MARC MÁRQUEZ

**ABOVE, LEFT-RIGHT** | *Miller scored his first dry-weather front row; there was no home-race salvation for Rossi; Pirro was back on the grid for the first time since his huge Mugello prang*

**MAIN** | *Lorenzo chases Márquez as Márquez chases Dovizioso*

limits to stay with the Desmosedicis, hoping for an opportunity in the final stages.

"Ducati are very strong here," said the world championship leader after practice. "They have very good stability at the brake points, they have good turning, so they don't lose there like before, and they have the acceleration. But they can't use all their torque when their rear tyre is used, so I feel I can follow them in the race."

Dovizioso took the lead after six of 27 laps, convinced he could run a faster pace than Lorenzo, while saving his tyres. By half-distance he was 1.1 seconds ahead, then Lorenzo made a mistake, allowing Márquez past. The two Spaniards spent the next six laps duking it out, no quarter asked, none given. Finally, Lorenzo made a pass stick, but the pair's infighting had allowed Dovizioso to double his advantage.

Undeterred, Lorenzo set off in pursuit, apparently prepared to risk everything for victory. With two laps to go he had reduced the gap to 1.4 seconds and was still charging. Entering turn eight for the last-but-one time he got too greedy. The medium tyres he had chosen didn't give him the grip he needed to go as fast as he wanted – the rear slithered around, he applied more front brake, the rear lifted off the track, the bike became unsettled and down he went.

"Dovizioso has a different style to me, so he has a very good feeling with the medium front and he is experienced in dealing with the medium rear," explained Lorenzo. "I use more corner speed and lean angle, so I need softer tyres. At the last races I was able to brake later than him, but today I couldn't stop the bike with the front or the rear."

That left Dovizioso enough breathing space to allow him an uncharacteristic wave to the crowd on the final lap. He was justifiably delighted with his first success at his home track.

"I tried to save the tyre and understand the situation about how comfortable I was when I pushed," he said. "I didn't really take maximum risks, so I understood I had a chance. At the end Jorge tried to catch me, he was coming very fast, so I pushed again, started taking some risks and on that same lap he crashed."

This was the first time Ducati had won three consecutive races since Casey Stoner's rampant 2007 season and the first time they'd ever taken three wins in a row with different riders. The championship, of course, looked like a long shot, but Dovizioso was now second overall and wasn't ready to surrender just yet. "We have to work on the details to be faster to try and stop Marc," he said. "If we can do something important this year, okay, but if we can't we have to be more ready for next year."

Márquez was happy enough with second, which increased his title lead to 67 points. And this was the first time all year that he had shared the podium with a fellow Honda rider.

## MARC'S LATEST LAZARUS MOMENT

Marc Márquez has always been famous for Lazarus-style comebacks. First there was his sighting-lap crash at Estoril in 2010, which had him starting the race from last place. It didn't matter. He won anyway.

Then there was his COTA 2015 pole-position lap. Forced to abandon his number-one bike on the track, he jumped the pit wall and sprinted 200 metres to grab his spare bike. He had time for one flying lap and took pole, despite almost crashing. Then there was Assen 2016, when he crashed in qualifying and borrowed a photographer's scooter to race back to the paddock.

Crutchlow may have inherited third place from Lorenzo's mistake, but there was no doubt that he deserved his place in the podium party. A close-run fifth at Brno and a strong fourth in Austria, he had become the best of the rest. This time he spent the early laps with Álex Rins, who ran wide at one-third distance, allowing the Briton through. With a clear road ahead, Crutchlow raised his pace and for several laps was the fastest man on track, closing on the duelling Spaniards. But the gap was too big to bridge and he had settled for a decent fourth-place finish when Lorenzo skated into the gravel.

Yamaha were once again in all kinds of trouble. Useful tests at Misano and Aragón had convinced both Maverick Viñales and Valentino Rossi that they were making progress. "The bike has improved, so I can ride my own way," said Viñales during practice. "Like this I feel like the bike can be in the top three."

In fact the Spaniard took the flag in fifth place, almost nine seconds behind Crutchlow, while Rossi was three seconds and two places further back. It was a gloomy result for the local hero, who had nothing to offer his hordes of yellow-uniformed fans.

"In yesterday's FP4 I wasn't too bad," said Rossi. "But for some reason, which we don't understand, everything today was more difficult. I was struggling very much from warm-up, also Maverick and Johann Zarco. The feeling with the bike and the tyres was worse. We don't know if it's the Moto2 rubber, but that's the same for Ducati and Yamaha, so it's strange if the Moto2 rubber is only bad for Yamaha, but it could be. Sincerely, we don't know if that's true and if it's true then we don't know why."

**CLOCKWISE FROM TOP LEFT** | *The awkward moment of the weekend as Márquez offers to shake Rossi's hand, but Rossi doesn't want to know; Tito Rabat sub Christophe Ponsson also caused controversy; Rins found more speed to chase the leading trio; that's a lot of VR46 merchandise; Dovizioso took his second win in three races; Márquez in full-attack mode, about to pounce on Lorenzo*

Q2 at Misano was similar but different. Márquez crashed at the 145kmh/90mph turn 15 and was already up and running for his second bike before he had even stopped rolling. He ran down the service road, found a marshal riding a scooter, hopped on the back, returned to the paddock, sprinted into his garage and jumped on his remaining RC213V. During those two minutes and 17 seconds he never once stopped moving.

"The guy on the scooter was pushing a lot; it was scary because I thought we would crash, but he did a great job," he laughed. "Unfortunately I wasn't able to improve my lap time — I had some dust in my eye. In the crash I lost the front too early, so this time I wasn't ready with my elbow."

# 13 | SAN MARINO

# RACE RESULTS

**WINNER** *ANDREA DOVIZIOSO*

**CIRCUIT LENGTH** *4.2 KM | 2.63 MILES*

**NO. OF LAPS** *27*

**RACE DISTANCE** *114.1 KM | 71.0 MILES*

**CIRCUIT RECORD LAP** *1'32.678 | 164.1 KM/H*
*ANDREA DOVIZIOSO (2018)*

**CIRCUIT BEST LAP** *1'31.629 | 166.0 KM/H*
*JORGE LORENZO (2018)*

**RACE CONDITION** *DRY*

**AIR** *27°C*

**HUMIDITY** *57%*

**GROUND** *41°C*

**TISSOT** SWISS WATCHES SINCE 1853 / MotoGP
**OFFICIAL** TIMEKEEPER

**MICHELIN** / MotoGP
**OFFICIAL** MotoGP™ CLASS TYRE

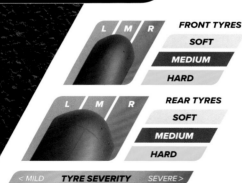

| FRONT TYRES |
| SOFT |
| MEDIUM |
| HARD |

| REAR TYRES |
| SOFT |
| MEDIUM |
| HARD |

< MILD  **TYRE SEVERITY**  SEVERE >

## QUALIFYING RESULTS

| | RIDER | NAT | TEAM | MACHINE | QP/TIME | GAP 1ST/PREV | |
|---|---|---|---|---|---|---|---|
| 1 | Jorge Lorenzo | SPA | Ducati Team | DUCATI | Q2 1'31.629 | | |
| 2 | Jack Miller | AUS | Alma Pramac Racing | DUCATI | Q2 1'31.916 | 0.287 | 0.287 |
| 3 | Maverick Viñales | SPA | Movistar Yamaha MotoGP | YAMAHA | Q2 1'31.950 | 0.321 | 0.034 |
| 4 | Andrea Dovizioso | ITA | Ducati Team | DUCATI | Q2 1'32.003 | 0.374 | 0.053 |
| 5 | Marc Márquez | SPA | Repsol Honda Team | HONDA | Q2 1'32.016 | 0.387 | 0.013 |
| 6 | Cal Crutchlow | GBR | LCR Honda CASTROL | HONDA | Q2 1'32.025 | 0.396 | 0.009 |
| 7 | Valentino Rossi | ITA | Movistar Yamaha MotoGP | YAMAHA | Q2 1'32.028 | 0.399 | 0.003 |
| 8 | Danilo Petrucci | ITA | Alma Pramac Racing | DUCATI | Q2 1'32.136 | 0.507 | 0.108 |
| 9 | Johann Zarco | FRA | Monster Yamaha Tech 3 | YAMAHA | Q2 1'32.250 | 0.621 | 0.114 |
| 10 | Álex Rins | SPA | Team SUZUKI ECSTAR | SUZUKI | Q2 1'32.338 | 0.709 | 0.088 |
| 11 | Dani Pedrosa** | SPA | Repsol Honda Team | HONDA | Q2 1'32.369 | 0.740 | 0.031 |
| 12 | Franco Morbidelli** | ITA | EG 0,0 Marc VDS | HONDA | Q1 1'32.454 | *0.065 | 0.065 |
| 13 | Andrea Iannone | ITA | Team SUZUKI ECSTAR | SUZUKI | Q1 1'32.566 | *0.177 | 0.112 |
| 14 | Michele Pirro | ITA | Ducati Team | DUCATI | Q1 1'32.624 | *0.235 | 0.058 |
| 15 | Álvaro Bautista | SPA | Ángel Nieto Team | DUCATI | Q1 1'32.792 | *0.403 | 0.168 |
| 16 | Aleix Espargaró | SPA | Aprilia Racing Team Gresini | APRILIA | Q1 1'33.084 | *0.695 | 0.292 |
| 17 | Bradley Smith | GBR | Red Bull KTM Factory Racing | KTM | Q1 1'33.085 | *0.696 | 0.001 |
| 18 | Stefan Bradl | GER | EG 0,0 Marc VDS | HONDA | Q1 1'33.361 | *0.972 | 0.276 |
| 19 | Takaaki Nakagami | JPN | LCR Honda IDEMITSU | HONDA | Q1 1'33.437 | *1.048 | 0.076 |
| 20 | Pol Espargaró | SPA | Red Bull KTM Factory Racing | KTM | Q1 1'33.502 | *1.113 | 0.065 |
| 21 | Scott Redding | GBR | Aprilia Racing Team Gresini | APRILIA | Q1 1'33.572 | *1.183 | 0.070 |
| 22 | Xavier Siméon | GER | Reale Avintia Racing | DUCATI | Q1 1'33.705 | *1.316 | 0.133 |
| 23 | Thomas Lüthi | SWI | EG 0,0 Marc VDS | HONDA | Q1 1'33.755 | *1.366 | 0.050 |
| 24 | Karel Abraham | CZE | Ángel Nieto Team | DUCATI | Q1 1'33.812 | *1.423 | 0.057 |
| 25 | Hafizh Syahrin | MAL | Monster Yamaha Tech 3 | YAMAHA | Q1 1'34.080 | *1.691 | 0.268 |
| 26 | Christophe Ponsson | FRA | Reale Avintia Racing | DUCATI | Q1 1'37.180 | *4.791 | 3.100 |

*\* Gap to the fastest rider in the Q1 session  \*\* Went forward from Q1 to Q2*

**1 ANDREA DOVIZIOSO**
Ducati's first Misano victory since their rampant 2007 season proved once again that the Bologna factory had made a significant step. Dovizioso had fixed his tyre-wear issues and rode a perfect race, risking only when necessary.

**2 MARC MÁRQUEZ**
Unlike Ducati and Yamaha, Repsol Honda hadn't tested at Misano, so he knew this would be another tough one. Took a while to get his tyres up to full temperature. Hoped he might profit from a Ducati-on-Ducati duel.

**3 CAL CRUTCHLOW**
Had set his heart on winning at Silverstone, so his first podium since Argentina was some compensation for his home-race disappointment. Was the fastest man on track once he'd used some fuel and got his hard front tyre working right.

**4 ÁLEX RINS**
Tested at Aragon, where he made some important improvements to braking stability, which had been an issue at previous races. Chose the soft tyre, which lasted fine, thanks to his smooth throttle technique.

**5 MAVERICK VIÑALES**
Felt confident of fighting for the podium after setting a good pace in the FP4 session, but didn't have the same grip or feel in the race. Had no idea what made the difference: was it Moto2 rubber or a three-degree increase in track temperature?

**6 DANI PEDROSA**
Dominated Misano in 2016 and perhaps thought this might be a good chance to continue his record of winning at least one race a year since 2002. Didn't win, but not a bad result, considering he was 14th in FP4.

**7 VALENTINO ROSSI**
Rossi's promising FP4 pace evaporated, so his side of the Movistar garage were scratching their heads as hard as those on the other side. After the race he was moved to suggest that perhaps Yamaha should build a V4 M1.

**8 ANDREA IANNONE**
An FP2 crash didn't help his weekend and he failed to make it into Q2, leaving him with his worst grid position of the year so far. Came through from 13th on lap one and ran a good pace until his tyres dropped.

**9 ÁLVARO BAUTISTA**
A seventh consecutive top-ten finish was reason to celebrate for the Spaniard. Chose soft front and rear tyres, which worked well for him. Ended the first lap in 14th position and spent much of the race chasing Iannone's factory Suzuki.

**10 JOHANN ZARCO**
FP3 was the highlight of his weekend, when he booked a place in Q2, despite a slightly damp track. In the race he tried too hard to make up for his M1's poor acceleration and ran wide, losing several positions.

**11 DANILO PETRUCCI**
Struggled all weekend at his home Grand Prix. Didn't make the first two rows for the first time since Germany and had to start from eighth on the grid. Chose the medium rear tyre and never had a good feeling with it, a bit like fellow GP18 rider Lorenzo.

**12 FRANCO MORBIDELLI**
An impressive result from the rookie. Made it into Q2 for the second time and spent the early stages of the race chasing Pedrosa. But he was risking too much and eased his pace slightly as the race went on.

## RACE LAP CHART

Dashed line: Lapped rider

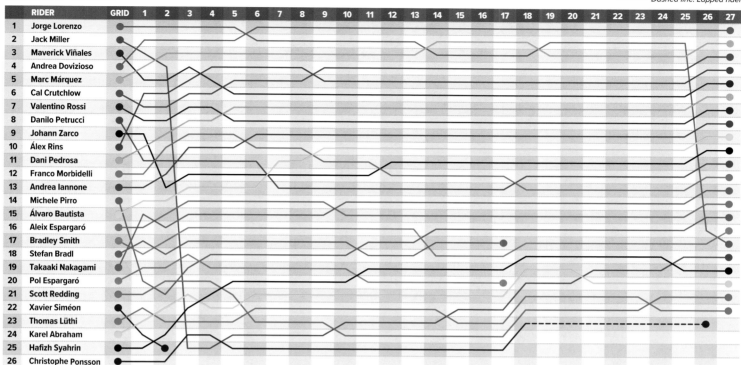

| | RIDER | GRID | 1 | 2 | 3 | 4 | 5 | 6 | 7 | 8 | 9 | 10 | 11 | 12 | 13 | 14 | 15 | 16 | 17 | 18 | 19 | 20 | 21 | 22 | 23 | 24 | 25 | 26 | 27 |
|---|---|---|---|---|---|---|---|---|---|---|---|---|---|---|---|---|---|---|---|---|---|---|---|---|---|---|---|---|---|
| 1 | Jorge Lorenzo | | | | | | | | | | | | | | | | | | | | | | | | | | | | |
| 2 | Jack Miller | | | | | | | | | | | | | | | | | | | | | | | | | | | | |
| 3 | Maverick Viñales | | | | | | | | | | | | | | | | | | | | | | | | | | | | |
| 4 | Andrea Dovizioso | | | | | | | | | | | | | | | | | | | | | | | | | | | | |
| 5 | Marc Márquez | | | | | | | | | | | | | | | | | | | | | | | | | | | | |
| 6 | Cal Crutchlow | | | | | | | | | | | | | | | | | | | | | | | | | | | | |
| 7 | Valentino Rossi | | | | | | | | | | | | | | | | | | | | | | | | | | | | |
| 8 | Danilo Petrucci | | | | | | | | | | | | | | | | | | | | | | | | | | | | |
| 9 | Johann Zarco | | | | | | | | | | | | | | | | | | | | | | | | | | | | |
| 10 | Álex Rins | | | | | | | | | | | | | | | | | | | | | | | | | | | | |
| 11 | Dani Pedrosa | | | | | | | | | | | | | | | | | | | | | | | | | | | | |
| 12 | Franco Morbidelli | | | | | | | | | | | | | | | | | | | | | | | | | | | | |
| 13 | Andrea Iannone | | | | | | | | | | | | | | | | | | | | | | | | | | | | |
| 14 | Michele Pirro | | | | | | | | | | | | | | | | | | | | | | | | | | | | |
| 15 | Álvaro Bautista | | | | | | | | | | | | | | | | | | | | | | | | | | | | |
| 16 | Aleix Espargaró | | | | | | | | | | | | | | | | | | | | | | | | | | | | |
| 17 | Bradley Smith | | | | | | | | | | | | | | | | | | | | | | | | | | | | |
| 18 | Stefan Bradl | | | | | | | | | | | | | | | | | | | | | | | | | | | | |
| 19 | Takaaki Nakagami | | | | | | | | | | | | | | | | | | | | | | | | | | | | |
| 20 | Pol Espargaró | | | | | | | | | | | | | | | | | | | | | | | | | | | | |
| 21 | Scott Redding | | | | | | | | | | | | | | | | | | | | | | | | | | | | |
| 22 | Xavier Siméon | | | | | | | | | | | | | | | | | | | | | | | | | | | | |
| 23 | Thomas Lüthi | | | | | | | | | | | | | | | | | | | | | | | | | | | | |
| 24 | Karel Abraham | | | | | | | | | | | | | | | | | | | | | | | | | | | | |
| 25 | Hafizh Syahrin | | | | | | | | | | | | | | | | | | | | | | | | | | | | |
| 26 | Christophe Ponsson | | | | | | | | | | | | | | | | | | | | | | | | | | | | |

## RACE CLASSIFICATION AFTER 27 LAPS = 114.102 KM

| | RIDER | NAT | TEAM | MACHINE | TIME | + GAP | TYRES |
|---|---|---|---|---|---|---|---|
| 1 | Andrea Dovizioso | ITA | Ducati Team | DUCATI | 42'05.426 | | M/M |
| 2 | Marc Márquez | SPA | Repsol Honda Team | HONDA | 42'08.248 | 2.822 | H/M |
| 3 | Cal Crutchlow | GBR | LCR Honda CASTROL | HONDA | 42'12.695 | 7.269 | H/M |
| 4 | Álex Rins | SPA | Team SUZUKI ECSTAR | SUZUKI | 42'20.113 | 14.687 | M/S |
| 5 | Maverick Viñales | SPA | Movistar Yamaha MotoGP | YAMAHA | 42'21.442 | 16.016 | M/S |
| 6 | Dani Pedrosa | SPA | Repsol Honda Team | HONDA | 42'22.834 | 17.408 | H/M |
| 7 | Valentino Rossi | ITA | Movistar Yamaha MotoGP | YAMAHA | 42'24.512 | 19.086 | M/M |
| 8 | Andrea Iannone | ITA | Team SUZUKI ECSTAR | SUZUKI | 42'27.230 | 21.804 | M/S |
| 9 | Álvaro Bautista | SPA | Ángel Nieto Team | DUCATI | 42'29.345 | 23.919 | S/S |
| 10 | Johann Zarco | FRA | Monster Yamaha Tech 3 | YAMAHA | 42'32.985 | 27.559 | S/S |
| 11 | Danilo Petrucci++ | ITA | Alma Pramac Racing | DUCATI | 42'36.124 | 30.698 | M/M |
| 12 | Franco Morbidelli | ITA | EG 0,0 Marc VDS | HONDA | 42'38.367 | 32.941 | H/M |
| 13 | Takaaki Nakagami | JPN | LCR Honda IDEMITSU | HONDA | 42'38.887 | 33.461 | H/M |
| 14 | Aleix Espargaró | SPA | Aprilia Racing Team Gresini | APRILIA | 42'41.112 | 35.686 | M/S |
| 15 | Michele Pirro | ITA | Ducati Team | DUCATI | 42'41.238 | 35.812 | S/M |
| 16 | Bradley Smith | GBR | Red Bull KTM Factory Racing | KTM | 42'51.926 | 46.500 | M/S |
| 17 | Jorge Lorenzo | SPA | Ducati Team | DUCATI | 42'52.040 | 46.614 | M/M |
| 18 | Jack Miller | AUS | Alma Pramac Racing | DUCATI | 42'56.019 | 50.593 | M/M |
| 19 | Hafizh Syahrin | MAL | Monster Yamaha Tech 3 | YAMAHA | 43'00.594 | 55.168 | M/S |
| 20 | Karel Abraham | CZE | Ángel Nieto Team | DUCATI | 43'07.681 | 62.255 | M/S |
| 21 | Scott Redding | GBR | Aprilia Racing Team Gresini | APRILIA | 43'14.901 | 69.475 | M/S |
| 22 | Thomas Lüthi | SWI | EG 0,0 Marc VDS | HONDA | 43'18.034 | 72.608 | M/S |
| 23 | Christophe Ponsson | FRA | Reale Avintia Racing | DUCATI | 43'02.996 | 1 lap | S/S |
| NC | Stefan Bradl | GER | EG 0,0 Marc VDS | HONDA | 6'55.496 | 10 laps | H/H |
| NC | Pol Espargaró | SPA | Red Bull KTM Factory Racing | KTM | 27'06.725 | 10 laps | M/S |
| NC | Xavier Siméon | GER | Reale Avintia Racing | DUCATI | 3'21.298 | 25 laps | M/S |

+ New race distance for 2018   ++ FIM MotoGP Stewards Race penalty - Danilo Petrucci 1.1 seconds penalty imposed

## CHAMPIONSHIP STANDINGS

| | RIDER | NAT | TEAM | POINTS |
|---|---|---|---|---|
| 1 | Marc Márquez | SPA | Repsol Honda Team | 221 |
| 2 | Andrea Dovizioso | ITA | Ducati Team | 154 |
| 3 | Valentino Rossi | ITA | Movistar Yamaha MotoGP | 151 |
| 4 | Jorge Lorenzo | SPA | Ducati Team | 130 |
| 5 | Maverick Viñales | SPA | Movistar Yamaha MotoGP | 124 |
| 6 | Cal Crutchlow | GBR | LCR Honda CASTROL | 119 |
| 7 | Johann Zarco | FRA | Monster Yamaha Tech 3 | 110 |
| 8 | Danilo Petrucci | ITA | Alma Pramac Racing | 110 |
| 9 | Andrea Iannone | ITA | Team SUZUKI ECSTAR | 92 |
| 10 | Álex Rins | SPA | Team SUZUKI ECSTAR | 79 |
| 11 | Dani Pedrosa | SPA | Repsol Honda Team | 76 |
| 12 | Álvaro Bautista | SPA | Ángel Nieto Team | 64 |
| 13 | Jack Miller | AUS | Alma Pramac Racing | 61 |
| 14 | Tito Rabat | SPA | Reale Avintia Racing | 35 |
| 15 | Pol Espargaró | SPA | Red Bull KTM Factory Racing | 32 |
| 16 | Franco Morbidelli | ITA | EG 0,0 Marc VDS | 26 |
| 17 | Hafizh Syahrin | MAL | Monster Yamaha Tech 3 | 24 |
| 18 | Aleix Espargaró | SPA | Aprilia Racing Team Gresini | 19 |
| 19 | Bradley Smith | GBR | Red Bull KTM Factory Racing | 15 |
| 20 | Takaaki Nakagami | JPN | LCR Honda IDEMITSU | 14 |
| 21 | Scott Redding | GBR | Aprilia Racing Team Gresini | 12 |
| 22 | Mika Kallio | FIN | Red Bull KTM Factory Racing | 6 |
| 23 | Karel Abraham | CZE | Ángel Nieto Team | 4 |
| 24 | Michele Pirro | ITA | Ducati Team | 1 |
| 25 | Thomas Lüthi | SWI | EG 0,0 Marc VDS | |
| 26 | Stefan Bradl | GER | Honda Racing Corporation | |
| 27 | Xavier Siméon | GER | Reale Avintia Racing | |
| 28 | Sylvain Guintoli | FRA | Team SUZUKI ECSTAR | |
| 29 | Christophe Ponsson | FRA | Reale Avintia Racing | |

**13 | TAKAAKI NAKAGAMI**
A good start moved him into 15th at the end of the first lap, after starting 19th. From there the rookie kept plugging away, running a very consistent pace that allowed him to get the better of Aleix Espargaró in the late stages of the race.

**14 | ALEIX ESPARGARÓ**
This was his best result since his ninth-place finish at Le Mans in May. Chased Petrucci and Zarco during the early laps but didn't quite have the pace to stay with them. Struggled most through the faster corners.

**15 | MICHELE PIRRO**
His first MotoGP outing since his huge tumble at Mugello, Ducati's main test rider ruined his race with a bad start that left him 20th on the first lap. His greatest satisfaction was seeing his hard work rewarded by Dovizioso's victory.

**16 | BRADLEY SMITH**
His first two worst races of 2017 at Misano and the RC16 struggled again on their second visit. Smith tried a new spec machine which at least reduced the gap to the leaders and gave hope for the future.

**17 | JORGE LORENZO**
Rued his decision to choose medium tyres instead of the soft option rear, which worked so well for Rins and others. Lost time battling with Márquez, then pushed too hard and fell. Remounted to chase Smith past the chequered flag.

**18 | JACK MILLER**
The Aussie's second place on the grid in perfect conditions was more important than his first pole in Argentina, on a damp track. He got a good enough start in the race, only to slide off at turn 14 on lap three.

**19 | HAFIZH SYAHRIN**
Haunted by continuing front-end issues that caused him to crash in FP2 and FP4, the Malaysian went into safety mode for the race, which left him outside the points and thus relinquishing the lead in the Rookie of the Year contest to Morbidelli.

**20 | KAREL ABRAHAM**
Struggled with a lack of front grip, which had him close to crashing on several occasions. Felt better once the fuel load had reduced and tried following Miller when he came past, but didn't have the speed.

**21 | SCOTT REDDING**
Was once again caught between two different front tyres; the hard was too risky and the medium too soft. Raced with the medium option.

**22 | THOMAS LÜTHI**
Crashed in FP3. Struggled with turning performance, so his crew gambled on a radical adjustment for the race, which didn't work.

**23 | CHRISTOPHE PONSSON**
Tito Rabat's substitute was criticised by many MotoGP full-timers. Was five seconds off the pace in the race.

**DNF | STEFAN BRADL**
His third MotoGP race of 2018 at least lasted longer than Brno. This time he lost the front and crashed with ten laps remaining.

**DNF | POL ESPARGARÓ**
An inflamed spinal cord prevented plating of the collarbone he broke at Brno, so he was far from full strength. Was unable to make race distance.

**DNF | XAVIER SIMÉON**
Graduated to Rabat's GP17 but didn't find the better machinery made much difference to his performance.

*Márquez has had enough of breathing Dovizioso's exhaust fumes and is planning his final attack*

# MÁRQUEZ FOILS DUCATI'S MOMENTUM

**Márquez won his first race in more than two months but controversy was never that far away**

The battle of Aragon lasted 41 minutes and 55.949 seconds but will mostly be remembered for what happened during its first ten seconds. Marc Márquez divebombed Jorge Lorenzo at the first corner, Lorenzo ran wide onto the dirty part of the track and got flicked to the moon.

The race favourite was out, stretchered away with two mangled toes and much ill feeling. Meanwhile the race continued, no doubt the worse for losing the man who had fought like his life depended on it at Brno, Red Bull Ring and Misano. At Aragon, Lorenzo wanted to make history: Ducati's first run of four consecutive MotoGP victories.

With the pole sitter down and out, Márquez and Andrea Dovizioso went about their business, chased all the way by the unlikely combination of both Suzukis.

Márquez and Dovizioso were strongest, but whatever Andrea Iannone and Álex Rins lost to the Honda and Ducati on Aragon's one-kilometre straight, they regained over the mountain, the GSX-RR flaunting its sweet-handling chassis through the twists and turns.

Márquez had pounced into turn one, but when he ran wide he was relegated to second by Dovizioso and briefly to third by

**MAIN** | Márquez's stunning getaway took him into the lead, while Lorenzo found the dirty part of the track and paid the price

**BELOW, LEFT-RIGHT** | Both Suzukis ran with the leaders throughout, proof of more progress at Hamamatsu; Pedrosa gets taped for his best race in more than three months; Aleix Espargaró transformed Aprilia's miserable season

## 'MARC DESTROYED MY RACE AND MY FOOT'

*JORGE LORENZO*

Iannone. Rins was also pushing hard, slicing past his team-mate and running faster than anyone at one-quarter distance. But the Suzukis didn't quite have the straight-line speed to overcome the leading duo.

Dovizioso was his usual cerebral self. He had chosen hard/hard tyres – for only the second time in 13 races – and waited for his fuel load to decrease and his grip to increase before he tried to escape. At half-distance he rode two consecutive fastest laps to leave Márquez seven tenths behind, but the Spaniard was soon back on the GP18's tailpipes, swooping through the downhill turn ten (named in his honour a few days earlier) to take the lead at turn 12, his front tyre skating across the asphalt.

The next few laps were a full-on brawl, the champion and world number two biting chunks out of each other while Iannone and Rins were right on them, like vultures waiting for a kill. With five laps to go Márquez and Dovizioso nearly tangled at the bus-stop chicane, allowing Iannone to grab the lead onto the main straight. The Suzuki, Honda and Ducati were side by side, front wheels in the air, pointing this way and that. "This was the best moment," grinned Márquez. "It was exciting on the bike!"

The final act was played out as the group raced up the mountain with three laps to go. Dovizioso got better drive out of turn three, snuck under Márquez at turn four, only for Márquez to sit him up at turn five. And that was that. Márquez hadn't won a race since Germany and didn't want to get beaten in front of his fans. It seemed he had decided it was worth throwing 25 points into the gravel, then defending a diminished points lead at the last five races. And this despite another high-speed crash in practice, which wore right through his leathers.

"I woke up this morning and said I want to take a risk," said Márquez after the race. This didn't only apply to his riding, it also applied to tyre choice. At the last minute he chose the soft rear, even though he hadn't tried it in the heat of an afternoon session. The tyre gave him more grip on corner entry as well as on corner exit.

"I believed in this tyre because I thought it was my only chance to fight with the Ducatis," he added. "In the race I saw Dovi struggling more than usual, so I knew I could go with him. I pushed to the limit and took a lot of risks. It was my only chance, but I was using the front too much."

Dovizioso also took risks, because he is happy to do so when he feels he has enough control of the bike.

"I'm aggressive when I can be aggressive and when I need to be aggressive," said the Misano winner, who had always struggled with the Ducati at Aragon. "I'm so happy with how much we improved our weak points here. We've made a huge step. What happened is more important than what happened at Misano, because it confirms our improvement and it's good for the future."

## LORENZO: 'LIFE IS A ROLLERCOASTER'

Lorenzo was mad about his crash. "Marc destroyed my race and my foot... He didn't allow me to enter the corner. He made me go to the dirt, where I opened the throttle and crashed. He didn't care about me, he just braked very late and didn't think about the exit of the corner."

The next day he was more philosophical. "I have always thought that life and sport are like a rollercoaster, a mixture of moments and emotions," he wrote on his Instagram account, @jorgelorenzo99. "As in the famous fairground attraction, we can find ourselves on a long, stable climb. When you are a novice, you think your life will

Márquez knew where Ducati had the advantage. The GP18 doesn't use a lot of lean angle through the corners, which puts more rubber on the ground for faster exits. "They don't lean the bike, they just use the drive," he said. "It's another style of motorcycle – this is why our battles are so nice to see."

The Suzuki is another kind of motorcycle again. It is more agile than the GP18 and the RC213V, making up time through the corners and on the brakes.

"In the corners our bike is unbelievable and we have very good front and rear grip," said Iannone. "We can recover a lot in the fast corners because we can enter very deep with a lot of speed, compared to the others. The negative point is that we use a lot of corner speed, so we use the edge of the tyres a lot."

Suzuki didn't win this race but the result was historic – the first time two Suzukis had finished within three seconds of victory in the dry since Assen, 1979.

Suzuki's rise coincided, not entirely coincidentally, with Yamaha's fall. Just as this was a historic day for the Hamamatsu factory, so too was it a historic day for its Iwata neighbour, but not in a good way. While Suzuki had made its inline-four GSX-RR into a corner-speed rocket, Yamaha's similar YZR-M1 was once again hopelessly lost.

Valentino Rossi qualified 18th fastest, his worst performance since Assen 2006, when he rode with a broken wrist. He recovered to eighth in the race, two places ahead of team-mate Maverick Viñales. This was the brand's 23rd consecutive defeat, its longest losing streak since it entered the premier class in 1973.

**CLOCKWISE FROM TOP LEFT** | *MotoGP's podium Instagram feed goes into action; Smith, Nakagami and Zarco spent the final laps fighting for the last points; Nakagami missed beating Morbidelli for top rookie status by a fraction; Rossi showed his old fire, fighting back from his worst grid position in a dozen years; Espargaró was aware that he had done something very special*

always be like this: in continuous ascendance. You think, naively, that the descents your parents or your friends have suffered won't happen to you. Even those who, like me, have been up and down hundreds of times, like to ignore what we already know: everything that goes up must come down.

"Thanks to that contrast of emotions one gets to feel alive and that is why rollercoasters are so addictive. In order to appreciate the satisfaction of an ascent, you need to go through the anguish generated by a descent. On Sunday I lived my latest descent. I did not like it. In fact I hated it with all my might, while I was cursing myself for not having foreseen it. Now, I cannot stop thinking about how I can improve my next rollercoaster and if I will live it better."

# 14 | ARAGÓN

# RACE RESULTS

**WINNER** | *MARC MÁRQUEZ*

**CIRCUIT LENGTH** | *5.1 KM* | *3.15 MILES*

**NO. OF LAPS** | *23*

**RACE DISTANCE** | *116.8 KM* | *72.5 MILES*

**CIRCUIT RECORD LAP** | *1'48.120* | *169.0 KM/H*
*JORGE LORENZO (2015)*

**CIRCUIT BEST LAP** | *1'46.635* | *171.4 KM/H*
*MARC MÁRQUEZ (2015)*

**RACE CONDITION** | *DRY*

**AIR** | *30°C*

**HUMIDITY** | *36%*

**GROUND** | *45°C*

**TISSOT** SWISS WATCHES SINCE 1853 | **MotoGP**

**OFFICIAL** TIMEKEEPER

**MICHELIN** | **MotoGP**

**OFFICIAL** MotoGP™ CLASS TYRE

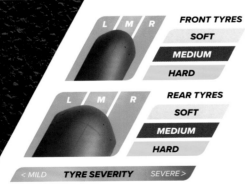

**FRONT TYRES**
- SOFT
- MEDIUM
- HARD

**REAR TYRES**
- SOFT
- MEDIUM
- HARD

< MILD | **TYRE SEVERITY** | SEVERE >

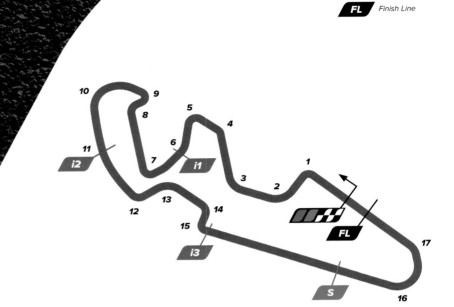

Start Line | Sectors | S Speed Trap | FL Finish Line

## QUALIFYING RESULTS

| | RIDER | NAT | TEAM | MACHINE | QP/TIME | | GAP 1ST/PREV |
|---|---|---|---|---|---|---|---|
| 1 | Jorge Lorenzo | SPA | Ducati Team | DUCATI | Q2 | 1'46.881 | | |
| 2 | Andrea Dovizioso | ITA | Ducati Team | DUCATI | Q2 | 1'46.895 | 0.014 | 0.014 |
| 3 | Marc Márquez | SPA | Repsol Honda Team | HONDA | Q2 | 1'46.960 | 0.079 | 0.065 |
| 4 | Cal Crutchlow | GBR | LCR Honda CASTROL | HONDA | Q2 | 1'47.146 | 0.265 | 0.186 |
| 5 | Andrea Iannone | ITA | Team SUZUKI ECSTAR | SUZUKI | Q2 | 1'47.169 | 0.288 | 0.023 |
| 6 | Dani Pedrosa | SPA | Repsol Honda Team | HONDA | Q2 | 1'47.224 | 0.343 | 0.055 |
| 7 | Danilo Petrucci | ITA | Alma Pramac Racing | DUCATI | Q2 | 1'47.351 | 0.470 | 0.127 |
| 8 | Álvaro Bautista | SPA | Ángel Nieto Team | DUCATI | Q2 | 1'47.678 | 0.797 | 0.327 |
| 9 | Álex Rins | SPA | Team SUZUKI ECSTAR | SUZUKI | Q2 | 1'47.737 | 0.856 | 0.059 |
| 10 | Jack Miller | AUS | Alma Pramac Racing | DUCATI | Q2 | 1'47.792 | 0.911 | 0.055 |
| 11 | Maverick Viñales** | SPA | Movistar Yamaha MotoGP | YAMAHA | Q2 | 1'47.810 | 0.929 | 0.018 |
| 12 | Takaaki Nakagami** | JPN | LCR Honda IDEMITSU | HONDA | Q2 | 1'48.284 | 1.403 | 0.474 |
| 13 | Franco Morbidelli | ITA | EG 0,0 Marc VDS | HONDA | Q1 | 1'48.009 | *0.186 | 0.063 |
| 14 | Johann Zarco | FRA | Monster Yamaha Tech 3 | YAMAHA | Q1 | 1'48.052 | *0.229 | 0.043 |
| 15 | Aleix Espargaró | SPA | Aprilia Racing Team Gresini | APRILIA | Q1 | 1'48.181 | *0.358 | 0.129 |
| 16 | Bradley Smith | GBR | Red Bull KTM Factory Racing | KTM | Q1 | 1'48.216 | *0.393 | 0.035 |
| 17 | Karel Abraham | CZE | Ángel Nieto Team | DUCATI | Q1 | 1'48.398 | *0.575 | 0.182 |
| 18 | Valentino Rossi | ITA | Movistar Yamaha MotoGP | YAMAHA | Q1 | 1'48.627 | *0.804 | 0.229 |
| 19 | Hafizh Syahrin | MAL | Monster Yamaha Tech 3 | YAMAHA | Q1 | 1'48.975 | *1.152 | 0.348 |
| 20 | Thomas Lüthi | SWI | EG 0,0 Marc VDS | HONDA | Q1 | 1'48.988 | *1.165 | 0.013 |
| 21 | Scott Redding | GBR | Aprilia Racing Team Gresini | APRILIA | Q1 | 1'49.303 | *1.480 | 0.315 |
| 22 | Xavier Siméon | GER | Reale Avintia Racing | DUCATI | Q1 | 1'49.699 | *1.876 | 0.396 |
| 23 | Jordi Torres | SPA | Reale Avintia Racing | DUCATI | Q1 | 1'50.336 | *2.513 | 0.637 |

*\* Gap to the fastest rider in the Q1 session*
*\*\* Went forward from Q1 to Q2*

**1 | MARC MÁRQUEZ**
Didn't only want to win for the points, but to stop Ducati's momentum. Used the green runoff at turn one but the FIM stewards took no action because they usually "disregard unclear green runoff incidents in the first two laps".

**2 | ANDREA DOVIZIOSO**
Tried to break away but couldn't maintain the pace of his mid-race spurt. Perhaps he would've had a better chance if he had run the soft rear. But was happy that the Desmosedici was no longer a nightmare around Aragon.

**3 | ANDREA IANNONE**
Worked all weekend to allow him to use the soft rear and tamed his throttle hand in the race. Drafted Márquez and Dovizioso, attacking whenever he could, especially in the final laps when he led very briefly.

**4 | ÁLEX RINS**
During pre-race tests at Aragon worked a lot on increasing braking stability, to allow him to brake later and compensate for the Suzuki's lack of top speed. Learned lots of new tricks by racing so close with the world champion.

**5 | DANI PEDROSA**
His best result since Barcelona and Le Mans could have been better if he had chosen the soft rear instead of the hard. No one raced the medium rear because it degraded more than the hard and soft.

**6 | ALEIX ESPARGARÓ**
Less than ten seconds behind the winner, he named this one of his best-ever rides. Had recently asked Aprilia to switch to the 2017 RS-GP but had been refused. Instead his crew revised bike balance to improve turning.

**7 | DANILO PETRUCCI**
Had aerodynamic outers fitted to his front forks for the first time. Qualified a strong seventh and tried to go with the lead group, but was slowed by rear-tyre chatter which forced him to ease his pace for a safe finish.

**8 | VALENTINO ROSSI**
As usual, found something extra for the race, fighting his way through from 13th place at the end of the first lap. Admitted afterwards that it was a struggle to make the top ten and his best lap was the tenth fastest of the race.

**9 | JACK MILLER**
Felt that he was continuing the return to form he had started during Silverstone practice and Misano qualifying. Made it into Q2 for the first time since Le Mans. Spent the last few laps of the race trying to keep Rossi behind him.

**10 | MAVERICK VIÑALES**
Found it difficult to maintain his focus, Yamaha's painful lack of progress affecting him more than his older team-mate. And once again, his FP4 pace disappeared on Sunday. Could the Moto2 rubber really be the culprit?

**11 | FRANCO MORBIDELLI**
Qualified 13th but was given a six-place grid penalty for riding slowly on the racing line in Q1. Mounted an impressive comeback from 18th position on lap one, riding the 11th fastest lap of the race.

**12 | TAKAAKI NAKAGAMI**
Made it into Q2 for the first time since Germany and didn't waste the opportunity. Got a good start and found a gap in the first-turn chaos to move further up the order. Had good battles with Espargaró and Rossi.

## RACE LAP CHART

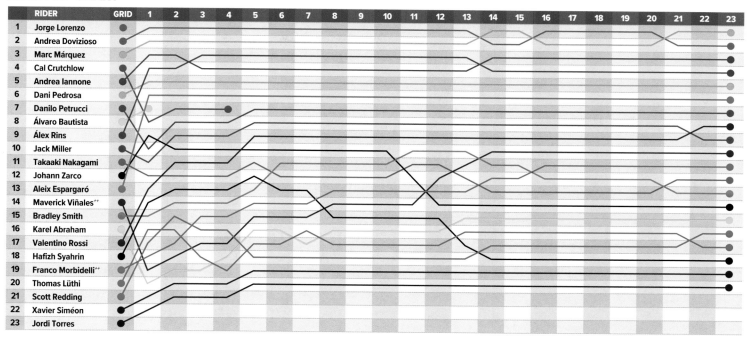

| | RIDER | GRID | 1 | 2 | 3 | 4 | 5 | 6 | 7 | 8 | 9 | 10 | 11 | 12 | 13 | 14 | 15 | 16 | 17 | 18 | 19 | 20 | 21 | 22 | 23 |
|---|---|---|---|---|---|---|---|---|---|---|---|---|---|---|---|---|---|---|---|---|---|---|---|---|---|
| 1 | Jorge Lorenzo | | | | | | | | | | | | | | | | | | | | | | | | |
| 2 | Andrea Dovizioso | | | | | | | | | | | | | | | | | | | | | | | | |
| 3 | Marc Márquez | | | | | | | | | | | | | | | | | | | | | | | | |
| 4 | Cal Crutchlow | | | | | | | | | | | | | | | | | | | | | | | | |
| 5 | Andrea Iannone | | | | | | | | | | | | | | | | | | | | | | | | |
| 6 | Dani Pedrosa | | | | | | | | | | | | | | | | | | | | | | | | |
| 7 | Danilo Petrucci | | | | | | | | | | | | | | | | | | | | | | | | |
| 8 | Álvaro Bautista | | | | | | | | | | | | | | | | | | | | | | | | |
| 9 | Álex Rins | | | | | | | | | | | | | | | | | | | | | | | | |
| 10 | Jack Miller | | | | | | | | | | | | | | | | | | | | | | | | |
| 11 | Takaaki Nakagami | | | | | | | | | | | | | | | | | | | | | | | | |
| 12 | Johann Zarco | | | | | | | | | | | | | | | | | | | | | | | | |
| 13 | Aleix Espargaró | | | | | | | | | | | | | | | | | | | | | | | | |
| 14 | Maverick Viñales[++] | | | | | | | | | | | | | | | | | | | | | | | | |
| 15 | Bradley Smith | | | | | | | | | | | | | | | | | | | | | | | | |
| 16 | Karel Abraham | | | | | | | | | | | | | | | | | | | | | | | | |
| 17 | Valentino Rossi | | | | | | | | | | | | | | | | | | | | | | | | |
| 18 | Hafizh Syahrin | | | | | | | | | | | | | | | | | | | | | | | | |
| 19 | Franco Morbidelli[++] | | | | | | | | | | | | | | | | | | | | | | | | |
| 20 | Thomas Lüthi | | | | | | | | | | | | | | | | | | | | | | | | |
| 21 | Scott Redding | | | | | | | | | | | | | | | | | | | | | | | | |
| 22 | Xavier Siméon | | | | | | | | | | | | | | | | | | | | | | | | |
| 23 | Jordi Torres | | | | | | | | | | | | | | | | | | | | | | | | |

## RACE CLASSIFICATION AFTER 23 LAPS = 116.771 KM

| | RIDER | NAT | TEAM | MACHINE | TIME | + GAP | TYRES |
|---|---|---|---|---|---|---|---|
| 1 | Marc Márquez | SPA | Repsol Honda Team | HONDA | 41'55.949 | | H/S |
| 2 | Andrea Dovizioso | ITA | Ducati Team | DUCATI | 41'56.597 | 0.648 | H/H |
| 3 | Andrea Iannone | ITA | Team SUZUKI ECSTAR | SUZUKI | 41'57.208 | 1.259 | M/S |
| 4 | Álex Rins | SPA | Team SUZUKI ECSTAR | SUZUKI | 41'58.587 | 2.638 | H/S |
| 5 | Dani Pedrosa | SPA | Repsol Honda Team | HONDA | 42'01.223 | 5.274 | H/H |
| 6 | Aleix Espargaró | SPA | Aprilia Racing Team Gresini | APRILIA | 42'05.345 | 9.396 | M/S |
| 7 | Danilo Petrucci | ITA | Alma Pramac Racing | DUCATI | 42'10.234 | 14.285 | H/H |
| 8 | Valentino Rossi | ITA | Movistar Yamaha MotoGP | YAMAHA | 42'11.148 | 15.199 | M/H |
| 9 | Jack Miller | AUS | Alma Pramac Racing | DUCATI | 42'12.324 | 16.375 | H/H |
| 10 | Maverick Viñales | SPA | Movistar Yamaha MotoGP | YAMAHA | 42'18.406 | 22.457 | H/H |
| 11 | Franco Morbidelli | ITA | EG 0,0 Marc VDS | HONDA | 42'22.974 | 27.025 | H/H |
| 12 | Takaaki Nakagami | JPN | LCR Honda IDEMITSU | HONDA | 42'23.906 | 27.957 | H/H |
| 13 | Bradley Smith | GBR | Red Bull KTM Factory Racing | KTM | 42'24.770 | 28.821 | H/H |
| 14 | Johann Zarco | FRA | Monster Yamaha Tech 3 | YAMAHA | 42'28.294 | 32.345 | M/S |
| 15 | Karel Abraham | CZE | Ángel Nieto Team | DUCATI | 42'33.588 | 37.639 | H/S |
| 16 | Scott Redding | GBR | Aprilia Racing Team Gresini | APRILIA | 42'35.534 | 39.585 | H/S |
| 17 | Thomas Lüthi | SWI | EG 0,0 Marc VDS | HONDA | 42'36.712 | 40.763 | H/H |
| 18 | Hafizh Syahrin | MAL | Monster Yamaha Tech 3 | YAMAHA | 42'52.245 | 56.296 | M/S |
| 19 | Xavier Siméon | GER | Reale Avintia Racing | DUCATI | 42'54.930 | 58.981 | M/H |
| 20 | Jordi Torres | SPA | Reale Avintia Racing | DUCATI | 42'55.462 | 59.513 | M/H |
| NC | Cal Crutchlow | GBR | LCR Honda CASTROL | HONDA | 7'21.099 | 19 laps | H/H |
| NC | Álvaro Bautista | SPA | Ángel Nieto Team | DUCATI | 1'53.554 | 22 laps | M/S |
| NC | Jorge Lorenzo | SPA | Ducati Team | DUCATI | | | S/H |

++ FIM MotoGP Stewards grid penalty for Franco Morbidelli and Maverick Viñales

## CHAMPIONSHIP STANDINGS

| | RIDER | NAT | TEAM | POINTS |
|---|---|---|---|---|
| 1 | Marc Márquez | SPA | Repsol Honda Team | 246 |
| 2 | Andrea Dovizioso | ITA | Ducati Team | 174 |
| 3 | Valentino Rossi | ITA | Movistar Yamaha MotoGP | 159 |
| 4 | Jorge Lorenzo | SPA | Ducati Team | 130 |
| 5 | Maverick Viñales | SPA | Movistar Yamaha MotoGP | 130 |
| 6 | Cal Crutchlow | GBR | LCR Honda CASTROL | 119 |
| 7 | Danilo Petrucci | ITA | Alma Pramac Racing | 119 |
| 8 | Johann Zarco | FRA | Monster Yamaha Tech 3 | 112 |
| 9 | Andrea Iannone | ITA | Team SUZUKI ECSTAR | 108 |
| 10 | Álex Rins | SPA | Team SUZUKI ECSTAR | 92 |
| 11 | Dani Pedrosa | SPA | Repsol Honda Team | 87 |
| 12 | Jack Miller | AUS | Alma Pramac Racing | 68 |
| 13 | Álvaro Bautista | SPA | Ángel Nieto Team | 64 |
| 14 | Tito Rabat | SPA | Reale Avintia Racing | 35 |
| 15 | Pol Espargaró | SPA | Red Bull KTM Factory Racing | 32 |
| 16 | Franco Morbidelli | ITA | EG 0,0 Marc VDS | 31 |
| 17 | Aleix Espargaró | SPA | Aprilia Racing Team Gresini | 29 |
| 18 | Hafizh Syahrin | MAL | Monster Yamaha Tech 3 | 24 |
| 19 | Bradley Smith | GBR | Red Bull KTM Factory Racing | 18 |
| 20 | Takaaki Nakagami | JPN | LCR Honda IDEMITSU | 18 |
| 21 | Scott Redding | GBR | Aprilia Racing Team Gresini | 12 |
| 22 | Mika Kallio | FIN | Red Bull KTM Factory Racing | 6 |
| 23 | Karel Abraham | CZE | Ángel Nieto Team | 5 |
| 24 | Michele Pirro | ITA | Ducati Team | 1 |
| 25 | Thomas Lüthi | SWI | EG 0,0 Marc VDS | |
| 26 | Stefan Bradl | GER | Honda Racing Corporation | |
| 27 | Xavier Siméon | GER | Reale Avintia Racing | |
| 28 | Sylvain Guintoli | FRA | Team SUZUKI ECSTAR | |
| 29 | Jordi Torres | SPA | Reale Avintia Racing | |
| 30 | Christophe Ponsson | FRA | Reale Avintia Racing | |

**13 BRADLEY SMITH**
Once again, found himself all alone in the KTM garage. Raced the latest spec of the reverse-crankshaft-rotation engine and had moved from 15th to tenth by mid-race. But when his rear tyre dropped he suffered more than most.

**14 JOHANN ZARCO**
The Frenchman's worst finish of the year so far came at the end of a difficult weekend for all the Yamahas. He tried to go with Petrucci but couldn't find enough acceleration grip, despite adjusting his riding technique.

**15 KAREL ABRAHAM**
Scored his first point since Barcelona. Had a lot of work to do after a hard pass by Rossi lost him several places. Passed Syahrin, Lüthi and Redding to get the last point. Like everyone, found the Moto2 rubber had reduced grip.

**16 SCOTT REDDING**
Improved his braking performance into the race but found it impossible to improve corner-exit grip. Worked hard to make fewer mistakes and keep things smooth but didn't have enough traction to either attack or defend.

**17 THOMAS LÜTHI**
Another who made the best out of the mess at the first corner to gain several positions. Was happy with his pace until the rear tyre dropped and then began chattering in the final laps. Missed his first MotoGP point by three seconds.

**18 HAFIZH SYAHRIN**
Made a good start and was determined to stay with Rossi, Morbidelli, Nakagami and Zarco. Lost rear grip sooner than he had expected, so he couldn't stop or turn the bike as he wanted and quickly dropped towards the back.

**19 XAVIER SIMÉON**
Rode Tito Rabat's GP17 for the second consecutive race but once again couldn't find a way to make the newer machine work for him. Found he could turn the bike better but couldn't get the power down fast enough.

**20 JORDI TORRES**
Reale Avintia hired the World Superbike rider and Moto2 podium man after its brief dalliance with Christophe Ponsson. He did an excellent job, adapting from Pirellis to Michelins, with a best lap 2.7 seconds slower than Márquez's.

**DNF CAL CRUTCHLOW**
One of those who came off worse due to Lorenzo's accident – had to shut off to miss the flying Spaniard and that lost him several places. Rode a good pace until he had the same turn-one crash that Márquez had had in warm-up.

**DNF ÁLVARO BAUTISTA**
Had high expectations after qualifying eighth fastest, but his hopes were dashed on the second lap of the race when he lost the front into turn 14, the first part of the bus-stop chicane before the main straight.

**DNF JORGE LORENZO**
Scored his first pole hat-trick since 2012 and had good reason to believe he could break away. Which is why Márquez had to get past him. Lost the rear when he got on the throttle in an attempt to avoid losing more positions.

# TRADING PLACES IN THAILAND

***Márquez and Dovizioso reversed roles, while Yamaha
were happy to be back in the game***

As usual, there was plenty of head-scratching in the factory Yamaha garage. But this time the question was different. This time they weren't asking, 'Why are we so slow?', but instead, 'Why are we so fast?'

The speed of the Yamahas remained a mystery to many throughout the first Thai Grand Prix, during which MotoGP fell in love with Thailand and Thailand fell in love with MotoGP. Sadly, the weekend went ahead without Jorge Lorenzo, who suffered a huge highside in FP2, which left him with a broken left radius bone.

This was always going to be a close-run race, with the short, tight layout offering nowhere to find a real advantage and Michelin telling all the riders to use the hard rear. The fastest 17 in free practice were covered by 0.977 seconds. Marc Márquez took pole position by one hundredth of a second from a revitalised Valentino Rossi; but pole didn't come easily. The reigning champion crashed at high speed in FP3 – his third big practice fall in as many races – and had to go through Q1. In the end he became the first Q1 graduate to take pole.

The fans got a sizzling race, which followed the now customary format: a leading gaggle running a steady pace, saving their tyres for later, then the fastest few increasing the tempo, splitting

*Echoes of Kevin Schwantz and Wayne Rainey: Dovizioso
out-brakes Márquez at the final corner, but this time it was
Márquez's turn to counterattack*

**MAIN** | Half-distance and the leading quartet are already laying rubber. Dovizioso admitted he was wrong to lead so much of the race: he should've taken the chance to study Márquez

**BOTTOM, LEFT-RIGHT** | Crutchlow ran with the leaders until he had to play a balancing act with his tyres — temperature increasing at the front, grip decreasing at the rear; Rossi was back with a bang, much to the delight of the local fans; to the delight of the riders, the fans supported all of them with equal enthusiasm

## 'TODAY WE SWAPPED STYLES — I WAS DOVI AND HE WAS MARC!'
*MARC MÁRQUEZ*

the lead group and readying themselves for the inevitable last-lap dogfight.

The fast few on this occasion were Márquez, Rossi, Andrea Dovizioso, Cal Crutchlow and Maverick Viñales. Márquez led, then Rossi, who swept past the Honda on the main straight. "I was losing two tenths accelerating out of the first and last corners," explained the world champion, whose Repsol Honda crew had for once struggled to find their way through the Magneti Marelli maze.

Crutchlow was the first of the few to wave the white flag, when he lost rear grip. As the Briton slipped backwards Viñales moved forwards, attacking his team-mate with seven laps to go and quickly closing the gap on the leading duo. But the Yamaha pair weren't the only comeback artists. Dani Pedrosa was shining brightly once again. Down in 11th place after three laps he was about to challenge Viñales and Rossi for a podium result when he lost the front on lap 19.

Meanwhile, Márquez seemed happy to let Dovizioso do the hard work. This wasn't an ideal strategy for either, because Dovizioso wasn't able to study his rival, while Márquez's front tyre overheated in the Ducati's burning-hot draft.

With three laps to go the fuse was lit, the leaders went for each other and swapped position four times in a few corners. With two laps to go Márquez was back in front, but he was running out of grip, which allowed Dovizioso to get better drive out of turn 11, get level and out-brake the leader into the final turn 12. On the last lap Márquez made a heavy block pass at turn five and tried to fend off another last-corner attack by eking more speed out of turn 11. So when Dovizioso launched his do-or-die effort he did so from just behind.

Both headed into the final corner with rear wheels in the air. Now it was Dovizioso's turn to block pass, but he couldn't quite get his GP18 stopped. And Márquez knew it. The youngster lifted his RC213V upright for an instant, applied the brakes again and scrubbed off more speed, so when they got into the corner Dovizioso was still on the side of his tyres, while Márquez was able to turn his bike and win the race to the finish line.

Márquez had done to Dovizioso what Dovizioso did to Márquez in Austria and Japan in 2017 and in Qatar in 2018.

"Today we swapped styles — I was Dovi and he was Marc!" laughed Márquez. "It's nice because we have some great battles and they always go to the last corner. I always try to give everything to the last metres, but Dovizioso is the same. We always respect each other, but we have different riding styles and different bikes, so we have different strong points, which allows us to play in a good way."

Márquez rode like he always does, as if the title was in jeopardy, when of course the only way he might jeopardise his crown was by crashing out. But he knows no other way.

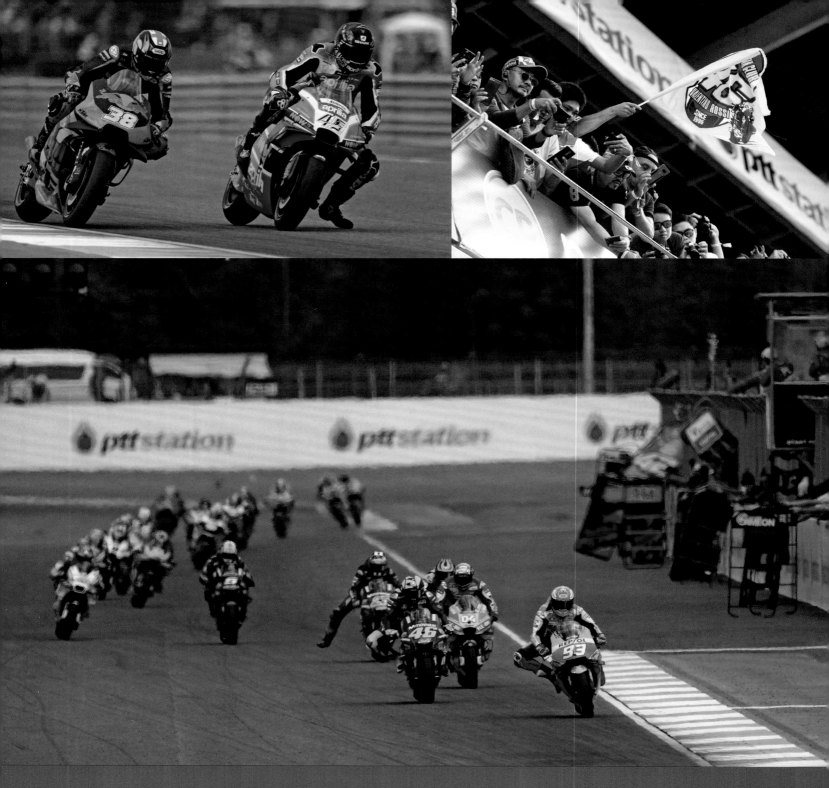

## MOTOGP'S SOUTH EAST ASIAN BOOM

Motorcycles are a bigger deal in South East Asia than anywhere else in the world. For several decades the region has used bikes, scooters and underbones for cheap transport, but now people are embracing the powered two wheeler as a cult machine.

Sales figures are huge: six million units annually in Indonesia, almost two million in Thailand, almost half a million in Malaysia. No wonder there's such enthusiasm for MotoGP, with more and more local riders in the Grand Prix paddock and the region's first MotoGP team preparing for 2019.

Dovizioso knew the championship was effectively out of reach, so he was already looking forward to 2019. "In the past we couldn't even fight for the podium at tracks like this where tyre consumption is so high, so I think we have made a huge step," said the Italian, who had tried but failed to make the break at two-thirds distance. "We aren't racing for the championship; we are racing to try to get the maximum results and to develop the bike for next year."

Viñales and Rossi were so close yet so far. The ducking and diving at the front had allowed them to catch the leading duo, Viñales ready to take advantage if there was a collision in the last-lap sort-out. In fact, the closest call was between the two Yamahas, when Rossi apparently attempted a divebomb move at the last corner and nearly rammed his team-mate.

The secret of Yamaha's speed turned out to be a special Michelin rear slick, with a stiffer carcass to resist the track surface and tropical heat. "We made some changes to the bike but for sure the rear tyre helped us a lot to turn," reported Viñales.

Rossi shared the same opinion. "I hope with all my heart that we can be strong at other tracks but unfortunately I think we are fast here because of the tyres and the track," he said.

Michelin's Buriram special also helped Tech 3 Yamaha riders Johann Zarco and Hafizh Syahrin, who finished top independent-team rider and top rookie.

**CLOCKWISE FROM TOP LEFT** | *Redding and Smith had a huge battle for the final point; the wonderful Thai fans made the first Thai GP an extra-special event; Torres impressed everyone; a stiffer rear Michelin revitalised Yamaha; Viñales smiling again with mechanics Ian Gilpin and Javier Ullate; Márquez and Rossi lead the early charge*

Riders and teams knew they could expect a special welcome at Thailand's first Grand Prix after they had visited Buriram for preseason testing, when several thousand fans turned up to see the riders and bikes with their own eyes for the first time. The race weekend was a sell-out and had the feel of a rock and roll festival, with a huge fan village constructed next to the track, where the fun continued into the night. "It's like a motorbike party!" said Márquez, who got in the mood by driving a tuk-tuk taxi around Bangkok during a pre-race media event.

The crowd was utterly unpartisan, a welcome relief from the fanatics who appear at some other races. "It's nice to see fans wearing shirts in red, yellow, or any colour they want, but supporting all the riders and not complaining about any of them," said Andrea Dovizioso. "In Europe, they've forgotten this."

# 15 | THAILAND

# RACE RESULTS

**WINNER** | MARC MÁRQUEZ

**CIRCUIT LENGTH** | 4.6 KM | 2.83 MILES

**NO. OF LAPS** | 26

**RACE DISTANCE** | 118.4 KM | 73.6 MILES

**CIRCUIT RECORD LAP** | 1'31.471 | 179.2 KM/H
MARC MÁRQUEZ (2018)

**CIRCUIT BEST LAP** | 1'30.031 | 182.0 KM/H
MARC MÁRQUEZ (2018)

**RACE CONDITION** | DRY

**AIR** | 32°C

**HUMIDITY** | 46%

**GROUND** | 49°C

**OFFICIAL** TIMEKEEPER

**OFFICIAL** MotoGP™ CLASS TYRE

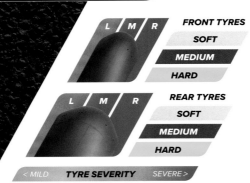

FRONT TYRES
SOFT
MEDIUM
HARD

REAR TYRES
SOFT
MEDIUM
HARD

< MILD   TYRE SEVERITY   SEVERE >

Start Line
Sectors
S  Speed Trap
FL  Finish Line

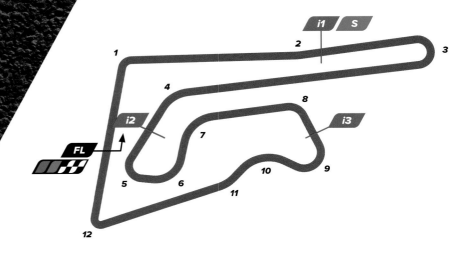

## QUALIFYING RESULTS

| | RIDER | NAT | TEAM | MACHINE | QP/TIME | | GAP 1ST/PREV | |
|---|---|---|---|---|---|---|---|---|
| 1 | Marc Márquez** | SPA | Repsol Honda Team | HONDA | Q2 | 1'30.088 | | |
| 2 | Valentino Rossi | ITA | Movistar Yamaha MotoGP | YAMAHA | Q2 | 1'30.099 | 0.011 | 0.011 |
| 3 | Andrea Dovizioso | ITA | Ducati Team | DUCATI | Q2 | 1'30.227 | 0.139 | 0.128 |
| 4 | Maverick Viñales | SPA | Movistar Yamaha MotoGP | YAMAHA | Q2 | 1'30.328 | 0.240 | 0.101 |
| 5 | Cal Crutchlow | GBR | LCR Honda CASTROL | HONDA | Q2 | 1'30.356 | 0.268 | 0.028 |
| 6 | Andrea Iannone | ITA | Team SUZUKI ECSTAR | SUZUKI | Q2 | 1'30.419 | 0.331 | 0.063 |
| 7 | Dani Pedrosa | SPA | Repsol Honda Team | HONDA | Q2 | 1'30.458 | 0.370 | 0.039 |
| 8 | Johann Zarco | FRA | Monster Yamaha Tech 3 | YAMAHA | Q2 | 1'30.471 | 0.383 | 0.013 |
| 9 | Danilo Petrucci | ITA | Alma Pramac Racing | DUCATI | Q2 | 1'30.599 | 0.511 | 0.128 |
| 10 | Jack Miller | AUS | Alma Pramac Racing | DUCATI | Q2 | 1'30.660 | 0.572 | 0.061 |
| 11 | Álex Rins** | SPA | Team SUZUKI ECSTAR | SUZUKI | Q2 | 1'30.738 | 0.650 | 0.078 |
| 12 | Álvaro Bautista | SPA | Ángel Nieto Team | DUCATI | Q2 | 1'30.976 | 0.888 | 0.238 |
| 13 | Franco Morbidelli | ITA | EG 0,0 Marc VDS | HONDA | Q1 | 1'30.923 | *0.892 | 0.002 |
| 14 | Takaaki Nakagami | JPN | LCR Honda IDEMITSU | HONDA | Q1 | 1'30.995 | *0.964 | 0.07 |
| 15 | Bradley Smith | GBR | Red Bull KTM Factory Racing | KTM | Q1 | 1'31.207 | *1.176 | 0.212 |
| 16 | Aleix Espargaró | SPA | Aprilia Racing Team Gresini | APRILIA | Q1 | 1'31.243 | *1.212 | 0.036 |
| 17 | Karel Abraham | CZE | Ángel Nieto Team | DUCATI | Q1 | 1'31.374 | *1.343 | 0.131 |
| 18 | Hafizh Syahrin | MAL | Monster Yamaha Tech 3 | YAMAHA | Q1 | 1'31.389 | *1.358 | 0.015 |
| 19 | Pol Espargaró | SPA | Red Bull KTM Factory Racing | KTM | Q1 | 1'31.399 | *1.368 | 0.010 |
| 20 | Xavier Siméon | GER | Reale Avintia Racing | DUCATI | Q1 | 1'31.686 | *1.655 | 0.287 |
| 21 | Jordi Torres | SPA | Reale Avintia Racing | DUCATI | Q1 | 1'31.819 | *1.788 | 0.133 |
| 22 | Thomas Lüthi | SWI | EG 0,0 Marc VDS | HONDA | Q1 | 1'31.830 | *1.799 | 0.011 |
| 23 | Scott Redding | GBR | Aprilia Racing Team Gresini | APRILIA | Q1 | 1'31.835 | *1.804 | 0.005 |

*Gap to the fastest rider in the Q1 session
** Went forward from Q1 to Q2

**1 | MARC MÁRQUEZ**
Paid back Dovizioso for their previous last-corner sort-outs. Ran out of tyre at the end but rode around the problem as only he knows how, despite electronics issues. Anyone else would've settled for 20 points, but settling isn't in his vocabulary.

**2 | ANDREA DOVIZIOSO**
Most riders would've been gutted at losing out at the last corner. But not the Italian, who saw the positives: saving the GP18's tyres to the end, which would have been impossible without recent improvements.

**3 | MAVERICK VIÑALES**
Michelin's stiffer rear slick, plus minor post-Aragon improvements to traction control and anti-wheelie put Yamaha back in contention for the first time in ages. But Viñales hadn't quite built up enough confidence to attack the leaders at the final corner.

**4 | VALENTINO ROSSI**
Closest he's been to pole position for a long, long time, and was able to back up his qualifying performance with impressive race pace. But like his team-mate, it had been a while since he had ridden the outer limits.

**5 | JOHANN ZARCO**
Like Viñales and Rossi, the Frenchman was revitalised by Michelin's stiffer rear slick, which gave him a better contact patch to use the M1's cornering speed. Managed to get the better of Crutchlow and Rins for his best result since May's Jerez GP.

**6 | ÁLEX RINS**
Tried very hard to go with the leaders in the early stages and in doing so he over-stressed his front tyre which left him unable to attack or defend. But in the end was very happy with another fast and consistent result.

**7 | CAL CRUTCHLOW**
Made the early running with the leaders and looked like he had the pace to stay with them. But after the first 15 laps he lost a lot of rear grip. He attempted to compensate by making up time into corners, but this only overheated his front tyre.

**8 | ÁLVARO BAUTISTA**
Came through from 12th place on the grid and could have done better if he hadn't lost time when he collided with Morbidelli. Very happy to finish just six seconds behind the winner on a year-old motorcycle.

**9 | DANILO PETRUCCI**
A third-row start compromised his race. Despite imperfect rear grip he pushed hard, overtook Rins and Miller, made a mistake that cost him three places, then regrouped and still had enough tyre life to take Iannone and repass his team-mate.

**10 | JACK MILLER**
Michelin advised the entire grid to run the hard rear tyre. Like many, Miller didn't feel good with the tyre in Buriram's five left-handers. Enjoyed his battle with Petrucci, Iannone and Bautista, but only bettered Iannone.

**11 | ANDREA IANNONE**
Wasted his second-row start by losing several places in the early laps. Spent most of the race chasing Petrucci. Briefly got ahead of the Italian, plus Bautista and Miller into eighth, then slipped back again. Still wanted more braking stability from the GSX-RR.

**12 | HAFIZH SYAHRIN**
This was an important weekend for the Malaysian rookie who had lost his way at previous races. His engine overheated, so he avoided drafting rivals, but he regained confidence in the front and could attack again.

## RACE LAP CHART

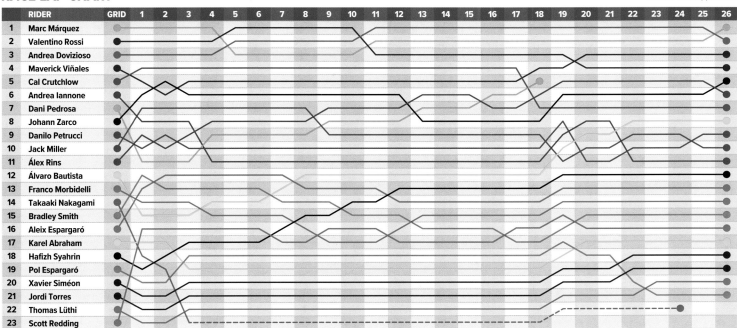

| | RIDER | GRID | 1 | 2 | 3 | 4 | 5 | 6 | 7 | 8 | 9 | 10 | 11 | 12 | 13 | 14 | 15 | 16 | 17 | 18 | 19 | 20 | 21 | 22 | 23 | 24 | 25 | 26 |
|---|---|---|---|---|---|---|---|---|---|---|---|---|---|---|---|---|---|---|---|---|---|---|---|---|---|---|---|---|
| 1 | Marc Márquez | | | | | | | | | | | | | | | | | | | | | | | | | | | |
| 2 | Valentino Rossi | | | | | | | | | | | | | | | | | | | | | | | | | | | |
| 3 | Andrea Dovizioso | | | | | | | | | | | | | | | | | | | | | | | | | | | |
| 4 | Maverick Viñales | | | | | | | | | | | | | | | | | | | | | | | | | | | |
| 5 | Cal Crutchlow | | | | | | | | | | | | | | | | | | | | | | | | | | | |
| 6 | Andrea Iannone | | | | | | | | | | | | | | | | | | | | | | | | | | | |
| 7 | Dani Pedrosa | | | | | | | | | | | | | | | | | | | | | | | | | | | |
| 8 | Johann Zarco | | | | | | | | | | | | | | | | | | | | | | | | | | | |
| 9 | Danilo Petrucci | | | | | | | | | | | | | | | | | | | | | | | | | | | |
| 10 | Jack Miller | | | | | | | | | | | | | | | | | | | | | | | | | | | |
| 11 | Álex Rins | | | | | | | | | | | | | | | | | | | | | | | | | | | |
| 12 | Álvaro Bautista | | | | | | | | | | | | | | | | | | | | | | | | | | | |
| 13 | Franco Morbidelli | | | | | | | | | | | | | | | | | | | | | | | | | | | |
| 14 | Takaaki Nakagami | | | | | | | | | | | | | | | | | | | | | | | | | | | |
| 15 | Bradley Smith | | | | | | | | | | | | | | | | | | | | | | | | | | | |
| 16 | Aleix Espargaró | | | | | | | | | | | | | | | | | | | | | | | | | | | |
| 17 | Karel Abraham | | | | | | | | | | | | | | | | | | | | | | | | | | | |
| 18 | Hafizh Syahrin | | | | | | | | | | | | | | | | | | | | | | | | | | | |
| 19 | Pol Espargaró | | | | | | | | | | | | | | | | | | | | | | | | | | | |
| 20 | Xavier Siméon | | | | | | | | | | | | | | | | | | | | | | | | | | | |
| 21 | Jordi Torres | | | | | | | | | | | | | | | | | | | | | | | | | | | |
| 22 | Thomas Lüthi | | | | | | | | | | | | | | | | | | | | | | | | | | | |
| 23 | Scott Redding | | | | | | | | | | | | | | | | | | | | | | | | | | | |

## RACE CLASSIFICATION AFTER 26 LAPS = 118.404 KM

| | RIDER | NAT | TEAM | MACHINE | TIME | + GAP | TYRES |
|---|---|---|---|---|---|---|---|
| 1 | Marc Márquez | SPA | Repsol Honda Team | HONDA | 39'55.722 | | H/H |
| 2 | Andrea Dovizioso | ITA | Ducati Team | DUCATI | 39'55.837 | 0.115 | H/H |
| 3 | Maverick Viñales | SPA | Movistar Yamaha MotoGP | YAMAHA | 39'55.992 | 0.270 | H/H |
| 4 | Valentino Rossi | ITA | Movistar Yamaha MotoGP | YAMAHA | 39'57.286 | 1.564 | H/H |
| 5 | Johann Zarco | FRA | Monster Yamaha Tech 3 | YAMAHA | 39'58.469 | 2.747 | M/H |
| 6 | Álex Rins | SPA | Team SUZUKI ECSTAR | SUZUKI | 39'58.745 | 3.023 | H/H |
| 7 | Cal Crutchlow | GBR | LCR Honda CASTROL | HONDA | 40'02.242 | 6.520 | H/H |
| 8 | Álvaro Bautista | SPA | Ángel Nieto Team | DUCATI | 40'02.413 | 6.691 | M/H |
| 9 | Danilo Petrucci | ITA | Alma Pramac Racing | DUCATI | 40'05.666 | 9.944 | H/H |
| 10 | Jack Miller | AUS | Alma Pramac Racing | DUCATI | 40'06.799 | 11.077 | M/H |
| 11 | Andrea Iannone | ITA | Team SUZUKI ECSTAR | SUZUKI | 40'11.210 | 15.488 | M/H |
| 12 | Hafizh Syahrin | MAL | Monster Yamaha Tech 3 | YAMAHA | 40'13.413 | 17.691 | H/H |
| 13 | Aleix Espargaró | SPA | Aprilia Racing Team Gresini | APRILIA | 40'17.135 | 21.413 | H/S |
| 14 | Franco Morbidelli | ITA | EG 0,0 Marc VDS | HONDA | 40'18.524 | 22.802 | H/H |
| 15 | Bradley Smith | GBR | Red Bull KTM Factory Racing | KTM | 40'19.350 | 23.628 | H/H |
| 16 | Scott Redding | GBR | Aprilia Racing Team Gresini | APRILIA | 40'19.526 | 23.804 | H/H |
| 17 | Karel Abraham | CZE | Ángel Nieto Team | DUCATI | 40'28.229 | 32.507 | H/H |
| 18 | Xavier Siméon | GER | Reale Avintia Racing | DUCATI | 40'32.938 | 37.216 | M/H |
| 19 | Jordi Torres | SPA | Reale Avintia Racing | DUCATI | 40'34.926 | 39.204 | M/H |
| 20 | Thomas Lüthi | SWI | EG 0,0 Marc VDS | HONDA | 40'35.143 | 39.421 | H/H |
| 21 | Pol Espargaró | SPA | Red Bull KTM Factory Racing | KTM | 40'49.110 | 53.388 | H/H |
| 22 | Takaaki Nakagami | JPN | LCR Honda IDEMITSU | HONDA | 40'21.117 | 2 laps | H/H |
| NC | Dani Pedrosa | SPA | Repsol Honda Team | HONDA | 27'40.766 | 8 laps | H/H |

## CHAMPIONSHIP STANDINGS

| | RIDER | NAT | TEAM | POINTS |
|---|---|---|---|---|
| 1 | Marc Márquez | SPA | Repsol Honda Team | 271 |
| 2 | Andrea Dovizioso | ITA | Ducati Team | 194 |
| 3 | Valentino Rossi | ITA | Movistar Yamaha MotoGP | 172 |
| 4 | Maverick Viñales | SPA | Movistar Yamaha MotoGP | 146 |
| 5 | Jorge Lorenzo | SPA | Ducati Team | 130 |
| 6 | Cal Crutchlow | GBR | LCR Honda CASTROL | 128 |
| 7 | Danilo Petrucci | ITA | Alma Pramac Racing | 126 |
| 8 | Johann Zarco | FRA | Monster Yamaha Tech 3 | 123 |
| 9 | Andrea Iannone | ITA | Team SUZUKI ECSTAR | 113 |
| 10 | Álex Rins | SPA | Team SUZUKI ECSTAR | 102 |
| 11 | Dani Pedrosa | SPA | Repsol Honda Team | 87 |
| 12 | Jack Miller | AUS | Alma Pramac Racing | 74 |
| 13 | Álvaro Bautista | SPA | Ángel Nieto Team | 72 |
| 14 | Tito Rabat | SPA | Reale Avintia Racing | 35 |
| 15 | Franco Morbidelli | ITA | EG 0,0 Marc VDS | 33 |
| 16 | Aleix Espargaró | SPA | Aprilia Racing Team Gresini | 32 |
| 17 | Pol Espargaró | SPA | Red Bull KTM Factory Racing | 32 |
| 18 | Hafizh Syahrin | MAL | Monster Yamaha Tech 3 | 28 |
| 19 | Bradley Smith | GBR | Red Bull KTM Factory Racing | 19 |
| 20 | Takaaki Nakagami | JPN | LCR Honda IDEMITSU | 18 |
| 21 | Scott Redding | GBR | Aprilia Racing Team Gresini | 12 |
| 22 | Mika Kallio | FIN | Red Bull KTM Factory Racing | 6 |
| 23 | Karel Abraham | CZE | Ángel Nieto Team | 5 |
| 24 | Michele Pirro | ITA | Ducati Team | 1 |
| 25 | Thomas Lüthi | SWI | EG 0,0 Marc VDS | |
| 26 | Stefan Bradl | GER | Honda Racing Corporation | |
| 27 | Xavier Siméon | GER | Reale Avintia Racing | |
| 28 | Jordi Torres | SPA | Reale Avintia Racing | |
| 29 | Sylvain Guintoli | FRA | Team SUZUKI ECSTAR | |
| 30 | Christophe Ponsson | FRA | Reale Avintia Racing | |

**13 | ALEIX ESPARGARÓ**
The only rider not to heed Michelin's advice to use the hard rear, found the soft worked perfectly. Chased Syahrin, lapping just 0.5 seconds off Márquez's best, but ultimately couldn't keep up with the rookie.

**14 | FRANCO MORBIDELLI**
Locked in a duel with Syahrin for the rookie of the year prize, Morbidelli was beaten by his rival for the first time in three races. Had issues with top speed and braking performance.

**15 | BRADLEY SMITH**
Made it into the points for the seventh time in 14 races, after a battle royal with Redding in the final laps, which proved how deep the fight goes in MotoGP. His hard rear tyre didn't feel great at first, but he realised most riders were having similar issues.

**16 | SCOTT REDDING**
Missed the last point by 0.176 seconds but was happy with his pace, after a crucial set-up change in warm-up. Made a stunning start from the back of the grid which gained

**17 | KAREL ABRAHAM**
Had a scary race due to a high-speed wobble that kept knocking back the brake pads, requiring him to constantly pump the brakes and sometimes lock the front tyre. Ran off the track on several occasions but managed to keep it out of the gravel.

**18 | XAVIER SIMÉON**
Started from the seventh row of the grid and had a clear track ahead, working hard throughout to keep substitute team-mate Torres behind him. Was content with his speed and rated this as his best race so far.

**19 | JORDI TORRES**
Worked well and rode well to reduce the gap to the winner from 59 seconds on his Aragon debut to 38 seconds. Found managing tyre wear and changing fuel maps a new challenge and never quite had the courage to show team-mate Siméon a wheel.

**20 | THOMAS LÜTHI**
Had an eventful race. Made a big mistake on the first lap that took him off track, onto the grass and into last place. Then lost more time when Nakagami crashed. Finally found enough pace to nearly catch Torres

**21 | POL ESPARGARÓ**
Remarkably this was his first finish since Assen. Had finally had his left collarbone plated (he broke it at Brno and again at Aragon) and understandably found the going particularly tough in the tropical conditions. Was happy to see the flag.

**22 | TAKAAKI NAKAGAMI**
Crashed at the last corner on the third lap after running in too hot and losing the front. Remounted, returned to the pits for some basic repairs and finished two laps down, with a bent right handlebar and footpeg.

**DNF | DANI PEDROSA**
A bittersweet race. In theory, the heat should've solved his tyre temperature woes, but in fact it took him several laps to get the hard rear to work. Was 11th after three laps and was about to pounce on Viñales when he lost the front with seven laps to go.

**DNS | JORGE LORENZO**
A mystery bike problem in FP2 locked the rear wheel at the end of the main straight, throwing him into orbit. He landed heavily, aggravating his Aragon injuries and fracturing the radius bone in his left arm

Seven steps to heaven – Márquez's Level 7 celebrations for his seventh title included a quick go on a custom-made videogame

# MÁRQUEZ ENTERS THE PANTHEON

**Motegi victory made the Spaniard the youngest rider in history to win five premier-class titles**

Motorcycle racing often looks easy from the outside. Most of us know how nice it feels to ride a motorcycle – sweeping through corners, enjoying the gentle push and pull of the g-forces and feeling that wonderful sensation of rapid motion through space.

Racing is very different: it's raw, vicious and overwhelming to mind and body. It takes someone very special to embrace that tumult and come out the other side smiling. But that was Marc Márquez at Motegi, even as he lay on the ground after the race with a dislocated left shoulder. He probably needed a good lie-down anyway. Ever since he landed in Tokyo he had been rushed from one PR event to another.

The big question that faced Márquez when he arrived at Motegi was could he delight Honda management by wrapping up the title at their home race or could Ducati spoil the party? The question was half answered just minutes into FP1 when Jorge Lorenzo returned to the pits, barely able to operate his GP18's clutch lever. After two tentative laps he knew it would be foolish to continue. "I felt unsafe on the bike," he said. "So if I pushed harder I could make a mistake and crash."

Now it was up to Dovizioso to try repeating his 2017 victory. He certainly had the speed, leading the first three practice sessions. But then everything changed in FP4. "I had a lot of issues with braking stability," said Márquez. "So my crew changed the set-up and I was able to ride in a good way and very consistently, but we did lose something in a few areas, like where I crashed."

The crash was no big deal — the usual case of easing open the throttle in the middle of the corner, removing load from the front tyre and the tyre losing grip. It was another fast crash — third gear at turn seven — so his crew couldn't fix the bike for Q2. He had to qualify with his other bike, with a standard set-up, which is why he ended up sixth fastest, with the front row shared by Dovizioso, Johann Zarco and Jack Miller.

It didn't matter. By the ninth corner of the first lap Márquez was second, behind Dovizioso. And so the game of chess commenced. And then Cal Crutchlow joined in. On lap five he surprised everyone when he sliced past his fellow HRC rider, with the intention of attacking Dovizioso. But the Italian had a surprise in store for him.

"The problem was that Dovi was yo-yoing the pace again," said the Briton. "He does two or three fast laps, then slows the pace, then does two or three fast laps again, then slows again. But there's nothing you can do because it's so difficult to pass."

Unless you're Márquez, of course. Two laps later he retook Crutchlow because Dovizioso was raising his pace, aiming to make good his escape. Márquez went after him, while Valentino Rossi, already suffering from tyre wear, succumbed to Andrea Iannone and Álex Rins. "Valentino destroyed the tyre," said Rins. "So I waited until he was suffering on the exits, then I overtook him because I had better traction."

Now things started to get interesting. Dovizioso's canny quick-slow-quick-quick-slow pace had allowed both Suzukis to catch the lead group, so it was time for decisive action. On lap 14 Márquez surged into the lead at turn nine, only to run wide exiting the hairpin, kicking dirt in the faces of his pursuers. His off-track excursion cost him vital drive, so Dovizioso immediately counter-attacked into the downhill turn 11. But not Crutchlow. "I wanted to keep half a second between me and Marc because I didn't want to run long in one of those braking zones at Honda's home GP with him challenging for the title."

Iannone wanted a podium — the perfect way to 'thank' Suzuki for dropping him. However, he wanted it too badly. The very next lap he locked the rear into the hairpin, the front folded and he was down. Bad news for Iannone was good news for Rins, who now had a clear run on Crutchlow and the rest.

Or at least on Crutchlow, because with nine laps to go Dovizioso decided he had enough tyre left to push harder. He set two fastest laps in a row, which Márquez immediately bettered. The leaders now gapped the others to fight their own duel, just like the previous year. With four laps to go Márquez put another block pass on Dovizioso at turn nine and this time he made it stick, but he couldn't make the break.

Dovizioso planned his victory attack for the penultimate lap. At the hairpin he tried to turn his GP18 earlier than usual, to lift the bike

'I NEEDED EXTRA MOTIVATION, SO I SET THE GOAL OF WINNING THE TITLE WITH MY FIRST MATCH BALL, AT MOTEGI'
MARC MÁRQUEZ

## MÁRQUEZ RIDES JAPAN'S NÜRBURGRING

Marc Márquez was in constant demand in Japan, but he did get to do two very cool PR jobs. On the Wednesday before the race he travelled south of Tokyo with a skeleton crew transporting one of his RC213V race bikes. The destination was the Hakone Turnpike road, known as Japan's Nürburgring. The turnpike is a public toll road that twists and turns through wooded countryside, rising from sea level to more than a thousand metres in a few kilometres.

This was a Red Bull stunt – the Austrian drinks company has a habit of pulling off thrilling PR coups. Márquez rode the turnpike

sooner for better drive, so he could attack Márquez at the bottom of the hill. But he lost the front and crashed. "I wanted to prepare the exit in a better way, but I was too early and asked too much of the front tyre," he said after his first DNF since Barcelona.

At the start of the last lap Márquez saw "DOVI OUT" on his pit board and knew he was champion. "I was very happy, but then disappointed because Dovi deserved to be on the podium — he's ridden an incredible race and season."

Crutchlow crossed the line 1.5 seconds back, with Rins on his rear wheel; another sign that Suzuki have overtaken Yamaha. Rossi was a distant fourth, after nearly succumbing to Álvaro Bautista who had charged through from 11th on lap one.

Yamaha's success at Buriram, with a stiffer rear tyre, had indeed been a mirage. "The current tyres are very soft," explained Rossi. "It looks like the other manufacturers work in a better way to use these soft tyres. The Yamaha needs something harder, so when we have a harder tyre like at Buriram it's an advantage for us."

And what of Márquez's dislocated shoulder? "I lay down and my brother and José [Luis Martinez] put it back in again. It's not the first time — during the season it dislocated many times during training at home. Maybe it was my weak point of the season."

**CLOCKWISE FROM TOP LEFT** | *Márquez celebrated with Honda Motor president Takahiro Hachigo; Dovizioso leads the charge through Motegi's first tunnel; Smith beat his team-mate by a fraction, but Morbidelli beat them both; Nakasuga did a good job, testing a revised-stiffness chassis and other new M1 parts; Márquez: #1 = Level 7; Miller chases the early freight train*

at impressive speed, looking like he was attacking the Isle of Man TT course. And he wasn't alone. The cameras made sure of that: he zoomed past a Honda Super Cub, cars, trucks and finally a group of stupefied bike riders.

The very next day he was at Motegi, visiting the Honda Collection Hall, the foremost collection of Honda road and race machinery, to mark the museum's 20th anniversary. His favourite bike was Mike Hailwood's legendary 22,000rpm 250 six of the 1960s. "This bike is amazing because Honda created all this new technology," he said, before moving on to look at one of Mick Doohan's NSR500s. "I feel similarly to Mick because he was really aggressive with the bike and he won five 500cc titles. Also, this is when the bikes started to be like our current bikes."

*Red Bull images supplied courtesy of www.redbullcontentpool.com*

# 16 | JAPAN

# RACE RESULTS

**WINNER** | *MARC MÁRQUEZ*

**CIRCUIT LENGTH** | *4.8 KM* | *2.98 MILES*

**NO. OF LAPS** | *24*

**RACE DISTANCE** | *115.2 KM* | *71.5 MILES*

**CIRCUIT RECORD LAP** | *1'45.350* | *164.0 KM/H*
*JORGE LORENZO (2014)*

**CIRCUIT BEST LAP** | *1'43.790* | *166.5 KM/H*
*JORGE LORENZO (2015)*

**RACE CONDITION** | *DRY*

**AIR** | *23°C*

**HUMIDITY** | *34%*

**GROUND** | *35°C*

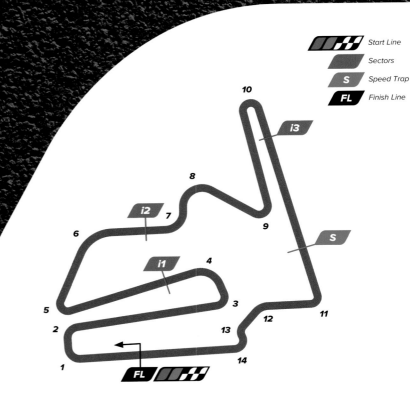

| | | Start Line |
| | | Sectors |
| S | | Speed Trap |
| FL | | Finish Line |

TISSOT | motoGP
SWISS WATCHES SINCE 1853
**OFFICIAL** TIMEKEEPER

MICHELIN | motoGP
**OFFICIAL** MotoGP™ CLASS TYRE

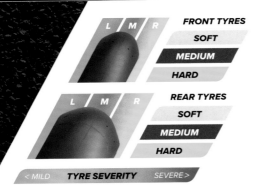

**FRONT TYRES**
SOFT
MEDIUM
HARD

**REAR TYRES**
SOFT
MEDIUM
HARD

< MILD  **TYRE SEVERITY**  SEVERE >

## QUALIFYING RESULTS

| | RIDER | NAT | TEAM | MACHINE | QP/TIME | GAP 1ST/PREV | |
|---|---|---|---|---|---|---|---|
| 1 | **Andrea Dovizioso** | ITA | Ducati Team | DUCATI | Q2 1'44.590 | | |
| 2 | **Johann Zarco** | FRA | Monster Yamaha Tech 3 | YAMAHA | Q2 1'44.658 | 0.068 | 0.068 |
| 3 | **Jack Miller** | AUS | Alma Pramac Racing | DUCATI | Q2 1'44.727 | 0.137 | 0.069 |
| 4 | **Cal Crutchlow** | GBR | LCR Honda CASTROL | HONDA | Q2 1'44.820 | 0.230 | 0.093 |
| 5 | **Andrea Iannone** | ITA | Team SUZUKI ECSTAR | SUZUKI | Q2 1'44.832 | 0.242 | 0.012 |
| 6 | **Marc Márquez** | SPA | Repsol Honda Team | HONDA | Q2 1'44.889 | 0.299 | 0.057 |
| 7 | **Maverick Viñales** | SPA | Movistar Yamaha MotoGP | YAMAHA | Q2 1'45.140 | 0.550 | 0.251 |
| 8 | **Álex Rins** | SPA | Team SUZUKI ECSTAR | SUZUKI | Q2 1'45.225 | 0.635 | 0.085 |
| 9 | **Valentino Rossi** | ITA | Movistar Yamaha MotoGP | YAMAHA | Q2 1'45.265 | 0.675 | 0.040 |
| 10 | **Álvaro Bautista**\*\* | SPA | Ángel Nieto Team | DUCATI | Q2 1'45.396 | 0.806 | 0.131 |
| 11 | **Dani Pedrosa** | SPA | Repsol Honda Team | HONDA | Q2 1'45.519 | 0.929 | 0.123 |
| 12 | **Takaaki Nakagami**\*\* | JPN | LCR Honda IDEMITSU | HONDA | Q2 1'46.168 | 1.578 | 0.649 |
| 13 | **Bradley Smith** | GBR | Red Bull KTM Factory Racing | KTM | Q1 1'45.722 | *0.293 | 0.066 |
| 14 | **Pol Espargaró** | SPA | Red Bull KTM Factory Racing | KTM | Q1 1'45.742 | *0.313 | 0.020 |
| 15 | **Danilo Petrucci** | ITA | Alma Pramac Racing | DUCATI | Q1 1'45.759 | *0.330 | 0.017 |
| 16 | **Hafizh Syahrin** | MAL | Monster Yamaha Tech 3 | YAMAHA | Q1 1'45.765 | *0.336 | 0.006 |
| 17 | **Franco Morbidelli** | ITA | EG 0,0 Marc VDS | HONDA | Q1 1'45.969 | *0.540 | 0.204 |
| 18 | **Karel Abraham** | CZE | Ángel Nieto Team | DUCATI | Q1 1'46.072 | *0.643 | 0.103 |
| 19 | **Aleix Espargaró** | SPA | Aprilia Racing Team Gresini | APRILIA | Q1 1'46.183 | *0.754 | 0.111 |
| 20 | **Katsuyuki Nakasuga** | JPN | Yamalube Yamaha Factory Racing | YAMAHA | Q1 1'46.441 | *1.012 | 0.258 |
| 21 | **Scott Redding** | GBR | Aprilia Racing Team Gresini | APRILIA | Q1 1'46.573 | *1.142 | 0.130 |
| 22 | **Xavier Siméon** | GER | Reale Avintia Racing | DUCATI | Q1 1'46.575 | *1.144 | 0.002 |
| 23 | **Thomas Lüthi** | SWI | EG 0,0 Marc VDS | HONDA | Q1 1'46.817 | *1.388 | 0.244 |
| 24 | **Sylvain Guintoli** | FRA | Team SUZUKI ECSTAR | SUZUKI | Q1 1'47.106 | *1.677 | 0.289 |
| 25 | **Jordi Torres** | SPA | Reale Avintia Racing | DUCATI | Q1 1'47.147 | *1.718 | 0.041 |

*\* Gap to the fastest rider in the Q1 session*
*\*\* Went forward from Q1 to Q2*

### 1 MARC MÁRQUEZ
Didn't really need to win, but clearly wanted to give Honda the crown at its home GP, so gave it everything and responded well to the pressure. As usual. Dialled in his RC213V to match Dovizioso's GP18 on braking.

### 2 CAL CRUTCHLOW
Once again ran with the lead group, but this time he stayed with them, because tyre life wasn't a serious issue at Motegi. Most riders used the medium rear. Was wary of causing problems for Márquez. Gave Honda their first one-two since Aragon 2017.

### 3 ÁLEX RINS
Another fine performance from the youngster who quietly gets better and better, always learning from his peers. Dovizioso's pace-changing game allowed him to catch the leaders but he couldn't out-brake Crutchlow.

### 4 VALENTINO ROSSI
Incorrect tyre pressure in his final Q2 run left him ninth on the grid but he made a great start to take fifth on lap one. However, the M1 once again used its rear tyre too quickly, making him an easy target for rivals.

### 5 ÁLVARO BAUTISTA
Fifth on a 2017 bike, half a second behind Rossi, once again showed why he deserves to be on the grid in 2019. Overheated his front tyre but was later able to attack Zarco and Rossi. Got his reward at the end of the day: Lorenzo's bikes at Phillip Island.

### 6 JOHANN ZARCO
Once again showed he was recovering from his traditional midseason slump. Struggled with cold tyres at the start but increased his pace. Was about to attack Rossi when he got divebombed by Bautista.

### 7 MAVERICK VIÑALES
Had the fastest top speed of the race but was compromised by corner-entry problems. Couldn't get the bike stopped effectively without the extra rear grip he enjoyed at Buriram. It was a far cry from his best Motegi results: victories in the 2002 125 GP, the 2004 250 GP and the 2011, 2012 and 2015 MotoGP races.

### 8 DANI PEDROSA
Another bitter disappointment, after the speed he had shown in the heat of Buriram. It was a far cry from his best Motegi results: victories in the 2002 125 GP, the 2004 250 GP and the 2011, 2012 and 2015 MotoGP races.

### 9 DANILO PETRUCCI
His size and weight can cause serious issues at Motegi, where the front tyre and brakes take a real hammering. Qualified down in 15th, then made a mistake on lap four which cost him more positions. Made the top ten thanks to crashes ahead of him.

### 10 HAFIZH SYAHRIN
The Malaysian rookie's first top-ten finish since April's chaotic Argentine GP showed confidence flowing back into his veins. Most importantly, got the better of Morbidelli in their ongoing Rookie of the Year duel.

### 11 FRANCO MORBIDELLI
Suffered a high-speed crash at turn 12 in Q1 which badly damaged his number-one machine and left him 17th on the grid. Lacked low-gear acceleration all weekend – a major handicap at Motegi – so he was happy enough with five points.

### 12 BRADLEY SMITH
Passed his team-mate, then chased Petrucci, but lost some edge grip which slowed his pace and made him easy prey for Syahrin. In the final laps came under pressure from Morbidelli, tried too hard and ran wide.

## RACE LAP CHART

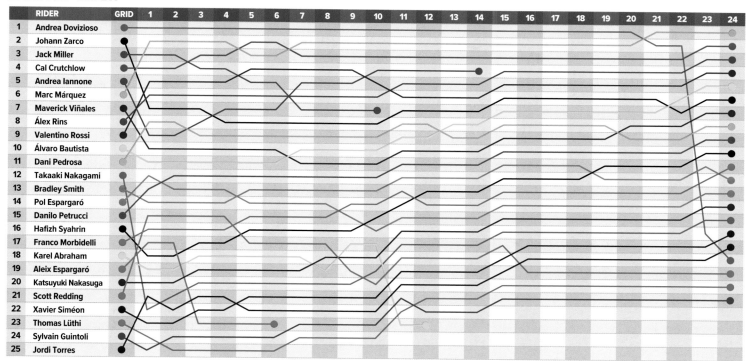

| | RIDER | GRID | 1 | 2 | 3 | 4 | 5 | 6 | 7 | 8 | 9 | 10 | 11 | 12 | 13 | 14 | 15 | 16 | 17 | 18 | 19 | 20 | 21 | 22 | 23 | 24 |
|---|---|---|---|---|---|---|---|---|---|---|---|---|---|---|---|---|---|---|---|---|---|---|---|---|---|---|---|
| 1 | Andrea Dovizioso | | | | | | | | | | | | | | | | | | | | | | | | | |
| 2 | Johann Zarco | | | | | | | | | | | | | | | | | | | | | | | | | |
| 3 | Jack Miller | | | | | | | | | | | | | | | | | | | | | | | | | |
| 4 | Cal Crutchlow | | | | | | | | | | | | | | | | | | | | | | | | | |
| 5 | Andrea Iannone | | | | | | | | | | | | | | | | | | | | | | | | | |
| 6 | Marc Márquez | | | | | | | | | | | | | | | | | | | | | | | | | |
| 7 | Maverick Viñales | | | | | | | | | | | | | | | | | | | | | | | | | |
| 8 | Álex Rins | | | | | | | | | | | | | | | | | | | | | | | | | |
| 9 | Valentino Rossi | | | | | | | | | | | | | | | | | | | | | | | | | |
| 10 | Álvaro Bautista | | | | | | | | | | | | | | | | | | | | | | | | | |
| 11 | Dani Pedrosa | | | | | | | | | | | | | | | | | | | | | | | | | |
| 12 | Takaaki Nakagami | | | | | | | | | | | | | | | | | | | | | | | | | |
| 13 | Bradley Smith | | | | | | | | | | | | | | | | | | | | | | | | | |
| 14 | Pol Espargaró | | | | | | | | | | | | | | | | | | | | | | | | | |
| 15 | Danilo Petrucci | | | | | | | | | | | | | | | | | | | | | | | | | |
| 16 | Hafizh Syahrin | | | | | | | | | | | | | | | | | | | | | | | | | |
| 17 | Franco Morbidelli | | | | | | | | | | | | | | | | | | | | | | | | | |
| 18 | Karel Abraham | | | | | | | | | | | | | | | | | | | | | | | | | |
| 19 | Aleix Espargaró | | | | | | | | | | | | | | | | | | | | | | | | | |
| 20 | Katsuyuki Nakasuga | | | | | | | | | | | | | | | | | | | | | | | | | |
| 21 | Scott Redding | | | | | | | | | | | | | | | | | | | | | | | | | |
| 22 | Xavier Siméon | | | | | | | | | | | | | | | | | | | | | | | | | |
| 23 | Thomas Lüthi | | | | | | | | | | | | | | | | | | | | | | | | | |
| 24 | Sylvain Guintoli | | | | | | | | | | | | | | | | | | | | | | | | | |
| 25 | Jordi Torres | | | | | | | | | | | | | | | | | | | | | | | | | |

## RACE CLASSIFICATION AFTER 24 LAPS = 115.224 KM

| | RIDER | NAT | TEAM | MACHINE | TIME | + GAP | TYRES |
|---|---|---|---|---|---|---|---|
| 1 | Marc Márquez | SPA | Repsol Honda Team | HONDA | 42'36.438 | | M/M |
| 2 | Cal Crutchlow | GBR | LCR Honda CASTROL | HONDA | 42'38.011 | 1.573 | M/M |
| 3 | Álex Rins | SPA | Team SUZUKI ECSTAR | SUZUKI | 42'38.158 | 1.720 | M/M |
| 4 | Valentino Rossi | ITA | Movistar Yamaha MotoGP | YAMAHA | 42'42.851 | 6.413 | M/M |
| 5 | Álvaro Bautista | SPA | Ángel Nieto Team | DUCATI | 42'43.357 | 6.919 | S/S |
| 6 | Johann Zarco | FRA | Monster Yamaha Tech 3 | YAMAHA | 42'44.462 | 8.024 | S/M |
| 7 | Maverick Viñales | SPA | Movistar Yamaha MotoGP | YAMAHA | 42'49.768 | 13.330 | S/M |
| 8 | Dani Pedrosa | SPA | Repsol Honda Team | HONDA | 42'52.020 | 15.582 | M/M |
| 9 | Danilo Petrucci | ITA | Alma Pramac Racing | DUCATI | 42'57.022 | 20.584 | S/M |
| 10 | Hafizh Syahrin | MAL | Monster Yamaha Tech 3 | YAMAHA | 43'01.423 | 24.985 | M/M |
| 11 | Franco Morbidelli | ITA | EG 0,0 Marc VDS | HONDA | 43'02.369 | 25.931 | M/M |
| 12 | Bradley Smith | GBR | Red Bull KTM Factory Racing | KTM | 43'03.313 | 26.875 | M/M |
| 13 | Pol Espargaró | SPA | Red Bull KTM Factory Racing | KTM | 43'03.507 | 27.069 | M/S |
| 14 | Katsuyuki Nakasuga | JPN | Yamalube Yamaha Factory Racing | YAMAHA | 43'08.988 | 32.550 | M/M |
| 15 | Takaaki Nakagami | JPN | LCR Honda IDEMITSU | HONDA | 43'14.156 | 37.718 | M/S |
| 16 | Xavier Siméon | GER | Reale Avintia Racing | DUCATI | 43'16.021 | 39.583 | S/M |
| 17 | Jordi Torres | SPA | Reale Avintia Racing | DUCATI | 43'16.277 | 39.839 | S/M |
| 18 | Andrea Dovizioso | ITA | Ducati Team | DUCATI | 43'19.136 | 42.698 | S/M |
| 19 | Scott Redding | GBR | Aprilia Racing Team Gresini | APRILIA | 43'26.381 | 49.943 | S/S |
| 20 | Thomas Lüthi | SWI | EG 0,0 Marc VDS | HONDA | 43'29.145 | 52.707 | M/M |
| 21 | Sylvain Guintoli | FRA | Team SUZUKI ECSTAR | SUZUKI | 43'38.286 | 1'01.848 | M/M |
| NC | Andrea Iannone | ITA | Team SUZUKI ECSTAR | SUZUKI | 24'55.602 | 10 laps | M/M |
| NC | Karel Abraham | CZE | Ángel Nieto Team | DUCATI | 22'38.296 | 12 laps | M/S |
| NC | Jack Miller | AUS | Alma Pramac Racing | DUCATI | 17'53.274 | 14 laps | S/S |
| NC | Aleix Espargaró | SPA | Aprilia Racing Team Gresini | APRILIA | 10'59.724 | 18 laps | M/S |

## CHAMPIONSHIP STANDINGS

| | RIDER | NAT | TEAM | POINTS |
|---|---|---|---|---|
| 1 | Marc Márquez | SPA | Repsol Honda Team | 296 |
| 2 | Andrea Dovizioso | ITA | Ducati Team | 194 |
| 3 | Valentino Rossi | ITA | Movistar Yamaha MotoGP | 185 |
| 4 | Maverick Viñales | SPA | Movistar Yamaha MotoGP | 155 |
| 5 | Cal Crutchlow | GBR | LCR Honda CASTROL | 148 |
| 6 | Johann Zarco | FRA | Monster Yamaha Tech 3 | 133 |
| 7 | Danilo Petrucci | ITA | Alma Pramac Racing | 133 |
| 8 | Jorge Lorenzo | SPA | Ducati Team | 130 |
| 9 | Álex Rins | SPA | Team SUZUKI ECSTAR | 118 |
| 10 | Andrea Iannone | ITA | Team SUZUKI ECSTAR | 113 |
| 11 | Dani Pedrosa | SPA | Repsol Honda Team | 95 |
| 12 | Álvaro Bautista | SPA | Ángel Nieto Team | 83 |
| 13 | Jack Miller | AUS | Alma Pramac Racing | 74 |
| 14 | Franco Morbidelli | ITA | EG 0,0 Marc VDS | 38 |
| 15 | Tito Rabat | SPA | Reale Avintia Racing | 35 |
| 16 | Pol Espargaró | SPA | Red Bull KTM Factory Racing | 35 |
| 17 | Hafizh Syahrin | MAL | Monster Yamaha Tech 3 | 34 |
| 18 | Aleix Espargaró | SPA | Aprilia Racing Team Gresini | 32 |
| 19 | Bradley Smith | GBR | Red Bull KTM Factory Racing | 23 |
| 20 | Takaaki Nakagami | JPN | LCR Honda IDEMITSU | 19 |
| 21 | Scott Redding | GBR | Aprilia Racing Team Gresini | 12 |
| 22 | Mika Kallio | FIN | Red Bull KTM Factory Racing | 6 |
| 23 | Karel Abraham | CZE | Ángel Nieto Team | 5 |
| 24 | Katsuyuki Nakasuga | JPN | Yamalube Yamaha Factory Racing | 2 |
| 25 | Michele Pirro | ITA | Ducati Team | 1 |
| 26 | Thomas Lüthi | SWI | EG 0,0 Marc VDS | |
| 27 | Xavier Siméon | GER | Reale Avintia Racing | |
| 28 | Stefan Bradl | GER | Honda Racing Corporation | |
| 29 | Jordi Torres | SPA | Reale Avintia Racing | |
| 30 | Sylvain Guintoli | FRA | Team SUZUKI ECSTAR | |
| 31 | Christophe Ponsson | FRA | Reale Avintia Racing | |

**13 | POL ESPARGARÓ**
Back to full physical strength after his collarbone surgery, so he was able to finish inside the points for the first time since Assen. Chose the soft rear (Smith used the medium) and found it difficult to manage the drop in grip during the final stages of the race.

**14 | KATSUYUKI NAKASUGA**
Yamaha equipped its 8 Hours hero and MotoGP test rider with a revised stiffness chassis, in the hope of improving tyre life. Spent the last half of the race successfully resisting attacks by compatriot Nakagami.

**14 | TAKAAKI NAKAGAMI**
His first MotoGP race at home was a big deal for Nakagami but sadly it all went awry on the first lap when a collision put him off track. He was lucky not to crash but found himself way back in 22nd place. It was a hard slog into the points from there.

**16 | XAVIER SIMÉON**
The best race of the year so far for the Belgian rookie, riding Tito Rabat's GP17 for the fourth time. A poor start left him 23rd at the end of the first lap and yet he crossed the line less than two seconds outside the points.

**17 | JORDI TORRES**
The former Moto2 winner had never made the top ten in a Motegi Moto2 race, so he knew this would be a tough weekend. Chased Siméon home again. His biggest positive was learning how to ride around the drop in grip in the closing stages.

**18 | ANDREA DOVIZIOSO**
Had the pace to prevent Márquez wrapping up the title at a track which amplifies the Ducati's braking and acceleration strengths. But had to push too hard to beat his rival and paid a high price for a minor error.

**19 | SCOTT REDDING**
Made his best start of the season so far, from 21st on the grid to 15th after one lap. However, he couldn't use the medium front, so raced with the soft, which started moving around too much from half-distance and his lap times slowed by up to a second.

**20 | THOMAS LÜTHI**
Once again, couldn't find a good feeling with his motorcycle and was last for several laps, until he was able to generate more temperature in the rear tyre, but by then the rest of the pack were way ahead of him.

**21 | SYLVAIN GUINTOLI**
Suzuki's tester finished last, but Rins' podium proved he had worked well during an earlier Motegi test session.

**DNF | ANDREA IANNONE**
Pushed hard but was troubled by rear-tyre vibration. Finally the problem caused him to lock the rear and then lose the front at the hairpin.

**DNF | KAREL ABRAHAM**
Was riding a promising race, battling with Yamaha's wild card Nakasuga when he lost the front at turn five.

**DNF | JACK MILLER**
Found the Moto2 rubber cost him edge grip. Made a mistake when Zarco came past and crashed at turn nine.

**DNF | ALEIX ESPARGARÓ**
His RS-GPs' dash flashing its front tyre temperature/pressure warnings and he kept locking the front, even in a straight line, so he retired.

**DNS | JORGE LORENZO**
Helped with Dorna TV commentary before flying home for keyhole surgery on a ligament in his left wrist.

# YAMAHA'S LOSING STREAK IS OVER

**Viñales rode a storming race, while Márquez and Zarco were the luckiest riders of the day**

Phillip Island is one of the jewels in MotoGP's crown: a mightily high-speed circuit where riders are on the throttle more than anywhere else, through 78 percent of each lap. Its fast, flowing layout gives everyone a better chance to run up front, even when their motorcycle lacks outright performance.

Yamaha hadn't won a race since Assen 2017, but Maverick Viñales, Valentino Rossi and even indie Yamaha rider Johann Zarco all thought they had a chance, because the YZR-M1's fine-handling chassis can make the difference through Phillip Island's super-fast curves.

But first they and everyone else had to deal with the typically tricky Island weather. It is a long-running paddock joke that MotoGP travels all the way to Australia, packing woolly hats, not beachwear. The thermometer never bettered 16 degrees all weekend. And on Friday and Saturday there was the added problem of gusting winds. This made for dangerous conditions, as many riders found to their cost; most of all Cal Crutchlow, who had his front wheel taken away by a gust as he attacked the first corner at over 200kmh/125mph. He badly broke his right ankle in the ensuing crash.

Qualifying was almost but not quite the scariest moment of the weekend. Scattered showers hit the circuit as riders readied

*Man, machine and racetrack in perfect harmony — finally it all came together for Viñales and Yamaha*

themselves for Q2, putting them in the unenviable position of attacking the track at full speed, while never quite sure of how much grip lay ahead at the next corner. Fortune favours the brave, so perhaps it was no surprise that Márquez came out on top.

The world champion led the early stages of the race but decided it was wiser to drop back into the pack, rather than risk overusing his tyres in attempting to break away. No doubt, he wished he had done otherwise, because at the start of lap six he was rammed from behind by Zarco, who crashed at 280kmh/175mph. The impact damaged Márquez's RC213V, forcing him to return to the pits and retire.

Viñales had a grandstand view of the terrifying collision and decided the last place he wanted to be was in the pack, so he charged forward, took the lead on lap eight and made the break, hoping his tyres would last.

They did. With five laps to go he was four seconds ahead of the chasing group: Andrea Iannone, Andrea Dovizioso, Rossi, Álex Rins and Jorge Lorenzo substitute Álvaro Bautista. The quartet fought back and forth, Bautista enjoying the extra performance of the factory GP18, despite two tumbles in practice. He looked good for a podium finish, but in the final laps Iannone and Dovizioso broke away from the others and hauled in the leader, but their final push came just too late.

"It feels amazing," said Viñales, who shed tears of delight after ending his own 18-month losing streak. "This win is so important because we need to be motivated to start next year really well and for sure this win gives us a lot of motivation. In some ways we did things different this weekend. We tried to maintain the same set-up and get used to the bike, so I could concentrate on my lines. Here, I know if the bike isn't perfect I can make it perfect, because I have some good lines and I can be fast."

Following Márquez's exit the only man who seemed capable of matching Viñales was Iannone, who had been super-fast throughout practice. The Maniac worked his way past Rossi into second on lap 11 and set about chasing the leader. But he ran wide at turn four – one of the track's few right-handers, where grip is always edgy – and slipped back to fifth. By lap 23 he had fought his way back into second once again and started carving chunks out of the leader's advantage. Then on the last lap he again ran wide at turn four, only just keeping Dovizioso at bay.

Perhaps the winner's secret was his choice of the soft front tyre, while his fellow podium finishers used the medium. "I was so happy we could make the soft front work," said Viñales, "because the medium was impossible for me – I couldn't turn in the corners."

Iannone was disappointed because he knew this was probably his best bet for a victory with Suzuki. "We had the potential to try to win the race," he said. "But I made a mistake at turn four, arriving into the corner with too much speed. I started to recover but I knew the situation wasn't good."

Dovizioso was very nearly as happy as the winner. Twelve

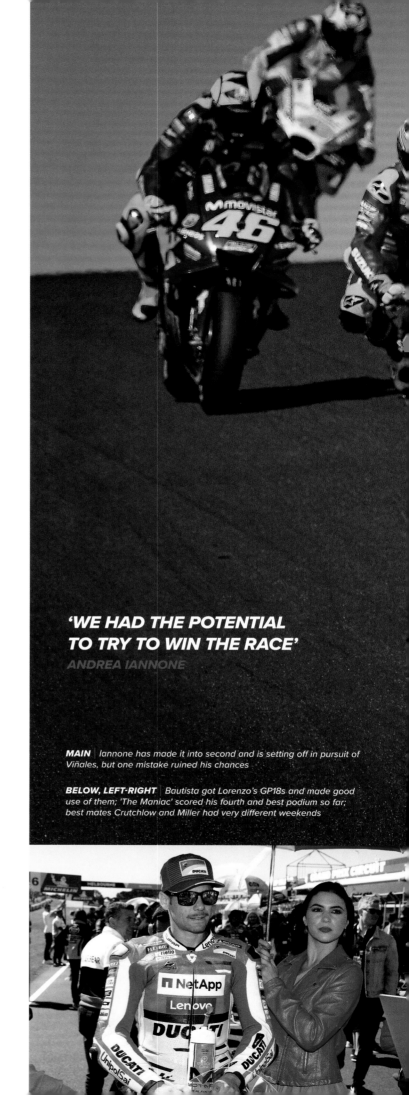

## 'WE HAD THE POTENTIAL TO TRY TO WIN THE RACE'
ANDREA IANNONE

**MAIN** | Iannone has made it into second and is setting off in pursuit of Viñales, but one mistake ruined his chances

**BELOW, LEFT-RIGHT** | Bautista got Lorenzo's GP18s and made good use of them; 'The Maniac' scored his fourth and best podium so far; best mates Crutchlow and Miller had very different weekends

## MOTOGP'S FASTEST SHUNT

Nowhere else is the lead group as closely packed as Phillip Island. The track boasts the closest premier-class top-three finish of all time — 0.124 seconds, between Tadayuki Okada, Max Biaggi and Regis Laconi at the 1999 Australian GP.

And nowhere do riders get closer than down the 340kmh/210mph start/finish straight, where they chase each other for slipstreams. Maverick Viñales may have dominated the 2018 Australian GP, but the race will most likely be remembered for what happened at the end of the start/finish straight on the sixth lap of the race.

Jack Miller, Marc Márquez and Johann Zarco were line astern, just behind leader Andrea Dovizioso. The Spaniard and the Frenchman

months earlier he had finished the Phillip Island race way down in 13th, 21 seconds behind winner Márquez, because the Ducati didn't like the track's long, sweeping corners. This time he was third, 1.8 seconds behind Viñales.

"This race was the last important test before the end of the season, because we always struggled at this track," he said. "We confirmed our improvement from last year, but we still struggled in the middle of the corners."

Bautista was delighted with fourth and his first factory Ducati MotoGP weekend, just weeks before he joined the marque's World Superbike squad. "In the factory team you have the same number of people working in the box, but behind the box you have another eight," he said. "In MotoGP the small details make the difference, and those small details are better in the factory team."

Rossi was the most disappointed of the lead group. Eight times a winner at Phillip Island, he burned the left side of his rear tyre and got sideways at turn six on the last lap, which allowed Rins to pounce. "After 15 laps I was in trouble because in the exits from the lefts I was spinning too much," Rossi explained.

**CLOCKWISE FROM TOP LEFT** | *Morbidelli and Aleix Espargaró had a great duel for eighth; Rins hitches a lift after a technical glitch in practice; local Mike Jones got the call to ride Abraham's GP16; Bautista impressed with his speed and commitment after two practice crashes; Rossi was bitterly disappointed with his race; the chasing group, before Dovizioso and Iannone upped the pace*

were drafting the Australian's faster Ducati, arriving at the turn one right-hander almost side by side. When Márquez moved to the left to take his normal line and braked, Zarco rammed him.

Zarco's M1 became airborne, luckily flying straight forward, rather than crossing the track. Even so, Andrea Iannone was just centimetres from disaster. Zarco rolled and rolled and rolled, then stood up and staggered away, a testament to modern riding gear. "At that speed I totally flew away," he said. "I was scared when I was sliding at that speed, I had the feeling I would never stop."

"I was behind Miller, getting a slipstream, then I braked and felt the contact," said Márquez. "At first I was angry, but when I saw the video I knew it was a racing incident. I feel really lucky today because we are both OK."

# ROUND 17 | AUSTRALIA

# RACE RESULTS

**WINNER** | MAVERICK VIÑALES

**CIRCUIT LENGTH** | 4.4 KM | 2.76 MILES

**NO. OF LAPS** | 27

**RACE DISTANCE** | 120.1 KM | 74.5 MILES

**CIRCUIT RECORD LAP** | 1'28.108 | 181.7 KM/H
MARC MÁRQUEZ (2013)

**CIRCUIT BEST LAP** | 1'27.899 | 182.1 KM/H
JORGE LORENZO (2013)

**RACE CONDITION** | DRY

**AIR** | 13°C

**HUMIDITY** | 55%

**GROUND** | 32°C

Start Line
Sectors
**S** Speed Trap
**FL** Finish Line

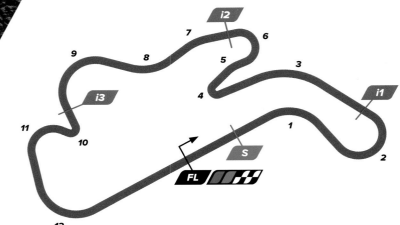

TISSOT / MotoGP
SWISS WATCHES SINCE 1853
**OFFICIAL** TIMEKEEPER

MICHELIN / MotoGP
**OFFICIAL** MotoGP™ CLASS TYRE

**FRONT TYRES**
SOFT
MEDIUM
HARD

**REAR TYRES**
SOFT
MEDIUM
HARD

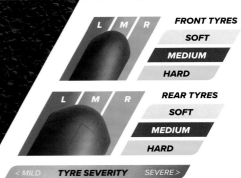

< MILD  **TYRE SEVERITY**  SEVERE >

## QUALIFYING RESULTS

|  | RIDER | NAT | TEAM | MACHINE | QP/TIME | | GAP 1ST/PREV | |
|---|---|---|---|---|---|---|---|---|
| 1 | Marc Márquez | SPA | Repsol Honda Team | HONDA | Q2 | 1'29.199 | | |
| 2 | Maverick Viñales | SPA | Movistar Yamaha MotoGP | YAMAHA | Q2 | 1'29.509 | 0.310 | 0.310 |
| 3 | Johann Zarco | FRA | Monster Yamaha Tech 3 | YAMAHA | Q2 | 1'29.705 | 0.506 | 0.196 |
| 4 | Andrea Iannone | ITA | Team SUZUKI ECSTAR | SUZUKI | Q2 | 1'29.712 | 0.513 | 0.007 |
| 5 | Álex Rins | SPA | Team SUZUKI ECSTAR | SUZUKI | Q2 | 1'30.026 | 0.827 | 0.314 |
| 6 | Jack Miller | AUS | Alma Pramac Racing | DUCATI | Q2 | 1'30.140 | 0.941 | 0.114 |
| 7 | Valentino Rossi | ITA | Movistar Yamaha MotoGP | YAMAHA | Q2 | 1'30.270 | 1.071 | 0.130 |
| 8 | Danilo Petrucci | ITA | Alma Pramac Racing | DUCATI | Q2 | 1'30.328 | 1.129 | 0.058 |
| 9 | Andrea Dovizioso | ITA | Ducati Team | DUCATI | Q2 | 1'30.519 | 1.320 | 0.191 |
| 10 | Hafizh Syahrin | MAL | Monster Yamaha Tech 3 | YAMAHA | Q2 | 1'30.593 | 1.394 | 0.074 |
| 11 | Pol Espargaró** | SPA | Red Bull KTM Factory Racing | KTM | Q2 | 1'30.640 | 1.441 | 0.047 |
| 12 | Álvaro Bautista** | SPA | Ducati Team | DUCATI | Q2 | 1'32.367 | 3.168 | 1.727 |
| 13 | Karel Abraham | CZE | Ángel Nieto Team | DUCATI | Q1 | 1'30.174 | *0.323 | 0.069 |
| 14 | Takaaki Nakagami | JPN | LCR Honda IDEMITSU | HONDA | Q1 | 1'30.452 | *0.601 | 0.278 |
| 15 | Franco Morbidelli | ITA | EG 0,0 Marc VDS | HONDA | Q1 | 1'30.518 | *0.667 | 0.066 |
| 16 | Bradley Smith | GBR | Red Bull KTM Factory Racing | KTM | Q1 | 1'30.646 | *0.795 | 0.128 |
| 17 | Xavier Siméon | GER | Reale Avintia Racing | DUCATI | Q1 | 1'30.679 | *0.828 | 0.033 |
| 18 | Dani Pedrosa | SPA | Repsol Honda Team | HONDA | Q1 | 1'30.770 | *0.919 | 0.091 |
| 19 | Aleix Espargaró | SPA | Aprilia Racing Team Gresini | APRILIA | Q1 | 1'30.911 | *1.060 | 0.141 |
| 20 | Thomas Lüthi | SWI | EG 0,0 Marc VDS | HONDA | Q1 | 1'30.958 | *1.107 | 0.047 |
| 21 | Jordi Torres | SPA | Reale Avintia Racing | DUCATI | Q1 | 1'31.141 | *1.290 | 0.183 |
| 22 | Scott Redding | GBR | Aprilia Racing Team Gresini | APRILIA | Q1 | 1'31.309 | *1.458 | 0.168 |
| 23 | Mike Jones | AUS | Ángel Nieto Team | DUCATI | Q1 | 1'32.639 | *2.788 | 1.330 |

*Gap to the fastest rider in the Q1 session
**Went forward from Q1 to Q2

**1 | MAVERICK VIÑALES**
Finally, after a year and a half of doubts and fallouts, Viñales got the job done again. Both the Spaniard and the M1 love Phillip Island and it showed. His choice of the soft front was a risk, but it paid off handsomely.

**2 | ANDREA IANNONE**
Some had him down as race favourite, but despite his speed in practice he didn't quite make it. Might it have been different if he had used the soft front? Victory would've been bittersweet for Suzuki, who had decided to replace him months earlier.

**3 | ANDREA DOVIZIOSO**
Interesting that he referred to this race as "a test". In other words, Phillip Island was a confirmation of Ducati's 2018 development work, which has substantially reduced the bike's mid-corner turning issues.

**4 | ÁLVARO BAUTISTA**
Bounced back from two practice crashes that would have sapped the confidence of many. This was an impressive ride on a motorcycle that was largely unfamiliar to him. It made many wonder why he hasn't got a MotoGP contract for 2019.

**5 | ÁLEX RINS**
Once again ran with the front group, unobtrusively as always. It was easy to forget that here was someone in only his second season, who still talked of learning so much while riding with Rossi and the rest.

**6 | VALENTINO ROSSI**
Was particularly crestfallen after missing the podium at a track that's been like a second home to him. His problem was the same as usual: he couldn't find the same race-long corner-exit grip that his team-mate conjured from the same rear tyre.

**7 | JACK MILLER**
Briefly led his home Grand Prix. In the middle of the race tried to save his rear tyre, but didn't have enough grip to attack at the end. Had the satisfaction of taking his place in Parce fermé as top indie rider.

**8 | FRANCO MORBIDELLI**
Top rookie, top Honda and his best MotoGP result made this a great day for the Moto2 champ. Battled with a factory Aprilia and KTM and beat them both. Like most, ran a medium/hard combination, but was able to look after them better than his rivals.

**9 | ALEIX ESPARGARÓ**
Rode a 2017/2018/2019 hybrid RS-GP that allowed him to attack throughout the race. However, his left hand was struck by debris from Márquez's bike, displacing a plate from an earlier injury, causing serious pain.

**10 | BRADLEY SMITH**
The Phillip Island layout is good for the KTM and Smith made the most of it. Another great first lap – during which he rode from 16th to eighth – had him fighting with Morbidelli but either the rider or the bike, didn't look after the rear tyre as well.

**11 | KAREL ABRAHAM**
Promoted to Bautista's GP17 for this one race the Czech rider scored his best result of 2018 and doubled his points score in a single afternoon! Won a four-man battle to the finish line, just fending off Petrucci.

**12 | DANILO PETRUCCI**
His best-ever start put him into the lead, but not for long. A clutch issue had him off the track and onto the grass at only the second corner and it was a long, long fightback from there. Only made it into the points with six laps remaining.

## RACE LAP CHART

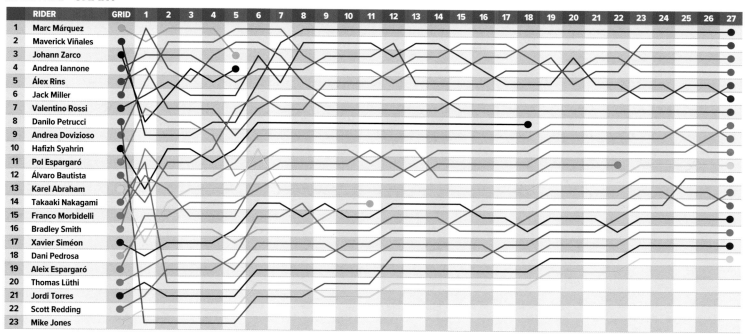

| | RIDER | GRID | 1 | 2 | 3 | 4 | 5 | 6 | 7 | 8 | 9 | 10 | 11 | 12 | 13 | 14 | 15 | 16 | 17 | 18 | 19 | 20 | 21 | 22 | 23 | 24 | 25 | 26 | 27 |
|---|---|---|---|---|---|---|---|---|---|---|---|---|---|---|---|---|---|---|---|---|---|---|---|---|---|---|---|---|---|
| 1 | Marc Márquez | | | | | | | | | | | | | | | | | | | | | | | | | | | | |
| 2 | Maverick Viñales | | | | | | | | | | | | | | | | | | | | | | | | | | | | |
| 3 | Johann Zarco | | | | | | | | | | | | | | | | | | | | | | | | | | | | |
| 4 | Andrea Iannone | | | | | | | | | | | | | | | | | | | | | | | | | | | | |
| 5 | Álex Rins | | | | | | | | | | | | | | | | | | | | | | | | | | | | |
| 6 | Jack Miller | | | | | | | | | | | | | | | | | | | | | | | | | | | | |
| 7 | Valentino Rossi | | | | | | | | | | | | | | | | | | | | | | | | | | | | |
| 8 | Danilo Petrucci | | | | | | | | | | | | | | | | | | | | | | | | | | | | |
| 9 | Andrea Dovizioso | | | | | | | | | | | | | | | | | | | | | | | | | | | | |
| 10 | Hafizh Syahrin | | | | | | | | | | | | | | | | | | | | | | | | | | | | |
| 11 | Pol Espargaró | | | | | | | | | | | | | | | | | | | | | | | | | | | | |
| 12 | Álvaro Bautista | | | | | | | | | | | | | | | | | | | | | | | | | | | | |
| 13 | Karel Abraham | | | | | | | | | | | | | | | | | | | | | | | | | | | | |
| 14 | Takaaki Nakagami | | | | | | | | | | | | | | | | | | | | | | | | | | | | |
| 15 | Franco Morbidelli | | | | | | | | | | | | | | | | | | | | | | | | | | | | |
| 16 | Bradley Smith | | | | | | | | | | | | | | | | | | | | | | | | | | | | |
| 17 | Xavier Siméon | | | | | | | | | | | | | | | | | | | | | | | | | | | | |
| 18 | Dani Pedrosa | | | | | | | | | | | | | | | | | | | | | | | | | | | | |
| 19 | Aleix Espargaró | | | | | | | | | | | | | | | | | | | | | | | | | | | | |
| 20 | Thomas Lüthi | | | | | | | | | | | | | | | | | | | | | | | | | | | | |
| 21 | Jordi Torres | | | | | | | | | | | | | | | | | | | | | | | | | | | | |
| 22 | Scott Redding | | | | | | | | | | | | | | | | | | | | | | | | | | | | |
| 23 | Mike Jones | | | | | | | | | | | | | | | | | | | | | | | | | | | | |

## RACE CLASSIFICATION AFTER 27 LAPS = 120.096 KM

| | RIDER | NAT | TEAM | MACHINE | TIME | + GAP | TYRES |
|---|---|---|---|---|---|---|---|
| 1 | Maverick Viñales | SPA | Movistar Yamaha MotoGP | YAMAHA | 40'51.081 | | S/H |
| 2 | Andrea Iannone | ITA | Team SUZUKI ECSTAR | SUZUKI | 40'52.624 | 1.543 | M/H |
| 3 | Andrea Dovizioso | ITA | Ducati Team | DUCATI | 40'52.913 | 1.832 | M/H |
| 4 | Álvaro Bautista | SPA | Ducati Team | DUCATI | 40'55.153 | 4.072 | S/H |
| 5 | Álex Rins | SPA | Team SUZUKI ECSTAR | SUZUKI | 40'56.098 | 5.017 | M/H |
| 6 | Valentino Rossi | ITA | Movistar Yamaha MotoGP | YAMAHA | 40'56.213 | 5.132 | M/H |
| 7 | Jack Miller | AUS | Alma Pramac Racing | DUCATI | 40'57.837 | 6.756 | M/H |
| 8 | Franco Morbidelli | ITA | EG 0,0 Marc VDS | HONDA | 41'12.886 | 21.805 | M/H |
| 9 | Aleix Espargaró | SPA | Aprilia Racing Team Gresini | APRILIA | 41'13.985 | 22.904 | M/S |
| 10 | Bradley Smith | GBR | Red Bull KTM Factory Racing | KTM | 41'14.021 | 22.940 | S/H |
| 11 | Karel Abraham | CZE | Ángel Nieto Team | DUCATI | 41'25.467 | 34.386 | S/H |
| 12 | Danilo Petrucci | ITA | Alma Pramac Racing | DUCATI | 41'26.106 | 35.025 | S/H |
| 13 | Scott Redding | GBR | Aprilia Racing Team Gresini | APRILIA | 41'27.429 | 36.348 | S/S |
| 14 | Takaaki Nakagami | JPN | LCR Honda IDEMITSU | HONDA | 41'27.470 | 36.389 | M/S |
| 15 | Xavier Siméon | GER | Reale Avintia Racing | DUCATI | 41'35.295 | 44.214 | S/H |
| 16 | Thomas Lüthi | SWI | EG 0,0 Marc VDS | HONDA | 41'39.307 | 48.226 | M/H |
| 17 | Jordi Torres | SPA | Reale Avintia Racing | DUCATI | 41'56.046 | 64.965 | S/H |
| 18 | Mike Jones | AUS | Ángel Nieto Team | DUCATI | 42'10.898 | 1'19.817 | S/S |
| NC | Pol Espargaró | SPA | Red Bull KTM Factory Racing | KTM | 33'39.100 | 5 laps | S/S |
| NC | Hafizh Syahrin | MAL | Monster Yamaha Tech 3 | YAMAHA | 27'22.361 | 9 laps | M/H |
| NC | Dani Pedrosa | SPA | Repsol Honda Team | HONDA | 16'57.082 | 16 laps | M/S |
| NC | Marc Márquez | SPA | Repsol Honda Team | HONDA | 7'42.377 | 22 laps | M/H |
| NC | Johann Zarco | FRA | Monster Yamaha Tech 3 | YAMAHA | 7'42.395 | 22 laps | S/S |

## CHAMPIONSHIP STANDINGS

| | RIDER | NAT | TEAM | POINTS |
|---|---|---|---|---|
| 1 | Marc Márquez | SPA | Repsol Honda Team | 296 |
| 2 | Andrea Dovizioso | ITA | Ducati Team | 210 |
| 3 | Valentino Rossi | ITA | Movistar Yamaha MotoGP | 195 |
| 4 | Maverick Viñales | SPA | Movistar Yamaha MotoGP | 180 |
| 5 | Cal Crutchlow | GBR | LCR Honda CASTROL | 148 |
| 6 | Danilo Petrucci | ITA | Alma Pramac Racing | 137 |
| 7 | Johann Zarco | FRA | Monster Yamaha Tech 3 | 133 |
| 8 | Andrea Iannone | ITA | Team SUZUKI ECSTAR | 133 |
| 9 | Jorge Lorenzo | SPA | Ducati Team | 130 |
| 10 | Álex Rins | SPA | Team SUZUKI ECSTAR | 129 |
| 11 | Álvaro Bautista | SPA | Ángel Nieto Team | 96 |
| 12 | Dani Pedrosa | SPA | Repsol Honda Team | 95 |
| 13 | Jack Miller | AUS | Alma Pramac Racing | 83 |
| 14 | Franco Morbidelli | ITA | EG 0,0 Marc VDS | 46 |
| 15 | Aleix Espargaró | SPA | Aprilia Racing Team Gresini | 39 |
| 16 | Tito Rabat | SPA | Reale Avintia Racing | 35 |
| 17 | Pol Espargaró | SPA | Red Bull KTM Factory Racing | 35 |
| 18 | Hafizh Syahrin | MAL | Monster Yamaha Tech 3 | 34 |
| 19 | Bradley Smith | GBR | Red Bull KTM Factory Racing | 29 |
| 20 | Takaaki Nakagami | JPN | LCR Honda IDEMITSU | 21 |
| 21 | Scott Redding | GBR | Aprilia Racing Team Gresini | 15 |
| 22 | Karel Abraham | CZE | Ángel Nieto Team | 10 |
| 23 | Mika Kallio | FIN | Red Bull KTM Factory Racing | 6 |
| 24 | Katsuyuki Nakasuga | JPN | Yamalube Yamaha Factory Racing | 2 |
| 25 | Xavier Siméon | GER | Reale Avintia Racing | 1 |
| 26 | Michele Pirro | ITA | Ducati Team | 1 |
| 27 | Thomas Lüthi | SWI | EG 0,0 Marc VDS | |
| 28 | Stefan Bradl | GER | Honda Racing Corporation | |
| 29 | Jordi Torres | SPA | Reale Avintia Racing | |
| 30 | Mike Jones | AUS | Ángel Nieto Team | |
| 31 | Sylvain Guintoli | FRA | Team SUZUKI ECSTAR | |
| 32 | Christophe Ponsson | FRA | Reale Avintia Racing | |

**13 SCOTT REDDING**
While in the middle of his group he found that the heat from other bikes brought his front tyre up to optimum temperature. But as soon as he got the front of the group, he lost temperature and grip again.

**14 TAKAAKI NAKAGAMI**
One of seven riders who chose the soft rear tyre, the Japanese rookie had great grip for the first two thirds of the race, but then found he had very little left for the last ten laps. Was disappointed by his race and by the result. Same as at Motegi.

**15 XAVIER SIMÉON**
The rash of crashes certainly helped, but the Belgian rookie was delighted to score his first MotoGP point. Last at the start, he came through well, until he had to ease his pace exiting the track's left-handers.

**16 THOMAS LÜTHI**
A near highside during practice left the Swiss rookie sore with severe bruising to his ribs. Struggled with understeer once the grip started to go away and wasn't happy to miss his first MotoGP championship point by one place for the fourth time.

**17 JORDI TORRES**
Felt good after a good pace in morning warm-up but complained that the windier afternoon conditions made it difficult to warm up his tyres. Twice nearly crashed and that affected his confidence a lot.

**18 MIKE JONES**
Last-minute Aussie substitute rode Abraham's GP16. Enjoyed the impossible task of learning to ride a MotoGP bike in just two days, getting steadily faster session after session and making it through the weekend without a single crash.

**DNF POL ESPARGARÓ**
Chose the soft rear and regretted it. Did plenty of laps on the tyre in practice and was confident it would last, but when it came to the race he found the bike dangerous to ride, so he retired with five laps to go.

**DNF HAFIZH SYAHRIN**
Started from his best grid position – tenth place – and fought his way towards what could've been his best MotoGP result, but finally got a bit too greedy and lost the front while trying to close the gap to Miller. Put a big dent in his Rookie of the Year hopes.

**DNF DANI PEDROSA**
The featherweight Spaniard often struggles at Phillip Island, where blustery winds and low temperatures are his enemy. Had a big practice crash at turn one, then lost the front again in the race, at turn four.

**DNF MARC MÁRQUEZ**
Surely would have given Viñales a hard time for the win, but it wasn't to be. High-speed contacts (like Rossi/Lorenzo at Assen) are the downsides of today's closer-than-ever premier-class racing. The champion did very well to stay onboard.

**DNF JOHANN ZARCO**
No one could really blame the Frenchman for what happened. There is considerable danger involved when riders draft so close at such high speeds – the huge amounts of buffeting can affect a rider's vision.

**DNS CAL CRUTCHLOW**
Went well again but was ruled out of the race by a heavy tumble in FP2 at turn one, caused by gusting winds that took his front wheel away. Suffered a very nasty fracture of his right ankle, which required two rounds of surgery in Melbourne.

# SO NEAR BUT SO FAR

**Veteran Valentino Rossi almost won his first race of the year, but in the end his young nemesis hunted him down**

Malaysia was the third flyaway race on as many Sundays. The tropical heat and humidity were intense, 169,000 fans poured through the gates and the weary, homesick paddock went about its business, dodging monsoon downpours.

The deluge that hit Sepang during Saturday's FP4 session flooded the track and delayed qualifying. But the recent works undertaken to improve drainage worked, so both Q1 and Q2 sessions went ahead; unlike 2006, when an epic rainstorm wiped out qualifying and grid positions were taken from free practice.

There was disappointment and joy for the huge crowd: local hero Hafizh Syahrin ended up on the back row of the grid, while global hero Valentino Rossi made it onto the front row.

Marc Márquez took pole in his own inimitable style. He qualified almost six tenths faster than Johann Zarco, crashed his number-one bike, rode it back to the pits, took his second bike and recorded the second-best lap of the session. But it was all for nothing. On his second out-lap he had impeded Andrea Iannone, so he was handed a six-place penalty; a bigger-than-usual sanction, because he had committed the same crime at COTA. Márquez being Márquez, he turned this into extra motivation: he had yet to win a MotoGP race from the third row.

The race schedule was brought forward to beat another

afternoon deluge; the thunder clouds already gathering as the lights went out.

Rossi got the holeshot, possibly inspired by the Moto2 race, at the end of which half-brother Luca Marini took his first Grand Prix victory and Francesco 'Pecco' Bagnaia secured the Sky VR46 team's first world title. But in fact this wasn't the best race preparation. "It was a great emotion, but I needed to sit down for maybe three hours to recover!" Rossi laughed. "So it was a difficult way to prepare for my race."

But he made it work. Rossi set a hot pace, so he was almost half a second ahead of pole-starter Zarco by the end of the first lap. And by the time Márquez had got past the Frenchman at one-quarter distance, Rossi was laying down a series of stunningly fast, consistent laps that stretched his advantage to 1.2 seconds. Could he do it?

Yamaha certainly seemed to have found something. But Rossi's speed wasn't related to his team-mate's winning pace at Phillip Island. "We modified the bike a lot here to try to help the rear tyre," he said later.

Márquez had just eight laps to chase down Rossi and he was up for the challenge, despite very nearly crashing on the first lap, which panicked Andrea Iannone into falling.

"I could see Valentino was pushing really hard and I saved that crash with my elbow," he said. "Then I was pushing my tyres too much, so I overheated them. When you overheat the tyres it's so difficult to get them back to the correct temperature, because you start to spin, then you spin more and more. So I slowed down, then step by step I found my rhythm again."

In other words, Rossi probably got a false idea of the situation when he saw +1.2 on his dash. And yet when Márquez began his hunt he could only sneak a tenth a lap out of the leader, who hadn't led a race for so long since Barcelona 2016, his last win in the dry.

"I didn't have anything more," said Márquez. "If I had still been racing for the championship I would've finished third or fourth, or maybe second, but I didn't have that pressure, so I was pushing to the limit. This year I've saved one crash per race – today I saved three or four."

Rossi knew Márquez was coming and was ready for a battle. "I understood he would arrive, but I wanted him to arrive as late as possible," he said. "It could have been fun, because I was quite strong, so I could fight."

By now, both men were sweating buckets and risking everything to maintain their pace as the 53-degree track temperature began to affect the tyres. On lap 17 Rossi was halfway through the horseshoe first corner when he lost the rear.

"When I touched the throttle I slid the rear and I didn't expect it, because I was more worried about the front," he said. "I'm devastated about the crash, because it was my first mistake of the season and at the worst moment, but on the other side I'm happy because we lived the dream for 16 laps."

'I'M HAPPY BECAUSE WE LIVED THE DREAM FOR 16 LAPS'
VALENTINO ROSSI

**MAIN** The Rossi grandstand erupts as their hero grabs the holeshot from Miller, Iannone, Pedrosa and Dovizioso

**BELOW, LEFT-RIGHT** Rossi was fast all weekend; Viñales shaved his head following his Australian GP victory; Hafizh Syahrin made history as the first Malaysian to contest the premier class at home

## ROSSI SLOWS DOWN TO GO FAST

Yamaha had surely found something important to dig themselves out of their rut. Seven days after Maverick Viñales won in Australia, Valentino Rossi led much of the Malaysian GP. Surely, this wasn't coincidence.

In fact it was, up to a point. Rossi and Viñales ride differently and use different chassis balance. Both had profited from rider-controls improvements filtering through from the factory's electronics dept, but the main factor in their new-found speed was getting more out of the Michelins through better mechanical grip. And in Rossi's instance, focusing less on outright performance.

"Before we worked to keep the performance and save the tyre, but it's not possible," said Rossi's crew chief Silvano

Márquez relaxed and cruised home for win number nine. The capacity crowd had groaned loudly when Rossi fell and now focused its interest on the battle for second, as Zarco attempted to fend off a fast-approaching Álex Rins. The young Spaniard had lost time dealing with Dani Pedrosa and the rocket-fast Ducatis of Andrea Dovizioso and Jack Miller, but once he had a clear track to play with he closed down a three-second gap to pounce on the final lap. As Márquez opined: Suzuki could challenge for the title in 2019.

Zarco may have lost second place but was delighted to be back on the podium for the first time since Jerez, despite a Phillip Island flashback when Márquez passed him. "æl was on the back straight, looking at his rear tyre. I said, no, I will keep away this time! After that I tried to stay with him and learn, but I was two or three tenths slower."

Dani Pedrosa enjoyed the hot asphalt more than most, his tyres for once fully up to temperature. A podium looked possible, until Rins came past, followed later by Maverick Viñales, who had to find his way through from the fourth row, after a complicated Saturday.

Sepang 2016 and 2017 winner Andrea Dovizioso was never in the hunt. "I couldn't brake properly, the front was locking a lot," he said.

***CLOKWISE FROM TOP LEFT*** | *Márquez had it relatively easy once Rossi had crashed out; Rins set the fastest lap, further proof of the GSX-RR's burgeoning speed; Dovizioso was out of the hunt for the first time in eight races; Márquez celebrates Honda's 24th premier-class constructors title with Masayuki Igarashi, Asian Honda CEO; Zarco was back up to speed for his first podium in 13 races; Syahrin gives thanks for his brilliant tenth-place finish*

Galbusera. "So now we lose some performance and try to keep the consistency of the tyre. Valentino can be stronger with this different setting. But the racing becomes more like endurance than MotoGP!

"We have worked on the geometry to put less stress on the rear tyre because our problem was always tyre life. Valentino complained about the consistency of the tyres. He could not use the Michelins the way he wants to because the tyres are too soft and they overheat. It's different for Maverick [Viñales]: he is a different size and uses a different style.

"Our new way is also to try to use a softer tyre from the allocation. Valentino usually feels better with a hard tyre because it gives him more support and better stability, whereas with a soft tyre he feels some movement in the bike, like in a streetbike, so he doesn't feel so comfortable. But this is the only way to be strong.

"Valentino says it's not easy to ride the bike like it is now, but it's the only way to save the tyres. We try to follow a different way, to make the bike not the best performer but more consistent with the rear tyre and it seems to work well. Now we have a bit more mechanical grip, but we have to be careful because the mechanical grip of the Yamaha has always been good, but if we use too much it overheats the tyre and the tyre will give up. So now we have to make the bike load the rear tyre a little more slowly."

On the other hand, circumstances may have helped Rossi as much as set-up. For once, tyre wear wasn't a big issue and Michelin's Malaysian tyre allocation suited all the Yamahas, because Johann Zarco and Viñales were also fast.

# ROUND 18 | MALAYSIA

# RACE RESULTS

**WINNER** | MARC MÁRQUEZ

**CIRCUIT LENGTH** | 5.5 KM  3.44 MILES

**NO. OF LAPS** | 20

**RACE DISTANCE** | 110.9 KM  68.8 MILES

**CIRCUIT RECORD LAP** | 2'00.606  165.4 KM/H
JORGE LORENZO (2015)

**CIRCUIT BEST LAP** | 1'59.053  167.6 KM/H
DANI PEDROSA (2015)

**RACE CONDITION** | DRY

**AIR** | 34°C

**HUMIDITY** | 55%

**GROUND** | 53°C

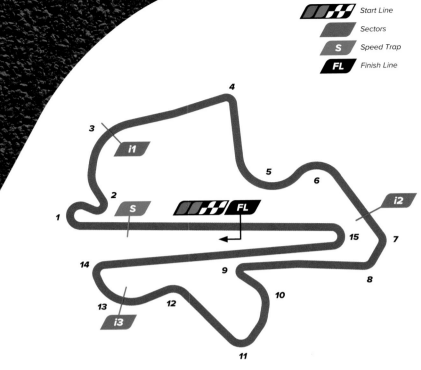

Start Line
Sectors
S — Speed Trap
FL — Finish Line

**TISSOT** SWISS WATCHES SINCE 1853 / motoGP
**OFFICIAL** TIMEKEEPER

**MICHELIN** / motoGP
**OFFICIAL** MotoGP™ CLASS TYRE

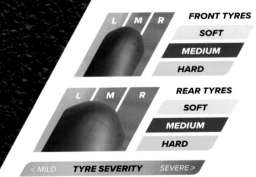

**FRONT TYRES**
SOFT
MEDIUM
HARD

**REAR TYRES**
SOFT
MEDIUM
HARD

< MILD  **TYRE SEVERITY**  SEVERE >

## QUALIFYING RESULTS

| | RIDER | NAT | TEAM | MACHINE | QP/TIME | GAP 1ST/PREV | |
|---|---|---|---|---|---|---|---|
| 1 | Marc Márquez | SPA | Repsol Honda Team | HONDA | Q2 2'12.161 | | |
| 2 | Johann Zarco | FRA | Monster Yamaha Tech 3 | YAMAHA | Q2 2'12.709 | 0.548 | 0.548 |
| 3 | Valentino Rossi | ITA | Movistar Yamaha MotoGP | YAMAHA | Q2 2'13.009 | 0.848 | 0.300 |
| 4 | Andrea Iannone | ITA | Team SUZUKI ECSTAR | SUZUKI | Q2 2'13.097 | 0.936 | 0.088 |
| 5 | Andrea Dovizioso | ITA | Ducati Team | DUCATI | Q2 2'13.183 | 1.022 | 0.086 |
| 6 | Jack Miller | AUS | Alma Pramac Racing | DUCATI | Q2 2'13.274 | 1.113 | 0.091 |
| 7 | Danilo Petrucci | ITA | Alma Pramac Racing | DUCATI | Q2 2'13.413 | 1.252 | 0.139 |
| 8 | Álex Rins | SPA | Team SUZUKI ECSTAR | SUZUKI | Q2 2'13.463 | 1.302 | 0.050 |
| 9 | Álvaro Bautista | SPA | Ángel Nieto Team | DUCATI | Q2 2'14.185 | 2.024 | 0.722 |
| 10 | Dani Pedrosa | SPA | Repsol Honda Team | HONDA | Q2 2'14.443 | 2.282 | 0.258 |
| 11 | Maverick Viñales | SPA | Movistar Yamaha MotoGP | YAMAHA | Q2 2'14.856 | 2.695 | 0.413 |
| 12 | Aleix Espargaró | SPA | Aprilia Racing Team Gresini | APRILIA | Q2 2'15.340 | 3.179 | 0.484 |
| 13 | Scott Redding | GBR | Aprilia Racing Team Gresini | APRILIA | Q1 2'13.786 | *0.475 | 0.451 |
| 14 | Michele Pirro | ITA | Ducati Team | DUCATI | Q1 2'13.823 | *0.512 | 0.037 |
| 15 | Xavier Siméon | GER | Reale Avintia Racing | DUCATI | Q1 2'13.971 | *0.660 | 0.148 |
| 16 | Pol Espargaró | SPA | Red Bull KTM Factory Racing | KTM | Q1 2'14.132 | *0.821 | 0.161 |
| 17 | Bradley Smith | GBR | Red Bull KTM Factory Racing | KTM | Q1 2'14.332 | *1.021 | 0.200 |
| 18 | Thomas Lüthi | SWI | EG 0,0 Marc VDS | HONDA | Q1 2'14.843 | *1.532 | 0.511 |
| 19 | Franco Morbidelli | ITA | EG 0,0 Marc VDS | HONDA | Q1 2'14.994 | *1.683 | 0.151 |
| 20 | Stefan Bradl | GER | LCR Honda CASTROL | HONDA | Q1 2'15.364 | *2.053 | 0.370 |
| 21 | Karel Abraham | CZE | Ángel Nieto Team | DUCATI | Q1 2'15.679 | *2.368 | 0.315 |
| 22 | Takaaki Nakagami | JPN | LCR Honda IDEMITSU | HONDA | Q1 2'16.558 | *3.247 | 0.879 |
| 23 | Hafizh Syahrin | MAL | Monster Yamaha Tech 3 | YAMAHA | Q1 2'16.825 | *3.514 | 0.267 |
| 24 | Jordi Torres | SPA | Reale Avintia Racing | DUCATI | FP2 2'01.940 | 2.332 | |

*\* Gap to the fastest rider in the Q1 session*
*\*\* Went forward from Q1 to Q2*

**1 | MARC MÁRQUEZ**
Risked it all to win, because he clearly wanted to erase the bad memories of 2015. Nearly crashed several times, but finally put enough pressure on Rossi to take him over the edge. Another almost superhuman victory.

**2 | ÁLEX RINS**
Rode the fastest lap of the race in the early stages, but then had to find a way past two Desmosedicis and a factory Honda, which wasn't easy and cost him time. Equalled his best result. Another super-smooth ride from the quietest talent on the grid.

**3 | JOHANN ZARCO**
Bounced back from his Phillip Island smash and usual midseason slump to take his first podium in 13 races. He was the only indie rider in the top six and assumed the lead of the independent-rider championship.

**4 | MAVERICK VIÑALES**
Would surely have been in the fight for victory once again, if he hadn't had to come through from the fourth row. Three of the six fastest laps of the race were set by Yamahas, which suggested the tyre allocation suited the M1 better than usual.

**5 | DANI PEDROSA**
If only MotoGP spent more time in the tropics, he would've enjoyed an even greater career. Like Buriram, he was on a charge, but it's not easy to find that final tenth when you struggle to find the limit at most races.

**6 | ANDREA DOVIZIOSO**
Just missed the front row in qualifying, so everyone was expecting him to be up front in the race. But it wasn't to be and he was nonplussed by his lack of speed, compared to his pace in practice. Perhaps he was delayed by a bike or tyre problem?

**7 | ÁLVARO BAUTISTA**
Back on his GP17 after a one-off ride on Jorge Lorenzo's GP18 in Australia, the Spaniard still rode the crest of a wave. Despite a lack of exit-grip he eventually got the better of fellow indie Duke men Petrucci and Miller.

**8 | JACK MILLER**
The only man to choose the medium rear instead of the soft option hoped his gamble might give him an advantage. But it didn't. Suffered from vibration throughout the race and had to concede seventh place to Bautista with only five laps remaining.

**9 | DANILO PETRUCCI**
Started from the second row, thanks to Márquez, but the heaviest rider on the grid was always going to struggle with tyres in such heat. The high point was Alma Pramac securing the independent-teams title.

**10 | HAFIZH SYAHRIN**
Most importantly, made history as the first Malaysian to contest a premier-class Malaysian GP. An amazing first lap took him from last on the grid to 11th. Chased Petrucci for much of the race and was promoted to the top-ten when Rossi crashed.

**11 | ALEIX ESPARGARÓ**
A disastrous first-corner dropped him to 17th at the end of lap one, with plenty of work to achieve his target of a top-ten finish. Very nearly made it, once again riding a hybrid RS-GP, basically a 2019 development bike.

**12 | FRANCO MORBIDELLI**
His minimal experience in riding a MotoGP bike in the rain told in qualifying, which put him way back on the grid. Completed lap one 19th, passed Redding and Lüthi, then won a big battle with Bradl. Finished less than two seconds behind Espargaró.

## RACE LAP CHART

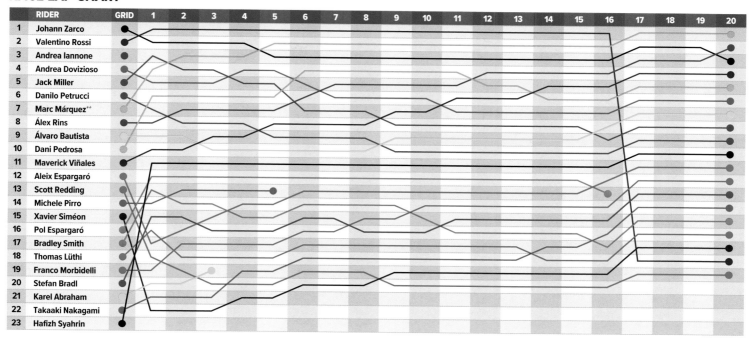

| | RIDER | GRID | 1 | 2 | 3 | 4 | 5 | 6 | 7 | 8 | 9 | 10 | 11 | 12 | 13 | 14 | 15 | 16 | 17 | 18 | 19 | 20 |
|---|---|---|---|---|---|---|---|---|---|---|---|---|---|---|---|---|---|---|---|---|---|---|---|
| 1 | Johann Zarco | | | | | | | | | | | | | | | | | | | | | |
| 2 | Valentino Rossi | | | | | | | | | | | | | | | | | | | | | |
| 3 | Andrea Iannone | | | | | | | | | | | | | | | | | | | | | |
| 4 | Andrea Dovizioso | | | | | | | | | | | | | | | | | | | | | |
| 5 | Jack Miller | | | | | | | | | | | | | | | | | | | | | |
| 6 | Danilo Petrucci | | | | | | | | | | | | | | | | | | | | | |
| 7 | Marc Márquez++ | | | | | | | | | | | | | | | | | | | | | |
| 8 | Álex Rins | | | | | | | | | | | | | | | | | | | | | |
| 9 | Álvaro Bautista | | | | | | | | | | | | | | | | | | | | | |
| 10 | Dani Pedrosa | | | | | | | | | | | | | | | | | | | | | |
| 11 | Maverick Viñales | | | | | | | | | | | | | | | | | | | | | |
| 12 | Aleix Espargaró | | | | | | | | | | | | | | | | | | | | | |
| 13 | Scott Redding | | | | | | | | | | | | | | | | | | | | | |
| 14 | Michele Pirro | | | | | | | | | | | | | | | | | | | | | |
| 15 | Xavier Siméon | | | | | | | | | | | | | | | | | | | | | |
| 16 | Pol Espargaró | | | | | | | | | | | | | | | | | | | | | |
| 17 | Bradley Smith | | | | | | | | | | | | | | | | | | | | | |
| 18 | Thomas Lüthi | | | | | | | | | | | | | | | | | | | | | |
| 19 | Franco Morbidelli | | | | | | | | | | | | | | | | | | | | | |
| 20 | Stefan Bradl | | | | | | | | | | | | | | | | | | | | | |
| 21 | Karel Abraham | | | | | | | | | | | | | | | | | | | | | |
| 22 | Takaaki Nakagami | | | | | | | | | | | | | | | | | | | | | |
| 23 | Hafizh Syahrin | | | | | | | | | | | | | | | | | | | | | |

## RACE CLASSIFICATION AFTER 20 LAPS = 110.86 KM

| | RIDER | NAT | TEAM | MACHINE | TIME | + GAP | TYRES |
|---|---|---|---|---|---|---|---|
| 1 | Marc Márquez | SPA | Repsol Honda Team | HONDA | 40'32.372 | | M/S |
| 2 | Álex Rins | SPA | Team SUZUKI ECSTAR | SUZUKI | 40'34.270 | 1.898 | M/S |
| 3 | Johann Zarco | FRA | Monster Yamaha Tech 3 | YAMAHA | 40'34.846 | 2.474 | M/S |
| 4 | Maverick Viñales | SPA | Movistar Yamaha MotoGP | YAMAHA | 40'37.039 | 4.667 | M/S |
| 5 | Dani Pedrosa | SPA | Repsol Honda Team | HONDA | 40'38.562 | 6.190 | M/S |
| 6 | Andrea Dovizioso | ITA | Ducati Team | DUCATI | 40'43.620 | 11.248 | M/S |
| 7 | Álvaro Bautista | SPA | Ángel Nieto Team | DUCATI | 40'47.983 | 15.611 | M/S |
| 8 | Jack Miller | AUS | Alma Pramac Racing | DUCATI | 40'51.381 | 19.009 | M/M |
| 9 | Danilo Petrucci | ITA | Alma Pramac Racing | DUCATI | 40'55.293 | 22.921 | M/S |
| 10 | Hafizh Syahrin | MAL | Monster Yamaha Tech 3 | YAMAHA | 40'59.291 | 26.919 | M/S |
| 11 | Aleix Espargaró | SPA | Aprilia Racing Team Gresini | APRILIA | 41'01.875 | 29.503 | M/S |
| 12 | Franco Morbidelli | ITA | EG 0,0 Marc VDS | HONDA | 41'03.305 | 30.933 | H/S |
| 13 | Stefan Bradl | GER | LCR Honda CASTROL | HONDA | 41'07.694 | 35.322 | M/S |
| 14 | Takaaki Nakagami | JPN | LCR Honda IDEMITSU | HONDA | 41'10.284 | 37.912 | M/S |
| 15 | Bradley Smith | GBR | Red Bull KTM Factory Racing | KTM | 41'12.047 | 39.675 | M/S |
| 16 | Thomas Lüthi | SWI | EG 0,0 Marc VDS | HONDA | 41'14.192 | 41.820 | M/S |
| 17 | Xavier Siméon | GER | Reale Avintia Racing | DUCATI | 41'16.350 | 43.978 | M/S |
| 18 | Valentino Rossi | ITA | Movistar Yamaha MotoGP | YAMAHA | 41'30.660 | 58.288 | M/S |
| 19 | Scott Redding | GBR | Aprilia Racing Team Gresini | APRILIA | 41'32.563 | 60.191 | H/S |
| NC | Pol Espargaró | SPA | Red Bull KTM Factory Racing | KTM | 32'49.371 | 4 laps | M/S |
| NC | Michele Pirro | ITA | Ducati Team | DUCATI | 10'20.138 | 15 laps | M/S |
| NC | Karel Abraham | CZE | Ángel Nieto Team | DUCATI | 6'18.930 | 17 laps | M/S |
| NC | Andrea Iannone | ITA | Team SUZUKI ECSTAR | SUZUKI | | | M/S |

*++ FIM MotoGP Stewards grid penalty for Marc Márquez*

## CHAMPIONSHIP STANDINGS

| | RIDER | NAT | TEAM | POINTS |
|---|---|---|---|---|
| 1 | Marc Márquez | SPA | Repsol Honda Team | 321 |
| 2 | Andrea Dovizioso | ITA | Ducati Team | 220 |
| 3 | Valentino Rossi | ITA | Movistar Yamaha MotoGP | 195 |
| 4 | Maverick Viñales | SPA | Movistar Yamaha MotoGP | 193 |
| 5 | Álex Rins | SPA | Team SUZUKI ECSTAR | 149 |
| 6 | Johann Zarco | FRA | Monster Yamaha Tech 3 | 149 |
| 7 | Cal Crutchlow | GBR | LCR Honda CASTROL | 148 |
| 8 | Danilo Petrucci | ITA | Alma Pramac Racing | 144 |
| 9 | Andrea Iannone | ITA | Team SUZUKI ECSTAR | 133 |
| 10 | Jorge Lorenzo | SPA | Ducati Team | 130 |
| 11 | Dani Pedrosa | SPA | Repsol Honda Team | 106 |
| 12 | Álvaro Bautista | SPA | Ángel Nieto Team | 105 |
| 13 | Jack Miller | AUS | Alma Pramac Racing | 91 |
| 14 | Franco Morbidelli | ITA | EG 0,0 Marc VDS | 50 |
| 15 | Aleix Espargaró | SPA | Aprilia Racing Team Gresini | 44 |
| 16 | Hafizh Syahrin | MAL | Monster Yamaha Tech 3 | 40 |
| 17 | Tito Rabat | SPA | Reale Avintia Racing | 35 |
| 18 | Pol Espargaró | SPA | Red Bull KTM Factory Racing | 35 |
| 19 | Bradley Smith | GBR | Red Bull KTM Factory Racing | 30 |
| 20 | Takaaki Nakagami | JPN | LCR Honda IDEMITSU | 23 |
| 21 | Scott Redding | GBR | Aprilia Racing Team Gresini | 15 |
| 22 | Karel Abraham | CZE | Ángel Nieto Team | 10 |
| 23 | Mika Kallio | FIN | Red Bull KTM Factory Racing | 6 |
| 24 | Stefan Bradl | GER | Honda Racing Corporation | 3 |
| 25 | Katsuyuki Nakasuga | JPN | Yamalube Yamaha Factory Racing | 2 |
| 26 | Xavier Siméon | GER | Reale Avintia Racing | 1 |
| 27 | Michele Pirro | ITA | Ducati Team | 1 |
| 28 | Thomas Lüthi | SWI | EG 0,0 Marc VDS | |
| 29 | Jordi Torres | SPA | Reale Avintia Racing | |
| 30 | Mike Jones | AUS | Ángel Nieto Team | |
| 31 | Sylvain Guintoli | FRA | Team SUZUKI ECSTAR | |
| 32 | Christophe Ponsson | FRA | Reale Avintia Racing | |

**13 | STEFAN BRADL**
HRC's test rider rode Cal Crutchlow's RC213V and did a good job, scoring his first points in his fourth race of 2018. LCR was a home from home for the German, who raced MotoGP with the team from 2012 to 2014.

**14 | TAKAAKI NAKAGAMI**
Had a great pace in FP3, which made him confident of challenging for a top-ten finish. However, the Japanese rookie found race day's higher track temperatures prevented him from replicating his Saturday morning pace. Took home two points.

**15 | BRADLEY SMITH**
Had a good FP3 session but Sunday wasn't the same. The first laps went well but then he went backwards, overtaken by Bradl, Aleix Espargaró and Nakagami. Made it into the points for the fifth consecutive race.

**16 | THOMAS LÜTHI**
This was the former Sepang Moto2 winner's fifth finish in 16th place, once again a tantalising single position away from scoring his first MotoGP point. He struggled a lot with edge grip and came very close to crashing at the final corner.

**17 | XAVIER SIMÉON**
One week after achieving his first MotoGP championship point the Belgian rookie wasn't in the hunt this time. He held last position for almost half the race until he finally overtook the struggling Redding.

**18 | VALENTINO ROSSI**
So near but so far. The nine-time world champion didn't deserve this ending. Like Márquez he had been fighting to lay the ghosts of Sepang 2015 to rest. Although if they had clashed on the final lap, who knows what might have happened?

**19 | SCOTT REDDING**
Was unable to magic any grip from his RS-GP all weekend. In the race he ran out of grip soon after one-quarter distance and found it impossible to better his lap times, however he rode, so he focused on finishing.

**DNF | POL ESPARGARÓ**
Completed a nightmare Pacific Rim trip with another retirement, seven days after his Australian DNF. A mystery electronics problem was probably at fault, causing his RC16 to progressively lose power. Called it a day with four laps remaining.

**DNF | MICHELE PIRRO**
Donned his leathers on Saturday morning to ride Lorenzo's GP18. Was an impressive 11th fastest in FP4 and started the race well, running just outside the top-ten. But lost the front at the final corner and crashed out.

**DNF | KAREL ABRAHAM**
Another let-down after a great Australian Grand Prix. Had a huge FP4 crash when the rain came down, which left him hurting badly. Decided to start the race, but an electronics fault put his motorcycle into shutdown mode after just three laps.

**DNF | ANDREA IANNONE**
Had a strong enough pace to fight for another podium. But when Márquez nearly crashed at the off-camber final turn on lap one he panicked and fell.

**DNS | JORDI TORRES**
His fourth MotoGP weekend got no further than FP4, when he crashed, fracturing a finger on his left hand.

**DNS | JORGE LORENZO**
Flew to Sepang hopeful of racing, but was 3.6 seconds off the pace in FP2, so he withdrew from the event.

## 19 | **VALENCIA**

**GRAN PREMIO MOTUL DE LA COMUNITAT VALENCIANA**
*CIRCUIT RICARDO TORMO*
*16/17/18 NOVEMBER*

# DOVIZIOSO STAYS AFLOAT TO WIN AGAIN

**The season finale was the first fully wet race day of 2018. And wet races often bring surprises**

Rainy races are a good thing, now and again. They allow the underdog to shine through the gloom and prove the impossible isn't always impossible.

The 2018 MotoGP season had been drier than most until the circus arrived at Valencia, where dark, brooding clouds gathered, unleashing biblical downpours throughout the weekend. Of course, the weather saved its best for Sunday, shortly after the MotoGP race got underway and while 15-year-old prodigy Can Öncü was still celebrating rewriting history with his impeccably mature Moto3 victory. He was now the youngest Grand Prix winner, the first Turk to win a GP and the first debutant to make it to the top step of the podium since Noboru Ueda won the 1991 Japanese 125cc GP. No doubt a few MotoGP riders were already wondering how fast Öncü might be around 2022.

The rain was already lashing down as MotoGP assembled on the grid. Álex Rins took full profit from his first front row start by leaping into the lead and leaving everyone spluttering in his spray. After four laps the 22-year-old was 3.5 seconds ahead of Andrea Dovizioso, while Marc Márquez battled back and forth with a very lively Pol Espargaró.

After six laps the rain intensified. Rins' lap times dropped dramatically, Dovizioso closed for the kill and Valentino Rossi carved his way towards the front, never mind the gathering flood. The crashes were coming quickly by now: Franco Morbidelli, Jack Miller, Aleix and Pol Espargaró, Andrea Iannone, Marc Márquez, Danilo Petrucci and Maverick Viñales, who took a huge tumble through the high-speed turn 13.

Pol Espargaró was able to get going again aboard his mud-spattered RC16 and was charging through the pack as Rins succumbed to Dovizioso and Rossi, who led for half a corner. When Dovizioso retook the lead his GP18 was aquaplaning wildly down the start/finish straight and he raised his left hand, signalling enough is enough. Immediately the red flags came out. The race hadn't reached three-quarters distance, so the riders had to go again, once the rain had eased and Race Direction had decided conditions had improved somewhat.

The world champion wasn't one of them. Márquez had fallen during qualifying, dislocating his left shoulder for the umpteenth time; which didn't stop him scooting back to the paddock, where the shoulder was popped in and he returned to the track, all within the space of seven minutes. But his race crash was bigger. He had chosen the medium rear, gambling the weather would get better, not worse. As soon as the rain increased his tyres cooled, the rear came around and he was flicked over the handlebars. "Choosing the medium was my worst mistake of the season," he said.

The restart got underway with just 16 bikes on the grid, while the rest of the riders tended their aches and pains in the pits. Once again, Rins led, his super-smooth throttle control and the Suzuki's sweet-handling chassis putting him ahead of Dovizioso after one lap. But this time there was no escape. Dovizioso eased his way past on lap two, followed six laps later by Rossi, while Pol Espargaró engaged with the surviving Repsol Honda rider, little Dani Pedrosa, contesting his 295th and last Grand Prix.

Dovizioso's pace was devastating but Rossi was determined to assuage the memory of an otherwise dismal season. His doomed chase ended on lap ten of 14, when he crashed at turn 12, which had already claimed several victims. "This is a bad emotion – very bad, very bad!" he said after his second consecutive race crash.

Now Rins was all alone in second, nursing his used rear tyre because, like many riders, he had exhausted his allocation of new rain tyres during the soaking weekend. Some way behind him was Espargaró, who had dealt with Pedrosa and was now holding on tight to complete an historic day for KTM: winners in Moto3 and Moto2 and their first podium in the big class.

Dovizioso's fourth win of the year came in ideal conditions for the Desmosedici, which could take full advantage of its braking and acceleration superiority on a slimy track, using the fatter part of the tyres, rather than risking in the corners when the contact patch is reduced. That and the fact that his crew had been clever enough to keep a spare soft rear rain tyre, having calculated that a restart wouldn't be out of the question in the ever-changing conditions.

**ABOVE, LEFT-RIGHT** Rookie Nakagami was top indie rider for the first time; Just seeing where you were going was a major issue; Rins started from the front row and led race one, raising a bow wave as conditions went from dodgy to dangerous

**MAIN** Rossi prepares to throw it up the inside of Dovizioso, moments before the red flags came out

**BELOW, LEFT-RIGHT** The start of an historic day for KTM – Öncü made history in Moto3, then Pol Espargaro fought like a tiger for the factory's first MotoGP podium; the rear Michelin of Viñales' M1 clearing four litres of water every second

'IN THE FIRST RACE I WAS WORRIED BECAUSE VALENTINO WAS SO FAST WHEN THE RAIN GOT HEAVIER'
ANDREA DOVIZIOSO

2018 FIM MotoGP™ WORLD CHAMPIONS

## GOODBYE 2018, HELLO 2019

Racing got underway at Valencia following some demo laps that signalled changes to MotoGP for 2019. Four-times GP world champion Jorge Aspar Martinez rode a MotoE bike, while former World Superbike champion and MotoGP rider James Toseland rode a Moto2 bike powered by the category's new engine supplier, Triumph.

The arrival of Triumph's 765cc triple will change Moto2, not only due to the engine's different power characteristics, but also due to the introduction of unified Magneti Marelli electronics. Both technical updates will bring the class closer to MotoGP so that riders are better prepared when they graduate to the premier-class.

"In the first race I was worried because Valentino was so fast when the rain got heavier," explained Dovizioso. "For the second race we made a small change to the set-up, used new soft tyres front and rear, and I was able to put up a good rhythm."

Rins was delighted with his fifth podium, which gave Suzuki four consecutive top-three finishes for the first time since 1994; the days of Kevin Schwantz! "I took a lot of risks when the rain got heavier in the first race, because it was so difficult to stay on the bike," said Rins after securing fifth in the championship.

Espargaró was even happier – this was his first-ever MotoGP podium and his first top-ten of an injury-blighted season. "It was a bit wild," he grinned. "I don't know how I did it – I couldn't even see on the straights. But after KTM's Moto2 and Moto3 wins I told myself, you're going to look ridiculous if you don't do something good!"

Pedrosa finished his career finale in fifth, behind a hard-charging Michele Pirro. He felt little emotion after the race because he had struggled so much in the rain. "I was on top of the water, the tyres weren't even touching the track," he said. "I was just trying not to crash, so I couldn't give everything I wanted. That's why I wasn't so emotional at the end."

**CLOCKWISE FROM TOP LEFT** | *This was Márquez's seventh time in the world champions' photo-call, but the first for Francesco Bagnaia and Jorge Martin; two weeks after crashing out of the lead at Sepang, Rossi's hopes of race-two victory ended in the Valencia mud; brotherly love as Aleix congratulates Pol; the BMW safety car checks the depth; Suzuki celebrate – this was the first time they'd scored four consecutive podiums since 1994; it really was very wet before the red flags came out*

"There will be a big change in riding style," says Alex Baumgartel of Kalex, winners of the previous six Moto2 riders and constructors titles. "There will be more torque at lower rpm and therefore more acceleration, so the riders won't need to carry all that speed through the corners, living on the edge of the tyres. Instead they will use less corner speed, so that they can better prepare the exit to use the acceleration, so in this way the riding style will be more like MotoGP."

The FIM Enel MotoE™ World Cup buzzes into action for the first time at the 2019 Spanish GP, with further rounds at the French, German, Austrian and San Marino events. The one-make series will use 160 horsepower/120Kw Energica bikes, charged by an onsite solar-panel charging system.

# ROUND 19 | VALENCIA

# RACE RESULTS

**WINNER** ANDREA DOVIZIOSO

**CIRCUIT LENGTH** 4.0 KM 2.49 MILES

**NO. OF LAPS** 27

**RACE DISTANCE** 108.1 KM 67.2 MILES

**CIRCUIT RECORD LAP** 1'31.171 158.1 KM/H
JORGE LORENZO (2016)

**CIRCUIT BEST LAP** 1'29.401 161.2 KM/H
JORGE LORENZO (2016)

**RACE CONDITION** WET

**AIR** 13°C

**HUMIDITY** 98%

**GROUND** 13°C

Start Line
Sectors
S Speed Trap
FL Finish Line

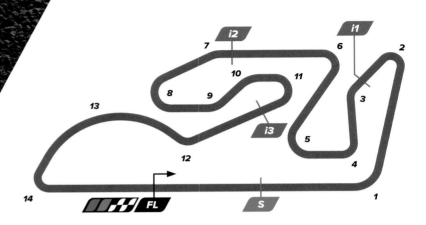

**OFFICIAL** TIMEKEEPER

**OFFICIAL** MotoGP™ CLASS TYRE

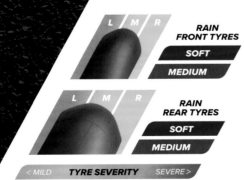

**RAIN FRONT TYRES**
SOFT
MEDIUM

**RAIN REAR TYRES**
SOFT
MEDIUM

< MILD **TYRE SEVERITY** SEVERE >

## QUALIFYING RESULTS

| | RIDER | NAT | TEAM | MACHINE | QP/TIME | | GAP 1ST/PREV | |
|---|---|---|---|---|---|---|---|---|
| 1 | Maverick Viñales** | SPA | Movistar Yamaha MotoGP | YAMAHA | Q2 | 1'31.312 | | |
| 2 | Álex Rins | SPA | Team SUZUKI ECSTAR | SUZUKI | Q2 | 1'31.380 | 0.068 | 0.068 |
| 3 | Andrea Dovizioso | ITA | Ducati Team | DUCATI | Q2 | 1'31.392 | 0.080 | 0.012 |
| 4 | Danilo Petrucci | ITA | Alma Pramac Racing | DUCATI | Q2 | 1'31.414 | 0.102 | 0.022 |
| 5 | Marc Márquez | SPA | Repsol Honda Team | HONDA | Q2 | 1'31.442 | 0.130 | 0.028 |
| 6 | Pol Espargaró | SPA | Red Bull KTM Factory Racing | KTM | Q2 | 1'31.577 | 0.265 | 0.135 |
| 7 | Andrea Iannone** | ITA | Team SUZUKI ECSTAR | SUZUKI | Q2 | 1'31.629 | 0.317 | 0.052 |
| 8 | Aleix Espargaró | SPA | Aprilia Racing Team Gresini | APRILIA | Q2 | 1'31.630 | 0.318 | 0.001 |
| 9 | Dani Pedrosa | SPA | Repsol Honda Team | HONDA | Q2 | 1'32.140 | 0.828 | 0.510 |
| 10 | Jack Miller | AUS | Alma Pramac Racing | DUCATI | Q2 | 1'32.145 | 0.833 | 0.005 |
| 11 | Johann Zarco | FRA | Monster Yamaha Tech 3 | YAMAHA | Q2 | 1'32.179 | 0.867 | 0.034 |
| 12 | Michele Pirro | ITA | Ducati Team | DUCATI | Q2 | 1'32.310 | 0.998 | 0.131 |
| 13 | Jorge Lorenzo | SPA | Ducati Team | DUCATI | Q1 | 1'31.900 | *0.518 | 0.042 |
| 14 | Takaaki Nakagami | JPN | LCR Honda IDEMITSU | HONDA | Q1 | 1'31.928 | *0.546 | 0.028 |
| 15 | Franco Morbidelli | ITA | EG 0,0 Marc VDS | HONDA | Q1 | 1'32.385 | *1.003 | 0.457 |
| 16 | Valentino Rossi | ITA | Movistar Yamaha MotoGP | YAMAHA | Q1 | 1'32.452 | *1.070 | 0.067 |
| 17 | Thomas Lüthi | SWI | EG 0,0 Marc VDS | HONDA | Q1 | 1'32.545 | *1.163 | 0.093 |
| 18 | Karel Abraham | CZE | Ángel Nieto Team | DUCATI | Q1 | 1'32.547 | *1.165 | 0.002 |
| 19 | Álvaro Bautista | SPA | Ángel Nieto Team | DUCATI | Q1 | 1'32.568 | *1.186 | 0.021 |
| 20 | Stefan Bradl | GER | LCR Honda CASTROL | HONDA | Q1 | 1'32.708 | *1.326 | 0.140 |
| 21 | Hafizh Syahrin | MAL | Monster Yamaha Tech 3 | YAMAHA | Q1 | 1'32.749 | *1.367 | 0.041 |
| 22 | Bradley Smith | GBR | Red Bull KTM Factory Racing | KTM | Q1 | 1'33.011 | *1.629 | 0.262 |
| 23 | Jordi Torres | SPA | Reale Avintia Racing | DUCATI | Q1 | 1'34.427 | *3.045 | 1.416 |
| 24 | Scott Redding | GBR | Aprilia Racing Team Gresini | APRILIA | Q1 | 1'35.171 | *3.789 | 0.744 |

*\* Gap to the fastest rider in the Q1 session*
*\*\* Went forward from Q1 to Q2*

**1 | ANDREA DOVIZIOSO**
Firstly, had the talent, bravery and the cool-headedness to ride faster than everyone else in truly treacherous conditions, without falling. Secondly, the team's strategy ensured that he had a brand-new soft rear for the restart.

**2 | ÁLEX RINS**
Another excellent ride from a fast-improving motorcycle. 'Won' the first race because he was leading the lap before the red flags came out. Rode an inch-perfect restart to make a little bit of history for Suzuki.

**3 | POL ESPARGARÓ**
Completed an historic day for the Austrian factory. The KTM showed its pace in the wet, apparently able to find grip where other bikes struggled. And it's not every day a MotoGP rider recovers from a crash to finish on the podium.

**4 | MICHELE PIRRO**
Perhaps MotoGP's fastest regular test rider had a slight advantage because he had tested at Valencia two weeks earlier, but nonetheless he rode a brilliant race, closing to within 1.2 seconds of a podium finish. Remounted after a race-one fall.

**5 | DANI PEDROSA**
Chose the soft front and rear for the restart but didn't have the grip or the feeling to ride as fast as he wanted, so had no chance of pushing his hardest towards completing his illustrious career with a podium in his last race.

**6 | TAKAAKI NAKAGAMI**
Said he felt scared at every corner, but managed to keep going and score by far the best result of his rookie season. His previous best was two 12th-place finishes at Jerez and Aragon. Helped by a strategy texted to him by injured Cal Crutchlow!

**7 | JOHANN ZARCO**
Happy with seventh, considering the conditions. Completed his time with Tech 3 as top independent-team rider, ahead of Crutchlow and Petrucci, a perfect way to end his first two years in MotoGP before joining the KTM factory.

**8 | BRADLEY SMITH**
Crashed out of the top ten in race one, restarting to end the race in last position. Made another of his great starts in race two to complete the first lap in tenth. Spent the entire 14 laps chasing Zarco and crossing the line three tenths down.

**9 | STEFAN BRADL**
Rode his fifth MotoGP race of 2018 and scored his first top-ten since Motegi 2016, when he was an Aprilia rider. Had even less recent experience of racing in the rain than most of his rivals, so made sure he built confidence slowly.

**10 | HAFIZH SYAHRIN**
This was 'Pescao's' first fully wet MotoGP race, so the Malaysian rookie did well to bring it home in the top ten. Had an outside chance of winning Rookie of the Year, after Franco Morbidelli's crash in race one, but came up five points short.

**11 | SCOTT REDDING**
Like many, considered the conditions to be too tricky. Completed his final MotoGP race in the points and celebrated by stripping off and throwing his helmet and leathers into the crowd. Finished the slowdown lap in his undies.

**12 | JORGE LORENZO**
Ducati's three-time winner started the weekend confident his wrist injury wouldn't be a problem, but it was. Most importantly he didn't want to risk falling, when he needed to be fit for his first Honda RC213V ride two days later.

## RACE LAP CHART

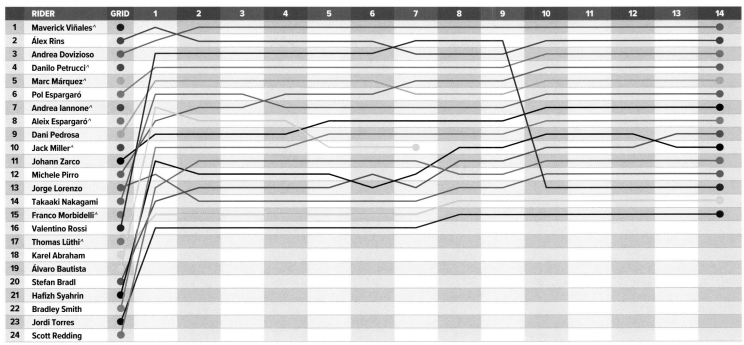

| | RIDER | GRID | 1 | 2 | 3 | 4 | 5 | 6 | 7 | 8 | 9 | 10 | 11 | 12 | 13 | 14 |
|---|---|---|---|---|---|---|---|---|---|---|---|---|---|---|---|---|
| 1 | Maverick Viñales^ | | | | | | | | | | | | | | | |
| 2 | Álex Rins | | | | | | | | | | | | | | | |
| 3 | Andrea Dovizioso | | | | | | | | | | | | | | | |
| 4 | Danilo Petrucci^ | | | | | | | | | | | | | | | |
| 5 | Marc Márquez^ | | | | | | | | | | | | | | | |
| 6 | Pol Espargaró | | | | | | | | | | | | | | | |
| 7 | Andrea Iannone^ | | | | | | | | | | | | | | | |
| 8 | Aleix Espargaró^ | | | | | | | | | | | | | | | |
| 9 | Dani Pedrosa | | | | | | | | | | | | | | | |
| 10 | Jack Miller^ | | | | | | | | | | | | | | | |
| 11 | Johann Zarco | | | | | | | | | | | | | | | |
| 12 | Michele Pirro | | | | | | | | | | | | | | | |
| 13 | Jorge Lorenzo | | | | | | | | | | | | | | | |
| 14 | Takaaki Nakagami | | | | | | | | | | | | | | | |
| 15 | Franco Morbidelli^ | | | | | | | | | | | | | | | |
| 16 | Valentino Rossi | | | | | | | | | | | | | | | |
| 17 | Thomas Lüthi^ | | | | | | | | | | | | | | | |
| 18 | Karel Abraham | | | | | | | | | | | | | | | |
| 19 | Álvaro Bautista | | | | | | | | | | | | | | | |
| 20 | Stefan Bradl | | | | | | | | | | | | | | | |
| 21 | Hafizh Syahrin | | | | | | | | | | | | | | | |
| 22 | Bradley Smith | | | | | | | | | | | | | | | |
| 23 | Jordi Torres | | | | | | | | | | | | | | | |
| 24 | Scott Redding | | | | | | | | | | | | | | | |

## RACE 2 CLASSIFICATION AFTER 14 LAPS = 56.07 KM

| | RIDER | NAT | TEAM | MACHINE | TIME | + GAP | TYRES |
|---|---|---|---|---|---|---|---|
| 1 | Andrea Dovizioso | ITA | Ducati Team | DUCATI | 24'03.408 | | RS/RS |
| 2 | Álex Rins | SPA | Team SUZUKI ECSTAR | SUZUKI | 24'06.158 | 2.750 | RM/RS |
| 3 | Pol Espargaró | SPA | Red Bull KTM Factory Racing | KTM | 24'10.814 | 7.406 | RS/RS |
| 4 | Michele Pirro | ITA | Ducati Team | DUCATI | 24'12.055 | 8.647 | RS/RS |
| 5 | Dani Pedrosa | SPA | Repsol Honda Team | HONDA | 24'16.759 | 13.351 | RS/RS |
| 6 | Takaaki Nakagami | JPN | LCR Honda IDEMITSU | HONDA | 24'35.696 | 32.288 | RS/RS |
| 7 | Johann Zarco | FRA | Monster Yamaha Tech 3 | YAMAHA | 24'36.214 | 32.806 | RS/RS |
| 8 | Bradley Smith | GBR | Red Bull KTM Factory Racing | KTM | 24'36.519 | 33.111 | RS/RS |
| 9 | Stefan Bradl | GER | LCR Honda CASTROL | HONDA | 24'39.784 | 36.376 | RS/RS |
| 10 | Hafizh Syahrin | MAL | Monster Yamaha Tech 3 | YAMAHA | 24'40.606 | 37.198 | RS/RS |
| 11 | Scott Redding | GBR | Aprilia Racing Team Gresini | APRILIA | 24'47.734 | 44.326 | RS/RS |
| 12 | Jorge Lorenzo | SPA | Ducati Team | DUCATI | 24'49.554 | 46.146 | RS/RS |
| 13 | Valentino Rossi | ITA | Movistar Yamaha MotoGP | YAMAHA | 24'56.217 | 52.809 | RS/RS |
| 14 | Karel Abraham | CZE | Ángel Nieto Team | DUCATI | 25'14.036 | 70.628 | RS/RS |
| 15 | Jordi Torres | SPA | Reale Avintia Racing | DUCATI | 25'20.147 | 76.739 | RS/RS |
| NC | Álvaro Bautista | SPA | Ángel Nieto Team | DUCATI | 12'19.932 | 7 laps | RS/RS |
| - | Maverick Viñales^ | SPA | Movistar Yamaha MotoGP | YAMAHA | | | |
| - | Danilo Petrucci^ | ITA | Alma Pramac Racing | DUCATI | | | |
| - | Marc Márquez ^ | SPA | Repsol Honda Team | HONDA | | | |
| - | Andrea Iannone^ | ITA | Team SUZUKI ECSTAR | SUZUKI | | | |
| - | Aleix Espargaró^ | SPA | Aprilia Racing Team Gresini | APRILIA | | | |
| - | Jack Miller^ | AUS | Alma Pramac Racing | DUCATI | | | |
| - | Franco Morbidelli^ | ITA | EG 0,0 Marc VDS | HONDA | | | |
| - | Thomas Lüthi ^ | SWI | EG 0,0 Marc VDS | HONDA | | | |

*Race 1 red flagged after 13 laps due to weather conditions*
*^ Not on restart grid, hence DNS notations below*
*Michelin wet tyre options : Rain Soft / Rain Medium*

## CHAMPIONSHIP STANDINGS

| | RIDER | NAT | TEAM | POINTS |
|---|---|---|---|---|
| 1 | Marc Márquez | SPA | Repsol Honda Team | 321 |
| 2 | Andrea Dovizioso | ITA | Ducati Team | 245 |
| 3 | Valentino Rossi | ITA | Movistar Yamaha MotoGP | 198 |
| 4 | Maverick Viñales | SPA | Movistar Yamaha MotoGP | 193 |
| 5 | Álex Rins | SPA | Team SUZUKI ECSTAR | 169 |
| 6 | Johann Zarco | FRA | Monster Yamaha Tech 3 | 158 |
| 7 | Cal Crutchlow | GBR | LCR Honda CASTROL | 148 |
| 8 | Danilo Petrucci | ITA | Alma Pramac Racing | 144 |
| 9 | Jorge Lorenzo | SPA | Ducati Team | 134 |
| 10 | Andrea Iannone | ITA | Team SUZUKI ECSTAR | 133 |
| 11 | Dani Pedrosa | SPA | Repsol Honda Team | 117 |
| 12 | Álvaro Bautista | SPA | Ángel Nieto Team | 105 |
| 13 | Jack Miller | AUS | Alma Pramac Racing | 91 |
| 14 | Pol Espargaró | SPA | Red Bull KTM Factory Racing | 51 |
| 15 | Franco Morbidelli | ITA | EG 0,0 Marc VDS | 50 |
| 16 | Hafizh Syahrin | MAL | Monster Yamaha Tech 3 | 46 |
| 17 | Aleix Espargaró | SPA | Aprilia Racing Team Gresini | 44 |
| 18 | Bradley Smith | GBR | Red Bull KTM Factory Racing | 38 |
| 19 | Tito Rabat | SPA | Reale Avintia Racing | 35 |
| 20 | Takaaki Nakagami | JPN | LCR Honda IDEMITSU | 33 |
| 21 | Scott Redding | GBR | Aprilia Racing Team Gresini | 20 |
| 22 | Michele Pirro | ITA | Ducati Team | 14 |
| 23 | Karel Abraham | CZE | Ángel Nieto Team | 12 |
| 24 | Stefan Bradl | GER | Honda Racing Corporation | 10 |
| 25 | Mika Kallio | FIN | Red Bull KTM Factory Racing | 6 |
| 26 | Katsuyuki Nakasuga | JPN | Yamalube Yamaha Factory Racing | 2 |
| 27 | Xavier Siméon | GER | Reale Avintia Racing | 1 |
| 28 | Jordi Torres | SPA | Reale Avintia Racing | 1 |
| 29 | Thomas Lüthi | SWI | EG 0,0 Marc VDS | |
| 30 | Mike Jones | AUS | Ángel Nieto Team | |
| 31 | Sylvain Guintoli | FRA | Team SUZUKI ECSTAR | |
| 32 | Christophe Ponsson | FRA | Reale Avintia Racing | |

**13 VALENTINO ROSSI**
Admitted the conditions were dangerous when the red flag came out but no doubt would've been happy to continue because he was the fastest man on the track at the time! Had too much of a gap to close on Dovizioso in race two.

**14 KAREL ABRAHAM**
Enjoyed the first race more than the second, but finished in the same position under the chequered flag as he had under the red flag. This was his third-best result of 2018 in his last race with the Ángel Nieto team before joining Avintia.

**15 JORDI TORRES**
Still recovering from the injury he sustained at Sepang, Tito Rabat's sub felt better with the lower physical stresses of racing in the wet. Achieved his goal of scoring a MotoGP point, bringing the total of points scorers to 28 riders.

**DNF ÁLVARO BAUTISTA**
Finished the null-and-void race one in seventh and felt better in the slightly drier race two. Was chasing Smith and fighting to set up a pass when he went down at turn 12. This was his last MotoGP race before moving to World Superbikes.

**DNS MAVERICK VIÑALES**
Was the last of the riders to crash out in race one, before the red flags came out. Lost control of his Yamaha as he rode through the waterlogged turn 13. Suffered a heavy highside, was hit by his bike and lucky to escape injury.

**DNS DANILO PETRUCCI**
His extra weight might be a real handicap for horsepower and traction in the dry, but some extra load in the rain can be a bonus. Was chasing Pol Espargaró for fourth in race one, when he overdid it. Wasn't able to get going again.

**DNS MARC MÁRQUEZ**
Made his own decision to switch to the medium rear for race one, while everyone else that mattered opted for the soft. Fell heavily when he lost the rear and was flicked off. Lucky not to dislocate his shoulder once again.

**DNS ANDREA IANNONE**
Pushed hard for a good result in his last race with Suzuki, so there was no option of switching to cruise mode when the rain intensified in race one. When he crashed, was one of four riders to go down at turn 12.

**DNS FRANCO MORBIDELLI**
Started race one from 15th and fought his way through to fifth place, for what should've been his best MotoGP result. Didn't ease his pace when the track became flooded and paid the price. Won the Rookie of the Year prize anyway.

**DNS THOMAS LÜTHI**
Started his final MotoGP race before reverting to Moto2 hoping that the dismal conditions might allow him to achieve his first point in the MotoGP world championship. But it wasn't to be: he was one of the first riders to crash, at turn 12.

**DNS JACK MILLER**
The Australian fell four times during practice, including twice on Saturday at the high-speed first corner. Then crashed out of race one.

**DNS ALEIX ESPARGARÓ**
Was angry following his early exit from race one, after showing good speed throughout practice on his 2017/2018/2019 lab RS-GP.

**DNS XAVIER SIMÉON**
The Belgian rookie didn't make it to the grid for his MotoGP finale after two big falls during the first practice sessions. Hit his head both times.

# THE RESULTS

## MotoGP™ WORLD CHAMPIONSHIP CLASSIFICATION

| | RIDER | NAT | POINTS | QAT | ARG | AME | ESP | FRA | ITA | CAT | NED | GER | CZE | AUT | GBR | RSM | ARA | THA | JPN | AUS | MAL | VAL |
|---|---|---|---|---|---|---|---|---|---|---|---|---|---|---|---|---|---|---|---|---|---|---|
| 1 | Marc Márquez | SPA | 321 | 20 | 0 | 25 | 25 | 25 | 0 | 20 | 25 | 25 | 16 | 20 | - | 20 | 25 | 25 | 25 | - | 25 | - |
| 2 | Andrea Dovizioso | ITA | 245 | 25 | 10 | 11 | - | - | 20 | - | 13 | 9 | 25 | 16 | - | 25 | 20 | 20 | 0 | 16 | 10 | 25 |
| 3 | Valentino Rossi | ITA | 198 | 16 | 0 | 13 | 11 | 16 | 16 | 16 | 11 | 20 | 13 | 10 | - | 9 | 8 | 13 | 13 | 10 | 0 | 3 |
| 4 | Maverick Viñales | SPA | 193 | 10 | 11 | 20 | 9 | 9 | 8 | 10 | 16 | 16 | - | 4 | - | 11 | 6 | 16 | 9 | 25 | 13 | - |
| 5 | Álex Rins | SPA | 169 | - | 16 | - | - | 6 | 11 | - | 20 | - | 5 | 8 | - | 13 | 13 | 10 | 16 | 11 | 20 | 20 |
| 6 | Johann Zarco | FRA | 158 | 8 | 20 | 10 | 20 | - | 6 | 9 | 8 | 7 | 9 | 7 | - | 6 | 2 | 11 | 10 | - | 16 | 9 |
| 7 | Cal Crutchlow | GBR | 148 | 13 | 25 | 0 | - | 8 | 10 | 13 | 10 | - | 11 | 13 | - | 16 | - | 9 | 20 | - | - | - |
| 8 | Danilo Petrucci | ITA | 144 | 11 | 6 | 4 | 13 | 20 | 9 | 8 | - | 13 | 10 | 11 | - | 5 | 9 | 7 | 7 | 4 | 7 | - |
| 9 | Jorge Lorenzo | SPA | 134 | - | 1 | 5 | - | 10 | 25 | 25 | 9 | 10 | 20 | 25 | - | 0 | - | - | - | - | - | 4 |
| 10 | Andrea Iannone | ITA | 133 | 7 | 8 | 16 | 16 | - | 13 | 6 | 5 | 4 | 6 | 3 | - | 8 | 16 | 5 | - | 20 | - | - |
| 11 | Dani Pedrosa | SPA | 117 | 9 | - | 9 | - | 11 | - | 11 | 1 | 8 | 8 | 9 | - | 10 | 11 | - | 8 | - | 11 | 11 |
| 12 | Álvaro Bautista | SPA | 105 | 3 | 0 | 1 | 8 | - | 7 | 7 | 7 | 11 | 7 | 6 | - | 7 | - | 8 | 11 | 13 | 9 | - |
| 13 | Jack Miller | AUS | 91 | 6 | 13 | 7 | 10 | 13 | - | - | 6 | 2 | 4 | 0 | - | 0 | 7 | 6 | - | 9 | 8 | - |
| 14 | Pol Espargaró | SPA | 51 | - | 5 | 3 | 5 | 5 | 5 | 5 | 4 | - | - | - | - | - | - | 0 | 3 | - | - | 16 |
| 15 | Franco Morbidelli | ITA | 50 | 4 | 2 | 0 | 7 | 3 | 1 | 2 | - | - | 3 | 0 | - | 4 | 5 | 2 | 5 | 8 | 4 | - |
| 16 | Hafizh Syahrin | MAL | 46 | 2 | 7 | - | 0 | 4 | 4 | - | 0 | 5 | 2 | 0 | - | 0 | 0 | 4 | 6 | - | 6 | 6 |
| 17 | Aleix Espargaró | SPA | 44 | 0 | - | 6 | - | 7 | - | - | 3 | - | 1 | 0 | - | 2 | 10 | 3 | - | 7 | 5 | - |
| 18 | Bradley Smith | GBR | 38 | 0 | - | 0 | 3 | 2 | 2 | - | 0 | 6 | - | 2 | - | 0 | 3 | 1 | 4 | 6 | 1 | 8 |
| 19 | Tito Rabat | SPA | 35 | 5 | 9 | 8 | 2 | - | 3 | - | 0 | 3 | - | 5 | - | - | - | - | - | - | - | - |
| 20 | Takaaki Nakagami | JPN | 33 | 0 | 3 | 2 | 4 | 1 | 0 | - | 0 | - | 0 | 1 | - | 3 | 4 | 0 | 1 | 2 | 2 | 10 |
| 21 | Scott Redding | GBR | 20 | 0 | 4 | 0 | 1 | - | - | 4 | 2 | 1 | - | 0 | - | 0 | 0 | 0 | 0 | 3 | 0 | 5 |
| 22 | Michele Pirro | ITA | 14 | - | - | - | - | - | - | - | - | - | - | - | - | 1 | - | - | - | - | - | 13 |
| 23 | Karel Abraham | CZE | 12 | 1 | - | - | 0 | 0 | - | 3 | - | 0 | 0 | 0 | - | 0 | 1 | 0 | - | 5 | - | 2 |
| 24 | Stefan Bradl | GER | 10 | - | - | - | - | - | - | - | - | 0 | - | - | - | - | - | - | - | - | 3 | 7 |
| 25 | Mika Kallio | FIN | 6 | - | - | - | 6 | - | - | - | - | - | - | - | - | - | - | - | - | - | - | - |
| 26 | Katsuyuki Nakasuga | JPN | 2 | - | - | - | - | - | - | - | - | - | - | - | - | - | - | - | 2 | - | - | - |
| 27 | Xavier Siméon | BEL | 1 | 0 | 0 | 0 | 0 | 0 | 0 | - | 0 | 0 | - | - | - | 0 | 0 | 0 | 0 | 1 | 0 | - |
| 28 | Jordi Torres | SPA | 1 | - | - | - | - | - | - | - | - | - | - | - | - | 0 | 0 | 0 | 0 | - | 1 | - |
| 29 | Thomas Lüthi | SWI | 0 | 0 | 0 | 0 | - | 0 | - | - | 0 | 0 | 0 | 0 | - | 0 | 0 | 0 | 0 | 0 | 0 | - |
| 30 | Mike Jones | AUS | 0 | - | - | - | - | - | - | - | - | - | - | - | - | - | - | - | - | 0 | - | - |
| 31 | Sylvain Guintoli | FRA | 0 | - | - | - | - | - | - | - | - | - | 0 | - | - | - | - | - | 0 | - | - | - |
| 32 | Christophe Ponsson | FRA | 0 | - | - | - | - | - | - | - | - | - | - | - | - | 0 | - | - | - | - | - | - |
| 33 | Loris Baz | FRA | 0 | - | - | - | - | - | - | - | - | - | - | - | - | - | - | - | - | - | - | - |

## CONSTRUCTORS

| | MANUFACTURER | POINTS | QAT | ARG | AME | ESP | FRA | ITA | CAT | NED | GER | CZE | AUT | GBR | RSM | ARA | THA | JPN | AUS | MAL | VAL |
|---|---|---|---|---|---|---|---|---|---|---|---|---|---|---|---|---|---|---|---|---|---|
| 1 | Honda | 375 | 20 | 25 | 25 | 25 | 25 | 10 | 20 | 25 | 25 | 16 | 20 | - | 20 | 25 | 25 | 25 | 8 | 25 | 11 |
| 2 | Ducati | 335 | 25 | 13 | 11 | 13 | 20 | 25 | 25 | 13 | 13 | 25 | 25 | - | 11 | 20 | 20 | 11 | 16 | 10 | 25 |
| 3 | Yamaha | 281 | 16 | 20 | 20 | 20 | 16 | 16 | 16 | 16 | 20 | 13 | 10 | - | 11 | 8 | 16 | 13 | 25 | 16 | 9 |
| 4 | Suzuki | 233 | 7 | 16 | 16 | 16 | 6 | 13 | 6 | 20 | 4 | 6 | 8 | - | 13 | 16 | 10 | 16 | 20 | 20 | 20 |
| 5 | KTM | 72 | - | 5 | 3 | 6 | 5 | 5 | 5 | 4 | 6 | - | 2 | - | - | 3 | 1 | 4 | 6 | 1 | 16 |
| 6 | Aprilia | 59 | - | 4 | 6 | 1 | 7 | - | 4 | 3 | 1 | 1 | - | - | 2 | 10 | 3 | - | 7 | 5 | 5 |

## TEAMS

| | TEAM | POINTS | QAT | ARG | AME | ESP | FRA | ITA | CAT | NED | GER | CZE | AUT | GBR | RSM | ARA | THA | JPN | AUS | MAL | VAL |
|---|---|---|---|---|---|---|---|---|---|---|---|---|---|---|---|---|---|---|---|---|---|
| 1 | Repsol Honda Team | 438 | 29 | - | 34 | 25 | 36 | - | 31 | 26 | 33 | 24 | 29 | - | 30 | 36 | 25 | 33 | - | 36 | 11 |
| 2 | Ducati Team | 392 | 25 | 11 | 16 | - | 10 | 45 | 25 | 22 | 19 | 45 | 41 | - | 25 | 20 | 20 | - | 29 | 10 | 29 |
| 3 | Movistar Yamaha MotoGP | 391 | 26 | 11 | 33 | 20 | 25 | 24 | 26 | 27 | 36 | 13 | 14 | - | 20 | 14 | 29 | 22 | 35 | 13 | 3 |
| 4 | Team SUZUKI ECSTAR | 302 | 7 | 24 | 16 | 16 | 6 | 24 | 6 | 25 | 4 | 11 | 11 | - | 21 | 29 | 15 | 16 | 31 | 20 | 20 |
| 5 | Alma Pramac Racing | 235 | 17 | 19 | 11 | 23 | 33 | 9 | 8 | 6 | 15 | 14 | 11 | - | 5 | 16 | 13 | 7 | 13 | 15 | - |
| 6 | Monster Yamaha Tech 3 | 204 | 10 | 27 | 10 | 20 | 4 | 10 | 9 | 8 | 12 | 11 | 7 | - | 6 | 2 | 15 | 16 | - | 22 | 15 |
| 7 | LCR Honda | 191 | 13 | 28 | 2 | 4 | 9 | 10 | 13 | 10 | - | 11 | 14 | - | 19 | 4 | 9 | 21 | 2 | 5 | 17 |
| 8 | Ángel Nieto Team | 104 | 4 | - | 1 | 8 | - | 7 | 10 | 7 | 11 | 7 | 6 | - | 7 | 1 | 8 | 11 | 5 | 9 | 2 |
| 9 | Red Bull KTM Factory Racing | 89 | - | 5 | 3 | 8 | 7 | 7 | 5 | 4 | 6 | - | 2 | - | - | 3 | 1 | 7 | 6 | 1 | 24 |
| 10 | Aprilia Racing Team Gresini | 64 | - | 4 | 6 | 1 | 7 | - | 4 | 5 | 1 | 1 | - | - | 2 | 10 | 3 | - | 10 | 5 | 5 |
| 11 | EG 0,0 Marc VDS | 50 | 4 | 2 | - | 7 | 3 | 1 | 2 | - | - | 3 | - | - | 4 | 5 | 2 | 5 | 8 | 4 | - |
| 12 | Reale Avintia Racing | 37 | 5 | 9 | 8 | 2 | - | 3 | - | - | 3 | - | 5 | - | - | - | - | - | 1 | - | 1 |

# EXPERIENCE SUPERIOR ACCELERATION WITH **CASTROL POWER1**

IT'S MORE THAN JUST OIL. IT'S LIQUID ENGINEERING.™

The Official Oil of the LCR Honda Castrol MotoGP team

**CASTROL POWER1 RACING** WITH RACE DERIVED TECHNOLOGY FOR **ULTIMATE PERFORMANCE AND RACING ACCELERATION.**

# A NEW ERA BEGINS...

FIM MotoGP™ WORLD CHAMPIONSHIP

POWERED BY
Moto2™ EXCLUSIVE ENGINE SUPPLIER 2019

## POWERING THE FIM Moto2™ WORLD CHAMPIONSHIP FROM 2019.

Based on the class-leading Street Triple our dedicated race tuned 765cc Triumph Triple engine has been developed for a new era of triple-powered Moto2™ racing. With a step change in performance, a thrilling, responsive torque delivery and a major step up in power, the new 765cc Moto2™ Triple has been designed to take the championship to a whole new level. Triumph's racing future starts here.

To find out more visit triumph.co.uk

FOR THE RIDE

# BAGNAIA: VR46'S SECOND MOTO2 CHAMP

**Mentored by a nine time world champion, Bagnaia was the driving force in Moto2, dismissing a strong challenge from Miguel Oliveira.**

Franco 'Pecco' Bagnaia became the VR46 Academy's second world champion when he beat Miguel Oliveira to the 2018 Moto2 title, following 2017 champ Franco Morbidelli. The 21-year-old Italian and 23-year-old Portuguese battled all season, until Bagnaia finally put it beyond doubt at the penultimate Malaysian GP.

The Bagnaia/Oliveira duel was significant because Moto2 isn't merely its own world championship, it's a production line for MotoGP apprentices. The pair are two of four 2018 Moto2 riders who will graduate to the premier class in 2019, along with Barcelona winner Fabio Quartararo and rookie of the year Joan Mir.

The promotion of Bagnaia and Oliveira is particularly significant because they are the product of two systems established for this very purpose. Firstly, VR46 (aka the Tavullia brotherhood), which was created to foster a new generation of Italian talent to follow in the wheel tracks of Valentino Rossi. Secondly, Red Bull KTM, which aims to conquer MotoGP, just as it has conquered pretty much every other category it has tackled, off-road and on.

Oliveira was the pre-season favourite for Moto2's final year with Honda CBR600RR power. He went into 2018 having completed the 2017 campaign with three consecutive victories that suggested KTM had found the secret to beating Kalex, which

**CLOCKWISE, FROM TOP LEFT** | Bagnaia and Oliveira at it; Binder came on strong; Pasini showed flashes of speed; Oliveira needed more wins; Quartararo was the big surprise; Sky VR46 celebrate race and title victories; Baldassarri lacked consistency; Oliveira leads the champ; Bagnaia celebrates the title at Sepang

had won every riders and constructors title since Marc Márquez moved to MotoGP at the end of 2012.

KTM's late-2017 advantage came from better rear-tyre management at the end of races, but Kalex responded well. "Our 2018 chassis has different front/rear stiffness balance to increase the self-turning effect, so now the bike turns better, so the rider doesn't need to stress the front tyre when braking into the corner or spin the rear tyre to finish the corner," explained Kalex engineer Alex Baumgartel.

Bagnaia had also improved. From four podiums in his rookie Moto2 season the 21-year-old won three of the first five races to open a 25-point lead over Oliveira, whose main problem was qualifying. Moto2 qualifying was unique in 2018. Rubber laid during the previous MotoGP FP4 and qualifying sessions increased grip for Moto2 riders, at least until the Moto2 bikes had cleaned it off. Thus pole positions were often established in the first few laps of qualifying, instead of the last laps. Oliveira's issue was the KTM struggled to take advantage of that brief moment of extra grip.

Then Bagnaia ran into his own problems. At Mugello a pre-race massage inflamed the arm he had injured at COTA and he struggled to fourth. At Barcelona his rear tyre gave up and at the Sachsenring he ran off the track when Mattia Pasini crashed and ended up 12th. Oliveira, who had won his first race at Mugello, had closed the gap to just eight points. And when he won at Brno, where Bagnaia finished third, the KTM man took the championship lead, by two points. The duel was on…

Bagnaia's greatest strength was leading from the front, laying down his lap times with metronomic precision.

"I realised that it's very important for me to be alone on track, so I can control the race, make my own pace and concentrate on my lines," said the former Moto3 winner. "One of my secrets is sector times – I control the gap by looking at my time and the gap in every sector on my dash. When I am behind it's difficult because my style is very different to Miguel's. He stops the bike more than me, so if I'm in front it's very difficult for him to follow me because I used more corner speed. And if I'm behind I can't use my corner speed, because he stops his bike so much."

And yet Bagnaia could do it the other way too. Seven days after Oliveira had taken the championship lead he put his KTM in front at the brand's home race in Austria. He led until the penultimate corner when Bagnaia divebombed him. Oliveira got back ahead into the final turn, but ran slightly wide and Bagnaia didn't need a written invitation; he dived past again, lifting up his rival, to win by two tenths.

Perhaps that was the championship turning point. Bagnaia had stalled Oliveira's momentum. Next time out at Misano, Bagnaia led from start to finish, while his title rival fought through from a third-row start to finish second. Further victories in Thailand and Japan sealed the deal for the VR46 rider. Even a 12th-place finish at the end of a complicated Australian GP didn't upset his rhythm, because Oliveira had a similarly difficult weekend, ending the race 11th.

Oliveira was philosophical about his defeat. "We came into Moto2 last year with a brand-new bike, with zero racing kilometres. Last year helped us understand the strong points and weak points of the bike, so we could make a compromise. The last part of 2017 came easy, so we thought we would be similarly strong this year, but Kalex made a good step. Our bike is still very young, while Kalex have been doing Moto2 for many years with many good riders, so they have a lot of data.

"But the differences between my bike and Pecco's are tiny. My problem was being able to use the edge of the tyres to turn the bike, with good grip and drive. Pecco rode a great season – he was strong in every situation – riding alone and fighting. And he clicked really well with his team."

Both title fighters had strong team-mates, especially Brad Binder on the other Red Bull KTM. The 23-year-old South African had a sluggish start to his second year with the team, never seeing the podium until he took his career first Moto2 victory at Sachsenring. Like Oliveira he had struggled in qualifying and didn't really get everything right until Aragon, where he took pole position and victory over Bagnaia. The secret to the transformation was a test session at Valencia, where he made vital tweaks to his set-up. "At other races it always seemed like something wasn't gelling," he revealed.

Binder's strong finish to the season lifted him from seventh overall to third, making him one of the favourites for 2019, when the series will use three-cylinder Triumph 765 engines.

Bagnaia's Sky VR46 team-mate Marini won his first GP at Sepang and was one of four other riders to win Moto2 races. The youngster, the second fastest rider at Rossi's ranch (after the man himself!), found impressive speed in the second half of the season, taking third place at Sachsenring, pole and second place at Brno (just seven hundredths of a second behind Oliveira), third place at the Red Bull Ring and second at Buriram, where he bettered Oliveira on the final lap to gift his team-mate some vital extra points.

Veteran Pasini took the flag at Termas Rio Honda, Lorenzo Baldassari won at Jerez, his first success with Sito Pons' team, and 2013 CEV Moto3 champ Quartararo came out of nowhere to take victory for Speed Up at Barcelona, his first Grand Prix success since he joined the world championships in 2015. Quartararo's victory followed a test session at Mugello and was the catalyst to his MotoGP deal with the new Petronas SIC Yamaha squad.

Moto3 world champion of 2017 Mir was rookie of the year, adapting quickly enough to climb a Moto2 podium for the first time at Le Mans. It was no coincidence that he signed a Suzuki MotoGP contract at around the same time. However, Mir's results were up and down for the rest of the year. The highlights were two runner-up finishes at Sachsenring and Phillip Island, chasing Binder over the line on both occasions.

Mir ended the championship in sixth, behind 0,0 Estrella Galicia Marc VDS team-mate Álex Márquez, who failed to add to the three wins he achieved in 2017, and Baldassarri. Next in the points chase were Luca Marini and Marcel Schrötter, who scored his first podium in ten and a half years of trying at Misano.

Moto2 will be different in 2019. Triumph's 765cc triple makes more torque, which will shift riding-technique focus from mid-corner speed to exit speed. New electronic rider controls will also affect technique. Frames will be slightly different because the triple is taller, so the engine hangers, which provide lateral flex, will be shorter. Finally, test teams will no longer be allowed in Moto2.

## Moto2™ WORLD CHAMPIONSHIP STANDING

| | RIDER | NAT | MANUFACTURER | POINTS |
|---|---|---|---|---|
| 1 | Francesco Bagnaia | ITA | KALEX | 306 |
| 2 | Miguel Oliveira | POR | KTM | 297 |
| 3 | Brad Binder | RSA | KTM | 201 |
| 4 | Álex Márquez | SPA | KALEX | 173 |
| 5 | Lorenzo Baldassarri | ITA | KALEX | 162 |
| 6 | Joan Mir | SPA | KALEX | 155 |
| 7 | Luca Marini | ITA | KALEX | 147 |
| 8 | Marcel Schrötter | GER | KALEX | 147 |
| 9 | Mattia Pasini | ITA | KALEX | 141 |
| 10 | Fabio Quartararo | FRA | SPEED UP | 138 |
| 11 | Xavi Vierge | SPA | KALEX | 131 |
| 12 | Iker Lecuona | SPA | KTM | 80 |
| 13 | Jorge Navarro | SPA | KALEX | 58 |
| 14 | Simone Corsi | ITA | KALEX | 53 |
| 15 | Andrea Locatelli | ITA | KALEX | 52 |
| 16 | Sam Lowes | GBR | KTM | 49 |
| 17 | Dominique Aegerter | SWI | KTM | 47 |
| 18 | Augusto Fernandez | SPA | KALEX | 45 |
| 19 | Remy Gardner | AUS | Tech 3 | 40 |
| 20 | Tetsuta Nagashima | JPN | KALEX | 27 |
| 21 | Romano Fenati | ITA | KALEX | 14 |
| 22 | Jesko Raffin | SWI | KALEX | 10 |
| 23 | Hector Barbera | SPA | KALEX | 10 |
| 24 | Stefano Manzi | ITA | SUTER | 8 |
| 25 | Danny Kent | GBR | SPEED UP | 8 |
| 26 | Isaac Viñales | SPA | SUTER | 7 |
| 27 | Joe Roberts | USA | NTS | 5 |
| 28 | Steven Odendaal | RSA | NTS | 4 |
| 29 | Bo Bendsneyder | NED | TECH 3 | 2 |
| 30 | Khairul Idham Pawi | MAL | KALEX | 1 |
| 31 | Edgar Pons | SPA | SPEED UP | 1 |
| 32 | Niki Tuuli | FIN | KALEX | 1 |
| 33 | Xavi Cardelus | AND | KALEX | |
| 34 | Jules Danilo | FRA | KALEX | |
| 35 | Thitipong Warokorn | THA | KALEX | |
| 36 | Federico Fuligni | ITA | KALEX | |
| 37 | Eric Granado | BRA | SUTER | |
| 38 | Lukas Tulovic | GER | SUTER | |
| 39 | Hector Garzo | SPA | TECH 3 | |
| 40 | Bryan Staring | AUS | TECH 3 | |
| 41 | Dimas Ekky Pratama | INA | TECH 3 | |
| 42 | Tommaso Marcon | ITA | - | |
| 43 | Alejandro Medina | SPA | KALEX | |
| 44 | Sheridan Morais | POR | KALEX | |
| 45 | Corentin Perolari | FRA | TRANSFORMERS | |
| 46 | Zulfahmi Khairuddin | MAL | KALEX | |
| 47 | Rafid Topan Sucipto | INA | SUTER | |
| 48 | Cedric Tangre | FRA | TECH 3 | |

Maverick Viñales

### History. Family. Dedication.

It doesn't matter what you ride or where you ride it, protection is our priority in every helmet we create. That is Arai's unshakeable foundation which you can rely on.

Even if you never use an Arai helmet for its intended purpose, the hand-crafted comfort which only Arai can deliver will let you enjoy every ride even more.

And look darn good while doing it too!

araihelmet.eu

**Arai**
HELMET®

*there is a difference*

# MARTIN IS A CLASS APART

*Young Spaniard Jorge Martin had an up-and-down fourth season in Moto3 but he was the standout rider of the championship*

Moto3 is by far the closest-fought racing category in the history of Grand Prix motorcycle racing. Since the world championships were created 70 years ago, 17 of the 20 closest top-15 finishes have been recorded in Moto3, which only came into existence seven seasons ago. That is quite a statistic, facilitated by a rulebook written specifically to prevent any manufacturer from spending more money than its competitors to leave its rivals behind.

In 2018 it was more of the same, with five races won by less than a tenth of a second and a further four by less than a second. Unsurprisingly, the wide, open spaces of Phillip Island produced the closest top-15, with all the points scorers crossing the finish line within two seconds of each other. The last lap was like the first lap of most races.

"Moto3 is always a big confusion!" laughs former 125cc world champion Valentino Rossi, who mentors several Moto3 youngsters in his VR46 Academy, including 2018 championship third place finisher Marco Bezzecchi.

Nevertheless, there was one man who stood out during the 2018 season. Twenty-year-old Spaniard Jorge Martin was mostly a class apart. He was a genius at qualifying with an ability to magic pole position out of nowhere, pretty much whenever he wanted. He started from pole on 11 occasions and won seven races. His victory tally would surely have been greater if it

**CLOCKWISE, FROM TOP LEFT** | Bastianini takes out Bezzecchi in Thailand; Canet was fast but crashed too often; just another normal Moto3 ride out; Bezzecchi came out of nowhere to challenge for the title; Bastianini was another who blew hot and cold; Bezzecchi nurses a wrist injury; Martin's just been taken out at Le Mans; mass pile-ups were nothing unusual; Martin basks in well-deserved glory at Sepang

hadn't been for some horrible luck and a couple of mistakes. This was a great triumph for Martin, who came close to quitting racing following his 2013 Red Bull Rookies campaign, due to money worries. Luckily, he hung in there and won the Rookies title the following year, beating 2017 Moto3 world champion Joan Mir. In 2015 he got his first Grand Prix ride, with Mahindra.

After winning two of the first three races of 2018, in Qatar and the Americas, Martin (Del Conca Gresini Honda) was taken out at the next two races - by Aron Canet at Jerez and by Bezzecchi at Le Mans. This, of course, is the nature of Moto3: riders are so closely packed that when someone goes down they invariably take someone with them. This didn't happen again to Martin for the remainder of the year, so perhaps he had learned to keep out of trouble.

At Mugello he won by 0.019 seconds and at Assen by 0.66 seconds. He could also run away from the pack when he felt he had it in him. At the Sachsenring he put 2.5 seconds between himself and runner-up Bezzecchi (Redox PrustelGP KTM), who had become his greatest rival following his DNFs in Spain and France. And at Aragon he destroyed his rivals, leaving the pack almost six seconds behind him.

His greatest victory probably came at Sepang, where he finally put the title out of Bezzecchi's reach. This was Martin at his aggressive, intelligent best. In the early laps he seemed to have lost his head — perhaps the championship pressure had finally got to him. He started the race from pole but was swamped in the early laps, dropping him to tenth place at half-distance. However, Martin had a plan. He was waiting for a few damp patches to dry out before unleashing everything he had, which took 3.5 seconds out of the pack during the last four laps. This should not be possible in Moto3.

"There are a lot of tactics in Moto3," he explained. "If you have a few tenths more than the others, maybe you can break away, if you can save your tyres. But if you are in a big group, you stay there and plan the best places to overtake at the end of the race. But it can be dangerous, because there are always some riders in the group who aren't fighting for the championship and have nothing to lose, so they can cause you problems. This is one reason I had such an up-and-down season. The year started well for us, then we had some bad luck, then I got injured."

Martin crashed out of the lead at Barcelona, but it was during Brno practice that he got hurt, breaking his left forearm. This could not have happened at a worse moment, because Brno and the Red Bull Ring were the only back-to-back races of the European season. So he rushed home to Spain, had the fracture plated and was back in business the following weekend, when he finished a Lazarus-like third, just behind winner Bezzecchi and Enea Bastianini (Leopard Honda). "That race was a lot of pain and a lot of emotion," said Martin. "It was a hard year but I never gave up, never lost my faith."

However, his injury woes weren't over. Two months later

in Thailand a nerve in his forearm became inflamed and he couldn't fully grip the handlebars. He wore a special glove for the race, which eased the problem, and he managed to finish a very close fourth. Bezzecchi's chance to take advantage of his rival's troubles was ruined by Bastianini, who took out his fellow Italian at the final corner.

This wasn't Bezzecchi's first last-lap tumble. He had crashed out of his own accord at Le Mans, where he took Martin with him, and at Assen, where his mistake put his Spanish rival back into the championship lead, which Martin had lost with those DNFs in Spain and France. And at his home race at Misano, Bezzecchi highsided out of the lead with just a lap to go.

There was more drama to follow. At Motegi it was Martin's turn to crash out in the final stages, allowing Bezzecchi to close the gap to just a single point with three races remaining. However, the very next weekend at Phillip Island it was Bezzecchi's turn to get taken out, by fellow KTM rider Gabriel Rodrigo. With two races left, Martin was back in control.

The Moto3 technical landscape remained much the same as previous years: Honda's NSF250RW had the sweetest-handling chassis, while KTM's RC250 had the best straight-line speed.

"The KTM was always faster than our bike, but we could beat them with our better handling," explained Martin. "We could use more corner speed, plus the Honda used its tyres less at the end of races."

KTM brought its one-per-year chassis update at Brno, with revised frame stiffness to improve corner-entry feel, but Honda still had the upper hand in the twists and turns.

Bezzecchi was the Austrian company's only title contender and he used his RC250 well. This was only the 19-year-old's second Grand Prix season, which followed a difficult rookie campaign with Mahindra, during which he was able to showcase his talent just once, at a rain-soaked Motegi, where he finished on the podium.

Rossi was impressed with Bezzecchi's 2018 campaign. "We picked him up after a tough season with Mahindra and he did more than I expected, he surprised me," said Rossi. "I think his biggest improvement was his mental improvement, which came from him, not from us."

The title fight was a straight two-way duel for much of the season, until Martin's Gresini team-mate Fabio Di Giannantonio came on strong in the final stages. He won his first Grand Prix at Brno and his second at Buriram, which he backed up with a runner-up finish at Phillip Island to put himself within striking distance of the championship lead. The young Roman's progression was impressive and he will surely figure in the 2019 title contest.

Bastianini won his first Grand Prix in almost two years at Barcelona, but was too up and down – both literally and metaphorically – to challenge for the title. He will need to stay on board more often next year if he is to fulfil his promise.

While Bastianini seemed to take a small step backwards, his Leopard Honda team-mate Lorenzo Dalla Porta took a giant leap forward. The former 125cc Italian champion had barely made it into the top ten until 2018, when he out-rode Martin to win his first Grand Prix at Misano and scored a handful of other podiums. He made it five Hondas in the top six of the championship, with Canet just behind on final points.

Rodrigo (RBA BOE Skull Rider) was the next KTM rider in seventh, followed by four others on the Austrian machines: Bezzecchi's team-mate Jakub Kornfeil, Albert Arenas (Ángel Nieto Team), Marcos Ramirez (Bester Capital Dubai) and Andrea Migno (Ángel Nieto Team).

## Moto3™ WORLD CHAMPIONSHIP STANDING

|  | RIDER | NAT | MANUFACTURER | POINTS |
|---|---|---|---|---|
| 1 | Jorge Martin | SPA | HONDA | 260 |
| 2 | Fabio Di Giannantonio | ITA | HONDA | 218 |
| 3 | Marco Bezzecchi | ITA | KTM | 214 |
| 4 | Enea Bastianini | ITA | HONDA | 177 |
| 5 | Lorenzo Dalla Porta | ITA | HONDA | 151 |
| 6 | Aron Canet | SPA | HONDA | 128 |
| 7 | Gabriel Rodrigo | ARG | KTM | 116 |
| 8 | Jakub Kornfeil | CZE | KTM | 116 |
| 9 | Albert Arenas | SPA | KTM | 107 |
| 10 | Marcos Ramirez | SPA | KTM | 102 |
| 11 | Andrea Migno | ITA | KTM | 84 |
| 12 | John Mcphee | GBR | KTM | 78 |
| 13 | Jaume Masia | SPA | KTM | 76 |
| 14 | Tatsuki Suzuki | JPN | HONDA | 71 |
| 15 | Niccolò Antonelli | ITA | HONDA | 71 |
| 16 | Philipp Oettl | GER | KTM | 58 |
| 17 | Darryn Binder | RSA | KTM | 57 |
| 18 | Tony Arbolino | ITA | HONDA | 57 |
| 19 | Dennis Foggia | ITA | KTM | 55 |
| 20 | Ayumu Sasaki | JPN | HONDA | 50 |
| 21 | Adam Norrodin | MAL | HONDA | 46 |
| 22 | Kaito Toba | JPN | HONDA | 37 |
| 23 | Alonso Lopez | SPA | HONDA | 36 |
| 24 | Can Öncü | TUR | KTM | 25 |
| 25 | Celestino Vietti | ITA | KTM | 24 |
| 26 | Nicolo Bulega | ITA | KTM | 18 |
| 27 | Vicente Perez | SPA | KTM | 16 |
| 28 | Raul Fernandez | SPA | KTM | 16 |
| 29 | Nakarin Atiratphuvapat | THA | HONDA | 12 |
| 30 | Makar Yurchenko | KAZ | HONDA | 9 |
| 31 | Kazuki Masaki | JPN | KTM | 9 |
| 32 | Livio Loi | BEL | KTM | 8 |
| 33 | Somkiat Chantra | THA | HONDA | 7 |
| 34 | Manuel Pagliani | ITA | HONDA | 6 |
| 35 | Stefano Nepa | ITA | KTM | 4 |
| 36 | Ai Ogura | JPN | HONDA | 1 |
| 37 | Yari Montella | ITA | HONDA | |
| 38 | Apiwath Wongthananon | THA | KTM | |
| 39 | Jeremy Alcoba | SPA | HONDA | |
| 40 | Kevin Zannoni | ITA | TM Racing | |
| 41 | Luca Grünwald | GER | KTM | |
| 42 | Shizuka Okazaki | JPN | HONDA | |
| 43 | Izam Ikmal | MAL | - | |
| 44 | Yuto Fukushima | JPN | HONDA | |
| 45 | Filip Salac | CZE | KTM | |
| 46 | Ryan Van De Lagemaat | NED | KTM | |
| 47 | Maximilian Kofler | AUT | KTM | |

# Take them all on.

Join today
**0800 201 2201** or
visit **bt.com/sport**

**BT Sport**
Be There

# THE NAME IS ÖNCÜ, CAN AND DENIZ

ROOKIESCUP.REDBULL.COM

*There is more than one way to dominate a championship but if you can finish the first ten of twelve races on the podium, winning five and finishing second four times, there is not much the opposition can do. And so it was that 15-year-old Turk Can Öncü wrapped up the 2018 Red Bull MotoGP Rookies Cup in Misano, with two races still remaining.*

His twin brother Deniz then did the double at Motorland Aragón to secure second in the Cup and conclude a truly remarkable second season for the decidedly dynamic duo. That made history and what made it truly impressive was the strength of the opposition.

Right from the start of the season in Jerez it was clear that the Öncü twins, while favourites after their great 2017 seasons, were in for a tough time. Still 14 back in May, curly haired Can, the larger of the twins, won Race 1 in Spain but pole man, Spaniard Carlos Tatay, also 14, battled him all the way and crossed the line just 0.144 seconds behind.

Typical Rookies Cup, the 16-lap contest had featured an eight man lead battle with the pair only breaking away towards the end. Czech 16-year-old Filip Salač chased them to complete the podium with Deniz Öncü a frustrated fourth.

Rookies newcomer Tatay pushed even harder in Race 2 and came out ahead with a perfect out-braking move on Can Öncü at the final turn. There was some confusion as the circuit lap board had shown two laps-to-go the previous time round and, while Tatay knew it was the last lap from his own

pit board, both the Öncü twins and Salač thought there was another still to go.

Carlos Tatay celebrated his 15th birthday the day after the race as joint Rookies points leader with Can Öncü. Deniz Öncü and third-year Rookie Salač shared third.

Suddenly there was a new Cup hero; Tatay had looked super smooth and comfortable at home. When the series moved on to Mugello he was just as smooth, was again in the lead battle but that struggle went all the way to the line and he crossed it fourth, with Japanese 15-year-old Yuki Kunii at the head and the top 13 covered by just 1.5 seconds.

Can Öncü was second and 15-year-old Spaniard Adrián Carrasco third. Kunii had been eleventh and sixth in Jerez and the superb Italian win launched him into possible Cup contention. He was as just as smooth and stylish as Tatay; a real challenger.

Sadly he was denied the chance to show how much of a challenge he would have made when a FIM CEV Repsol Moto3 Junior World Championship crash resulted in a broken hand that demanded surgery. He missed the next four Cup races.

Can Öncü was also doing the CEV races but managing to keep himself out of serious trouble and he came back to the Cup to score a double at Assen, matching his 2017 achievement. In Race 1 he dominated from pole while twin brother Deniz was embroiled in a chasing five-man battle. It was Xavi Artigas and Ryusei Yamanaka who took the podium places.

All three on the podium were second-year Rookies and while Spanish 15-year-old Artigas was there for the first time, Yamanaka, the 16-year-old Japanese, had stood there in 2017.

Artigas had not been stunning in 2017 but he had been intelligently improving through the season, while Yamanaka was at times faster but less consistent.

Can Öncü continued to win and did so in Race 2 at Assen after some furious opening laps. He then reeled off a string of near perfect circuits to replicate his Saturday domination and thus extended his points lead to 49.

It was Salač who got the best of the chasing KTM RC 250 Rs to better his fourth from Saturday by taking second ahead of Artigas, who stepped onto the podium for the second time.

Just as he had in 2017 Can was moving in to put a first hand on the Cup. The others were a long way short of giving up, including brother Deniz who made a wonderful job of taking Race 1 in Germany. He headed twin brother Can by 4.455 seconds after 19 laps.

Can wasn't perfectly happy with the bike in Race 1 but still took second, hounded across the line by Yamanaka, Salač, Carrasco and 18-year-old Colombian Steward Garcia, all blanketed by half a second.

The Öncüs also dominated the Sunday race but with Can heading Deniz and just a fraction of a second separating them. Three seconds back, the battle for third was even more intense with Salač snatching it after another great battle with Carrasco, Artigas and Yamanaka.

On to the Red Bull Ring with just five races remaining. Having turned 15 on July 26th, the Turkish twins were looking good. Can had a 52-point advantage over Deniz after they had scored equally in Germany and both were gaining on the rest. Salač was closest, 13 points behind Deniz.

Can had been in this position before: he was already grabbing for the Cup in 2017 but things unravelled in the second half of the season. He scored points in just half of the last six races and ended the year third overall. So everyone, the brothers especially, knew how quickly it could all change.

Adding another dimension, the weather mixed things up in Austria. Friday morning was dry but FP2 in the afternoon was cut short by a deluge. As the track dried through qualifying, Yamanaka judged it perfectly for pole ahead of Artigas and 16-year-old Brazilian Meikon Kawakami. Can Öncü was only eighth and Deniz 14th.

From first pole to first victory makes Yamanaka's Saturday sound easy but it certainly wasn't. He fought all the way and it was only a decisive move on the last lap that secured him the win. Snapping at his heels were Artigas and Can Öncü. Deniz had quickly cut through to the front but it took Can longer. He finished better though, as Deniz stumbled at the end and took fourth.

Deniz got the same finish on Sunday while Artigas claimed his first win by matching Yamanaka's last lap plan and finished ahead of Can Öncü and Salač. The top nine were separated by only 1.3 seconds.

That third and second enhanced Can Öncü's Cup position and made it possible for him to clinch the title in Italy. On the other hand, brother Deniz was under increased pressure for second from both Artigas and Salač.

At Misano it was even more of a family thing than usual for the Öncüs, with them chasing each other around in qualifying to secure first and second. Yamanaka completed the front row ahead of Kawakami.

The single Italian race followed that form with Deniz doing most of the front running, heading another fabulous nine-rider lead battle. Yet again it was the final lap or so that was his undoing and he was deeply frustrated with eighth while Can won the race and the Cup.

Just 1.3 seconds covered the top eight across the line as Salač took second ahead of Carrasco. The battle for the runner-up position in the Cup intensified with Salač and Deniz equal second and Artigas just seven points adrift in fourth.

No doubting that Can Öncü was a worthy champion, that run of ten podium finishes was just incredible and only one of them was a third. Surely he would go into the final two races in Motorland Aragón with plans to complete the perfect season.

Whatever he might have intended, it didn't happen. He was tenth in qualifying, placed the same in Race 1 and eighth in Race 2. He said that both he and the bike were off form.

Dad might not have been happy but his other son saved the family honour completely with two classic wins from P2 on the grid.

He had not been impressed by being chased round in qualifying and was upset with Artigas even though the Spaniard set a time almost half-a-second quicker. Deniz made use of the frustration he felt and avoided the end-of-race errors that had cost him so dearly earlier in the season.

On Saturday he won from Artigas and Tatay then on Sunday secured second in the Cup with a second win from Tatay and Yamanaka. Salač had been brought down on Saturday so Artigas took third in the Cup.

That brought the total number of 2018 Öncü wins to eight. Very special, and it left only four victories to be taken by Artigas, Tatay, Yamanaka and Kunii. With Tatay doing the podium double in Aragón, as he had in Jerez, he is looking good for a possible Cup-winning second season in 2019 as is Kunii, up to speed again following his injury.

The other top men all move on to further challenges - the Moto3 World Championship and the Junior World Championship where they will race other former Rookies, all building an incredible legacy.

**MAIN** | *Can Öncü takes the win in Race 2 at the Sachsenring ahead of brother Deniz*

**LEFT-RIGHT** | *Can Öncü (61) heads Filip Salač (12), Deniz Öncü (53) and the pack at Mugello; Deniz and curly haired twin brother Can share the celebration in Germany; Xavier Artigas (24) and Carlos Tatay (99), both Rookies Cup winners*

# TWO WHEELS FOR LIFE

## WHAT WE DO

***Two Wheels for Life supports programmes that ensure healthcare reaches the poorest and most remote communities in Sub-Saharan Africa.***

Health workers immunise newborns, diagnose disease, educate in childhood nutrition, provide preventative measures to combat disease and help women in dangerous labour.

There are few roads, fuels stations or other infrastructure that are commonplace in economically developed countries and which mean making vehicles run reliably is relatively simple. Without these services transport is haphazard. Vehicles break down, clinics don't get run, tests are delayed, women with complications give birth unaided. The consequences are deadly.

Operating in countries including Lesotho, Malawi, Nigeria, Zimbabwe and The Gambia, the programmes we support focus on the single issue of transport for health workers, an essential but neglected aspect of healthcare in Africa. The programmes ensure vehicles are always reliable through maintenance, fuelling, monitoring and training.

## HOW WE DO IT

This year we've raised more than £250,000 at Day of Champions, a record amount and our biggest turn-out ever. We've also worked with each of the MotoGP™ teams to give our supporters the chance to bid on exclusive moto-memorabilia and once-in-a-lifetime experiences in our online auction.

We work with the motorcycle community throughout the year to raise money to fund these vital programmes. With the support of the MotoGP™ paddock, Two Wheels for Life runs unique events for motorcycle racing fans. These include exclusive paddock experiences across Europe, internationally renowned online and team auctions, and our annual Day of Champions family day out.

From bidding on our online auctions, attending Day of Champions, setting up regular donations or taking part in a fundraising challenge, our supporters are essential to our success.

## FIND OUT MORE

***To find out how you can support Two Wheels for Life, or just find out more about what we do, visit twowheelsforlife.org.uk***

## THE PLAGUE THAT WON'T GIVE UP, AND WHY MOTORCYCLES ARE THE SOLUTION

### by Barry Coleman, co-founder of Riders for Health and advisor to Two Wheels for Life

Malaria. Such a pretty word. Like a flower. But of course there is nothing pretty about this ruthless killer disease.

In some places, there is almost no escape. Everybody has it. It may not always kill you, but it will always make you seriously ill. Violent headaches, nausea, dizziness and disorientation.

You can barely see, can hardly stand and you most certainly will not be able to work. Imagine the effects on the family, with the children ill and the bread-winners effectively disabled. And in poor countries everyone is a bread winner because bread

And yet there is good news, not least from history. Malaria was once common in Europe and yet it has gone. It was common too in the US, particularly in the sub-tropical South. But they said goodbye to the last endemic case in Florida in 1953.

There are relatively effective preventative drugs, and there are bed nets which are a successful solution if people are educated to use them properly and they are regularly replaced (as the medication they are treated with eventually wears away). Plus, the disease, spread by sucking-in and squirting-out infected blood, is transmitted only by female mosquitoes and once they have been eliminated – as in the US case – it is extremely difficult for any area to be re-infected.

So what's the problem? Well, as usual it's the transport. There are wonderfully effective drugs and nets but they don't spontaneously fly through the air and deliver themselves.

The programmes we support train and provide reliable transport to motorcycling health workers who are able to reach villages and families whenever needed with medical supplies and the education that must go alongside them.

Motorcycles are far more effective than any other transport in this fight. Because insecticide-impregnated bed nets are so light, a health worker on a bike can carry hundreds of them at a time. And because malaria prevention and treatment call for permanent follow-up, motorcycles are perfectly suited because of their versatility and cost-effectiveness.

As with any huge problem, there is no single answer. But one thing is clear enough: if the people cannot be reached, the plague will rage on. A pretty name, but a far from pretty picture.

TWO WHEELS FOR LIFE

## 500cc

| YEAR | RIDER | NAT | MANUFACTURER |
|---|---|---|---|
| 1949 | Leslie Graham | GBR | AJS |
| 1950 | Umberto Masetti | ITA | GILERA |
| 1951 | Geoff Duke | GBR | NORTON |
| 1952 | Umberto Masetti | ITA | GILERA |
| 1953 | Geoff Duke | GBR | GILERA |
| 1954 | Geoff Duke | GBR | GILERA |
| 1955 | Geoff Duke | GBR | GILERA |
| 1956 | John Surtees | GBR | MV AGUSTA |
| 1957 | Libero Liberati | ITA | GILERA |
| 1958 | John Surtees | GBR | MV AGUSTA |
| 1959 | John Surtees | GBR | MV AGUSTA |
| 1960 | John Surtees | GBR | MV AGUSTA |
| 1961 | Gary Hocking | CAF | MV AGUSTA |
| 1962 | Mike Hailwood | GBR | MV AGUSTA |
| 1963 | Mike Hailwood | GBR | MV AGUSTA |
| 1964 | Mike Hailwood | GBR | MV AGUSTA |
| 1965 | Mike Hailwood | GBR | MV AGUSTA |
| 1966 | Giacomo Agostini | ITA | MV AGUSTA |
| 1967 | Giacomo Agostini | ITA | MV AGUSTA |
| 1968 | Giacomo Agostini | ITA | MV AGUSTA |
| 1969 | Giacomo Agostini | ITA | MV AGUSTA |
| 1970 | Giacomo Agostini | ITA | MV AGUSTA |
| 1971 | Giacomo Agostini | ITA | MV AGUSTA |
| 1972 | Giacomo Agostini | ITA | MV AGUSTA |
| 1973 | Phil Read | GBR | MV AGUSTA |
| 1974 | Phil Read | GBR | MV AGUSTA |
| 1975 | Giacomo Agostini | ITA | YAMAHA |
| 1976 | Barry Sheene | GBR | SUZUKI |
| 1977 | Barry Sheene | GBR | SUZUKI |
| 1978 | Kenny Roberts | USA | YAMAHA |
| 1979 | Kenny Roberts | USA | YAMAHA |
| 1980 | Kenny Roberts | USA | YAMAHA |
| 1981 | Marco Lucchinelli | ITA | SUZUKI |
| 1982 | Franco Uncini | ITA | SUZUKI |
| 1983 | Freddie Spencer | USA | HONDA |
| 1984 | Eddie Lawson | USA | YAMAHA |
| 1985 | Freddie Spencer | USA | HONDA |
| 1986 | Eddie Lawson | USA | YAMAHA |
| 1987 | Wayne Gardner | AUS | HONDA |
| 1988 | Eddie Lawson | USA | YAMAHA |
| 1989 | Eddie Lawson | USA | HONDA |
| 1990 | Wayne Rainey | USA | YAMAHA |
| 1991 | Wayne Rainey | USA | YAMAHA |
| 1992 | Wayne Rainey | USA | YAMAHA |
| 1993 | Kevin Schwantz | USA | SUZUKI |
| 1994 | Mick Doohan | AUS | HONDA |
| 1995 | Mick Doohan | AUS | HONDA |
| 1996 | Mick Doohan | AUS | HONDA |
| 1997 | Mick Doohan | AUS | HONDA |
| 1998 | Mick Doohan | AUS | HONDA |
| 1999 | Àlex Crivillé | ESP | HONDA |
| 2000 | Kenny Roberts, Jr. | USA | SUZUKI |
| 2001 | Valentino Rossi | ITA | HONDA |

## 250cc

| YEAR | RIDER | NAT | MANUFACTURER |
|---|---|---|---|
| 1949 | Bruno Ruffo | ITA | MOTO GUZZI |
| 1950 | Dario Ambrosini | ITA | BENELLI |
| 1951 | Bruno Ruffo | ITA | MOTO GUZZI |
| 1952 | Enrico Lorenzetti | ITA | MOTO GUZZI |
| 1953 | Werner Haas | GER | NSU |
| 1954 | Werner Haas | GER | NSU |
| 1955 | Hermann Paul Müller | GER | NSU |
| 1956 | Carlo Ubbiali | ITA | MV AGUSTA |
| 1957 | Cecil Sandford | GBR | MONDIAL |
| 1958 | Tarquinio Provini | ITA | MV AGUSTA |
| 1959 | Carlo Ubbiali | ITA | MV AGUSTA |
| 1960 | Carlo Ubbiali | ITA | MV AGUSTA |
| 1961 | Mike Hailwood | GBR | HONDA |
| 1962 | Jim Redman | CAF | HONDA |
| 1963 | Jim Redman | CAF | HONDA |
| 1964 | Phil Read | GBR | YAMAHA |
| 1965 | Phil Read | GBR | YAMAHA |
| 1966 | Mike Hailwood | GBR | HONDA |
| 1967 | Mike Hailwood | GBR | HONDA |
| 1968 | Phil Read | GBR | YAMAHA |
| 1969 | Kel Carruthers | AUS | BENELLI |
| 1970 | Rodney Gould | GBR | YAMAHA |
| 1971 | Phil Read | GBR | YAMAHA |
| 1972 | Jarno Saarinen | FIN | YAMAHA |
| 1973 | Dieter Braun | GER | YAMAHA |
| 1974 | Walter Villa | ITA | HARLEY DAVIDSON |
| 1975 | Walter Villa | ITA | HARLEY DAVIDSON |
| 1976 | Walter Villa | ITA | HARLEY DAVIDSON |
| 1977 | Mario Lega | ITA | MORBIDELLI |
| 1978 | Kork Ballington | ZAF | Kawasaki |
| 1979 | Kork Ballington | ZAF | Kawasaki |
| 1980 | Anton Mang | GER | Kawasaki |
| 1981 | Anton Mang | GER | Kawasaki |
| 1982 | Jean-Louis Tournadre | FRA | YAMAHA |
| 1983 | Carlos Lavado | VEN | YAMAHA |
| 1984 | Christian Sarron | FRA | YAMAHA |
| 1985 | Freddie Spencer | USA | HONDA |
| 1986 | Carlos Lavado | VEN | YAMAHA |
| 1987 | Anton Mang | GER | HONDA |
| 1988 | Sito Pons | ESP | HONDA |
| 1989 | Sito Pons | ESP | HONDA |
| 1990 | John Kocinski | USA | YAMAHA |
| 1991 | Luca Cadalora | ITA | HONDA |
| 1992 | Luca Cadalora | ITA | HONDA |
| 1993 | Tetsuya Harada | JPN | YAMAHA |
| 1994 | Max Biaggi | ITA | APRILIA |
| 1995 | Max Biaggi | ITA | APRILIA |
| 1996 | Max Biaggi | ITA | APRILIA |
| 1997 | Max Biaggi | ITA | HONDA |
| 1998 | Loris Capirossi | ITA | APRILIA |
| 1999 | Valentino Rossi | ITA | APRILIA |
| 2000 | Olivier Jacque | FRA | YAMAHA |
| 2001 | Daijiro Kato | JPN | HONDA |

## 125cc

| YEAR | RIDER | NAT | MANUFACTURER |
|---|---|---|---|
| 1949 | Nello Pagani | ITA | MONDIAL |
| 1950 | Bruno Ruffo | ITA | MONDIAL |
| 1951 | Carlo Ubbiali | ITA | MONDIAL |
| 1952 | Cecil Sandford | GBR | MV AGUSTA |
| 1953 | Werner Haas | GER | NSU |
| 1954 | Rupert Hollaus | AUT | NSU |
| 1955 | Carlo Ubbiali | ITA | MV AGUSTA |
| 1956 | Carlo Ubbiali | ITA | MV AGUSTA |
| 1957 | Tarquinio Provini | ITA | MONDIAL |
| 1958 | Carlo Ubbiali | ITA | MV AGUSTA |
| 1959 | Carlo Ubbiali | ITA | MV AGUSTA |
| 1960 | Carlo Ubbiali | ITA | MV AGUSTA |
| 1961 | Tom Phillis | AUS | HONDA |
| 1962 | Luigi Taveri | CHE | HONDA |
| 1963 | Hugh Anderson | AUS | SUZUKI |
| 1964 | Luigi Taveri | CHE | HONDA |
| 1965 | Hugh Anderson | AUS | SUZUKI |
| 1966 | Luigi Taveri | CHE | HONDA) |
| 1967 | Bill Ivy | GBR | YAMAHA |
| 1968 | Phil Read | GBR | YAMAHA |
| 1969 | Dave Simmonds | GBR | Kawasaki |
| 1970 | Dieter Braun | GER | SUZUKI |
| 1971 | Ángel Nieto | ESP | DERBI |
| 1972 | Ángel Nieto | ESP | DERBI |
| 1973 | Kent Andersson | SWE | YAMAHA |
| 1974 | Kent Andersson | SWE | YAMAHA |
| 1975 | Paolo Pileri | ITA | MORBIDELLI |
| 1976 | Pier Paolo Bianchi | ITA | MORBIDELLI |
| 1977 | Pier Paolo Bianchi | ITA | MORBIDELLI |
| 1978 | Eugenio Lazzarini | ITA | MBA |
| 1979 | Ángel Nieto | ESP | MINARELLI |
| 1980 | Pier Paolo Bianchi | ITA | MBA |
| 1981 | Ángel Nieto | ESP | MINARELLI |
| 1982 | Ángel Nieto | ESP | GARELLI |
| 1983 | Ángel Nieto | ESP | GARELLI |
| 1984 | Ángel Nieto | ESP | GARELLI |
| 1985 | Fausto Gresini | ITA | GARELLI |
| 1986 | Luca Cadalora | ITA | GARELLI |
| 1987 | Fausto Gresini | ITA | GARELLI |
| 1988 | Jorge Martínez | ESP | DERBI |
| 1989 | Àlex Crivillé | ESP | JJ COBAS |
| 1990 | Loris Capirossi | ITA | HONDA |
| 1991 | Loris Capirossi | ITA | HONDA |
| 1992 | Alessandro Gramigni | ITA | APRILIA |
| 1993 | Dirk Raudies | GER | HONDA |
| 1994 | Kazuto Sakata | JPN | APRILIA |
| 1995 | Haruchika Aoki | JPN | HONDA |
| 1996 | Haruchika Aoki | JPN | HONDA |
| 1997 | Valentino Rossi | ITA | APRILIA |
| 1998 | Kazuto Sakata | JPN | APRILIA |
| 1999 | Emilio Alzamora | ESP | HONDA |
| 2000 | Roberto Locatelli | ITA | APRILIA |
| 2001 | Manuel Poggiali | RSM | GILERA |

## MotoGP™

| YEAR | RIDER | NAT | MANUFACTURER |
|---|---|---|---|
| 2002 | Valentino Rossi | ITA | HONDA |
| 2003 | Valentino Rossi | ITA | HONDA |
| 2004 | Valentino Rossi | ITA | YAMAHA |
| 2005 | Valentino Rossi | ITA | YAMAHA |
| 2006 | Nicky Hayden | USA | HONDA |
| 2007 | Casey Stoner | AUS | DUCATI |
| 2008 | Valentino Rossi | ITA | YAMAHA |
| 2009 | Valentino Rossi | ITA | YAMAHA |

## 250cc

| YEAR | RIDER | NAT | MANUFACTURER |
|---|---|---|---|
| 2002 | Marco Melandri | ITA | APRILIA |
| 2003 | Manuel Poggiali | SMR | APRILIA |
| 2004 | Dani Pedrosa | ESP | HONDA |
| 2005 | Dani Pedrosa | ESP | HONDA |
| 2006 | Jorge Lorenzo | ESP | APRILIA |
| 2007 | Jorge Lorenzo | ESP | APRILIA |
| 2008 | Marco Simoncelli | ITA | GILERA |
| 2009 | Hiroshi Aoyama | JPN | HONDA |

## 125cc

| YEAR | RIDER | NAT | MANUFACTURER |
|---|---|---|---|
| 2002 | Arnaud Vincent | FRA | APRILIA |
| 2003 | Dani Pedrosa | ESP | HONDA |
| 2004 | Andrea Dovizioso | ITA | HONDA |
| 2005 | Thomas Lüthi | CHE | HONDA |
| 2006 | Álvaro Bautista | ESP | APRILIA |
| 2007 | Gábor Talmácsi | ITA | APRILIA |
| 2008 | Mike di Meglio | FRA | DERBI |
| 2009 | Julián Simón | ESP | APRILIA |

## MotoGP™

| YEAR | RIDER | NAT | MANUFACTURER |
|---|---|---|---|
| 2010 | Jorge Lorenzo | ESP | YAMAHA |
| 2011 | Casey Stoner | AUS | HONDA |

## Moto2™

| YEAR | RIDER | NAT | MANUFACTURER |
|---|---|---|---|
| 2010 | Toni Elías | ESP | MORIWAKI |
| 2011 | Stefan Bradl | GER | KALEX |

## 125cc

| YEAR | RIDER | NAT | MANUFACTURER |
|---|---|---|---|
| 2010 | Marc Márquez | ESP | DERBI |
| 2011 | Nicolás Terol | ESP | APRILIA |

## MotoGP™

| YEAR | RIDER | NAT | MANUFACTURER |
|---|---|---|---|
| 2012 | Jorge Lorenzo | ESP | YAMAHA |
| 2013 | Marc Márquez | ESP | HONDA |
| 2014 | Marc Márquez | ESP | HONDA |
| 2015 | Jorge Lorenzo | ESP | YAMAHA |
| 2016 | Marc Márquez | ESP | HONDA |
| 2017 | Marc Márquez | ESP | HONDA |
| 2018 | Marc Márquez | ESP | HONDA |

## Moto2™

| YEAR | RIDER | NAT | MANUFACTURER |
|---|---|---|---|
| 2012 | Marc Márquez | ESP | SUTER |
| 2013 | Pol Espargaró | ESP | KALEX |
| 2014 | Esteve Rabat | ESP | KALEX |
| 2015 | Johann Zarco | FRA | KALEX |
| 2016 | Johann Zarco | FRA | KALEX |
| 2017 | Franco Morbidelli | ITA | KALEX |
| 2018 | Francesco Bagnaia | ITA | KALEX |

## Moto3™

| YEAR | RIDER | NAT | MANUFACTURER |
|---|---|---|---|
| 2012 | Sandro Cortese | GER | KTM |
| 2013 | Maverick Viñales | ESP | KTM |
| 2014 | Alex Márquez | ESP | HONDA |
| 2015 | Danny Kent | GBR | HONDA |
| 2016 | Brad Binder | ZAF | KTM |
| 2017 | Joan Mir | SPA | HONDA |
| 2018 | Jorge Martin | SPA | HONDA |